# Good Housekeeping

# ALL NEW
# COOKBOOK

# Good Housekeeping
## ALL NEW
# COOKBOOK

TED SMART

A TED SMART Publication 1995

1 3 5 7 9 10 8 6 4 2

First published in the United Kingdom in 1995 by Ebury Press
Random House, 20 Vauxhall Bridge Road, London, SW1V 2SA

Random House Australia (Pty) Limited
20 Alfred Street, Milsons Point, Sydney,
New South Wales 2061, Australia

Random House New Zealand Limited
18 Poland Road, Glenfield,
Auckland 10, New Zealand

Random House South Africa (Pty) Limited
PO Box 337, Bergvlei, South Africa

Random House UK Limited Reg. No. 954009

A CIP catalogue record for this book is available from the British
Library.

ISBN 0 09 181144 9

**Managing Editor:** Julia Canning
**Design:** Sara Kidd, Jerry Goldie

**Contributing authors:** Jacqueline Clark, Joanna Farrow,
Louise Pickford, Janet Smith, Louise Steele
**Contributing editors:** Helen Southall, Donna Wood
**Additional editorial research and assistance:** Hilary Bird,
Fiona Hunter, Sara Lewis
**Recipe testing:** Emma-Lee Gow, Patricia Stone

**Special photography:** Karl Adamson, Graham Kirk
**Photographic styling:** Helen Payne
**Food for photography:** Louise Pickford
**Colour illustrations:** Madeleine David

Printed and bound in Spain by Printer Barcelona

# CONTENTS

# COOKERY NOTES

✦

Both metric and imperial measures are given for the recipes. Follow either metric or imperial throughout as they are not interchangeable.

✦

All spoon measures are level unless otherwise stated. Sets of measuring spoons are available in metric and imperial for accurate measurements of small quantities.

✦

Ovens should be preheated to the specified temperature. Grills should also be preheated. The cooking times given in the recipes assume that this has been done.

✦

Where a stage is specified in brackets under freezing, the dish should be frozen at the end of that stage.

✦

Size 2 eggs should be used except where otherwise specified. Free-range eggs are recommended.

✦

Use freshly ground black pepper and sea salt unless otherwise specified.

✦

Use fresh rather than dried herbs unless dried herbs are suggested in the recipe.

✦

Stocks should be freshly made if possible. Alternatively buy ready-made stocks or use good quality stock cubes.

# COLOUR INDEX

# COLOUR INDEX

In this Colour Index you will find a photograph of every recipe in the book, plus the following information:
- a brief description of the dish
- the number of servings
- page on which recipe appears
- useful, at-a-glance symbols

SYMBOLS
✳ Freeze-ahead
☺ Recipe can be prepared and cooked in 30 minutes or under
♡ Under 350 cals per portion for main courses; under 200 cals for starters, accompaniments and desserts

USING THE COLOUR INDEX
Where a photograph of the finished dish does not appear next to a recipe, you will find a reference to a page in the Colour Index. Just turn to the page number indicated and you will see a photograph of the dish.

**Asparagus Soup**
Delicately flavoured creamy smooth soup topped with almonds and parsley.

SERVES 4 . PAGE 62 . ✳

**Creamy Carrot and Celeriac Soup**
Velvety smooth carrot and celeriac soup with a hint of orange and soy.

SERVES 6 . PAGE 59 . ♡ . ✳

**Lettuce and Sorrel Soup**
Delicately flavoured soup, garnished with Parmesan and served hot.

SERVES 4 . PAGE 63 . ✳

**Parsnip and Apple Soup**
Creamy, smooth soup bursting with distinctive autumnal flavours.

SERVES 6 . PAGE 60 . ♡ . ✳

**Broccoli and Watercress Soup**
Deliciously smooth, deep green soup, full of fresh flavour.

SERVES 6 . PAGE 58 . ✳

**Jerusalem Artichoke and Parmesan Soup**
Lightly curried, creamy soup.

SERVES 6 . PAGE 61 . ♡ . ✳

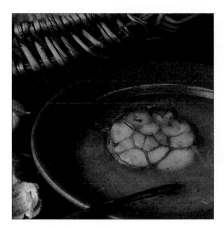

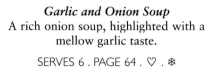

### Garlic and Onion Soup
A rich onion soup, highlighted with a
mellow garlic taste.

SERVES 6 . PAGE 64 . ♡ . ✳

### Spiced Dal Soup
Coarsely textured split pea soup
spiced with cumin and chillies.

SERVES 4-6 . PAGE 59 . ♡ . ✳

### Bouillabaisse
Mediterranean-style chunky seafood
soup with saffron and garlic.

SERVES 6 . PAGE 60

### Thai Chicken Soup
Chunky chicken soup spiced with
chilli, ginger and coconut.

SERVES 4 . PAGE 62 . ◔ . ✳

### Chilled Tomato and Vodka Soup
Wonderfully refreshing and very low
in calories, perfect for a hot day.

SERVES 6 . PAGE 65 . ♡

### Chilled Avocado and Lime Soup
Elegant soup with a velvety smooth
texture and just a hint of lime.

SERVES 4 . PAGE 65

### Pâté de Campagne
Coarse pork pâté, speckled with
black olives and layered with bacon.

SERVES 10-12 . PAGE 68 . ✳

### Chicken Liver and Pistachio Pâté
This tasty pâté is made with butter
and low fat cheese for a lighter texture.

SERVES 8-10 . PAGE 69 . ✳

### Peppered Mackerel and Apple Mousses
Individual mousses served with slices
of apple and horseradish sauce.

SERVES 6 . PAGE 72 . ✳

### Spicy Crab Dip
Perfect partnered with crudités and a glass of white wine, alfresco style.

SERVES 4 . PAGE 70 . ♡

### Nutty Chicken Bites, Smoked Salmon Roulade, Nan Bread with Spicy Prawns.
Three delicious canapés - tiny chicken kebabs with satay-style sauce; delicate smoked salmon and cheese rolls; little curried prawn bites.

MAKES 60-70 . PAGE 66/67

### Little Spanish Savouries
Irresistible hot cheesy pastries topped with anchovies, olives and pesto.

MAKES 24 . PAGE 66 . ✳

### Corn Scones with Avocado
Bite-sized scones with tasty toppings - ideal for serving with drinks.

MAKES 30 . PAGE 68 . ✳

### Courgette and Pesto Rounds
Colourful layers of tomato, courgette and basil baked in the oven.

SERVES 6 . PAGE 80 . ♡ . ⏱

### Vegetable Samosas
Deep-fried crispy parcels of spicy vegetables - an Indian speciality.

MAKES 24 . PAGE 74 . ✳

### Potato Pancakes with Smoked Salmon
Warming pancakes with a topping.

MAKES 6 . PAGE 75 . ✳

**Carpaccio of Salmon**
Deliciously light, wafer thin slices of
salmon in a lime and chive dressing.

SERVES 10 . PAGE 77 . ♡ . ⊕

**Soy-glazed Chicken Livers with
Chinese Leaves**
Chicken livers on shredded pak choi.

SERVES 4 . PAGE 76

**Bruschetta**
Full of Mediterranean flavour, this
hot tasty starter is quick to make.

SERVES 6 . PAGE 70 . ⊕

**Skewered Tiger Prawns with
Parma Ham**
Grilled kebabs - an easy starter.

SERVES 4 . PAGE 71 . ♡

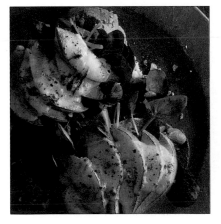

**Deep-fried Whitebait with Hot Sauce**
Crispy fried whitebait served with a
fiery paprika and chilli sauce.

SERVES 4 . PAGE 73

**Grilled Pears with Stilton**
An amazingly quick to make savoury
pear starter.

SERVES 4 . PAGE 78 . ⊕

**Golden Stuffed Mushrooms**
Bite-sized mushrooms filled with
bacon, cashews, garlic and parsley.

SERVES 4 . PAGE 75 . ⊕

**Bulghur Wheat Salad with Dried Fruit**
Deliciously tangy salad speckled with
figs, apricots, peaches and herbs.

SERVES 4-6 . PAGE 78

**Warm Seafood Salad with
Toasted Polenta**
Delicious haddock and prawn starter.

SERVES 6 . PAGE 72

**Toasted Bacon and Goats' Cheese Salad**
Crisp bacon coating concealing a melting soft cheese centre, perfect with salad.

SERVES 6 . PAGE 79

**Spinach, Bacon and
Roquefort Salad**
A fresh-tasting French starter.

SERVES 8 . PAGE 80 . ⏲

**Grapefruit and Chicory Salad
with Prawns**
A refreshing salad starter.

SERVES 4 . PAGE 79 . ♡ . ⏲

**Mango and Prawn Salads**
New twist to an old favourite, with
mango and fromage frais added.

SERVES 4 . PAGE 81 . ♡ . ⏲

**Cucumber and Strawberry Salad**
Refreshing mix of summer ingredients complement each other beautifully.

SERVES 4 . PAGE 81 . ♡

**Grilled Pepper and Aubergine Salad**
Contrasting salad of black aubergine
slices and red pepper with garlic.

SERVES 4 . PAGE 77 . ♡ . ⏲

***Cod Fillet Wrapped in Filo Pastry
with Rocket***
Crisp parcels of tasty fish.
SERVES 6 . PAGE 86 . ♡ . ❄ .

***Cod Cutlets Provençale***
Robust flavours and bright colours
characterize this French dish.
SERVES 4 . PAGE 88 . ♡

***Pan-fried Cod with Chanterelle
Mushrooms***
Seared cod on a crisp bread croûte.
SERVES 4 . PAGE 85

***Cod in Orange and Cider Sauce***
Deliciously tangy and colourful, this
fish dish is very easy to prepare.
SERVES 4 . PAGE 84 . ♡ . ❄

***Fish Plaki with Root Vegetables***
Tasty Greek-style dish flavoured with
lemon, white wine and thyme.
SERVES 4 . PAGE 84 . ♡ . ❄

***Roasted Fish with Garlic-herb Crumbs***
Buttery baked white fish steaks
sprinkled with crisp garlicky crumbs.
SERVES 6 . PAGE 95

***Haddock and Corn Chowder***
This hearty main meal soup is packed
with fish and vegetables.
SERVES 4 . PAGE 90

***Kedgeree with Lentils***
Lentils and lime add a new twist to
the traditional kedgeree.
SERVES 6 . PAGE 91 . ♡

***Thai Grilled Caramelized Fish***
Rolled plaice fillets on a bed of salad
leaves served with a hot chilli sauce.
SERVES 4 . PAGE 90

***Plaice with Grapes***
Plaice fillets poached in wine and
herbs, with a surprise grape filling.

SERVES 4 . PAGE 89 . ♡

***Fish with Lemon and Ginger***
Spicy marinated sole fillets stuffed with coriander, in a creamy saffron sauce.

SERVES 6 . PAGE 92 . ♡

***Lemon Sole with Spinach Hollandaise***
Melt-in-the-mouth grilled sole, served
with a tangy lime and spinach sauce.

SERVES 4 . PAGE 92

***Whiting in Soured Cream***
Grilled whiting bathed in a cheesy
cream sauce - simplicity itself.

SERVES 2 . PAGE 88 . ☻

***Grilled Halibut with Stir-fried
Vegetables***
Stylish and speedy combination.

SERVES 4 . PAGE 93 . ♡ . ☻

***Pan-roasted Monkfish with Sweet
Potatoes and Onions***
Stuffed monkfish all-in-one meal.

SERVES 4 . PAGE 94

***Light Monkfish and Prawn Sauté***
Quick-and-easy combination of
seafood and vegetables.

SERVES 4 . PAGE 104 . ♡ . ☻

***Normandy Skate with Caper Sauce***
A more unusual but very successful
way of serving skate.

SERVES 4 . PAGE 96 . ♡ . ☻

**Red Mullet with Spinach and Bacon**
This colourful treatment traps in the
full flavour of the fish.

SERVES 4 . PAGE 95

**Pan-fried Mullet with Citrus and Basil**
Marinated fish fillets served in a
tangy orange and lemon sauce.

SERVES 4 . PAGE 102

**Spiced Barbecued Salmon**
Melt-in-the-mouth salmon fillet with
a crisp and spicy skin.

SERVES 6 . PAGE 100 . ♡ . ⊕

**Baked Salmon with Walnut
Oil and Herbs**
Marinated salmon with a rich sauce.

SERVES 4 . PAGE 100

**Roast Salmon with a Peanut Crust**
Nutty topped salmon fillets served
with ginger and chilli butter.

SERVES 4 . PAGE 102 . ⊕ . ❇

**Roast Salmon in Mustard Butter**
Simplicity itself - thick slices of hot
buttery salmon on a bed of crisp salad.

SERVES 6 . PAGE 98 . ⊕

**Salmon Pie with Parmesan Crust**
Freeze ahead this luxurious fish pie
for effortless Christmas entertaining.

SERVES 8 . PAGE 98 . ❇

**Smoked Salmon Fishcakes**
These upmarket fishcakes are an
excellent freezer standby.

SERVES 12 . PAGE 101 . ❇

**Salmon Trout with Herb Sauce**
A decorated whole fish makes a
splendid centrepiece.

SERVES 4 . PAGE 99

15

***Poached Trout with Fennel***
Buttery baked trout on a bed of
thinly sliced fennel and potato.

SERVES 2 . PAGE 97

***Tuna Steaks with Parmesan
Basil Butter***
Grilled tuna with flavoured butter.

SERVES 6 . PAGE 105

***Trout with Dill and Horseradish Mayonnaise***
Poached trout served with mayonnaise,
mixed with dill, horseradish and apple.

SERVES 4 . PAGE 97

***Grilled Sardines with Tomato Sauce***
Herby spiked sardines, grilled and
served with a garlicky tomato sauce.

SERVES 4 . PAGE 105 . ♡

***Oatmeal Crusted Herrings***
Traditional Scottish recipe updated
and flavoured with lemon and dill.

SERVES 4 . PAGE 104 . ⏱

***Coconut Fish Pilau***
Colourful rice dish enhanced with
nuts, curry paste and prawns.

SERVES 4 . PAGE 106

***Paella with Peppers***
Packed with pieces of fish and peppers,
delicately flavoured with saffron.

SERVES 6 . PAGE 106

***Spiced Fish Kebabs with
Avocado Salsa***
The salsa offsets the spicy fish perfectly.

SERVES 4-6 . PAGE 107

***Fresh Seafood Stew***
Chunky Mediterranean fish stew
gently cooked with wine and herbs.

SERVES 6 . PAGE 109 . ♡

***Creamy Fish and Pumpkin Pie***
Break through the crisp filo topping to
reveal a delicious chunky fish filling.

SERVES 4 . PAGE 87

***Fisherman's Pie***
Chunky pieces of fish cooked in
tomato sauce, topped with potato.

SERVES 4 . PAGE 87 . ❊

***Winter Fish Stew***
Hearty Mediterranean-style fish stew,
perfect for informal entertaining.

SERVES 8 . PAGE 103

***Chillied Mediterranean Prawns***
Quick and spicy luxury prawn dish,
ideal for a romantic dinner for two.

SERVES 2 . PAGE 109 . ♡ . ⏲

***Charred Scallops with
Fennel and Pernod***
Fast and flavourful scallop dish.

SERVES 4 . PAGE 115 . ⏲

***Warm Scallop and Basil Salad***
Sautéed scallops tossed in walnut oil
and served on a bed of salad leaves.

SERVES 6 . PAGE 110 . ⏲

**Steamed Mussels in Saffron Cream Sauce**
Mussels bathed in a wine sauce.
SERVES 4-6 . PAGE 113

**Mussels in Tomato Sauce**
Shelled mussels in a chunky tomato sauce flavoured with oregano.
SERVES 4 . PAGE 112 . ♡ . ⏱

**Mussels with Ginger, Chilli and Coriander**
An exotic blend of spicy flavours.
SERVES 2 . PAGE 111 . ♡ . ⏱

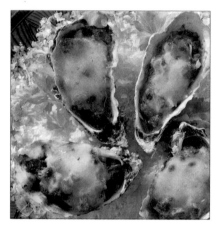

**Oysters au Gratin**
Stretch a dozen oysters by topping with bacon, artichokes and mozzarella.
SERVES 4-6 . PAGE 111 . ♡ . ⏱

**Dressed Crab**
Classically decorated crab always makes an impressive centrepiece.
SERVES 2-3 . PAGE 114 . ♡

**Grilled Lobster**
Simply grilling with butter brings out the true taste of this prized shellfish.
SERVES 4 . PAGE 110 . ♡ . ⏱

**Mixed Seafood Gratin**
Rich seafood cocktail coated in a cheese sauce, topped with tortillas.
SERVES 4 . PAGE 108 . ⏱

**Mixed Seafood Salad**
Colourful, chunky main meal salad served with warm crusty bread.
SERVES 6 . PAGE 114

**Seafood Risotto**
Mixed flavourful seafood combined with creamy rice.
SERVES 4 . PAGE 112

18

**French Roast Chicken**
Succulent tarragon roast chicken
served with garlic-flavoured gravy.

SERVES 4 . PAGE 135

**Roasted Pecan Chicken**
Creamy goats' cheese and ground
pecans transform a roast chicken.

SERVES 4 . PAGE 118

**Chicken Breasts with Spinach
and Ricotta**
Spinach-wrapped chicken with cheese.

SERVES 4 . PAGE 129

**Chicken Breasts with Apples
and Thyme**
Apple-flavoured roasted chicken.

SERVES 4 . PAGE 126 . ♡

**Herb Marinated Chicken with Spring
Vegetables in a Warm Dressing**
Herby oven-baked chicken breasts.

SERVES 4 . PAGE 123

**Poached Chicken in Watercress Sauce**
Chicken wrapped in Parma ham, served
in a creamy watercress sauce.

SERVES 4 . PAGE 130 . ♡ . ⏱

**Sweet Gingered Chicken**
Sticky soy and ginger glazed chicken
breasts roasted with aubergine.

SERVES 6 . PAGE 120

**Garlic Chicken with Roast
Pepper Purée**
Colourful peppers adorn baked chicken.

SERVES 6 . PAGE 125

**Chicken in Smoky Bacon Sauce**
Quick chicken dish with bacon,
apples and crème fraîche

SERVES 4 . PAGE 119 . ♡ . ⏱

19

***Spring Chicken Fricassee***
Stuffed chicken breasts, pan-fried in a
creamy vermouth sauce.

SERVES 4 . PAGE 124

***Spicy Coconut Chicken***
Pan-fried chicken simmered with Thai spices, tomatoes and creamed coconut.

SERVES 6 . PAGE 122 . ♡

***Oriental Chicken Parcels***
Orange-marinated chicken, baked in
foil to seal in the flavour.

SERVES 4 . PAGE 122 . ♡

***Savoury Crumbed Chicken***
Crispy baked chicken thighs - delicious
spring meal served hot or cold.

SERVES 4-6 . PAGE 128

***Southern Fried Chicken with
Corn Fritters***
American-style golden chicken.

SERVES 4-6 . PAGE 126

***Cheesy Chicken and Bacon Rolls***
Prepare these tasty rolls ahead, then
bake just before serving.

SERVES 4 . PAGE 132 . ❋

20

**Lime-peppered Chicken**
Marinated chicken kebabs with a chilli
dipping sauce, ideal for barbecues.

SERVES 6 . PAGE 131 . ♡

**Stir-fried Chicken with Courgettes**
Thin strips of chicken quickly fried
and tossed in sherry and soy sauce.

SERVES 4 . PAGE 130 . ♡ . ⏱

**Hot Red Jungle Curry**
Colourful Thai-style chicken curry
with fragrant Kaffir lime leaves.

SERVES 4 . PAGE 128 . ♡ . ⏱

**Chicken and Apple Casserole**
Hearty chicken casserole packed with
vegetables, lentils and apples.

SERVES 4 . PAGE 127

**Country Chicken Casserole**
Slow-cooked chicken pieces flavoured
with bacon, mushrooms and wine.

SERVES 4 . PAGE 124 . ❄

**Chicken Hotpot with Leeks**
Potato-topped chicken hotpot with a
creamy sauce.

SERVES 4 . PAGE 119 . ♡

**Marinated Chicken with Prunes**
The prunes and wine add a rich
mellow flavour to this wintery dish.

SERVES 4 . PAGE 121

**Winter Chicken**
Colourful chicken casserole packed
with wintery vegetables.

SERVES 4 . PAGE 120 . ♡

**Smoked Chicken with Cucumber
and Mango**
Bright salad with unusual dressing.

SERVES 6 . PAGE 135

21

**Warm Asparagus and Chicken Salad**
Hot sliced chicken and asparagus with
a tomato, olive and caper dressing.

SERVES 4 . PAGE 134 . ☺

**Chicken with Spiced Wheat**
Lightly curried pieces of grilled chicken
make up this main meal salad.

SERVES 6 . PAGE 133 . ♡

**Grilled Chicken Salad**
Tomato and olive encrusted chicken,
sliced and tossed in a crunchy salad.

SERVES 4 . PAGE 134 . ♡

**Mediterranean Chicken**
Bursting with flavour, this tightly-
packed loaf is great for picnics.

SERVES 6 . PAGE 132

**Cinnamon Roast Poussin with
Couscous**
An unusual dish featuring pistachios.

SERVES 4 . PAGE 137

**Lemon and Ginger Poussin with
Onions**
Poussins on a bed of onions.

SERVES 6 . PAGE 138

**Mustard-roasted Turkey**
Full of flavour, this mustard-glazed
turkey is perfect for Christmas.

SERVES 8 . PAGE 140

**Oriental Turkey**
A tasty alternative to the traditional
Christmas roast turkey.

SERVES 6 . PAGE 140 . ❊

**Turkey Apricot and Hazelnut Pilaff**
Use up the turkey leftovers in this
delicious Middle-Eastern rice dish.

SERVES 4 . PAGE 141

22

**Pan-fried Turkey with Lemon**
Crunchy hazelnut coated escalopes
with a lemon and tarragon sauce.

SERVES 4 . PAGE 139 . ☉

**Roast Duckling with Sherry Vinegar**
Slices of roast duck on a colourful
bed of glazed winter vegetables.

SERVES 6 . PAGE 142

**Guinea Fowl with Rocket Sauce and Spring Vegetables**
Braised with wine and served with a rich creamy rocket sauce.

SERVES 6 . PAGE 138

**Duckling Breasts with Armagnac**
Marinated in Armagnac and herbs
for an exquisite flavour.

SERVES 6 . PAGE 142 . ♡

**Crispy Chinese Duck with Oriental
Vegetables**
Sliced duck on piquant vegetables.

SERVES 6 . PAGE 144 . ☉

**Warm Duck Salad**
Low in calories, this upmarket salad
is great for summer entertaining.

SERVES 8 . PAGE 143 . ♡

23

**Goose with Prune Stuffing**
A traditional alternative to turkey at
Christmas.

SERVES 10 . PAGE 136

**Pot-roasted Pheasant with Red
Cabbage**
A classic combination of flavours.

SERVES 4 . PAGE 145

**French Roast Pheasant with Grapes
and Nuts**
An unusual way to serve pheasant.

SERVES 6 . PAGE 146

**Christmas Pheasant**
Casseroled pheasant flavoured with
Madeira, chestnuts and cranberries.

SERVES 6 . PAGE 144 . ❄

**Casserole of Grouse with Red Wine**
Slow-cooked grouse in a rich wine,
celery and shallot sauce.

SERVES 4 . PAGE 146 . ♡ . ❄

**Quails on Gnocchi with Cream Sauce**
Roasted quail on a circle of potato
gnocchi, served with a creamy sauce.

SERVES 6 . PAGE 149

**Country-style Rabbit Casserole**
Sautéed rabbit, flamed in brandy and
slowly cooked with tomatoes and wine.

SERVES 6 . PAGE 148 . ♡ ❄

**Pan-fried Venison with
Blueberry Sauce**
Rich venison with a tangy sauce.

SERVES 6 . PAGE 148 . ♡ . 🕐 . ❄

**Raised Game Pie**
This impressive pie encases a richly
flavoured mixture of game.

SERVES 8-10 . PAGE 147 . ❄

### Spiced Rib of Beef
Always an impressive roast, here the fat is spread with spiced butter.

SERVES 6 . PAGE 153

### Grilled Steaks with Shallots and Wine
Quickly grilled beef steaks served with a rich buttery wine sauce.

SERVES 4 . PAGE 152 . ☺

### Beef Medallions with Stilton Mousse
Pan-fried fillet steaks topped with a creamy Stilton and chicken mousse.

SERVES 6 . PAGE 154 . ☺

### Pizzaiola Steak
Flash-fried steak with a summery basil and tomato sauce.

SERVES 4 . PAGE 159 . ♡ . ☺

### Beef Rendang
Melt-in-the-mouth beef cooked in a Thai spice paste with coconut.

SERVES 6 . PAGE 152 . ✽

### Rich Beef Daube
A delicious make-ahead casserole for easy entertaining.

SERVES 6 . PAGE 157 . ✽

### Country Beef with Barley
Beef slowly cooked with barley, root vegetables, wine and orange.

SERVES 4 . PAGE 155 . ♡ . ✽

### Festive Beef Casserole
Rich spicy beef and venison casserole, flavoured with orange and sherry.

SERVES 8 . PAGE 154 . ♡ . ✽

### Steak and Kidney Pudding
Traditional dish of slow-cooked steak and kidney encased in suet pastry.

SERVES 6 . PAGE 156 . ✽

25

**Classic Oxtail Casserole**
This warming, traditional casserole is
packed with wintery vegetables.

SERVES 6 . PAGE 156 . ❋

**Italian Meatloaf**
A hearty, wholesome dish, just right
for large family gatherings.

SERVES 8 . PAGE 161 . ❋

**Babotee**
Spicy South African meat loaf topped
with a cheesy turmeric custard.

SERVES 4 . PAGE 160

**Spicy Burgers**
Lightly spiced burgers flavoured with
parsley and coriander, served in pittas.

SERVES 4 . PAGE 161 . ♡ . ⏱ . ❋

**Middle Eastern Meat Skewers**
Spiced beef sausages pressed onto
skewers, served with a minty sauce.

SERVES 6 . PAGE 158 . ❋

**Roast Lamb with a Creamy
Fennel Sauce**
Split racks of lamb roasted quickly.

SERVES 6 . PAGE 162

**Sesame Beef Salad**
Hot strips of marinated beef, served with celery, onion and cucumber for a light
main course dish.

SERVES 6 . PAGE 159 . ♡

**Boned and Stuffed Shoulder of Lamb**
Dried fruit adds a wonderful flavour
to this favourite roast.

SERVES 6 . PAGE 163

***Roast Eye Fillet of Lamb with Candied Lemons***
Marinated lamb with lemon.
SERVES 8 . PAGE 162

***Honeyed Leg of Lamb with Winter Vegetables***
Lamb roasted with root vegetables.
SERVES 4 . PAGE 166

***Tomato-crusted Lamb with Summer Vegetables***
Rack of lamb with summer flavours.
SERVES 6 . PAGE 165

***Lamb Chops with Leeks and Lentils***
Orange marinated lamb chops served on a bed of red lentils and leeks.
SERVES 4 . PAGE 169

***Lamb Steaks in Herby Tomato Sauce***
Baked lamb on a bed of herby tomatoes and topped with lemon.
SERVES 4 . PAGE 164

***Minted Lamb Escalopes***
Lamb marinated with yogurt, mint, lemon and garlic for added flavour.
SERVES 4 . PAGE 165 . ♡

***Spiced Lamb Hot Pot***
Cinnamon spiced lamb cooked slowly with potato, red pepper and barley.
SERVES 6 . PAGE 169 . ❋

***Spicy Lamb Casserole***
Chunky pieces of lean lamb, lightly spiced with ginger, cumin and paprika.
SERVES 6 . PAGE 164 . ❋

***Fruity Lamb Casserole with Spices***
Marinated lamb, gently casseroled with dried fruit, saffron and sherry.
SERVES 8 . PAGE 166 . ❋

27

***Moussaka***
Greek minced lamb topped with fried
aubergines and a cheese sauce.

SERVES 6 . PAGE 168 . ❋

***Moroccan Lamb Pie with Spinach
and Sultanas***
Spicy mince with spinach in filo.

SERVES 4 . PAGE 170 . ❋

***Lamb and Lentil Bake***
Aromatic mince and raisin mixture
baked in golden layers of pastry.

SERVES 4 . PAGE 167 . ❋

***Kidneys in Sherry Sauce***
Garlicky lambs' kidneys pan-fried in olive oil and sherry
provide a rich Spanish-style main dish.

SERVES 4 . PAGE 171

***Autumn Spiced Kidneys***
Delicious combination of sautéed kidneys, mushrooms and double cream.

SERVES 4 . PAGE 172 . ⊘

***Sautéed Liver with Orange and Sage***
Quick to cook, pan-fried liver with
fresh sage, tangy orange rind and juice.

SERVES 4 . PAGE 171 . ♡ . ⊘

### Roast Pork with Apple Gravy
Garlic and rosemary marinated roast pork with a delicious cider gravy.

SERVES 6 . PAGE 173

### Herby Rack of Pork with Roast Vegetables
Pork roasted on a bed of vegetables.

SERVES 6 . PAGE 175

### Pork Loin Stuffed with Figs
Transform the Sunday joint with this easy-to-make stuffing.

SERVES 4 . PAGE 174

### Peppered Garlic Pork with Crème Fraîche
Stuffed fillet with a creamy sauce.

SERVES 6 . PAGE 177 . ♡

### Pork Chops with Rhubarb Chutney
Grilled pork chops topped with a quick-to-make rhubarb chutney.

SERVES 4 . PAGE 176 . ⏱

### Grilled Pork with Spiced Butter
Grilled pork chops spread with mustard butter, served with a cider sauce.

SERVES 4 . PAGE 172 . ⏱

### Braised Pork Chops with Plums and Ginger
Pork and ginger plums with yogurt.

SERVES 4 . PAGE 180 . ❄

### Chinese-style Spare Ribs
Pork ribs flavoured with five-spice powder, ginger and soy sauce.

SERVES 4-6 . PAGE 179 . ♡

### Pork and Lemon Brochettes
Marinated cubes of pork and lemon slices, threaded onto skewers.

SERVES 2 . PAGE 176

***Homemade Sausages with
Rocket Pesto***
Coarse pork sausages to barbecue.

SERVES 6 . PAGE 179 . ✳

***Spanish Pork and Bean Casserole***
Slowly cooked gammon joint with white
beans, chorizo and black pudding.

SERVES 6-8 . PAGE 174

***Harvest Pork Casserole***
Rich mellow-tasting casserole of
pork, parsnips and apples.

SERVES 4-6 . PAGE 178 . ✳

***Stir-fried Pork***
Strips of pork, Chinese vegetables and rice make up this bumper stir-fry.

SERVES 4 . PAGE 181 . ♡

***Maple-glazed Gammon with
Papaya Salsa***
Sweet gammon with tangy fruit salsa.

SERVES 10 -12 . PAGE 182

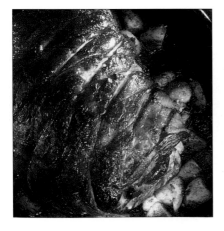

***Braised Ham with Madeira***
This Madeira-glazed ham joint is perfect for large Christmas gatherings.

SERVES 12-16 . PAGE 181 . ✳

***Mushroom and Ham Risotto***
Quick spring supper dish, perfect for
informal gatherings.

SERVES 4 . PAGE 183 . ⏱

***Saltimbocca***
Buttery fried veal escalopes and
Parma ham, with sage and wine.

SERVES 6 . PAGE 183 . ♡

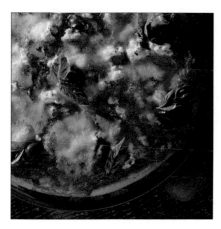

***Four Cheese Pizza***
Pizza base topped with mozzarella,
Dolcelatta, ricotta and Parmesan.

SERVES 6 . PAGE 186 . ♡ . ❊

***Feta and Oregano Tarts***
Individual tomato tarts flavoured
with feta, oregano and cream.

SERVES 4 . PAGE 191 . ❊

***Asparagus and Red Onion Tart***
This delicious tart makes a little
asparagus go a long way.

SERVES 8 . PAGE 189 . ❊

***Stilton, Walnut and Bacon Flan***
Crisp walnut pastry with a creamy
bacon, celery and Stilton filling.

SERVES 4-6 . PAGE 190 . ❊

***Melting Cheese and Ham Parcel***
Wonderful combination of melting
cheese, ham and crisp pastry.

SERVES 4 . PAGE 188

***Deep-fried Camembert with
Rhubarb Sauce***
Melting cheese in crisp coating.

SERVES 4 . PAGE 186

***Golden Cheese and Spinach Pudding***
Savoury version of bread and butter
pudding makes a tasty supper dish.

SERVES 4 . PAGE 190

***Aubergine and Pepper Parmigiana***
Oven-baked layers of grilled peppers,
aubergines, tomatoes and cheese.

SERVES 6 . PAGE 187 . ❊

***Goats' Cheese Puffs***
Rather like a double cooked cheese
soufflé, coated with chopped nuts.

SERVES 8 . PAGE 197 . ♡

**Chick-pea and Parsnip Soufflés**
Individual soufflés lightly spiced with
curry powder.

SERVES 4 . PAGE 188 . ♡

**Eggs in Poppadom Baskets**
Unusual poppadom baskets richly
filled with quails' eggs and hollandaise.

SERVES 6 . PAGE 197

**Poached Eggs on Smoked Haddock**
Smoked haddock with a poached
egg, croûtons and hot caper dressing.

SERVES 4 . PAGE 195

**Poached Eggs on Toasted Bacon
Baguette**
All-in-one supper dish.

SERVES 4 . PAGE 196 . ⊘

**Vegetable Egg Nests**
Individual rings of summer vegetables, filled with poached eggs.

SERVES 4 . PAGE 194 . ♡ . ⊘

**Courgette and Bacon Frittata**
Jumbo omelette flavoured with
courgettes, bacon and herbs.

SERVES 4 . PAGE 194 . ♡ . ⊘

**Caramelized Onion and Gruyère
Frittata**
An omelette with a difference!

SERVES 4 . PAGE 192 . ♡

**Stuffed Thai Omelette**
Folded omelette enclosing a gingered
pork filling.

SERVES 2 . PAGE 192 . ⊘

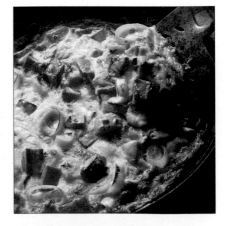

**Sweet Potato and Leek Tortilla**
Thick sweet potato and leek omelette
- delicious hot, cut into wedges.

SERVES 4 . PAGE 193 . ⊘

**Seafood Lasagne**
Always popular for informal entertaining or fork suppers.

SERVES 6 . PAGE 202

**Spaghetti with Clams**
Baby clams, wine, garlic and parsley
feature in this classic pasta dish.

SERVES 4-6 . PAGE 204 . ⏲

**Italian Seafood Pasta Salad**
Attractive salad bursting with
seafood, perfect for a light lunch.

SERVES 6 . PAGE 206

**Seafood Spaghetti with Pepper and
Almond Sauce**
Vibrant red sauce to top pasta.

SERVES 4 . PAGE 200 . ♡

**Pasta with Tuna and Olive Sauce**
Easy store-cupboard supper, richly
flavoured with fish and olives.

SERVES 4 . PAGE 204

**Pad Thai Noodles**
This is one of Thailand's favourite
noodle dishes.

SERVES 4 . PAGE 209 . ⏲

**Thai Chicken Noodle Salad**
Colourful main meal salad with all
the tastes of the East.

SERVES 6 . PAGE 203

**Noodles with Meatballs and Shallots**
Noodles tossed with pesto and shallots and served with meatballs.

SERVES 4 . PAGE 200 . ♡

**Gingered Chicken and Noodles**
Thai-style noodles flavoured with
ginger, curry paste and coconut.

SERVES 4 . PAGE 201 . ♡ . ⏲

### *Pastitsio*
Spicy minced lamb and pasta topped with a cheese sauce - a Greek classic.

SERVES 4 . PAGE 205 . ✳

### *Chilli Pork with Noodles*
Chillied pork cooked with noodles, broccoli and yellow pepper.

SERVES 4 . PAGE 201 . ♡ . ◷

### *Pasta in Sweet Pepper Sauce*
Finely chopped red peppers and salami flavour this easy-to-make sauce.

SERVES 4 . PAGE 203 . ✳

### *Pumpkin Ravioli with Herbs*
Tasty parcels filled with pumpkin, Parmesan, prosciutto and basil.

SERVES 4 . PAGE 214 . ✳

### *Linguine with Parma Ham and Sun-dried Tomatoes*
Creamy pasta with crisp ham.

SERVES 4 . PAGE 207 . ◷

### *Creamy Pasta Bake*
This luxurious version of macaroni cheese is flavoured with Gruyère.

SERVES 4 . PAGE 208

### *Roasted Vegetable and Pasta Gratin*
This colourful and tasty pasta dish is great for feeding a crowd.

SERVES 8 . PAGE 208 . ✳

### *Crespoline*
Spinach stuffed cannelloni on a tomato base, topped with a light sauce.

SERVES 4 . PAGE 211 . ♡

**Pasta Primavera**
Ribbon pasta perfectly offsets the
spring vegetables in this colourful dish.

SERVES 4-6 . PAGE 212

**Classic Tomato Sauce**
This tomato and basil pasta sauce
can be made in batches and frozen.

SERVES 4 . PAGE 212 . ♡ . ✳

**Pasta with Walnut and Basil Sauce**
Homemade tomato pesto-style sauce,
added to cream and walnuts.

SERVES 4 . PAGE 206 . ⏱

**Crunchy Courgette Pasta**
Lightly chillied courgette, red pepper
and tomato sauce on a bed of pasta.

SERVES 4 . PAGE 210 . ♡ . ⏱

**Pasta with Grilled Asparagus and
Broad Beans**
Pasta with summery flavours.

SERVES 4 . PAGE 215 . ⏱

**Tomato and Mozzarella Noodles**
Choose tomatoes with lots of flavour
for this quick summery supper dish.

SERVES 4 . PAGE 210 . ⏱

**Japanese Noodles with Pak Choi
and Mooli**
Soft noodles with a vegetable sauce.

SERVES 4 . PAGE 213 . ♡

**Calabrian Pasta**
Garlic-flavoured breadcrumbs and pine nuts, tossed with
broccoli, top this pasta dish.

SERVES 4-6 . PAGE 214 . ⏱

**Vegetable Strudel**
Cut through the crisp filo layers to
the hearty mix of vegetables inside.

SERVES 6 . PAGE 221 . ✳

**Leek Pancakes with Watercress
Sauce**
Stuffed pancakes baked in sauce.

MAKES 8 . PAGE 230 . ♡

**Vegetable Pithivier**
Attractive layered vegetable pie,
served in thick slices.

SERVES 6 . PAGE 218

**Tomato and Gruyère Pie**
Open pie made unusually with green
tomatoes, gruyère and mayonnaise.

SERVES 4 . PAGE 223

**Quick Tomato and Garlic Pizza**
Thin crispy base topped with tomatoes,
olives, garlic, herbs and feta cheese.

SERVES 2 . PAGE 220

**Crusty Mediterranean Parcels**
Puff pastry encases a rich vegetable
filling with a cheesy topping.

SERVES 8 . PAGE 225 . ✳

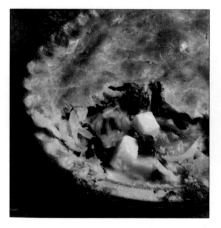

**Vegetable Cheese Pie with
Potato Crust**
Colourful pie with unusual topping.

SERVES 4 . PAGE 219 . ✳

**Mixed Mushroom Parcels**
Crisp filo purses with a tasty wild
mushroom and rice filling.

SERVES 6 . PAGE 228

**Gnocchi with Red Pesto**
Delicious red pesto sauce served with
potato gnocchi - a tasty combination.

SERVES 4-6 . PAGE 228

**Summer Couscous**
Herby trio of mint, coriander and
parsley flavour this tasty salad.

SERVES 6 . PAGE 223 . ♡ . ⏱

**Summer Risotto**
Colourful mixture of bright green
vegetables, tomatoes and wild rice.

SERVES 4 . PAGE 222 . ♡ . ⏱

**Vegetable Biryani**
Basmati rice mixed with Indian
spices, carrots and cauliflower.

SERVES 4 . PAGE 226

**Turkish Aubergines**
Chilled tomato stuffed aubergines,
flavoured with allspice and parsley.

SERVES 6 . PAGE 222

**Couscous-filled Aubergines with a Coriander Dressing**
Tasty stuffed aubergines bursting with minty couscous, apricots and pine nuts
for a satisfying vegetarian dish.

SERVES 4 . PAGE 232 . ♡

**Catalan Red Peppers**
Chilled red peppers with a rice
stuffing, tossed in a garlicky dressing.

SERVES 4 . PAGE 230 . ♡

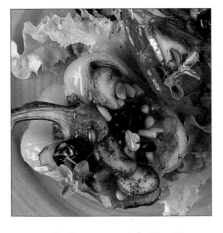

**Stuffed Peppers with Pine Nuts**
Vegetarian feast served with a tasty
tomato sauce.

SERVES 4 . PAGE 218 . ♡

**Baked Cabbage with Fruited
Bulghur Wheat Stuffing**
Tasty, stuffed cabbage parcels.

SERVES 4 . PAGE 226

37

**Filled Baked Potatoes**
Baked potatoes topped with two
delicious vegetarian fillings.

SERVES 8 . PAGE 229

**Baked Vegetables with a Spicy Sauce**
Roasted Mediterranean vegetables served with a chillied passata sauce.

SERVES 4-6 . PAGE 220

**Broccoli and Cheese Timbale**
Hot cheesy broccoli mould turned
out and served with a tomato sauce.

SERVES 6 . PAGE 232 . ♡

**Vegetable Kebabs with Mango Sauce
and Tropical Rice**
Colourful kebabs with tangy sauce.

SERVES 4 . PAGE 231

**Stir-fried Spring Vegetables with
Cashews**
Easy stir-fry to serve with noodles.

SERVES 4 . PAGE 233 . ♡ . ◔

**Mixed Vegetables and Tofu in
Coconut Sauce**
Quick Oriental-style supper dish.

SERVES 4 . PAGE 224

**Vegetable Stew with Rouille**
Mixed vegetable and bean stew,
served with a fiery pepper sauce.

SERVES 4 . PAGE 224

**Spiced Vegetable Tagine**
This fiery North African stew is
traditionally served with couscous.

SERVES 4 . PAGE 227 . ❊

**Spring Green Sauté**
Quickly fried shreds of garlicky
spring greens sprinkled with pine nuts.

SERVES 6 . PAGE 246 . ♡ . ⊕

**Crispy Chinese Greens**
Crisply-fried spring green shreds,
with a Chinese touch.

SERVES 4 . PAGE 246 . ⊕

**Cauliflower in Curry Sauce**
Cauliflower fried with spices, then
simmered with tomatoes.

SERVES 4 . PAGE 243 . ⊕

**Red Cabbage with Pine Nuts**
Sautéed red cabbage flavoured with
ginger, balsamic vinegar and pine nuts

SERVES 8 . PAGE 236 . ♡

**Chestnut and Sprout Sauté**
A classic combination and the perfect
accompaniment for roast turkey.

SERVES 8 . PAGE 237

**Citrus Leeks with Sugar Snap Peas**
Bright green leeks and peas tossed in
a tangy mustard dressing.

SERVES 6 . PAGE 237 . ♡ . ⊕

**Broad Beans in Herbed Lemon
Cream**
Creamy dish of baby broad beans.

SERVES 4-6 . PAGE 239

**Sweet and Hot Green Beans
with Peanuts**
Stir-fried green beans in a fiery sauce.

SERVES 4-6 . PAGE 238 . ♡ . ⊕

**Spicy Mushrooms**
Hot and spicy mushroom and
aubergine dish.

SERVES 6 . PAGE 238 . ♡

### Carrots in Spiced Dressing
Buttery young carrots tossed with
spices, honey and almonds.

SERVES 4 . PAGE 247 . ♡ . ⏱

### Mixed Onion Casserole with Juniper
Different types of onion baked slowly
for a wonderfully mellow flavour.

SERVES 4 . PAGE 240

### Marrow with Tomato and Onion
Chunky cubes of marrow simmered
in a garlic tomato sauce.

SERVES 4-6 . PAGE 240 . ♡

### Spiced Pumpkin Fritters
Sliced pumpkin fried in an Indian
spiced batter until crisp.

SERVES 4 . PAGE 241 . ⏱

### Squash with Nutty Gingered Crumbs
Soft cubes of squash coated in buttery
fried crumbs, ginger and pine nuts.

SERVES 4 . PAGE 242 . ⏱

### Parsnip and Carrot au Gratin
Smooth parsnip and carrot purée
topped with breadcrumbs.

SERVES 4-6 . PAGE 242 . ♡

### Parsnips in a Lime Glaze
The piquant, fresh taste of lime is
perfect with sweet parsnips.

SERVES 4 . PAGE 245 . ⏱

### Swede and Orange Purée
Creamy smooth swede purée with
just a hint of orange.

SERVES 4 . PAGE 243 . ♡ . ❄

### Aromatic Swede and Carrots
Stem ginger and mustard seeds
provide fragrant flavour.

SERVES 4 . PAGE 244 . ♡

***New Potatoes with Creamy
Mint Butter***
Sautéed new potatoes with herbs.

SERVES 4 . PAGE 246 . ☻

***Potato and Celeriac Galette***
Buttery layers of sliced potato and
celeriac, oven-baked until golden.

SERVES 4 . PAGE 244 . ♡

***Golden Potatoes***
Crisp, golden jacket roast potatoes,
spiked with garlic and rosemary.

SERVES 6 . PAGE 244

***Vegetable and Apple Stir-fry***
Quickly fried vegetables flavoured
with chopped apple and cashew nuts.

SERVES 4 . PAGE 249 . ☻

***Stir-fried Summer Vegetables***
Make the most of summer vegetables
in this colourful stir-fry.

SERVES 4-6 . PAGE 251 . ♡ . ☻

***Vegetable Medley***
Carrot sticks, baby sweetcorn and
asparagus cooked with lemon.

SERVES 4 . PAGE 250 . ♡ . ☻

***Roasted Tomatoes, Peppers and
Courgettes***
Full of Mediterranean flavour.

SERVES 4 . PAGE 253

***Pan-fried Tomatoes***
Serve this tasty salad with ciabatta
bread and goats' cheese.

SERVES 4 . PAGE 248 . ☻

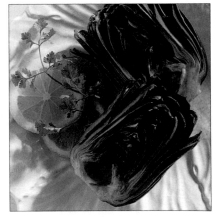

***Baked Artichokes***
Artichokes baked with olive oil and
served with lemon and parsley.

SERVES 6 . PAGE 248 . ♡

**Okra with Apricots**
Gently simmered okra with orange juice, tomatoes and sweet shreds of apricot.
SERVES 4 . PAGE 248

**Buckwheat and Lentil Pilaff**
Spiced lentils, nutty buckwheat and crispy bacon make up this pilaff.
SERVES 8 . PAGE 259

**Mixed Herb Salad**
Serve this pretty salad between courses to refresh the palate.
SERVES 4 . PAGE 252 . ♡ . ⏲

**Mixed Leaf, Orange and Strawberry Salad**
A tangy and colourful salad.
SERVES 6 . PAGE 252 . ♡ . ⏲

**Cucumber and Watercress Salad**
A cool, quick-to-make salad with chopped nuts for added texture.
SERVES 6 . PAGE 255 . ♡ . ⏲

**Tomato and Red Onion Salad**
Use a mixture of different tomatoes in this vibrant summer salad.
SERVES 6 . PAGE 252 . ♡ . ⏲

**Leeks and Asparagus in Vinaigrette**
Bright green vegetables tossed in a mustard dressing, topped with eggs.
SERVES 6 . PAGE 250 . ⏲

**Artichoke and Asparagus Salad**
Wonderful combination of flavours which improve with marinating.
SERVES 6 . PAGE 254 . ♡

**Minted Vegetable Salad**
A light fresh accompaniment to
barbecued meat or salmon.

SERVES 6 . PAGE 256 . ♡ . ⏱

**Grated Baby Beetroot Salad**
Young uncooked beetroot, grated and
tossed in horseradish dressing.

SERVES 4-6 . PAGE 257 . ⏱

**New Potato and Dill Salad**
Baby new potatoes tossed in a
yogurt and dill dressing.

SERVES 6 . PAGE 253 . ⏱

**Spiced Coleslaw with Pecans**
Fine shreds of cabbage tossed in a
spicy mayonnaise dressing.

SERVES 4 . PAGE 258

**Winter salad**
Crisp coleslaw-style salad with a
tangy lemon and yogurt dressing

SERVES 4 . PAGE 259 . ⏱

**Feta Cheese and Olive Salad**
Refreshing Greek-style mix of
cucumber, tomatoes, olives and feta.

SERVES 2 . PAGE 255 . ⏱

**Avocado and Chick-pea Salad**
A feast of flavours and textures,
topped with a light dressing.

SERVES 4 . PAGE 254 . ⏱

**Wild Mushroom and Lentil Salad**
Sautéed mushrooms and bacon
served on crisp sprouting lentils.

SERVES 4 . PAGE 258 . ♡ . ⏱

**Warm Chinese Salad**
Spicy stir-fried vegetables and
bamboo shoots on a bed of lettuce.

SERVES 4 . PAGE 257 . ♡ . ⏱

### Berry Compote
Sweet summer currants and strawberries served in a delicious syrup.

SERVES 6 . PAGE 263 . ♥ . ⊘

### Summer Pudding
This sublime British pudding captures
berry fruits in a thin bread casing.

SERVES 6-8 . PAGE 262 . ♥ . ❋

### Strawberry Mille Feuilles
Melt-in-the mouth pastry layers with
creamy crème pâtissière and fruit.

SERVES 6-8 . PAGE 263 . ❋

### Raspberry Fool
Swirls of fresh raspberry purée
combined with tangy fromage frais.

SERVES 4 . PAGE 262 . ♥

### Gooseberry Mousse
A delicate tasting dessert of puréed
gooseberries and yogurt.

SERVES 4 . PAGE 265 . ♥

### Cherry Brûlées
Crack through the brittle topping to
velvety custard and boozy cherries.

SERVES 8 . PAGE 265

### Poached Apricots
Halved apricots lightly poached in a
spiced wine and cinnamon syrup.

SERVES 6 . PAGE 266 . ♥

### Grilled Peaches with Chocolate and Marzipan
An unusual hot peach dessert.

SERVES 4 . PAGE 267 . ⊘

### Poached Pears with Apricots
Lightly poached pears and dried
apricots with Grand Marnier.

SERVES 4 . PAGE 271 . ♥ . ⊘

44

***Crispy Pear Clafoutis***
Sliced pears baked in a deliciously
crisp and golden batter.

SERVES 6 . PAGE 271

***Plum Custard Bake***
Melt-in-the-mouth plums in a light
custard, drizzled with warm honey.

SERVES 6 . PAGE 270 . ♡

***Bramley Apples with Ginger***
Baked apples, stuffed with a delicious
ginger filling.

SERVES 4 . PAGE 268

***Flambéed Pineapple***
Oven-baked pineapple wedges flamed
with brandy just before serving.

SERVES 4 . PAGE 273 . ♡

***Passion Fruit and Mango Soufflé***
Be a little exotic with this wonderfully
light, fruity soufflé.

SERVES 10 . PAGE 281 . ❋

***Clementines in Brandy***
Quick, refreshing dessert, perfect for
unexpected visitors.

SERVES 6 . PAGE 272 . ♡ . ⏱

***Fragrant Fruit Salad***
A divine concoction of exotic fruits,
producing a tantalizing fragrance.

SERVES 6 . PAGE 273 . ♡

***Pineapple and Date Salad with
Kumquats***
An exotic fruit salad steeped in tea.

SERVES 6 . PAGE 272

***Apple and Blackberry Upside-down
Pudding***
Autumnal fruit tops light sponge.

SERVES 8 . PAGE 270 . ❋

45

**Rhubarb and Cinnamon Cobbler**
Delicious buttery pastry surrounds
cinnamon spiced rhubarb.

SERVES 4 . PAGE 277 . ❄

**Banoffi Fudge Pie**
Wonderfully indulgent layers of
banana, fudge, cream and caramel.

SERVES 6 . PAGE 277

**Light Christmas Puddings**
Weight-watchers will love this lighter
festive pudding.

SERVES 8 . PAGE 274 . ❄

**Sticky Fudge and Walnut Pudding**
Moist walnut and date pudding
served with a rich fudge sauce.

SERVES 6 . PAGE 275

**Bread and Butter Pudding with Prunes**
A luxurious version of this well loved
English pudding.

SERVES 6 . PAGE 274

**Gooey Chocolate Pudding**
A chocolate treat - moist rich sponge
with a dark saucy layer.

SERVES 4 . PAGE 276

**Honey-toasted Rice**
Creamy rice pudding, sprinkled with
almonds and drizzled with honey.

SERVES 4 . PAGE 283

**Raisin and Orange Custard Tart**
Rich buttery pastry case filled with
custard and orange-soaked raisins.

SERVES 8 . PAGE 280

**Apple and Fig Strudel**
Sliced apples and moist figs flavoured
with lemon and encircled in filo.

SERVES 6 . PAGE 268 . ♡ . ❄

***Almond Tarte Tatin***
Melt-in-the-mouth almond pastry
topped with caramelized apples.

SERVES 6 . PAGE 269

***Higgledy-piggledy Apple Tart***
Buttery filo case filled with honeyed
mascarpone and caramelized apples.

SERVES 6 . PAGE 278

***Apple and Walnut Filo Pie***
Crisp golden layers of filo pastry con-
ceal the generous nutty apple filling.

SERVES 6 . PAGE 276

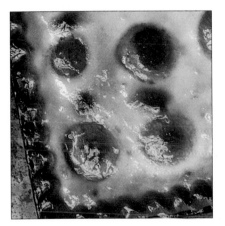

***Golden Nectarine Tart***
Rich tart filled with nectarines and a
creamy nutmeg and brandy custard.

SERVES 8 . PAGE 266 . ✱

***Lime Meringue Pies***
Individual pies filled with a tangy
lime sauce and topped with meringue.

SERVES 6 . PAGE 279

***Whisky Mocha Flan***
Heart-shaped flan coated with
chocolate, filled with coffee custard.

SERVES 6-8 . PAGE 285

***Chocolate Truffle Cake***
This rich, dense chocolate dessert is
ideal for parties.

SERVES 16 . PAGE 282 . ✱

***White Chocolate Torte***
Wonderfully decadent creamy
chocolate dessert with chocolate stars.

SERVES 12 . PAGE 284 . ✱

***Easter Cheesecake***
Baked cheesecake with a surprise
pear layer. Decorated with primroses.

SERVES 8 . PAGE 278 . ✱

**Strawberry Cheesecake**
Baked lemon cheesecake on an oaty
base, topped with strawberries.

SERVES 8 . PAGE 264 . ❋

**Saffron Meringues with Blueberry
Sauce**
Fruity sauce tops crispy meringue.

SERVES 6 . PAGE 282 . ❋

**Chocolate Chestnut Meringues**
Chocolate meringues filled with
chestnut cream.

SERVES 6 . PAGE 281 . ❋

**Crêpes with Orange Ice**
Hot lacy pancakes filled with orange
ice cream and flamed with liqueur.

SERVES 6 . PAGE 286 . ❋

**Frozen Strawberry Ice**
A lightweight ice, this pretty dessert
is perfect for hot balmy days.

SERVES 6 . PAGE 288 . ♡ . ❋

**Iced Orange and Lemon Terrine with
Burnt Sugar Sauce**
Citrus ice cream with rich sauce.

SERVES 6 . PAGE 288 . ❋

**Melon Ice**
Tiny balls of refreshing melon ice
cream with marinated melon.

SERVES 6-8 . PAGE 287 . ❋

**Lime and Cranberry Ice**
Refresh those festive palates with this
tangy ice cream.

SERVES 8 . PAGE 289 . ❋

**Vanilla Ice with Espresso**
The perfect instant dessert, hot
espresso tops cool ice cream.

SERVES 6 . PAGE 289 . ◷

48

***The Ultimate Chocolate Cake***
Wonderfully rich chocolate cake
coated in a creamy chocolate icing.

MAKES 25 . PAGE 294 . ✻

***Crumbly Apple and Cheese Cake***
Moist, crumbly fruit cake with a
surprise layer of Caerphilly cheese.

MAKES 10 SLICES . PAGE 292 . ✻

***Cinnamon Coffee Cake***
Spicy layered cake flavoured with
soured cream, perfect with coffee.

MAKES 8 SLICES . PAGE 292 . ✻

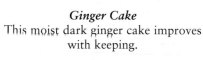

***Ginger Cake***
This moist dark ginger cake improves
with keeping.

MAKES 25 SLICES . PAGE 293 . ♡ . ✻

***Almond, Chocolate and Sweet
Potato Loaf***
A moist cake with sweet potato.

MAKES 8-10 SLICES . PAGE 293 . ✻

***Walnut Torte***
Nutty walnut cake flavoured with
orange and ricotta cheese.

MAKES 8-10 SLICES . PAGE 294

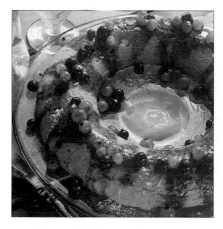

***Lemon Sponge with Kirsch and
Fresh Currants***
Delicious syrup-soaked sponge cake.

SERVES 8-10 . PAGE 295 . ♡ . ✻

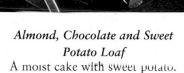

***Chocolate Roulade***
Everyone's favourite, soft moist chocolate sponge
encircling whipped cream.

SERVES 6-8 . PAGE 297 . ✻

49

**Simnel Cake**
Spiced fruit cake layered with
marzipan and traditionally decorated.

SERVES 20 . PAGE 301 . ❃

**Rich Christmas Cake**
The fruit for this traditional cake is
soaked in rum for extra flavour.

SERVES 12-16 . PAGE 298

**Stollen**
Rich, fruity yeast bread with a
marzipan filling.

SERVES 10 . PAGE 299 . ❃

**Bûche de Noël**
Chestnut filled Swiss roll, decorated
with a rich chocolate butter cream.

SERVES 8-10 . PAGE 306 . ❃

**Hazelnut Vacherin with Apricots**
Spirals of hazelnut meringue filled
with fresh apricots and cream.

SERVES 6 . PAGE 296

**Raspberry Mousse Gâteau**
Delicious layers of hazelnut sponge, cream and raspberry mousse.
SERVES 6-8 . PAGE 297 . ❃

***Sticky Orange Flapjacks***
This sticky tea-time bake is a great
favourite with all ages.

MAKES 18 . PAGE 303 . ❄

***Honey and Yogurt Muffins***
Wonderfully craggy, easy to make,
American-style muffins.

MAKES 12 . PAGE 300 . ♡ . ⏱ . ❄

***Berry Scones***
These moist crumbly scones are made with blackberries.

MAKES 16 . PAGE 300 . ♡ . ⏱ . ❄

***Mince Pies***
No need for special tins for these
festive fruit pies.

MAKES 24 . PAGE 299 . ❄

***Mini Hot Cross Buns***
Spicy buns speckled with currants
and marked with pastry crosses.

MAKES 25 . PAGE 302 . ❄

***Almond Squares***
A version of almond Bakewell tart,
topped with toasted flaked almonds.

MAKES 12 . PAGE 304 . ❄

### Honey Wafers
Wafer-thin sponge rounds, delicious served layered with cream and fruit.

MAKES 24 . PAGE 305 . ❀

### Orange Flower Biscuits
Crisp, buttery biscuits, delicately flavoured with orange flower water.

MAKES 20-24 . PAGE 305

### Easter Biscuits
Spiced currant biscuits flavoured with brandy and mixed peel.

MAKES 30 . PAGE 302 . ❀

### Shortbread
Home-made buttery shortbread makes an ideal Christmas gift.

MAKES 24-36 . PAGE 307

### Florentines
Dainty Italian fruit and nut biscuits coated with chocolate.

MAKES 30 . PAGE 306

### Oat and Sesame Biscuits
These crisp wholemeal biscuits are delicious with blue cheese.

MAKES 50 . PAGE 308 . ♡ . ❀

### Cottage Cheese and Brazil Nut Teabread
This nutty loaf is virtually fat free.

MAKES 12 SLICES . PAGE 308 . ♡ . ❀

### Olive and Walnut Bread
Serve warm and thickly sliced for a taste of the Mediterranean.

MAKES 2 LOAVES . PAGE 309 . ♡ . ❀

***Chocolate Eggs***
For Easter - one large egg, or 4 small
solid eggs.

MAKES 1 OR 4 EGGS . PAGE 313

***Chocolate Colettes with Frosted
Flowers***
Creamy-filled dark chocolate cases.

MAKES 16 . PAGE 312

***Summer Pickle***
Piquant vegetables, herbs and spices -
ideal with cold meats or cheese.

MAKES 450 G (1 LB) . PAGE 318

***Sweetcorn Relish***
Colourful American-style preserve,
good with cold roast meats or burgers.

MAKES 2.3 KG (5 LB) . PAGE 315

***Cranberry and Roast Shallot
Chutney***
Ideal accompaniment to cold turkey.

MAKES 900 G (2 LB) . PAGE 314

***Damson Chutney***
Mellow-tasting chutney captures all
the tastes of autumn.

MAKES 1.8 KG (4 LB) . PAGE 315

***Apple and Mint Jelly***
Clear, golden jelly, flecked with
fragrant chopped mint.

PAGE 316

***Marrow and Apricot Jam***
A good way to use and preserve gluts
of marrow.

MAKES 2.3 KG (5 LB) . PAGE 316

***Berry Jam***
A cream tea just wouldn't be complete without this favourite jam.

MAKES 1.8 KG (4 LB) . PAGE 318

<u>53</u>

### *Apricot Jam*
Delicious golden coloured jam, the
ideal breakfast choice.

MAKES 3 KG (6½ LB) . PAGE 318

### *Tangerine Jelly Marmalade*
Crystal clear marmalade, textured
with fine tangerine shreds.

MAKES 2.3 KG (5 LB) . PAGE 317

### *Seville Orange Marmalade*
The purist's marmalade with its
classic bitter-sweet taste.

MAKES 4.5 KG (10 LB) . PAGE 317

### *Brandy-soaked Cherries*
Capture the best of the cherry crop in
this boozy preserve.

MAKES 450 G (1 LB) . PAGE 319

### *Apricot Mincemeat*
An easy-to-make preserve for the
festive season.

MAKES 1.8 KG (4 LB) . PAGE 314

### *Summer Punch*
Refreshingly cool and bubbly, ideal
for entertaining.

SERVES 18-20 . PAGE 320

### *Mangoade*
Refreshingly non-alcoholic cocktail,
ideal for any time of day.

SERVES 4-6 . PAGE 320

### *Apricot Flip, Tropical Fruit Crush*
Two fruity and refreshing drinks for
summer days.

SERVES 2 OR 8-10 . PAGE 320/321

### *Redcurrant Rum*
Wonderfully decadent pale pink
liqueur made with redcurrants.

SERVES 16 . PAGE 321

# THE RECIPES

# SOUPS AND STARTERS

# BROCCOLI AND WATERCRESS SOUP

PREPARATION TIME 10 minutes
COOKING TIME 30 minutes
FREEZING Suitable
❊

**SERVES 6**
- *225 g (8 oz) broccoli*
- *75 g (3 oz) butter*
- *2 leeks, trimmed and sliced*
- *1-2 garlic cloves, peeled and halved*
- *2 bunches watercress, trimmed*
- *25 g (1 oz) white plain flour*
- *600 ml (1 pint) chicken stock*

**215 CALS/SERVING**
- *salt and pepper*
- *450 ml (15 fl oz) milk*
- *150 ml (5 fl oz) single cream*
- *Parmesan cheese shavings, to garnish*
- *a little freshly grated nutmeg, to taste*

**1** Divide the broccoli into florets and slice the stalks into even-sized pieces.
**2** Melt the butter in a saucepan, add the broccoli florets and stalks and stir in the leeks and garlic. Cook gently for 5 minutes, stirring occasionally.
**3** Add the watercress and cook for a further 3 minutes, stirring frequently. Stir in the flour and cook for 1 minute, then gradually add the stock and bring to the boil, stirring. Season with salt and pepper.
**4** Cover and simmer gently for 20 minutes or until all the vegetables are tender and cooked through. Remove from the heat and allow to cool slightly.
**5** Purée the soup in a blender or food processor. Return the mixture to the rinsed-out pan, check the seasoning, stir in the milk and cream, and heat through gently.
**6** Serve the soup hot, sprinkled with shavings of Parmesan and a pinch of freshly grated nutmeg.

**VARIATION** This soup is also delicious served cold, in which case thin the consistency with extra milk and cream.

# CREAMY CARROT AND CELERIAC SOUP

PREPARATION TIME 15 minutes
COOKING TIME 45 minutes
FREEZING Suitable (stage 3)
COLOUR INDEX Page 8
♡ ✱

**SERVES 6**
- *30 ml (2 tbsp) vegetable oil*
- *225 g (8 oz) onions, peeled and roughly chopped*
- *900 g (2 lb) carrots, peeled and roughly chopped*
- *900 g (2 lb) celeriac, peeled and roughly chopped*
- *1.7 litres (3 pints) chicken stock*

**200 CALS/SERVING**
- *5 ml (1 tsp) soy sauce*
- *finely grated rind and juice of 1 orange*
- *300 ml (10 fl oz) single cream*
- *salt and pepper*
- *croûtons and flat-leaf parsley, to garnish*

1 Heat the oil in a large saucepan and add the vegetables. Sauté for 5 minutes, stirring frequently. Add the chicken stock and bring to the boil. Cover and then leave to simmer gently for 20 minutes.
2 Stir in the soy sauce, orange rind and 60 ml (4 tbsp) orange juice. Cover and simmer for 20 minutes
3 Cool slightly, then blend in a food processor until smooth. For an extra-velvety texture, push through a sieve.
4 Stir in the cream and warm gently. Season to taste and serve garnished with croûtons and parsley.

# SPICED DAL SOUP

PREPARATION TIME 10 minutes, plus soaking
COOKING TIME 1½ hours
FREEZING Suitable
COLOUR INDEX Page 9
♡ ✱

**SERVES 4-6**
- *125 g (4 oz) yellow split peas*
- *5 ml (1 tsp) cumin seeds*
- *10 ml (2 tsp) coriander seeds*
- *3 dried red chillies*
- *15 ml (1 tbsp) desiccated unsweetened coconut*
- *30 ml (2 tbsp) ghee or vegetable oil*

**200-130 CALS/SERVING**
- *225 g (8 oz) tomatoes, skinned and roughly chopped*
- *2.5 ml (½ tsp) ground turmeric*
- *5 ml (1 tsp) treacle*
- *5 ml (1 tsp) salt*
- *coriander sprigs and lemon slices, to garnish*

1 Put the split peas into a sieve and wash thoroughly under cold running water. Drain well, then transfer to a bowl, cover with cold water and soak for 8 hours. Drain, place in a large saucepan, cover with 600 ml (1 pint) water and boil rapidly for 10 minutes. Cover and simmer for at least 1 hour, or until tender.
2 Finely grind the cumin, coriander, chillies and coconut in a small electric mill or with a pestle and mortar. Heat the ghee or oil in a heavy-based frying pan, add the spice mixture and fry, stirring, for 30 seconds. Set aside.
3 Mash the split peas and transfer to a large saucepan. Stir in the tomatoes, fried spices, turmeric, treacle, salt and 300 ml (10 fl oz) water.
4 Bring to the boil, then lower the heat, cover and simmer for about 20 minutes. Taste and adjust the seasoning and turn into a warmed serving dish. Garnish with coriander sprigs and lemon slices.

> ### *TIP*
> Poppadoms make an excellent accompaniment to this soup. To cook poppadoms, either fry for a few seconds in vegetable oil or brush with oil and grill for a few seconds on each side.

## BOUILLABAISSE

PREPARATION TIME 25 minutes, plus soaking
COOKING TIME 20-25 minutes
FREEZING Not suitable
COLOUR INDEX Page 9

SERVES 6     365 CALS/SERVING

- *900 g (2 lb) mixed fish and shellfish, such as monkfish, red mullet, John Dory, bass, prawns, cleaned*
- *few saffron strands*
- *150 ml (5 fl oz) olive oil*
- *2–3 onions, peeled and sliced*
- *1 celery stick, chopped*
- *225 g (8 oz) tomatoes, skinned and sliced*
- *2 garlic cloves, peeled and crushed*
- *1 bay leaf*
- *2.5 ml (½ tsp) dried thyme or fennel*
- *a few parsley sprigs*
- *finely shredded rind of ½ orange*
- *salt and pepper*
- *about 1.1 litres (2 pints) fish stock*
- *parsley sprigs, to garnish*

1 Skin and fillet the fish if necessary, then cut into fairly large, thick pieces. Remove the shellfish from their shells.
2 Put the saffron in a small bowl. Pour in 150 ml (5 fl oz) boiling water and leave to soak for 30 minutes.
3 Heat the oil in a large saucepan, add the onions and celery and fry gently for 5 minutes, until beginning to soften. Add the tomatoes to the pan with the garlic, herbs, orange rind and seasoning.
4 Arrange the fish in a layer over the vegetables, pour over the saffron liquid and just enough stock to cover the fish. Bring to the boil and simmer uncovered for about 8 minutes.
5 Add the shellfish and cook for a further 5–8 minutes, until the fish pieces are cooked but still hold their shape. Serve garnished with parsley.

**NOTE** Choose from the wealth of fish and shellfish available at this time of year to create your own version of this mediterranean-style chunky soup.

## PARSNIP AND APPLE SOUP

PREPARATION TIME 15 minutes
COOKING TIME 45 minutes
FREEZING Suitable (stage 3)
COLOUR INDEX Page 8

♡ ❄

SERVES 6     175 CALS/SERVING

- *25 g (1 oz) butter or margarine*
- *700 g (1½ lb) parsnips, peeled and roughly chopped*
- *1 cooking apple, peeled and roughly chopped*
- *1.1 litres (2 pints) vegetable stock*
- *4 sage leaves or 2.5 ml (½ tsp) dried sage*
- *2 cloves*
- *150 ml (5 fl oz) single cream*
- *salt and pepper*
- *sage leaves or parsley and croûtons, to garnish*

1 Melt the butter in a large saucepan; add the parsnips and apple, cover and cook gently for 10 minutes, stirring occasionally.
2 Pour in the stock, and add the sage and cloves. Bring to the boil, cover, then simmer for 30 minutes or until the parsnips are very soft.
3 Remove the sage leaves and cloves; leave the soup to cool slightly, then purée in a blender or food processor.
4 Return the soup to the saucepan, add the cream and reheat gently. Season with salt and pepper. Serve hot, garnished with the sage or parsley and croûtons.

---

### TIP
This autumnal soup freezes very well, so make a double quantity to save time. It's useful to freeze the soup in single or double portions in readiness for last-minute suppers. Add the cream when reheating.

## JERUSALEM ARTICHOKE AND PARMESAN SOUP

PREPARATION TIME 15 minutes
COOKING TIME 25 minutes
FREEZING Suitable

♡ ❊

**SERVES 6**

- *50 g (2 oz) butter*
- *2 shallots, peeled and diced*
- *5 ml (1 tsp) mild curry paste*
- *450 g (1 lb) Jerusalem artichokes, scrubbed clean and thinly sliced*
- *900 ml (1½ pints) chicken or vegetable stock*
- *150 ml (5 fl oz) single cream (or milk for a less rich soup)*
- *freshly grated nutmeg, to taste*

**190 CALS/SERVING**

- *pinch of cayenne pepper*
- *60 ml (4 tbsp) freshly grated Parmesan cheese*
- *salt and pepper*

PARMESAN TOAST

- *3-4 slices day-old softgrain white bread*
- *a little freshly grated Parmesan cheese, for sprinkling*
- *1.25 ml (¼ tsp) paprika*

1 Melt the butter in a large saucepan and add the shallots. Cook gently for 5 minutes until soft and golden. Stir in the curry paste and cook for 1 minute. Add the sliced artichokes and stock; stir well. Bring to the boil, cover and simmer for about 15 minutes or until the artichokes are tender.

2 Meanwhile, make the Parmesan toast. Toast the bread lightly on both sides. Quickly cut off the crusts and split each slice in two. Scrape off any doughy bits, then sprinkle with Parmesan and paprika. Place on a baking sheet and bake in the oven at 180°C (350°F) mark 4 for 10-15 minutes or until uniformly golden.

3 Add the cream, nutmeg and cayenne to the soup. Transfer to a blender or food processor and work until smooth, then pass through a sieve into a clean saucepan. Reheat the soup and stir in the Parmesan cheese. Taste and adjust the seasoning. Serve at once, with the hot toast.

**VARIATION** Replace the Jerusalem artichokes with 1 large cauliflower. Cut away the leaves and core, and discard. Divide the cauliflower into florets. Add to the shallots with the stock and bring to the boil. Simmer for about 10 minutes or until very soft, then continue as in stage 3.

# THAI CHICKEN SOUP

PREPARATION TIME 10 minutes
COOKING TIME 20 minutes
FREEZING Suitable
🕐 ❄

**SERVES 4**
- *125 g (4 oz) creamed coconut, chopped*
- *15 ml (1 tbsp) vegetable oil*
- *1 green chilli, deseeded and finely chopped*
- *2.5 cm (1 inch) piece fresh root ginger, peeled and finely chopped*
- *350 g (12 oz) skinless chicken breast, cut into chunks*

**265 CALS/SERVING**
- *2 garlic cloves, peeled and crushed*
- *750 ml (1½ pints) chicken stock*
- *45 ml (3 tbsp) fresh lime juice (about 2 limes)*
- *about 90 ml (6 tbsp) chopped fresh coriander*
- *225 g (8 oz) mangetout, sliced*
- *salt and pepper*
- *chopped spring onions, to garnish*

**1** Dissolve the chopped coconut in 300 ml (10 fl oz) boiling water.
**2** Heat the oil in a non-stick saucepan, add the chilli, ginger, chicken and garlic and cook for 1-2 minutes.
**3** Add the stock, coconut milk, lime juice and half the coriander. Bring to the boil. Cover and simmer for 15 minutes. Add the mangetout and cook for a further 5 minutes until the chicken is tender.
**4** Add the remaining coriander and season to taste. Garnish with chopped spring onions.

# ASPARAGUS SOUP

PREPARATION TIME 15 minutes
COOKING TIME 25 minutes
FREEZING Suitable
COLOUR INDEX Page 8
❄

**SERVES 4**
- *125 g (4 oz) blanched almonds*
- *1.1 litres (2 pints) vegetable stock or water*
- *15 ml (1 tbsp) vegetable oil*
- *4 celery sticks, diced*
- *450 g (1 lb) asparagus, trimmed and chopped*

**260 CALS/SERVING**
- *30 ml (2 tbsp) chopped fresh parsley*
- *45 ml (3 tbsp) single cream*
- *salt and pepper*
- *cream, toasted flaked almonds and parsley, to garnish*

**1** Place the almonds and stock in a blender or food processor and grind until very smooth. Sieve the mixture, reserving the liquid, and discard the grains.
**2** Heat the oil in a large saucepan and gently fry the celery for 5-6 minutes. Add the asparagus and cook for 5 minutes. Pour the stock over the top and add the parsley. Cover and simmer for 15 minutes.
**3** Cool slightly, then purée in a blender or food processor until smooth. Return to the pan and stir in the cream. Heat gently. Season and garnish with cream, toasted almonds and parsley.

# LETTUCE AND SORREL SOUP

PREPARATION TIME 15 minutes
COOKING TIME 20-25 minutes
FREEZING Suitable
❈

**SERVES 4**

- *60 ml (4 tbsp) extra-virgin olive oil*
- *6 spring onions, chopped*
- *1 garlic clove, peeled and crushed*
- *5 ml (1 tsp) chopped fresh thyme (lemon thyme preferably)*
- *50 g (2 oz) long-grain rice*
- *450 g (1 lb) cos lettuce, shredded*

**205 CALS/SERVING**

- *125 g (4 oz) sorrel, shredded*
- *1.2 litres (2 pints) vegetable stock*
- *30 ml (2 tbsp) chopped fresh chives*
- *pinch of grated nutmeg*
- *salt and pepper*
- *Parmesan cheese shavings, to garnish (optional)*

1 Heat 15 ml (1 tbsp) of the oil in a saucepan, add the spring onions, garlic and thyme and fry gently for 5 minutes until softened but not coloured. Add the rice and stir-fry for 1 minute.

2 Stir in the lettuce and the sorrel and pour in the stock. Bring to the boil, cover and simmer gently for 15 minutes until the rice is cooked.

3 Transfer to a blender or food processor, add the chives and nutmeg and purée until smooth. Return the soup to the pan, and heat through, whisking in the remaining oil and seasoning with salt and pepper. Serve hot, garnished with a little Parmesan.

**VARIATIONS** For a more substantial soup, omit the rice, reduce the lettuce to 225 g (8 oz) and add 225 g (8 oz) potatoes. If sorrel is not available, use spinach instead.

## GARLIC AND ONION SOUP

PREPARATION TIME 10 minutes
COOKING TIME 50 minutes
FREEZING Suitable (stage 2)
♡ ❊

**SERVES 6**
- *50 g (2 oz) butter*
- *450 g (1 lb) onions, peeled and thinly sliced*
- *8 large garlic cloves, peeled and thinly sliced*
- *30 ml (2 tbsp) white plain flour*

**115 CALS/SERVING**
- *2 litres (3½ pints) vegetable or chicken stock*
- *2 egg yolks*
- *15 ml (1 tbsp) red wine vinegar*
- *salt and pepper*

**1** Melt the butter in a saucepan; add the onions and garlic and cook until golden.

**2** Stir in the flour and cook for 1 minute. Remove from the heat and pour in the stock, then bring to the boil, stirring. Cover and simmer for about 30 minutes.

**3** Beat the egg yolks with the vinegar. Mix with a little hot soup, then stir the egg yolks into the rest of the soup. Cook over a gentle heat, stirring until the soup thickens slightly. Do not boil. Season to taste. Serve in individual bowls.

### TIP
A roast garlic garnish looks attractive and enhances the flavour of this soup. Leave the skins on three small garlic bulbs. Halve each one. Place on an oiled baking sheet. Roast at 170°C (325°F) mark 3 for about 45 minutes or until they are tender.

# CHILLED TOMATO AND VODKA SOUP

PREPARATION TIME 10 minutes plus chilling
FREEZING Not suitable
COLOUR INDEX Page 9
♡

**SERVES 6**
- *125 g (4 oz) celery, trimmed and chopped*
- *1 red pepper, deseeded and chopped*
- *900 ml (1½ pints) tomato juice*
- *60 ml (4 tbsp) vodka*
- *45 ml (3 tbsp) chopped fresh coriander*

**55 CALS/SERVING**
- *60 ml (4 tbsp) Worcestershire sauce*
- *juice of 2 lemons, about 45 ml (3 tbsp)*
- *2.5 ml (½ tsp) chilli sauce*
- *salt and pepper*
- *3 garlic cloves, peeled and crushed*
- *crushed ice, to serve (optional)*

1 Mix the celery and pepper with the remaining ingredients in a large bowl.
2 Cover and chill for at least 1 hour. Serve over a little crushed ice, if wished.

# CHILLED AVOCADO AND LIME SOUP

PREPARATION TIME 5-10 minutes, plus chilling
COOKING TIME 15-20 minutes
FREEZING Not suitable
COLOUR INDEX Page 9

**SERVES 4**
- *15 ml (1 tbsp) extra-virgin olive oil*
- *1 bunch spring onions, trimmed and sliced*
- *225 g (8 oz) potatoes, peeled and cubed*
- *900 ml (1½ pints) vegetable stock*

**235 CALS/SERVING**
- *1-2 limes*
- *2 ripe avocados*
- *salt and pepper*
- *90 ml (6 tbsp) very low-fat fromage frais*
- *snipped chives, to garnish*

1 Heat the oil in a large saucepan, add the spring onions and fry gently until softened.
2 Add the potato to the softened onions and fry, stirring, for 2 minutes. Add the stock and bring to the boil. Cover and simmer for 15-20 minutes.
3 Towards the end of the cooking time, remove a little zest from one of the limes, using a zester, and set aside for the garnish. Squeeze the juice from the lime. Halve, stone and peel the avocados, then chop roughly. Add the avocado to the soup with the lime juice. Taste and adjust the seasoning; add extra lime juice (from the other lime) if required.
4 Remove the soup from the heat, allow to cool slightly, then work until smooth in a blender or food processor. Add 30 ml (2 tbsp) fromage frais and stir to mix. Pour into soup bowls and chill for 3-4 hours. (The soup thickens as it is chilled.)
5 To serve, add a swirl of fromage frais and a squeeze of lime juice. Grind some black pepper on top and garnish with snipped chives and the lime zest. Serve with Melba Toast.

## TIP
To make Melba Toast, cut 4-5 thin slices from a day-old loaf of wholemeal bread. Toast lightly on both sides. Quickly cut off the crusts and split each slice in two horizontally. Bake in a 180°C (350°F) mark 4 oven for 10-15 minutes until crisp and curled.

# NAN BREAD WITH SPICY PRAWNS

PREPARATION TIME 20 minutes
COOKING TIME About 15 minutes
FREEZING Not suitable
COLOUR INDEX Page 10

**MAKES ABOUT 60**

- *15 ml (1 tbsp) vegetable oil*
- *1 garlic clove, peeled and crushed*
- *10 ml (2 tsp) mild curry powder*
- *4 spring onions, finely chopped*
- *350 g (12 oz) cooked peeled prawns, roughly chopped*

**25 CALS/SQUARE**

- *20 ml (4 tsp) mango chutney*
- *20 ml (4 tsp) natural yogurt*
- *salt and pepper*
- *2 large nan bread, about 300 g (10 oz) total weight*

1 Heat the oil in a frying pan and add the garlic, curry powder and onions. Cook for 1 minute, stirring, then add the prawns. Cook gently for a further 2-3 minutes. Off the heat, stir in the chutney and yogurt. Season to taste and set aside.
2 Heat the nan bread in the oven according to packet instructions, then cut into small squares and top with a little of the prawn mixture. Serve warm or cold.

# LITTLE SPANISH SAVOURIES

PREPARATION TIME 30 minutes, plus pastry
COOKING TIME 10 minutes
FREEZING Suitable (stage 2)

❄

**MAKES ABOUT 24**

- *225 g (8 oz) Puff Pastry (see page 370)*
- *butter for greasing*
- *125 g (4 oz) firm goats' cheese or mozzarella, diced*
- *50 g (2 oz) sun-dried tomatoes in oil, drained and roughly chopped*

**65 CALS/SAVOURY**

- *50 g (2 oz) capers, chopped*
- *50 g (2 oz) can anchovy fillets, chopped*
- *50 g (2 oz) pitted olives, quartered*
- *50 g (2 oz) pesto sauce*
- *salt and pepper*

1 Roll out the pastry to 3 mm (⅛ inch) thick. Stamp out 24 circles with a 5 cm (2 inch) cutter and place on a greased baking sheet.
2 Top with the cheese, sun-dried tomatoes, capers, anchovies and olives. Spoon pesto sauce over and season with salt and pepper.
3 Cook at 200°C (400°F) mark 6 for 10-15 minutes or until crisp. Serve hot.

## SMOKED SALMON ROULADE

PREPARATION TIME 30 minutes, plus chilling
FREEZING Not suitable

**MAKES 70 ROUNDS**
- *1 large bunch watercress*
- *225 g (8 oz) full-fat soft cheese with garlic and herbs*
- *10 ml (2 tsp) lemon juice*

**20 CALS/ROUND**
- *black pepper*
- *225 g (8 oz) smoked salmon*
- *lemon wedges, to garnish*

1 Finely chop the watercress, discarding any coarse stalks. Using an electric whisk, mix the watercress into the soft cheese with the lemon juice and plenty of black pepper.
2 Cut out a piece of greaseproof paper measuring 30 x 33 cm (12 x 13 inches). Lay the pieces of smoked salmon on top, overlapping each piece slightly to form a rectangle of about 30 x 28 cm (12 x 11 inches). Cut in half widthways to make two rectangles.
3 Spread the soft-cheese mixture over both rectangles, then carefully roll each one into a thin sausage, using the paper to help you. Cover and refrigerate overnight.
4 Cut each roll into 5 mm (¼ inch) slices and serve immediately, garnished with wedges of lemon.

## NUTTY CHICKEN BITES

PREPARATION TIME 40 minutes, plus marinating
COOKING TIME About 15 minutes
FREEZING Not suitable

**MAKES ABOUT 70**
- *900 g (2 lb) skinless chicken breast fillets*
- *125 g (4 oz) onion, peeled and finely chopped*
- *90 ml (6 tbsp) dark soy sauce*
- *50 ml (10 tsp) dark muscovado sugar*
DIP
- *15 ml (1 tbsp) vegetable oil*

**115 CALS/ BITE WITH DIP**
- *2 garlic cloves, peeled and crushed*
- *5 ml (1 tsp) mild curry powder*
- *10-15 ml (2-3 tsp) mild chilli powder*
- *450 g (1 lb) crunchy peanut butter*
- *pinch of salt*
- *½ cucumber*

1 Beat out the chicken breasts between sheets of greaseproof paper. Cut into 2.5 cm (1 inch) pieces.
2 Mix the onion with the soy sauce and 20 ml (4 tsp) sugar. Pour over the chicken and toss well. Cover and refrigerate overnight.
3 Meanwhile, make the dip. Heat the oil in a pan and add the garlic, curry and chilli powders. Cook for 1-2 minutes, then add the peanut butter, salt and remaining sugar with 450 ml (15 fl oz) water. Simmer for 5 minutes, stirring, until thick.
4 Thread the chicken onto cocktail sticks. Cook at 220°C (425°F) mark 7 for 10 minutes until cooked through. Cut the cucumber into 1 cm (½ inch) pieces and thread onto the sticks. Serve with the cold dip.

## PATE DE CAMPAGNE

PREPARATION TIME 20 minutes, plus chilling
COOKING TIME 2 hours
FREEZING Suitable
❅

**SERVES 10-12**
- *300 g (10 oz) rindless streaky bacon rashers*
- *450 g (1 lb) belly of pork*
- *300 g (10 oz) diced pie veal*
- *175 g (6 oz) lamb's liver*
- *1 onion, peeled*
- *1 garlic clove, peeled and crushed*

**380-310 CALS/SERVING**
- *50 g (2 oz) pitted black olives, chopped*
- *salt and pepper*
- *5 ml (1 tsp) chopped fresh sage*
- *30 ml (2 tbsp) olive oil*
- *15 ml (1 tbsp) lemon juice*
- *30 ml (2 tbsp) brandy*

**1** Stretch the bacon, using the back of a knife. Finely mince the pork, veal, liver and onion. Mix with the remaining ingredients.
**2** Layer the bacon and minced ingredients in a 1.1 litre (2 pint) terrine, topping with a layer of bacon rashers.
**3** Cover with foil or a lid and place in a roasting tin, half-filled with boiling water. Cook at 170°C (325°F) mark 3 for about 2 hours.
**4** Weight down the pâté and allow to cool, then refrigerate overnight. Leave at room temperature for 30 minutes before serving. Cut the pâté into slices and serve on individual plates.

## CORN SCONES WITH AVOCADO

PREPARATION TIME 40 minutes
COOKING TIME 7-8 minutes
FREEZING Suitable (stage 3)
COLOUR INDEX Page 10
❅

**MAKES ABOUT 30**
- *75 g (3 oz) white self-raising flour*
- *salt and pepper*
- *5 ml (1 tsp) baking powder*
- *25 g (1 oz) maize meal or fine semolina*
- *15 ml (1 tbsp) caster sugar*
- *25 g (1 oz) butter*
- *milk*
AVOCADO TOPPING
- *125 g (4 oz) full-fat soft cheese*

**25 CALS/SERVING**
- *1 avocado, roughly mashed*
- *1 hard-boiled egg, finely chopped*
- *15 ml (1 tbsp) lemon juice*
- *dash each of Worcestershire sauce and paprika*
- *175 g (6 oz) rindless lean bacon, grilled and crumbled*

**1** Sift the flour with a pinch of salt and the baking powder into a bowl. Stir in the maize meal and caster sugar. Rub in the butter until the mixture resembles fine breadcrumbs.
**2** Make a well in the centre and stir in enough milk to give a soft dough, about 45-60 ml (3-4 tbsp). Knead lightly, then roll out to 5 mm-1 cm (¼-½ inch) thickness. Cut into rounds using a 2.5 cm (1 inch) cutter. (Use a cap from a bottle if you do not have a cutter.) Place on a baking sheet and brush with milk.
**3** Bake at 220°C (425°F) mark 7 for about 7-8 minutes or until risen and light golden. Leave to cool.
**4** To make the avocado topping, mix the soft cheese with the avocado, hard-boiled egg, lemon juice, Worcestershire sauce and paprika. Season to taste and cover tightly.
**5** Split the cold scones in half and spoon on the avocado topping. Sprinkle with crumbled bacon and serve.

**VARIATION** For a tangy mackerel topping, finely chop a few capers or gherkins and mix with 150 ml (5 fl oz) crème fraîche. Season to taste. Spread onto the halved scones. Top with flakes of smoked mackerel and garnish with chives.

## CHICKEN LIVER AND PISTACHIO PATE

PREPARATION TIME 20 minutes, plus overnight chilling
COOKING TIME 15 minutes
FREEZING Suitable

❄

SERVES 8-10

- *2 rashers of rindless streaky bacon, finely chopped*
- *about 225 g (8 oz) butter*
- *700 g (1½ lb) chicken livers, chopped*
- *1-2 garlic cloves, peeled and chopped*
- *large pinch of ground allspice*
- *125 g (4 oz) flat mushrooms, finely chopped*
- *1 onion, peeled and finely chopped*
- *200 g (7 oz) low-fat soft cheese*

435-350 CALS/SERVING

- *30 ml (2 tbsp) double cream*
- *40 g (1½ oz) shelled pistachio nuts, roughly chopped*
- *45 ml (3 tbsp) chopped mixed fresh parsley, chives and thyme*
- *salt and pepper*

TO GARNISH

- *parsley or other herb leaves*
- *few shelled pistachio nuts*

1 Place the bacon in a heavy-based frying pan and cook until lightly browned.
2 Add 50 g (2 oz) of the butter to the pan and heat until just melted. Add the livers to the pan with the garlic and allspice, and cook briskly over a high heat until the livers are sealed and browned on the outside but still a little pink (but not bloody) on the inside. Remove the bacon and livers from the pan with a slotted spoon and set aside.
3 Add the mushrooms and onion to the pan and cook gently until the onion is softened. Remove from the heat.
4 Transfer the livers and bacon to a blender or food processor. Add the onion and mushrooms, along with any butter remaining in the pan. Add the soft cheese and cream and work until smooth. Turn into a mixing bowl.
5 Fold the nuts and herbs into the pâté. Season with salt and pepper to taste. Spoon the pâté into small individual dishes and level the tops.
6 Melt the remaining butter in a small saucepan over a very low heat. Slowly pour into a jug, leaving the milky sediment behind. Slowly pour the clarified butter onto the pâtés to cover them completely. Immerse herbs and pistachios in the butter to garnish. Chill overnight to set.

**VARIATION** To make a milder pâté, increase the cream cheese to 400 g (14 oz).

## SPICY CRAB DIP

PREPARATION TIME 10 minutes, plus chilling
FREEZING Not suitable
♡

SERVES 4
- *225 g (8 oz) white crab meat, flaked*
- *225 g (8 oz) soft cheese*
- *45 ml (3 tbsp) canned pimiento, finely chopped*
- *juice of ½ lemon*

135 CALS/SERVING
- *10 ml (2 tsp) Worcestershire sauce*
- *5 ml (1 tsp) anchovy essence*
- *1.25 ml (¼ tsp) cayenne pepper*
- *salt and pepper*
- *crudités, to serve*

1 Fold the crab meat into the soft cheese until evenly mixed.
2 Fold in the pimiento, then stir in the lemon juice, Worcestershire sauce, anchovy essence and cayenne and season with salt and pepper. Turn into a serving bowl and chill for at least 2 hours. Serve with crudités.

# BRUSCHETTA

PREPARATION TIME 20 minutes
COOKING TIME 4 minutes
FREEZING Not suitable
COLOUR INDEX Page 11
🕐

SERVES 6
- *12 slices Italian bread (such as Ciabatta), about 2 cm (¾ inch) thick*
- *salt and pepper*
- *1-2 garlic cloves, peeled*
- *90 ml (6 tbsp) olive oil*
- *lemon rind and basil leaves, to garnish*
*HERB AND LEMON TOPPING*
- *15 ml (1 tbsp) each chopped fresh mint and parsley*
- *15 ml (1 tbsp) lemon juice*

300 CALS/SERVING
*TOMATO TOPPING*
- *3 plum or very ripe tomatoes, skinned, deseeded and diced*
- *15 ml (1 tbsp) pesto sauce*
- *30 ml (2 tbsp) chopped fresh basil*
*TAPENADE TOPPING*
- *45-60 ml (3-4 tbsp) tapenade (black olive paste)*
- *4 pitted black olives, shredded*

1 To make the toppings, mix together the ingredients in three small separate bowls and season each with salt and pepper to taste.
2 Toast both sides of the slices of bread until golden. Press the garlic cloves with the blade of a large knife to bruise them and rub over one side of each slice. Drizzle the toast with olive oil, then spoon each of the toppings onto four of the slices.
3 Drizzle the remaining olive oil on top and garnish the Herb and Lemon Topping with lemon rind and the Tomato Topping with basil leaves. Serve while still hot and crisp.

## SKEWERED TIGER PRAWNS WITH PARMA HAM

PREPARATION TIME 20 minutes, plus marinating
COOKING TIME 4-6 minutes
FREEZING Not suitable

♡

**SERVES 4**

- *225 g (8 oz) raw tiger prawns*
- *65 g (2½ oz) sliced Parma ham*
- *coriander or flat-leaf parsley sprigs, to garnish*

*MARINADE*

- *1 shallot, peeled and finely chopped*
- *1 garlic clove, peeled and crushed*

**200 CALS/SERVING**

- *5 ml (1 tsp) wholegrain mustard*
- *1 small fresh red chilli, deseeded and very finely sliced*
- *15 ml (1 tbsp) olive oil*
- *juice of ½ lemon*
- *salt and pepper*

1 Peel the prawns, discarding the heads. Cut down the back of each prawn and remove the black intestinal vein. Wash and dry well. Thread the prawns onto 8 small bamboo skewers which have been previously soaked in warm water for 30 minutes.
2 Cut the Parma ham slices in half lengthways and wrap around the skewered prawns. Place the skewers in a glass or china dish and set aside.
3 Mix together the marinade ingredients and pour over the skewered prawns. Cover and marinate in the refrigerator for 1-2 hours, turning occasionally.
4 Drain the skewered prawns and place on a grill rack. Cook under a hot grill for 4-6 minutes, basting with the marinade and turning occasionally until the prawns are cooked and the ham is beginning to crisp and brown. Serve at once, garnished with coriander or parsley sprigs.

**VARIATION** Thread lemon wedges onto the skewers, in between the prawns.

# PEPPERED MACKEREL AND APPLE MOUSSES

PREPARATION TIME 30 minutes, plus chilling
COOKING TIME 13-18 minutes
FREEZING Suitable (stage 3)
COLOUR INDEX Page 9
❄

| SERVES 6 | 380 CALS/SERVING |
|---|---|
| • *15 ml (1 tbsp) vegetable oil* | • *60 ml (4 tbsp) lemon juice* |
| • *1 small onion, peeled and chopped* | • *15 ml (1 tbsp) powdered gelatine* |
| • *225 g (8 oz) cooking apples, peeled and chopped* | • *salt and pepper* |
| | • *3 red eating apples* |
| • *4 peppered mackerel fillets* | • *few sprigs of watercress or flat-leaf parsley* |
| • *30 ml (2 tbsp) creamed horseradish* | • *45 ml (3 tbsp) low-fat natural yogurt* |
| • *75 ml (5 tbsp) mayonnaise* | |

1 Heat the oil in a saucepan, add the onion and cook gently until softened. Add the cooking apples, cover, and cook for 10-15 minutes or until the apple has softened. Leave to cool.
2 Flake the mackerel, and put into a blender or food processor with half the creamed horseradish and 30 ml (2 tbsp) mayonnaise. Blend for a minute. Add the onion and apple, and blend until smooth.
3 Put 15 ml (1 tbsp) lemon juice and 15 ml (1 tbsp) water in a small bowl. Sprinkle the gelatine over it and leave to soak for 5 minutes. Stand the bowl in a pan of simmering water and stir until dissolved, then stir into the mackerel and apple purée. Season with salt and pepper. Spoon the mixture into six greased 150 ml (5 fl oz) ramekin dishes. Chill for 2 hours until set.
4 Core and thinly slice the red apples and toss in 30 ml (2 tbsp) of the lemon juice. Arrange on six plates with the watercress or parsley.
5 Dip the mousses briefly in hot water, then unmould them onto the plates. Grind a little pepper over the top. Mix the yogurt with the remaining horseradish, mayonnaise and lemon juice. Season and serve with the mousses.

# WARM SEAFOOD SALAD WITH TOASTED POLENTA

PREPARATION TIME 15 minutes, plus cooling
COOKING TIME 15 minutes
FREEZING Not suitable
COLOUR INDEX Page 12

| SERVES 6 | 285 CALS/SERVING |
|---|---|
| • *75 g (3 oz) polenta* | • *350 g (12 oz) smoked haddock fillet, thinly sliced* |
| • *150 ml (5 fl oz) salad dressing* | |
| • *1 garlic clove, peeled and crushed* | • *175 g (6 oz) cooked, peeled prawns* |
| • *30 ml (2 tbsp) chopped fresh herbs* | |

1 Make up the polenta according to packet instructions. Spoon onto a sheet of foil, cool slightly, then press into a rectangle about 1 cm (½ inch) thick. Leave to cool.
2 Whisk together the dressing, garlic and half of the herbs. Place the haddock and prawns in a single layer in a shallow, heatproof dish. Pour the dressing over. Cover and chill.
3 Cut the cooled polenta into 7.5 cm (3 inch) triangles. Grill for about 4 minutes on each side until golden.
4 Grill the fish for 1-2 minutes, basting, until the haddock turns opaque. Serve the polenta with the warm salad. Sprinkle the remaining herbs over.

***TIP***
Polenta is coarse-grained, yellow cornmeal which is cooked in water to a thick paste. The quick-cook variety is suitable for this recipe. Look for it in supermarkets and Italian delicatessens.

# DEEP-FRIED WHITEBAIT WITH HOT SAUCE

PREPARATION TIME 20 minutes
COOKING TIME About 15 minutes
FREEZING Not suitable

### SERVES 4

- *60 ml (4 tbsp) white plain flour*
- *700 g (1½ lb) whitebait*
- *oil for deep-frying*
- *chopped parsley, to garnish*
- *paprika, for sprinkling*
- *lime or lemon wedges, to serve*

HOT SAUCE
- *25 g (1 oz) ground hazelnuts*
- *2-3 hot red chillies, stems removed*

### 790 CALS/SERVING

- *1 small onion, peeled and quartered*
- *3 garlic cloves, peeled*
- *1 ripe tomato, skinned*
- *15 ml (1 tbsp) mild paprika*
- *salt and pepper*
- *10 ml (2 tsp) balsamic or red wine vinegar*
- *about 60 ml (4 tbsp) virgin olive oil*

1 To make the sauce, first spread the hazelnuts in the grill pan and toast until golden brown, shaking the pan occasionally.
2 Put all the sauce ingredients, except the olive oil, in a food processor or blender and process until smooth. Add a little of the olive oil if the mixture gets stuck around the blades. With the machine running, gradually add the olive oil in a thin stream to make a fairly thick sauce. Season to taste.
3 Put the flour in a bowl and season generously. Add the whitebait and toss to coat in the flour.
4 Heat the oil in a deep-fat fryer to 190°C (380°F) or until a cube of stale bread dropped into the oil turns golden brown in about 30 seconds.
5 Deep-fry the fish in the hot oil in batches for about 3 minutes or until golden brown. Drain on crumpled absorbent kitchen paper and keep hot while cooking the remainder.
6 Serve garnished with chopped parsley and a sprinkling of paprika, and accompanied by lime wedges and the sauce.

**VARIATION** If you're short of time, serve the whitebait with a spiced mayonnaise instead of the hot sauce. Flavour some homemade or good bought mayonnaise with grated lime rind, chopped chilli and chopped basil to taste.

# VEGETABLE SAMOSAS

PREPARATION TIME 45 minutes, plus cooling
COOKING TIME About 35 minutes
FREEZING Suitable

✳

**MAKES 24**

**150 CALS/SAMOSA**

- *450 g (1 lb) potatoes, peeled and halved*
- *salt and pepper*
- *15 ml (1 tbsp) vegetable oil*
- *1 onion, peeled and finely chopped*
- *1 garlic clove, peeled and crushed*
- *1-2 hot green chillies, deseeded and chopped*
- *10 ml (2 tsp) ground coriander*
- *10 ml (2 tsp) cumin seeds*
- *5 ml (1 tsp) ground fenugreek*
- *1 large ripe tomato, chopped*

- *50 g (2 oz) frozen peas*
- *30 ml (2 tbsp) chopped fresh coriander*
- *15 ml (1 tbsp) chopped fresh mint*
- *oil for deep-frying*
- *mint sprigs and lime halves, to garnish*
  PASTRY
- *450 g (1 lb) white plain flour*
- *5 ml (1 tsp) salt*
- *45 ml (3 tbsp) chopped fresh coriander (optional)*
- *60 ml (4 tbsp) vegetable oil, melted ghee or butter*

1 Cook the potatoes in boiling salted water until just tender. Drain and chop into fairly small pieces.
2 Heat the oil in a frying pan, add the onion and garlic and cook for about 5 minutes until softened. Add the spices and cook for 2 minutes, stirring continuously.

3 Add the tomato to the pan and simmer until softened. Add the potatoes and stir to coat in the spice mixture. Add the peas and cook for 1-2 minutes until thawed. Add the herbs and plenty of seasoning, then allow to cool.
4 To make the pastry, mix the flour with the salt and herbs, if using, in a bowl. Add the oil or melted fat and enough warm water to make a soft dough - about 200 ml (7 fl oz). Turn onto a lightly floured surface and knead for about 5 minutes.
5 Divide the dough into 12 pieces; keep covered with a damp cloth to prevent drying out. Roll one piece out to a 15 cm (6 inch) round and cut in half to make two semi-circles. Place a heaped teaspoon of filling on each semi-circle. Dampen the edges, fold over the filling and press together to seal. Repeat with the remaining pastry and filling.
6 Heat the oil in a deep-fat fryer to 180°C (350°F). Test the temperature by dropping a small piece of pastry into the oil - the pastry should sizzle immediately on contact and rise to the surface.
7 Deep-fry the samosas, about three at a time, for 3-5 minutes or until pale golden brown. Drain on crumpled absorbent kitchen paper. Serve warm, garnished with mint and lime halves.

**VARIATION** *Meat samosas* Omit the potato. After frying the spices, add 175 g (6 oz) minced lamb or beef and fry until browned. Add 5-10 ml (1-2 tsp) curry paste and a few spoonfuls of water, and cook for about 20 minutes or until the meat is tender. Add the peas and cook for 2 minutes. Cool and complete as above.

---

*TIP*
Make a quick chutney to accompany the samosas. Peel and finely slice a few spring onions, mix with a little crushed garlic, then toss with freshly torn mint and coriander leaves, a splash of lemon juice, a dash of oil and plenty of seasoning.

# POTATO PANCAKES WITH SMOKED SALMON

PREPARATION TIME 15 minutes, plus standing
COOKING TIME About 30 minutes
FREEZING Suitable (stage 5)
COLOUR INDEX Page 10
❄

**MAKES 6**
- *350 g (12 oz) potatoes, peeled*
- *salt and pepper*
- *45 ml (3 tbsp) milk*
- *2 whole eggs, 2 egg whites*
- *45 ml (3 tbsp) single cream*
- *45 ml (3 tbsp) white plain flour*

**340 CALS/SERVING**
- *oil for frying*
- *175 g (6 oz) sliced smoked salmon*
- *200 ml (7 fl oz) crème fraîche or soured cream*
- *40 g (1½ oz) jar salmon roe*
- *fresh chives and lemon wedges, to garnish*

1 Cook the potatoes in boiling, salted water for 20 minutes until tender. Drain and mash well.
2 Beat in the milk, whole eggs, cream and flour: season well.
3 Lightly whisk the egg whites and fold into the potato mixture. Cover, then leave in a cool place for about 1 hour.
4 Heat a little oil in a non-stick crêpe pan and spoon in about 75 ml (5 tbsp) of the pancake mixture. Cook for approximately 2-3 minutes, then carefully flip over and cook the underside for a further 2-3 minutes. Cook the remaining pancakes. You should have 6 in total.
5 Keep the pancakes hot in a low oven, layered with greaseproof paper and wrapped in foil.
6 To serve, arrange one pancake on individual plates and top with a slice of smoked salmon, a spoonful of crème fraîche and a little salmon roe. Garnish with fresh chives and lemon wedges.

# GOLDEN STUFFED MUSHROOMS

PREPARATION TIME 10 minutes
COOKING TIME About 25 minutes
FREEZING Not suitable
🕐

**SERVES 4**
- *12 cup mushrooms*
- *about 60 ml (4 tbsp) olive oil*
- *175 g (6 oz) rindless streaky bacon, roughly chopped*
- *1 small onion, peeled and finely chopped*
- *50 g (2 oz) salted cashews, chopped*
- *2 garlic cloves, peeled and crushed*

**320 CALS/SERVING**
- *75 g (3 oz) fresh white breadcrumbs*
- *45 ml (3 tbsp) chopped fresh parsley*
- *1 egg, beaten*
- *salt and pepper*
- *lemon slices and basil, to garnish*

1 Roughly chop the mushroom stems; rinse and drain the mushroom caps.
2 Heat 30 ml (2 tbsp) oil in a medium-sized frying pan and stir-fry the bacon for 2-3 minutes. Add the onion, mushroom stems, cashews and garlic. Cook for a further 3-4 minutes. Remove from the heat.
3 Stir the breadcrumbs, parsley and beaten egg into the mushroom mixture. Add plenty of pepper but only a little salt. Leave to cool.
4 Place the mushroom caps on an oiled edged baking tray. Fill with the mushroom mixture. Drizzle with oil.
5 Bake at 220°C (425°F) mark 7 for 15-20 minutes or until tender and lightly browned. Serve garnished with lemon slices and basil.

## SOY-GLAZED CHICKEN LIVERS WITH CHINESE LEAVES

PREPARATION TIME 10 minutes, plus marinating
COOKING TIME 5 minutes
FREEZING Not suitable

SERVES 4                    275 CALS/SERVING

- *30 ml (2 tbsp) dark soy sauce*
- *30 ml (2 tbsp) dry sherry*
- *1 garlic clove, peeled and crushed*
- *5 ml (1 tsp) grated fresh root ginger*
- *5 ml (1 tsp) sesame oil*
- *5 ml (1 tsp) clear honey*
- *1.25 ml ($^1/_4$ tsp) Chinese five-spice powder*
- *350 g (12 oz) chicken livers, thawed if frozen*
- *50 g (2 oz) watercress*

- *125 g (4 oz) pak choi or Chinese cabbage, shredded*
- *15 ml (1 tbsp) coriander leaves*
- *15 ml (1 tbsp) sesame seeds, toasted*
*DRESSING*
- *30 ml (2 tbsp) groundnut oil*
- *10 ml (2 tsp) chilli oil*
- *30 ml (2 tbsp) lime juice*
- *15 ml (1 tbsp) rice or wine vinegar*
- *10 ml (2 tsp) caster sugar*
- *salt and pepper*

1 Combine the soy sauce, sherry, garlic, ginger, sesame oil, honey and five-spice powder together until well blended. Wash and dry the chicken livers, discarding any discoloured parts. Toss the livers in the soy mixture and transfer to a shallow dish. Cover and marinate for 2 hours.
2 Meanwhile, make the dressing. Place all the ingredients in a small bowl and whisk until blended. Set aside.
3 Transfer the chicken livers, with all the juices, to a foil-lined grill pan and grill as close to the heat as possible for 1-2 minutes on each side until browned and just cooked through.
4 Place the salad leaves and coriander in a large bowl, add the dressing and toss until evenly coated. Divide the salad between individual plates, spoon on the chicken livers with their juices and serve at once, scattered with the sesame seeds.

**VARIATION** If preferred, you can fry the chicken livers – heat 30 ml (2 tbsp) sunflower oil in a frying pan, add the livers and fry quickly to seal. Add the marinade juices to the pan and simmer gently for 3 minutes.

## CARPACCIO OF SALMON

PREPARATION TIME 20 minutes
FREEZING Not suitable
COLOUR INDEX Page 11
♡ ⏱

**SERVES 10**
- *575 g (1¼ lb) salmon fillet, skinned*
- *125 ml (4 fl oz) olive oil*
- *225 g (8 oz) tomatoes, skinned, deseeded and finely chopped*
- *1 bunch fresh chives or spring onions, cut into long pieces*

**200 CALS/SERVING**
- *juice of 2 limes*
- *salt and pepper*
- *lime wedges, to garnish*
- *slices of brown bread and butter, to serve*

1 Cut the salmon into 20 slices. Bat out thinly between sheets of oiled clingfilm. It should be the thickness of sliced smoked salmon.
2 Mix the tomatoes and chives or spring onions with the lime juice, olive oil and seasoning.
3 Just before serving, arrange the salmon on individual serving plates and spoon the dressing over. Garnish with lime wedges and serve with slices of brown bread and butter.

**VARIATION** If the idea of eating raw salmon doesn't really appeal to you, serve the same quantity of sliced smoked salmon instead. Alternatively, place the thin salmon slices in single layers in ovenproof dishes and cook in the oven at 220°C (425°F) mark 7 for about 5 minutes or until the salmon just turns opaque. Serve warm, garnished with lime.

## GRILLED PEPPER AND AUBERGINE SALAD

PREPARATION TIME 20 minutes
COOKING TIME 10 minutes
FREEZING Not suitable
♡ ⏱

**SERVES 4**
- *30 ml (2 tbsp) French dressing*
- *15 ml (1 tbsp) extra-virgin olive oil*
- *2 small, fat aubergines, cut into slices*
- *2 large, long red peppers*

**120 CALS/SERVING**
- *10 ml (2 tsp) lemon juice*
- *30 ml (2 tbsp) chopped fresh basil*
- *1 garlic clove, peeled and thinly sliced*
- *salt and pepper*
- *fresh basil leaves, to garnish*

1 Mix together the French dressing and olive oil. Brush the aubergine slices with the dressing mixture and then grill with the whole peppers until blackened all over, turning the aubergine slices and brushing with more dressing. Put them in a bowl and immediately cover with a damp tea towel. Leave until cool enough to handle.
2 Remove the charred skins from the peppers and cut lengthways into quarters, removing the core and seeds and reserving any juices in a bowl. Stir the remaining cooking juices from the grill pan into the bowl, then add the lemon juice, basil and garlic. Season with salt and pepper. Drizzle the mixture over the vegetables. Serve at room temperature, garnished with basil leaves.

1 Place the bulghur wheat in a large bowl and pour over 300 ml (10 fl oz) boiling water. Leave to soak for 30 minutes until the bulghur has softened, then drain off any excess water.
2 Peel the lemon, being careful to remove all the pith. Cut the flesh into segments, discarding the pips. Finely dice the flesh.
3 Combine the bulghur wheat with the lemon and the next seven ingredients. Cover and chill for 1 hour for the flavours to develop.
4 Remove the salad from the refrigerator and stir in the pine nuts, olives and plenty of seasoning. Serve at once.

## GRILLED PEARS WITH STILTON

PREPARATION TIME 10 minutes
COOKING TIME 6-7 minutes
FREEZING Not suitable
COLOUR INDEX Page 11

SERVES 4
- *8 thick slices cut from a large baguette*
- *1 packet ready-washed watercress, trimmed*
- *2 large ripe pears, peeled, cored and sliced*

350 CALS/SERVING
- *225 g (8 oz) blue Stilton cheese*
- *freshly ground black pepper*

1 Toast the bread on both sides then transfer to a baking sheet that will hold the slices in a close single layer.
2 Cover with the watercress and place the pear slices on top. Slice the cheese and arrange over the pears.
3 Place under a hot grill until the cheese is just beginning to melt. Grind black pepper liberally over the top and serve at once.

**VARIATION** Substitute another blue cheese, such as Gorgonzola or Bleu d'Auvergne.

## BULGHUR WHEAT SALAD WITH DRIED FRUIT AND PINE NUTS

PREPARATION TIME 15 minutes, plus soaking and chilling
FREEZING Not suitable

SERVES 4-6
- *225 g (8 oz) bulghur wheat*
- *1 lemon*
- *1 large onion, peeled and finely chopped*
- *4 ripe tomatoes, skinned and diced*
- *75 g (3 oz) dried fruit, such as figs, apricots and peaches, chopped*
- *60 ml (4 tbsp) chopped fresh coriander*

635–425 CALS/SERVING
- *30 ml (2 tbsp) chopped fresh mint*
- *125 ml (4 fl oz) extra-virgin olive oil*
- *5 ml (1 tsp) clear honey*
- *50 g (2 oz) pine nuts, toasted*
- *50 g (2 oz) pitted black olives*
- *salt and pepper*

### TIP
To toast the pine nuts, place the nuts on a baking sheet and toast in the oven at 200°C (400°F) mark 6 for 6-8 minutes until golden.

# TOASTED BACON AND GOATS' CHEESE SALAD

PREPARATION TIME 30 minutes
COOKING TIME About 6 minutes
FREEZING Not suitable
COLOUR INDEX Page 12

SERVES 6

- *about 350 g (12 oz) soft, rindless goats' cheese*
- *2 bunches chives, finely chopped*
- *salt and pepper*
- *about 350 g (12 oz) thin-cut, rindless streaky bacon*
- *25 g (1 oz) toasted walnut pieces*
- *60 ml (4 tbsp) walnut oil*

320 CALS/SERVING

- *10 ml (2 tsp) balsamic or red-wine vinegar*
- *1.25 ml (¼ tsp) sugar*
- *75 g (3 oz) mixed green salad leaves or rocket*
- *toasted ciabatta, to serve*

1 With wet hands, shape the goats' cheese into six round patties.
2 Roll the patties in the chopped chives and season with black pepper only. Chill.
3 Stretch the rashers of bacon by running the back of a round-bladed knife along each piece. Carefully wrap each pattie in bacon, making sure all the cheese is hidden and the ends of bacon are tucked underneath the pattie (you will need 3 4 rashers per pattie). Cover and chill until required.
4 Roughly chop the walnuts and mix with the walnut oil, vinegar and sugar. Season to taste. Wash and dry the salad leaves.
5 Place the patties on a foil-lined grill pan and grill for about 6 minutes, until golden and crisp, turning once. (If a little cheese oozes out, scoop it onto the mixed salad leaves to serve.)
6 Toss the dressing with the mixed salad, arrange on six plates and top each one with a pattie. Serve immediately with ciabatta.

### TIP
Goats' cheese is most often sold in 125 g (4 oz) packs - just slice in half horizontally.

# GRAPEFRUIT AND CHICORY SALAD WITH PRAWNS

PREPARATION TIME 15 minutes
FREEZING Not suitable
♡ ⏲

SERVES 4

- *2 grapefruit*
- *2 heads of chicory, washed and trimmed*
- *30 ml (2 tbsp) sunflower oil*
- *freshly ground black pepper*

110 CALS/SERVING

- *12 cooked prawns with shells*
- *snipped fresh chives, to garnish*

1 Using a serrated knife, remove all the peel and pith from the grapefruit then, holding the grapefruit over a bowl to collect the juice, divide into segments, discarding the pips and as much of the membrane as possible. Put the segments in another bowl and reserve the grapefruit juice.
2 Slice one of the chicory heads widthways into thin slices and add to the grapefruit segments. Mix gently together then arrange on four plates with the whole leaves of the other chicory head.
3 Add the oil and pepper to the reserved grapefruit juice and whisk everything together until well blended.
4 Pour the dressing over the salads and arrange the prawns on top. Garnish with the chives.

# FISH AND SHELLFISH

# FISH PLAKI WITH ROOT VEGETABLES

PREPARATION TIME 15 minutes, plus cooling
COOKING TIME 35-45 minutes
FREEZING Suitable
COLOUR INDEX Page 13
♡ ❄

SERVES 4

290 CALS/SERVING

- *45 ml (3 tbsp) olive oil*
- *2 onions, peeled and sliced*
- *2 garlic cloves, peeled and crushed*
- *2 carrots, peeled, halved lengthways and sliced*
- *225 g (8 oz) celeriac, peeled and diced*
- *salt and pepper*
- *3 plum tomatoes, skinned, deseeded and diced*
- *1 lemon, sliced*
- *15 ml (1 tbsp) chopped fresh thyme*
- *75 ml (3 fl oz) dry white wine*
- *4 cod or tuna fish steaks, each weighing about 150 g (5 oz)*
- *45 ml (3 tbsp) chopped fresh parsley, to garnish*

1 Heat the oil in a large shallow saucepan, add the onions and cook over moderate heat for 5 minutes until softened and beginning to brown. Add the garlic, carrots and celeriac and cook for 8 minutes, stirring occasionally.
2 Stir in 150 ml (5 fl oz) water and season with salt and pepper to taste. Cover and simmer for 10-15 minutes, until the carrot and celeriac are very tender. Add the tomatoes, sliced lemon and thyme and simmer for 2-3 minutes. Add the wine.
3 Place the fish steaks in the sauce, cover and cook over a low heat for 10-15 minutes until the fish is cooked and flakes easily. Leave to cool for about 15 minutes, then sprinkle with the parsley to garnish and serve warm.

# COD IN ORANGE AND CIDER SAUCE

PREPARATION TIME 15 minutes
COOKING TIME 25-30 minutes
FREEZING Suitable
COLOUR INDEX Page 13
♡ ❄

SERVES 4

160 CALS/SERVING

- *4 cod fillets, skinned, each weighing about 175 g (6 oz)*
- *1 orange*
- *175 g (6 oz) onion, peeled and chopped*
- *black pepper*
- *150 ml (5 fl oz) medium-dry cider*
- *125 ml (4 fl oz) fish stock*
- *10 ml (2 tsp) chopped fresh coriander*
- *coriander sprigs and orange slices, to garnish*

1 Place the fish in a 1.1 litre (2 pint) ovenproof dish. Pare the rind from the orange and cut into 7.5 cm (3 inch) long thin strips. Place on top of the fish with the onion and season with black pepper.
2 Mix 30 ml (2 tbsp) orange juice with the cider and fish stock. Pour over the fish, cover and bake in the oven at 190°C (375°F) mark 5 for 20-25 minutes or until the fish is cooked through.
3 Carefully place the onion, orange strips and fish in a serving dish and keep them warm.
4 Strain the cooking liquid into a small saucepan and boil rapidly for about 5 minutes or until the liquid is reduced by half. Pour over the fish and sprinkle with the coriander. Garnish with coriander sprigs and orange slices and serve immediately.

## PAN-FRIED COD WITH CHANTERELLE MUSHROOMS

PREPARATION TIME 20 minutes
COOKING TIME About 20 minutes
FREEZING Not suitable

**SERVES 4**

- *4 slices white bread*
- *4 cod steaks, each weighing about 175 g (6 oz)*
- *75 g (3 oz) butter*
- *30 ml (2 tbsp) vegetable oil*
- *salt and pepper*
- *plain flour for dredging*
- *4 spring onions, finely chopped*

**480 CALS/SERVING**

- *225 g (8 oz) chanterelle mushrooms or mixed mushrooms*
- *1 garlic clove, peeled and crushed*
- *45 ml (3 tbsp) crème fraîche*
- *30 ml (2 tbsp) chopped fresh chives*

1 Remove the crusts from the bread and cut the slices into ovals, the same size as the cod steaks. Heat half the butter and the oil in a frying pan. Fry the bread slices on both sides until crisp and golden. Keep warm.

2 Season the cod, then coat with flour. Heat the remaining butter in the frying pan and fry the cod for about 5 minutes on each side until cooked through and lightly golden. Remove from the pan and keep warm.

3 Add the spring onions, mushrooms and garlic to the pan and sauté for 5 minutes until the juices are just beginning to escape from the mushrooms. Stir in the crème fraîche and heat through gently. Season and add half the chives.

4 Place a bread croûte on each plate, arrange a cod steak on top and spoon the mushroom mixture on top of the fish. Sprinkle with the remaining chives and serve at once.

**NOTE** Any other variety of wild mushroom can be used instead of chanterelles.

# COD FILLET WRAPPED IN FILO
## PASTRY WITH ROCKET

PREPARATION TIME 20 minutes
COOKING TIME 18-20 minutes
FREEZING Suitable (stage 2)

♡ ❊

**SERVES 6**

- *6 thick cod fillets, each weighing about 125 g (4 oz)*
- *salt and pepper*
- *50 g (2 oz) rocket leaves, roughly chopped*
- *50 g (2 oz) ricotta cheese*
- *25 g (1 oz) freshly grated Parmesan cheese*
- *1 garlic clove, peeled*

**335 CALS/SERVING**

- *30 ml (2 tbsp) chopped mixed herbs*
- *grated rind and juice of ½ lemon*
- *90 ml (6 tbsp) olive oil*
- *12 small sheets filo pastry*
- *beaten egg for brushing*
- *30 ml (2 tbsp) freshly grated Parmesan cheese*

**1** Wash and dry the cod fillets and season well on both sides. Place the rocket in a blender with the ricotta, 25 g (1 oz) Parmesan, the garlic, herbs, lemon rind and juice and 30 ml (2 tbsp) olive oil. Purée until smooth and season to taste.

**2** Take 1 sheet of pastry, brush with a little oil and top with a second sheet; brush with oil. Place 1 cod fillet in the middle of the pastry and spread over a sixth of the rocket paste. Wrap the pastry over and around the fish and press the edges together to seal. Place on a greased baking sheet, seam side down and repeat to make 6 parcels.

**3** Brush all the parcels with a little more oil and bake at 220°C (425°F) mark 7 for 10 minutes. Brush with egg, then sprinkle with the grated Parmesan and bake for 8-10 minutes until the pastry is crisp and golden and a skewer inserted into the centre of the fish comes out hot.

---

*TIP*
Make sure you buy thick fillets of cod from the head end of the fish.

## FISHERMAN'S PIE

PREPARATION TIME 10 minutes
COOKING TIME 54 minutes
FREEZING Suitable
COLOUR INDEX Page 17
❅

SERVES 4      390 CALS/SERVING

- *50 g (2 oz) butter or margarine*
- *1 red pepper, deseeded and thinly sliced*
- *1 green pepper, deseeded and thinly sliced*
- *1 small onion, peeled and sliced*
- *salt and pepper*
- *125 g (4 oz) button mushrooms, halved*
- *500 ml (16 fl oz) tomato juice*
- *575 g (1¼ lb) cod fillet, skinned*
- *450 g (1 lb) potatoes, peeled and very thinly sliced*
- *50 g (2 oz) Edam cheese, grated*

1 Melt 25 g (1 oz) of the butter in a frying pan, add the peppers and onion and fry gently for 10 minutes or until soft but not coloured. Using a slotted spoon, transfer to a 2.4 litre (4 pint) ovenproof dish. Season well with salt and pepper.
2 Add the mushrooms to the juices in the frying pan and cook for 3-4 minutes, stirring frequently, until evenly coloured.
3 Pour the tomato juice evenly over the pepper and onion mixture in the dish.
4 Cut the fish into large cubes. Arrange the cubes on top of the tomato juice, pressing down gently into the juice. Top with the mushrooms. Season again with salt and pepper to taste.
5 Arrange the potato slices on top of the mushrooms. Melt the remaining butter and brush over the potatoes. Bake in the oven at 190°C (375°F) mark 5 for 25 minutes.
6 Sprinkle the grated cheese over the pie, return to the oven and bake for a further 15 minutes or until the cheese has melted and is bubbling. Serve the pie hot.

## CREAMY FISH AND PUMPKIN PIE

PREPARATION TIME 10 minutes
COOKING TIME 30 minutes
FREEZING Not suitable
COLOUR INDEX Page 17

SERVES 4      395 CALS/SERVING

- *700 g (1½ lb) pumpkin or squash, peeled, deseeded and chopped*
- *salt and pepper*
- *350 g (12 oz) courgettes, roughly chopped*
- *450 g (1 lb) cod fillet, skinned and cut into large chunks*
- *125 ml (4 fl oz) milk*
- *3 peppercorns*
- *1 bay leaf*
- *30 ml (2 tbsp) butter or margarine*
- *45 ml (3 tbsp) white plain flour*
- *50 ml (2 fl oz) dry white wine*
- *75 g (3 oz) soft cheese with garlic and herbs*
- *30 ml (2 tbsp) chopped fresh tarragon or 5 ml (1 tsp) dried*
- *4 sheets filo pastry, about 50 g (2 oz) total weight*
- *15 ml (1 tbsp) melted butter or margarine*
- *15 ml (1 tbsp) sesame seeds*

1 Simmer the pumpkin in salted water for 5 minutes. Add the courgettes and simmer for a further 5 minutes or until just tender. Drain well.
2 Meanwhile, place the cod in a saucepan with the milk, peppercorns, bay leaf and 125 ml (4 fl oz) water and simmer for about 2 minutes until just tender. Drain well, reserving the cooking liquid.
3 Melt the butter in a saucepan, add the flour and cook gently for 1 minute, stirring. Remove from the heat and gradually stir in 275 ml (9 fl oz) reserved cooking liquid and the wine. Bring to the boil and cook, stirring, until the sauce thickens. Remove from the heat and stir in the cheese and tarragon. Season to taste.
4 Place the vegetables and fish in a 1.1 litre (2 pint) ovenproof dish. Spoon over the sauce. Crumple pastry on top and brush with melted butter. Sprinkle with sesame seeds.
5 Bake at 200°C (400°F) mark 6 for about 15 minutes until golden brown and piping hot.

scatter the olives between them. Cover and cook gently for 6 minutes, then turn the fish cutlets over and continue cooking for a further 4-5 minutes until cooked.

5 Adjust the seasoning, tear the basil leaves over the dish and serve immediately, garnished with extra basil sprigs.

**NOTE** Ricard is the best-known brand of pastis. Pernod is similarly flavoured with anise and has the same effect in cooking.

**VARIATION** Use other white fish steaks – such as swordfish or haddock. If you have no aniseed-flavoured liqueur, fry a teaspoonful of fennel seeds with the onion.

## COD CUTLETS PROVENCALE

PREPARATION TIME 10 minutes
COOKING TIME About 25 minutes
FREEZING Not suitable
♡

**SERVES 4**
- *4 cod cutlets, each weighing about 150 g (5 oz)*
- *75 ml (5 tbsp) olive oil*
- *1 Spanish onion, peeled and finely chopped*
- *5 ml (1 tsp) dried oregano*
- *3 garlic cloves, peeled and crushed*

**325 CALS/SERVING**
- *400 g (14 oz) can plum tomatoes*
- *15 ml (1 tbsp) tomato purée*
- *10 ml (2 tsp) pastis, ouzo or other aniseed liqueur*
- *salt and pepper*
- *12 small black olives*
- *1-2 fresh basil sprigs*
- *extra basil sprigs, to garnish*

1 Rinse the fish cutlets and pat dry with absorbent kitchen paper; set aside.
2 Heat the olive oil in a large shallow frying pan. Add the onion with the oregano and cook over a very low heat for 10 minutes, stirring frequently. Add the garlic to the pan and cook for a further 2-3 minutes until the onion is translucent and beginning to turn pale golden.
3 Add the tomatoes to the pan, mashing with a fork. Add the tomato purée, bring to the boil and stir in the liqueur. Season to taste.
4 Bury the fish cutlets in the tomato sauce and

## WHITING IN SOURED CREAM

PREPARATION TIME 10 minutes
COOKING TIME 6 minutes
FREEZING Not suitable
COLOUR INDEX Page 14
🕐

**SERVES 2**
- *25 g (1 oz) butter*
- *350 g (12 oz) whiting fillet, skinned*
- *salt and pepper*
- *1 large firm tomato*
- *30 ml (2 tbsp) chopped parsley and chives, mixed*

**620 CALS/SERVING**
- *150 ml (5 fl oz) soured cream*
- *75 g (3 oz) Gruyère cheese, grated*
- *herb sprigs, to garnish*

1 Choose a shallow serving dish that fits under the grill and is just large enough to take the fish in a single layer. Put the butter in the dish and grill until melted.
2 Remove the dish from the grill and put in the fish. Turn the fish so it is buttered side up, then sprinkle with salt and pepper to taste. Grill for 2-3 minutes.
3 Meanwhile, chop the tomato finely, place in a bowl and combine with the herbs and soured cream. Add 40 g (1½ oz) of the cheese, salt and pepper to taste, and mix again.
4 When the fish has cooked for about 3 minutes, spoon the cream mixture on top. Sprinkle a little more cheese over and grill for a further 2 minutes until bubbling. Serve at once, garnished with sprigs of herbs.

## PLAICE WITH GRAPES

PREPARATION TIME 30 minutes
COOKING TIME 25 minutes
FREEZING Not suitable
♡

**SERVES 4**                    **270 CALS/SERVING**

- *175 g (6 oz) green grapes, skinned, halved and deseeded*
- *8 large plaice fillets, each weighing about 125 g (4 oz), skinned*
- *125 ml (4 fl oz) dry white wine*
- *125 ml (4 fl oz) fish stock*
- *10 ml (2 tsp) finely chopped fresh basil or 5 ml (1 tsp) dried basil*
- *2-3 bay leaves*
- *5 ml (1 tsp) cornflour*
- *125 ml (4 fl oz) milk*
- *salt and pepper*
- *30 ml (2 tbsp) Greek yogurt*
- *chopped fresh parsley, to garnish*

**1** Place 2-3 grape halves on the skinned side of each plaice fillet. Roll up from the narrow end, secure with cocktail sticks and arrange close together in a poaching pan or large saucepan.
**2** Mix together the wine, stock, basil and bay leaves and pour over the fish. Bring to the boil, lower the heat, cover and poach gently for 10 minutes until the fish is cooked.
**3** Using a slotted spoon, transfer the fish rolls to a serving dish, draining well. Remove the cocktail sticks if wished, and keep warm. Simmer the cooking liquid for about 10 minutes to reduce by half. Remove the bay leaves.
**4** Blend the cornflour with the milk, then stir into the cooking liquid. Season and bring back to the boil, stirring continuously until slightly thickened. Simmer for a further 5 minutes to give a pouring consistency. Stir in the yogurt.
**5** Add the remaining grapes. Pour the sauce over the fish rolls and sprinkle with parsley. Serve at once.

### TIP
To make skinning grapes an easier task, nick each one with a sharp knife and cover with boiling water for 30 seconds. Then drain and peel away the skins.

## THAI GRILLED CARAMELIZED FISH

PREPARATION TIME 15 minutes, plus standing
COOKING TIME 30 minutes
FREEZING Not suitable

SERVES 4

- 4 whole plaice fillets, skinned and halved
- 5 ml (1 tsp) salt
- juice of 2 limes
- 60-90 ml (4-6 tbsp) demerara sugar
- salad leaves, lime wedges and 5 ml (1 tsp) finely chopped red chilli, to garnish

SWEET AND SOUR CHILLI SAUCE

- 400 g (14 oz) red peppers, deseeded and chopped

375 CALS/SERVING

- 50 g (2 oz) red chillies, deseeded and chopped
- 2 garlic cloves, peeled and chopped
- 30 ml (2 tbsp) olive oil
- 60 ml (4 tbsp) sugar
- 90 ml (6 tbsp) distilled malt vinegar

1 First make the sauce. Place the peppers, chillies and garlic in a blender or food processor with 30 ml (2 tbsp) water and blend until smooth.
2 Put the remaining ingredients in a saucepan and add the chilli paste with 125 ml (4 fl oz) water. Bring to the boil and simmer for about 20 minutes or until reduced by half.
3 Meanwhile, sprinkle each half-fillet with salt and lime juice and roll up. Secure with wooden cocktail sticks. Set aside for 30 minutes. Just before grilling, rub fish all over with the sugar.

4 Cook under the grill for 4-5 minutes on each side, or until cooked and caramelized. Remove cocktail sticks.
5 Serve immediately on a bed of salad leaves and garnished with lime wedges and chopped red chilli, with the sweet and sour sauce poured over.

## HADDOCK AND CORN CHOWDER

PREPARATION TIME 20 minutes
COOKING TIME About 20 minutes
FREEZING Not suitable
COLOUR INDEX Page 13

SERVES 4

- 25-50 g (1-2 oz) butter or margarine
- 450 g (1 lb) old potatoes, peeled and diced
- 225 g (8 oz) onion, peeled and thinly sliced
- 2.5 ml (½ tsp) chilli powder
- 600 ml (1 pint) vegetable stock
- 600 ml (1 pint) milk
- salt and pepper

430 CALS/SERVING

- 225 g (8 oz) fresh haddock fillet, skinned and broken into bite-sized pieces
- 225 g (8 oz) smoked haddock fillet, skinned and broken into bite-sized pieces
- 200 g (7 oz) can sweetcorn kernels
- 125 g (4 oz) cooked peeled prawns
- chopped fresh parsley

1 Heat the butter in a large saucepan and fry the vegetables and the chilli powder for 2-3 minutes until beginning to soften.
2 Pour in the stock and milk with a little seasoning. Bring to the boil, then cover and simmer for 10 minutes.
3 Add the haddock to the pan with the corn. Return to the boil, then cover and simmer until the potatoes are tender and the fish begins to flake apart. Skim the surface as necessary.
4 Stir in the prawns with plenty of parsley. Adjust the seasoning and serve at once.

**VARIATION** This hearty, meal-in-a-bowl chowder is equally delicious made with other fish. You can use cod or whiting, or fresh salmon if you are feeling extravagant. For extra colour, sauté a finely diced red pepper with the other vegetables.

## KEDGEREE WITH LENTILS

PREPARATION TIME 15 minutes
COOKING TIME About 45 minutes
FREEZING Not suitable

♡

**SERVES 6**

- *75 g (3 oz) green lentils, rinsed in cold water and drained*
- *450 g (1 lb) smoked haddock fillets*
- *300 ml (10 fl oz) milk*
- *1 onion, peeled and sliced*
- *175 g (6 oz) basmati or long-grain rice*
- *10 ml (2 tsp) coriander seeds*

**305 CALS/SERVING**

- *2 cloves*
- *2 cardamom pods*
- *15 ml (1 tbsp) vegetable oil*
- *finely grated rind and juice of 1 lime*
- *2 eggs, hard-boiled and cut into wedges*
- *chopped fresh coriander or parsley and lime slices, to garnish*

**1** Put the lentils in a pan with enough cold water to cover generously. Bring to the boil and boil vigorously for 10 minutes, then simmer for about 15 minutes or until tender. Set on one side.

**2** Meanwhile, put the smoked haddock into a wide saucepan, pour the milk over and add the onion. Bring to the boil and cook, covered, for 20-25 minutes, depending on the thickness of the fish, until the flesh flakes easily. Set on one side.

**3** Rinse the rice several times in cold water to remove the starch.

**4** Crush the coriander seeds, cloves and cardamom pods. Heat the oil in a large saucepan, and add the spices. Cook for 1 minute, then add the rice. Stir until the grains are coated in oil, then add 600 ml (1 pint) water. Bring to the boil and simmer gently, covered, for about 20 minutes, until the rice is tender.

**5** Remove the fish skin and flake the flesh.

**6** Add the lime juice and rind to the rice. Stir in the eggs. Drain the lentils and add to the rice with the fish. Reheat briefly, stirring. To serve, sprinkle with coriander or parsley and garnish with lime.

blended. Add the remaining spinach and blend. Season to taste. Arrange the fish on plates, spoon over the sauce and garnish with lime

## FISH WITH LEMON AND GINGER

PREPARATION TIME 20 minutes, plus marinating
COOKING TIME 20-25 minutes
FREEZING Not suitable
COLOUR INDEX Page 14
♡

### SERVES 6    295 CALS/SERVING
- *5 ml (1 tsp) garam masala or curry powder*
- *5 cm (2 inch) piece fresh root ginger, peeled and finely chopped*
- *2 garlic cloves, peeled and crushed*
- *12 sole fillets, skinned, about 1.1 kg (2½ lb) total weight*
- *175 g (6 oz) spring onions, chopped*
- *45 ml (3 tbsp) chopped fresh coriander*
- *finely grated rind and juice of 1 lemon*
- *salt and pepper*
- *50 g (2 oz) creamed coconut*
- *2.5 ml (½ tsp) saffron strands*
- *25 g (1 oz) salted cashew nuts*
- *15 ml (1 tbsp) vegetable oil*
- *150 ml (5 fl oz) single cream*
- *fresh coriander, spring onions and lime slices, to garnish*

1 Mix together the garam masala, ginger and garlic. Place the sole fillets in a flat, non-metallic dish and rub over with the spice mixture. Cover tightly and marinate in the refrigerator overnight.
2 Mix half the spring onions with the coriander, lemon rind, 45 ml (3 tbsp) lemon juice and seasoning. Place the fillets, skinned-sides up, on a plate and spoon a little of the onion mixture into the centre of each one. Roll up and secure with a cocktail stick.
3 In a food processor, blend the coconut, saffron and cashew nuts with 200 ml (7 fl oz) water.
4 Heat the oil in a large shallow flameproof casserole and fry the remaining spring onions for 2-3 minutes. Add the coconut liquid and fish with any remaining marinade. Bring to the boil, cover and simmer very gently for 15-20 minutes or until the fish is cooked but still tender.
5 Add the cream and heat gently without boiling for 2-3 minutes. Season, garnish and serve hot.

## LEMON SOLE WITH SPINACH AND LIME HOLLANDAISE

PREPARATION TIME 15 minutes
COOKING TIME 20 minutes
FREEZING Not suitable

### SERVES 4    680 CALS/SERVING
- *oil for brushing*
- *4 lemon sole, each weighing 225 g (8 oz)*
- *45 ml (3 tbsp) wine vinegar*
- *4 black peppercorns*
- *4 egg yolks*
- *250 g (9 oz) unsalted butter, melted*
- *10 ml (2 tsp) lime juice*
- *grated rind of ½ lime*
- *50 g (2 oz) young spinach leaves*
- *salt and pepper*
- *lime wedges, to garnish*

1 Lightly oil a baking tray. Place the fish on the tray in a single layer, with the brown sides uppermost. Brush with oil.
2 Place the fish under a hot grill, about 10-15 cm (4-6 inches) from the heat source, and cook for 15-20 minutes, without turning.
3 Meanwhile, boil the vinegar and peppercorns in a heavy-based saucepan until reduced to 22 ml (1½ tbsp). Remove from the heat, then lift out and discard the peppercorns. Place the egg yolks in a blender and process for 1-2 minutes. Keeping the machine running, add the reduced vinegar, then very slowly add the hot melted butter, adding at intervals the lime juice, lime rind and 30 ml (2 tbsp) hot water.
4 Add half the spinach and process until well

## GRILLED HALIBUT
## WITH STIR-FRIED VEGETABLES

PREPARATION TIME 15 minutes
COOKING TIME 6-10 minutes
FREEZING Not suitable
♡ ⏲

**SERVES 4**

- *4 halibut steaks*
- *melted butter for basting*
- *15 ml (1 tbsp) oil*
- *25 g (1 oz) butter*
- *1 large courgette, cut into matchstick strips*
- *1 red pepper, deseeded and cut into matchstick strips*

**280 CALS/SERVING**

- *15 ml (1 tbsp) sun-dried tomato paste*
- *10 ml (2 tsp) chopped fresh thyme*
- *10 ml (2 tsp) chopped fresh tarragon or chervil*
- *salt and pepper*
- *tarragon or chervil sprigs, to garnish*

**1** Brush the halibut steaks with a little melted butter and grill for about 3-5 minutes on each side or until cooked through.

**2** Meanwhile, heat the oil and butter in a frying pan and stir-fry the courgette and pepper strips for about 2 minutes. Stir in the sun-dried tomato paste and chopped herbs, then season with salt and pepper.

**3** Serve the halibut with the stir-fried vegetables, garnished with sprigs of herbs.

## PAN-ROASTED MONKFISH WITH SWEET POTATOES AND ONIONS

PREPARATION TIME 20 minutes
COOKING TIME 40-45 minutes
FREEZING Not suitable

SERVES 4

490 CALS/SERVING

- *700 g (1½ lb) monkfish tail, skinned*
- *50 g (2 oz) can anchovies in oil, drained and washed*
- *salt and pepper*
- *4 slices Parma ham*
- *juice of ½ lemon*
- *700 g (1½ lb) sweet potatoes, scrubbed*
- *2 red onions, peeled and cut into wedges*
- *12 whole garlic cloves, peeled*
- *2 sprigs rosemary*
- *60 ml (4 tbsp) olive oil*
- *225 g (8 oz) baby tomatoes*
- *tapenade (black olive paste), to serve*

### TIP
If preferred, ask your fishmonger to fillet the fish for you.

1 Wash and dry the monkfish and, using a sharp knife, cut down each side of the bone and discard. Arrange the fillets back together and place the anchovy fillets in the gap left by the bone. Season with pepper.
2 Wrap the Parma ham around the fish and secure with cocktail sticks. Squeeze over the lemon juice and set aside.
3 Cut the potatoes into wedges and place in a large roasting pan with the onions, garlic and rosemary sprigs. Season well and stir in the olive oil. Transfer to the oven and roast at 230°C (450°F) mark 8 on the top shelf for 15 minutes.
4 Remove the pan from the oven and arrange the monkfish tail well down amongst the vegetables. Arrange the tomatoes on top of the vegetables, return to the oven and roast for a further 25-30 minutes until the fish is firm to the touch and the vegetables are tender.
5 Cover with foil and allow to rest for 5 minutes before slicing and serving the fish with the roasted vegetables and a little tapenade.

**VARIATION** For a Mediterranean flavour, spread olive paste along the centre of the fish with the anchovies and roast with red peppers, aubergines and courgettes as well as the garlic and onions.

# ROASTED FISH WITH GARLIC-HERB CRUMBS

PREPARATION TIME 20 minutes
COOKING TIME 25 minutes
FREEZING Not suitable
COLOUR INDEX Page 13

SERVES 6      430 CALS/SERVING

- 900 g (2 lb) firm-textured, chunky white fish fillets, such as monkfish or cod
- salt and pepper
- 15 ml (1 tbsp) chopped fresh thyme or 5 ml (1 tsp) dried
- juice of 1 lemon
- 175 g (6 oz) butter, plus a knob for finishing
- 300 g (10 oz) baby courgettes, thickly sliced
- 3 garlic cloves, peeled and crushed
- 125 g (4 oz) fresh brown breadcrumbs
- 60 ml (4 tbsp) chopped fresh parsley and basil
- 6 plum tomatoes, about 700 g (1½ lb), thickly sliced
- lemon wedges, to garnish

1 Trim the fish fillets of any skin and membrane, cut into large steaks and place in a single layer in a non-stick roasting tin. Season with pepper and thyme and sprinkle with the lemon juice.
2 Melt 125 g (4 oz) butter and pour over the fish. Cover with foil and cook at 220°C (425°F) mark 7 for 10-15 minutes.
3 Meanwhile, cook the courgettes in boiling, salted water for 4-5 minutes or until just tender. Drain well. Melt 50 g (2 oz) butter in a frying pan, then add the garlic and breadcrumbs. Fry until golden brown, stirring occasionally. Take off the heat, add the herbs and season well. Set aside.
4 Uncover the fish and scatter the courgettes and tomatoes around it. Season well and baste the vegetables with the fish juices. Cook, uncovered, for a further 10 minutes. Reheat the garlic crumbs with a knob of butter and sprinkle over the fish to serve. Garnish with lemon wedges.

**NOTE** Monkfish takes about 5-10 minutes longer to cook then flakier fish, such as haddock.

# RED MULLET WITH SPINACH AND BACON

PREPARATION TIME 30 minutes
COOKING TIME 8 minutes
FREEZING Not suitable

SERVES 4      440 CALS/SERVING

- 4 red mullet, scaled, cleaned and heads removed
- salt and pepper
- 16 small fresh spinach leaves
- 1 garlic clove, peeled and crushed
- 60 ml (4 tbsp) chopped fresh parsley
- 75 ml (5 tbsp) olive oil
- 4 streaky bacon rashers
- coriander or flat-leaf parsley sprigs and lemon rind strips, to garnish

1 Rinse the fish in cold water and pat dry with absorbent kitchen paper. Season to taste.
2 Finely shred 8 of the spinach leaves and place in a small bowl. Add the garlic, parsley and 15 ml (1 tbsp) olive oil and mix well, then use to stuff the fish.
3 Stretch the bacon rashers with the back of a knife and wrap one around each fish, interleaving 2 of the remaining spinach leaves into each.
4 Heat the remaining oil in a large frying pan, add the fish and fry for about 4 minutes on each side until the fish is cooked and the bacon is golden brown. Serve at once, garnished with coriander or flat-leaf parsley sprigs and lemon rind strips.

## NORMANDY SKATE WITH CAPER SAUCE

PREPARATION TIME 5 minutes
COOKING TIME 15-20 minutes
FREEZING Not suitable

♡ ⏲

**SERVES 4**

- *4 pieces of skate wing, each weighing about 200 g (7 oz)*
- *1 celery stick*
- *2 shallots, peeled and roughly chopped*
- *2 bay leaves*
- *5 ml (1 tsp) black peppercorns*
- *75 ml (5 tbsp) cider vinegar*

**330 CALS/SERVING**

- *10 ml (2 tsp) capers, chopped*
- *150 ml (5 fl oz) double cream*
- *30 ml (2 tbsp) chopped fresh parsley*
- *salt and pepper*
- *parsley sprigs, to garnish*

1 Ask your fishmonger to skin the skate wings if necessary, and cut to the right portion size.
2 Break the celery stick into 3 or 4 pieces. Put them into a large saucepan with the shallots, bay leaves, peppercorns and 60 ml (4 tbsp) of the cider vinegar. Add 1.1 litres (2 pints) cold water, slide in the skate and slowly bring to just below the boil.
3 Cover the pan, lower the heat and cook for 7-10 minutes, until the skate flesh just parts from the central cartilaginous layer.
4 While the fish is cooking, put the capers into a small pan with the cream. Stir in the parsley and season with salt and pepper. Bring to the boil, lower the heat and simmer for 1 minute. Take off the heat and stir in the remaining vinegar. Check the seasoning.
5 Lift the skate from the poaching liquor onto warmed serving plates. Spoon on the cream sauce and garnish with parsley sprigs. Serve immediately.

**NOTE** Drain the skate scrupulously as you lift it from the poaching liquor and flick off any flavouring debris adhering to the fish.

# POACHED TROUT WITH FENNEL

PREPARATION TIME 15 minutes
COOKING TIME 40 minutes
FREEZING Not suitable
COLOUR INDEX Page 16

**SERVES 2**

**545 CALS/SERVING**

- *1 small head fennel, about 175 g (6 oz) total weight*
- *350 g (12 oz) potatoes, peeled and thinly sliced*
- *1 bay leaf*
- *60 ml (4 tbsp) dry vermouth*
- *salt and pepper*
- *2 fresh gutted trout, each weighing about 225 g (8 oz)*
- *25 g (1 oz) butter or margarine*
- *lemon slices, to garnish*

1 Trim the green feathery tops from the fennel and reserve for the garnish. Slice the fennel thinly and scatter over the bottom of a shallow ovenproof dish.
2 Cover the fennel with the slices of potato and place the bay leaf on top. Pour the vermouth and 60 ml (4 tbsp) water over, then season to taste.
3 Place the prepared trout on top of the fennel and potato and dot with the butter.
4 Cover tightly with foil. Bake in the oven at 180°C (350°F) mark 4 for about 40 minutes.
5 Remove the foil to serve. Chop the reserved fennel tops finely, then sprinkle over the dish. Serve immediately, garnished with lemon slices.

# TROUT WITH DILL AND HORSERADISH MAYONNAISE

PREPARATION TIME 10 minutes, plus cooling
COOKING TIME 20 minutes
FREEZING Not suitable
COLOUR INDEX Page 16

**SERVES 4**

**560 CALS/SERVING**

- *100 ml (3½ fl oz) white wine vinegar*
- *10 ml (2 tsp) black peppercorns*
- *10 ml (2 tsp) dill seeds (optional)*
- *3 bay leaves*
- *5 ml (1 tsp) salt*
- *4 fresh gutted trout, each weighing about 200 g (7 oz)*

MAYONNAISE
- *1 Bramley apple, weighing about 150 g (5 oz)*
- *150 ml (5 fl oz) mayonnaise*
- *45 ml (3 tbsp) chopped fresh dill leaves*
- *10 ml (2 tsp) grated horseradish or horseradish sauce*
- *Cos lettuce leaves, to serve*
- *dill sprigs, bay leaves and lime wedges, to garnish*

1 Fill a large roasting tin with boiling water. Add the wine vinegar, peppercorns, dill seeds if using, bay leaves and salt. Immerse the fish in the liquid and bring back to the boil. Turn off the heat and leave the fish undisturbed in the liquid for at least 20 minutes.
2 To make the mayonnaise, peel, quarter, core and slice the apple. Place in a small pan with 45 ml (3 tbsp) water. Cover and cook until the apple is softened to a purée. Beat until smooth and allow to cool, then mix with the mayonnaise, chopped dill and horseradish.
3 Lift the trout from the poaching liquor, remove the skin, and their heads if preferred. Lay each fish in a long lettuce leaf on a serving plate and spoon some of the dill and apple mayonnaise alongside. Garnish with dill sprigs, bay leaves and lime wedges.

## SALMON PIE WITH PARMESAN CRUST

PREPARATION TIME 30 minutes, plus chilling
COOKING TIME About 55 minutes
FREEZING Suitable

❋

**SERVES 8**

- 225 g (8 oz) butter
- 50 g (2 oz) onion, peeled and finely chopped
- 400 g (14 oz) white plain flour
- 450 ml (15 fl oz) fish stock
- 150 ml (5 fl oz) dry white wine
- 900 g (2 lb) salmon fillet, skinned and cut into chunks

**720 CALS/SERVING**

- 225 g (8 oz) queen scallops (optional)
- 125 g (4 oz) Gruyère cheese
- salt and pepper
- 75 g (3 oz) freshly grated Parmesan cheese
- 1 egg, beaten
- beaten egg, to glaze
- chopped fresh herbs, to garnish (optional)

1 Melt 50 g (2 oz) butter in a medium saucepan. Sauté the onion, stirring, for 5-6 minutes or until softened but not coloured.
2 Off the heat, stir in 50 g (2 oz) flour, the stock and wine. Bring to the boil, stirring, then simmer for 3-4 minutes until thickened. Remove from the heat, and allow to cool slightly.
3 Add the salmon, the scallops (if using) and the Gruyère cheese. Season to taste, then turn into a 1.7 litre (3 pint) shallow, ovenproof dish and leave to cool.

4 Rub the remaining butter into the rest of the flour, then stir in the Parmesan. Add the beaten egg and 45-60 ml (3-4 tbsp) cold water. Bind the pastry together with your hands, adding extra water, if necessary.
5 Turn out onto a floured surface and knead lightly until smooth. Cover and chill for about 15 minutes.
6 Roll out the pastry and cover the filling, pressing the edges down well. Trim any excess pastry and re-roll.
7 Cut out holly leaves from the trimmings. Brush the pie with beaten egg and cover with the leaves. Brush with egg again, then chill for 15-20 minutes.
8 Bake at 190°C (375°F) mark 5 for 45-50 minutes or until crisp, covering loosely with foil if necessary. Serve immediately, sprinkling herbs over each serving, if wished.

## ROAST SALMON IN MUSTARD BUTTER

PREPARATION TIME 10 minutes
COOKING TIME 20 minutes
FREEZING Not suitable
COLOUR INDEX Page 15

🕐

**SERVES 6**

- 1.1 kg (2½ lb) piece of boned middle cut of salmon
- 175 g (6 oz) butter, melted
- 45 ml (3 tbsp) wholegrain mustard

**560 CALS/SERVING**

- 20 ml (4 tsp) dried dill
- salt and pepper
- 300 g (10 oz) fresh spinach, rocket or mixed salad leaves

1 Open out the salmon like a book until almost flat by pressing along the backbone area. Place skin-side up in a shallow ovenproof dish just large enough to hold it.
2 Mix together the butter, mustard, dill and seasoning. Pour over the salmon. Cook at 230°C (450°F) mark 8 for about 20 minutes or until just tender.
3 Toss the salad leaves and season well. Place on large plates.
4 Cut the salmon into thick slices and serve on top of the salad leaves with the mustard butter spooned over the top.

## SALMON TROUT WITH HERB SAUCE

PREPARATION TIME 25 minutes, plus cooling
COOKING TIME 40 minutes
FREEZING Not suitable

**SERVES 4**

- *1 salmon or sea trout, about 900 g (2 lb), cleaned*
- *45 ml (3 tbsp) lemon juice*
- *50 g (2 oz) butter or margarine*
- *salt and pepper*
- *1 bunch watercress, roughly chopped*
- *125 g (4 oz) spinach leaves, roughly chopped*

**575 CALS/SERVING**

- *45 ml (3 tbsp) chopped fresh parsley*
- *30 ml (2 tbsp) chopped fresh chervil*
- *5 ml (1 tsp) chopped fresh dill*
- *150 ml (5 fl oz) mayonnaise*
- *herb sprigs and lemon rind shapes, to garnish*

1 Place the fish in the centre of a large piece of foil. Add 30 ml (2 tbsp) of the lemon juice, then dot with 25 g (1 oz) of the butter. Season with salt and pepper.

2 Seal the foil, weigh the fish and place on a baking sheet. Calculate the cooking time at 15 minutes per 450 g (1 lb), plus 10 minutes. Bake at 180°C (350°F) mark 4 until tender.

3 Remove the fish from the foil, reserving the cooking liquor, then carefully remove the skin while still warm. Place the fish on a serving dish and leave to cool.

4 To make the sauce, put the cooking liquor and the remaining 25 g (1 oz) butter in a saucepan and heat gently. Add the watercress, spinach, parsley, chervil and dill, then cook for 2-3 minutes or until softened.

5 Put the sauce in a blender or food processor and blend until smooth. Transfer to a bowl, add the remaining lemon juice and season to taste. Leave to cool, then fold in the mayonnaise. Turn into a small serving jug and refrigerate until required.

6 Garnish the fish decoratively with herbs and lemon rind shapes, and serve with the herb sauce.

# SPICED BARBECUED SALMON

PREPARATION TIME 15 minutes
COOKING TIME 15 minutes
FREEZING Not suitable
COLOUR INDEX Page 15
♡ ⌚

**SERVES 6**

- *900 g (2 lb) salmon fillet, with skin on and scales removed*
- *6 cardamom pods*
- *5 ml (1 tsp) cumin seeds*
- *5 ml (1 tsp) coriander seeds*

**295 CALS/SERVING**

- *2.5 ml (½ tsp) black peppercorns*
- *2.5 ml (½ tsp) coarse salt*
- *30 ml (2 tbsp) olive oil*

1 Remove any remaining salmon bones with tweezers. Using a sharp knife, slash the skin side into diamonds.
2 Remove the dark seeds from the cardamom pods and discard the pods. Finely grind the seeds with the cumin seeds, coriander seeds, peppercorns and coarse salt in a grinder or with a pestle and mortar.
3 Brush the salmon with the oil and press the spices firmly onto the skin side. Place the salmon in a fish griller and cook on the barbecue for 10-15 minutes, turning halfway through, until brown and crisp but just cooked on the inside.

**VARIATIONS** The fish can be cooked in the oven, if wished. Place the salmon on an oiled baking sheet and cook at 230°C (450°F) mark 8 for 10-15 minutes.

For an unusual touch, dip a small bunch of mixed herbs into a bowl of olive oil and brush lightly over the fish as it cooks.

> *TIP*
> If you barbecue fish frequently it's a good idea to invest in a fish grill, which encloses the fish and makes it much easier to handle.

# BAKED SALMON WITH WALNUT OIL AND HERBS

PREPARATION TIME 35 minutes, plus marinating
COOKING TIME 15-20 minutes
FREEZING Not suitable
COLOUR INDEX Page 15

**SERVES 4**

- *575 g (1¼ lb) salmon fillet, skinned*
- *125 ml (4 fl oz) white wine*
- *50 ml (2 fl oz) walnut oil*
- *60 ml (4 tbsp) chopped fresh mixed herbs, such as parsley and chives*
- *2 garlic cloves, peeled and crushed*
- *large pinch of paprika*

**490 CALS/SERVING**

- *salt and pepper*
- *4 sticks celery, cut into matchsticks*
- *225 g (8 oz) young turnips, peeled and cut into matchsticks*
- *olive oil*
- *90 ml (6 tbsp) double cream*
- *lime juice to taste*
- *cooked shrimps or prawns, to garnish*

1 Cut the fillet into four even-size pieces and place in a shallow non-metallic dish. Mix the wine, walnut oil, herbs, garlic, paprika and seasoning. Spoon the mixture over the fish, cover and chill in the refrigerator for at least 4 hours or overnight, turning occasionally.
2 Meanwhile, blanch the celery and turnips together in boiling, salted water for 1 minute, then drain under cold water to cool quickly.
3 Lightly oil a shallow ovenproof dish. Place the celery and turnips in it in a single layer and season well. Lift the salmon out of the marinade and place on top of the vegetables. Reserve the marinade.
4 Bake the salmon and vegetables at 220°C (425°F) mark 7 for 15-20 minutes or until the fish is cooked.
5 Meanwhile, place the marinade and the cream in a small saucepan and boil until reduced by about half. Off the heat, quickly whisk in the lime juice to taste and season with salt and pepper.
6 To serve, arrange the salmon and vegetables on individual serving plates. Spoon the sauce over the top and garnish with shrimps or prawns.

# SMOKED SALMON FISHCAKES

PREPARATION TIME 45 minutes, plus chilling
COOKING TIME About 45 minutes
FREEZING Suitable (stage 4)

❅

**SERVES 12**

- *1.1 kg (2½ lb) old potatoes*
- *salt and pepper*
- *450 g (1 lb) salmon fillet, skinned*
- *150 ml (5 fl oz) white wine*
- *juice of 1 lemon*
- *450 g (1 lb) smoked salmon pieces*
- *10 ml (2 tsp) anchovy essence*
- *30 ml (2 tbsp) chopped fresh dill or 10 ml (2 tsp) dried dill*

**380 CALS/SERVING**

- *1 spring onion, finely chopped*
- *flour for coating*
- *3 eggs, beaten*
- *350 g (12 oz) fresh white breadcrumbs*
- *oil for frying*
- *lemon wedges and fresh dill, to garnish*

**1** Boil the potatoes until tender, then drain, mash and season with salt and pepper. Keep warm.
**2** Meanwhile, poach the salmon fillet in a covered saucepan with wine and lemon juice for about 15 minutes or until just cooked. Cool the salmon in the liquid, then coarsely flake the fish. (The liquid can be frozen for stock.)
**3** Roughly chop the smoked salmon, then mix it with the fresh salmon, anchovy essence, dill and spring onion. Beat half the fish mixture into the warm potatoes. Fold in the remaining fish and season to taste. Spread the mixture on a baking sheet lined with greaseproof paper to a depth of 4 cm (1½ inches). Cover and chill for about 2 hours.
**4** Shape the mixture into 24 fishcakes. Dip them in the flour, beaten egg and breadcrumbs to coat.
**5** Shallow fry the fishcakes a batch at a time in 5 mm (¼ inch) of hot oil for about 4 minutes on each side or until golden and crisp. Drain on absorbent kitchen paper and keep warm while cooking the remainder. Garnish with lemon wedges and fresh dill to serve.

**NOTE** When coating any food in egg and breadcrumbs, it is best to have plates of flour, beaten egg and breadcrumbs lined up on the work surface. Use one hand for dipping and coating the

food into the dry ingredients and the other hand for dipping into the egg.

The fishcakes can be cooked in the oven if preferred – place on a lightly greased baking sheet, brush lightly with melted butter and cook at 220°C (425°F) mark 7 for about 25 minutes.

---

### TIPS
Smoked salmon trimmings can be bought from fishmongers more cheaply than slices. Quality varies, so check before buying.

These fishcakes freeze well, making an excellent standby for instant meals over the Christmas holiday period.

# ROAST SALMON WITH A PEANUT CRUST

PREPARATION TIME 5 minutes
COOKING TIME 20 minutes
FREEZING Suitable (stage 2)
COLOUR INDEX Page 15
🕐 ❄

SERVES 4      865 CALS/SERVING

- *1 red chilli, finely chopped*
- *2.5 cm (1 inch) piece fresh root ginger, peeled and grated*
- *175 g (6 oz) unsalted butter, softened*
- *45 ml (3 tbsp) chopped fresh parsley*
- *finely grated rind of 1 lime*

- *75 g (3 oz) salted roasted peanuts*
- *3-4 spring onions, trimmed and finely chopped*
- *125 g (4 oz) fresh white breadcrumbs*
- *salt and pepper*
- *4 salmon fillets, about 175 g (6 oz) each (skinned if wished)*

1 Beat the red chilli and the ginger into the unsalted butter with the fresh parsley and lime rind. Roughly process the peanuts in a blender or food processor.

2 Melt 50 g (2 oz) of the flavoured butter in a frying pan, add the spring onions, peanuts and breadcrumbs and fry until golden, stirring continuously to prevent the breadcrumbs from sticking together. Season to taste.

3 Arrange the salmon fillets, skin-side uppermost, in a roasting tin. Spoon the fried breadcrumb mixture on the top. Cook at 200°C (400°F) mark 6 for 10-15 minutes or until the salmon is just cooked.

4 Melt the remaining flavoured butter and serve with the roast salmon.

### TIP
To save cooking time, make up a batch of the spicy flavoured butter and the fried peanut and breadcrumb topping, and freeze ahead. Both of these mixtures can be used direct from the freezer; just allow an extra 2-3 minutes cooking time at stage 3.

# PAN-FRIED RED MULLET WITH CITRUS AND BASIL

PREPARATION TIME 10 minutes, plus marinating
COOKING TIME 10 minutes
FREEZING Not suitable
COLOUR INDEX Page 15

SERVES 4      430 CALS/SERVING

- *4 red mullet, each about 225 g (8 oz), filleted*
- *90 ml (6 tbsp) olive oil*
- *10 peppercorns, crushed*
- *2 oranges*

- *1 lemon*
- *30 ml (2 tbsp) plain flour*
- *salt and peppet*
- *15 g (½ oz) butter*
- *2 anchovies*
- *15 g (½ oz) shredded fresh basil*

1 Place the fish fillets in a shallow dish, in a single layer. Drizzle over the olive oil and sprinkle with the peppercorns. Peel one of the oranges, removing all of the skin and white pith, then cut into thin slices. Lay the orange slices over the fish. Cover and leave to marinate in the refrigerator for 4 hours.

2 Halve the lemon. Remove the skin and white pith from one half, then slice thinly. Squeeze the juice from the other half and reserve.

3 Using a fish slice lift the fish out of the marinade, reserving the marinade, and pat dry on absorbent kitchen paper. Season with salt and pepper, then dust lightly with flour.

4 Heat 45 ml (3 tbsp) of the marinade in a sauté pan or frying pan. Add the red mullet fillets and fry for 2 minutes on each side. Remove from the pan and set aside; keep warm. Discard the oil remaining in the pan.

5 Melt the butter in the pan with the remaining marinade. Add the anchovies and crush until dissolved. Add the juice of the remaining orange and the reserved lemon juice. Season and cook until slightly reduced. Lastly, stir in the shredded basil.

6 Pour the citrus sauce over the fish and garnish with the orange and lemon slices. Serve at once.

# WINTER FISH STEW

PREPARATION TIME 15 minutes, plus soaking
COOKING TIME 45-50 minutes
FREEZING Not suitable

**SERVES 8**

- *good pinch of saffron strands*
- *about 1.8 kg (4 lb) mixed fish fillets, such as red mullet, plaice or cod, skinned*
- *90 ml (6 tbsp) olive oil*
- *2 large onions, peeled and finely chopped*
- *4 garlic cloves, peeled and crushed*
- *1 red pepper, deseeded and sliced*
- *900 g (2 lb) tomatoes, skinned, deseeded and chopped*

**420 CALS/SERVING**

- *4 anchovy fillets, drained*
- *300 ml (10 fl oz) dry white wine*
- *4 bay leaves*
- *90 ml (6 tbsp) chopped fresh basil*
- *salt and pepper*
- *20-24 cooked peeled prawns*
- *150 g (5 oz) cooked shelled mussels*
- *8 slices of toast*
- *chopped fresh parsley, to garnish*

1 Soak the saffron strands in a little boiling water for 30 minutes.
2 Meanwhile, cut the fish into chunky pieces.
3 Heat the oil in a saucepan, add the onions, garlic and pepper, and fry gently for 5 minutes.
4 Add the tomatoes and anchovies and stir to break them up. Add the wine and 300 ml (10 fl oz) water, bring to the boil, then lower the heat and add the bay leaves and half the basil. Simmer, uncovered, for 20 minutes.
5 Add the firm-textured fish to the tomato mixture, strain in the saffron water and season to taste. Cook for 10 minutes, then add the delicate-textured fish and cook for 5 minutes more.
6 Add the prawns and mussels, cover and cook for 3-5 minutes until warm. Remove the bay leaves and discard.
7 Put one slice of toast in each of eight soup bowls and spoon over the stew. Serve garnished with chopped parsley.

cucumber half crosswise into 1 cm (½ inch) slices. Cut the lettuce crosswise into slices of about the same thickness.

4 Grill the herrings, coated side up, for 4-5 minutes.

5 Meanwhile, melt the butter in a frying pan and add the lemon juice. Add the cucumber and lettuce and cook, stirring, until the lettuce wilts. Add the chopped dill and season with salt and pepper.

6 Transfer the grilled herrings to warmed serving plates and spoon the wilted lettuce and cucumber alongside. Garnish with dill to serve.

## LIGHT MONKFISH AND PRAWN SAUTE

PREPARATION TIME 15 minutes
COOKING TIME 15 minutes
FREEZING Not suitable
COLOUR INDEX Page 14
♡ ⏰

## OATMEAL CRUSTED HERRINGS

PREPARATION TIME 10 minutes
COOKING TIME 5-6 minutes
FREEZING Not suitable
⏰

SERVES 4
- *4 herrings, gutted and filleted, heads removed, each weighing about 225 g (8 oz)*
- *15 ml (1 tbsp) olive oil*
- *45-60 ml (3-4 tbsp) pinhead oatmeal*
- *5 ml (1 tsp) dill seed*

700 CALS/SERVING
- *finely grated rind and juice of 1 lemon*
- *salt and pepper*
- *½ cucumber*
- *1 Little Gem lettuce*
- *50 g (2 oz) butter*
- *30 ml (2 tbsp) finely chopped fresh dill leaves*
- *dill sprigs, to garnish*

1 Rinse the herrings and pat dry with absorbent kitchen paper, then smear the fleshy surface of each fillet with olive oil. Line a grill rack with foil and arrange the fish flesh-side up on it.

2 Mix the oatmeal with the dill seed, grated lemon rind, and salt and pepper, then sprinkle the mixture evenly over the herring fillets. Pat down lightly to give a good coating.

3 Peel the cucumber, halve it lengthways and scoop out the seeds with a teaspoon. Cut each

SERVES 4
- *30 ml (2 tbsp) vegetable oil*
- *450 g (1 lb) monkfish fillet, skinned and cut into chunks*
- *1 bunch spring onions, sliced*
- *1 garlic clove, peeled and chopped*
- *2.5 cm (1 inch) piece fresh root ginger, peeled and finely chopped*

230 CALS/SERVING
- *300 g (10 oz) leeks, trimmed and sliced*
- *1 red pepper, deseeded and roughly chopped*
- *125 g (4 oz) cooked peeled prawns*
- *15 ml (1 tbsp) hoisin sauce*
- *15 ml (1 tbsp) light soy sauce*
- *15 ml (1 tbsp) dry sherry*
- *black pepper*

1 Heat the oil in a large non-stick frying pan and sauté the monkfish for 2-3 minutes. Remove using a slotted spoon. Add the onions, garlic and ginger to the pan and sauté for 2 minutes or until beginning to soften. Add the leeks and pepper and sauté for a further 10 minutes, stirring, until softened.

2 Return the monkfish to the pan with the prawns, hoisin sauce, soy sauce and sherry. Season with plenty of black pepper (the soy sauce is fairly salty). Cook for 30 seconds-1 minute, stirring. Serve at once.

# TUNA STEAKS WITH PARMESAN BASIL BUTTER

PREPARATION TIME 20 minutes, plus marinating
COOKING TIME 12-15 minutes
FREEZING Not suitable
COLOUR INDEX Page 16

**SERVES 6**     **500 CALS/SERVING**

- *6 tuna steaks, cut 2 cm (³/₄ inch) thick, each weighing about 175 g (6 oz)*
- *fresh herbs, to garnish*

*MARINADE*

- *100 ml (3¹/₂ fl oz) olive oil*
- *2 garlic cloves, peeled and crushed*
- *10 ml (2 tsp) balsamic or sherry vinegar*
- *30 ml (2 tbsp)*
- *chopped fresh mixed herbs, such as thyme and parsley*
- *salt and pepper*

*PARMESAN BASIL BUTTER*

- *75 g (3 oz) unsalted butter, softened*
- *30 ml (2 tbsp) freshly grated Parmesan cheese*
- *5 ml (1 tsp) balsamic or sherry vinegar*
- *5-6 fresh basil leaves*

1 Rinse the steaks and pat dry on absorbent kitchen paper. Place in a shallow non-metallic dish.
2 Whisk together all the marinade ingredients and pour over the steaks. Turn to coat, cover and leave to marinate in the refrigerator for 3-4 hours or overnight.
3 To make the basil butter, beat the butter until soft and creamy. Beat in the Parmesan cheese, vinegar and pepper to taste. Finely shred the basil and stir it into the butter mixture. Spoon into a sausage shape on wet non-stick baking parchment and roll up neatly. Chill for at least 1 hour or until firm enough to slice.
4 Lift the steaks out of the marinade and place directly over the barbecue or under the grill. Cook for 12-15 minutes or until firm and tender, turning once and brushing occasionally with the marinade. The flesh will turn a lighter colour when cooked. Pierce the centre with the tip of a sharp knife to see if it is cooked in the middle.
5 Serve the steaks topped with slices of Parmesan basil butter and garnished with fresh herbs.

**VARIATION** Use salmon for this dish if fresh tuna is not available.

# GRILLED SARDINES WITH TOMATO SAUCE

PREPARATION TIME 20 minutes
COOKING TIME About 20 minutes
FREEZING Not suitable
COLOUR INDEX Page 16
♡

**SERVES 4**     **295 CALS/SERVING**

- *16 small or 8 large sardines, cleaned*
- *30 ml (2 tbsp) olive oil*
- *few sprigs of thyme*
- *pepper*
- *juice of ¹/₂ lemon*
- *lemon rind shreds, to garnish*

*TOMATO SAUCE*

- *15 ml (1 tbsp) olive oil*
- *1 small onion, peeled and finely chopped*
- *1 garlic clove, peeled and finely chopped*
- *450 g (1 lb) ripe tomatoes, finely chopped*
- *15 ml (1 tbsp) chopped fresh parsley*
- *salt and pepper*

1 To make the tomato sauce, heat the oil in a frying pan, add the onion and garlic and fry gently until the onion is softened. Add the tomatoes and parsley, then season with salt and pepper to taste. Cook, uncovered, for 10-15 minutes until the tomatoes are just tender.
2 Meanwhile, score the fish with three or four diagonal cuts on each side. Brush with oil, and push a few sprigs of thyme into some of the cuts. Season with pepper and sprinkle with lemon juice.
3 Arrange the fish on a grill rack and grill for about 4 minutes on each side or until cooked, brushing frequently with the oil and juices.
4 Arrange the sardines on a platter, and pour over any juices from the grill pan. Garnish with lemon rind shreds, and serve with the tomato sauce.

**NOTE** The sardines can be barbecued, if wished. The sauce can be kept hot on the edge of the barbecue grid.

## PAELLA WITH PEPPERS

PREPARATION TIME 15 minutes
COOKING TIME About 25 minutes
FREEZING Not suitable

SERVES 6      365 CALS/SERVING

- *15-30 ml (1-2 tbsp) vegetable oil*
- *175 g (6 oz) onion, peeled and thinly sliced*
- *1 small red pepper, deseeded and chopped*
- *1 small green pepper, deseeded and chopped*
- *1 small yellow pepper, deseeded and chopped*
- *225 g (8 oz) chicken breast fillet, chopped*
- *300 g (10 oz) long-grain white rice*
- *600 ml (1 pint) chicken stock*
- *225 g (8 oz) ripe tomatoes, skinned, deseeded and chopped*
- *finely grated rind and juice of 1 lemon*
- *pinch of saffron strands*
- *350 g (12 oz) fish fillet, skinned and chopped*
- *salt and pepper*
- *225 g (8 oz) packet cooked mixed seafood*
- *125 g (4 oz) frozen peas*
- *lemon wedges and fresh parsley, to garnish*

1 Heat the oil in a large sauté pan or flameproof casserole and fry the onion and peppers for 3-4 minutes until softened.
2 Using a slotted spoon, remove the vegetables, then add the chicken and the rice, with a little more oil if necessary. Cook, stirring, for 1-2 minutes.
3 Return the vegetables to the pan with the stock, tomatoes, lemon rind and juice and a pinch of saffron. Bring to the boil and boil for 1 minute, then reduce the heat and add the fish. Season to taste.
4 Cover and simmer for about 15 minutes, or until the rice is almost tender, adding more stock if necessary (there should be little free liquid).
5 Stir the mixed seafood and peas into the rice. Cover the pan tightly and cook for a further 2-3 minutes or until all the fish is heated through. Adjust the seasoning, garnish and serve immediately.

## COCONUT FISH PILAU

PREPARATION TIME 10 minutes
COOKING TIME 30 minutes
FREEZING Not suitable
COLOUR INDEX Page 16

SERVES 4      375 CALS/SERVING

- *15 ml (1 tbsp) vegetable oil*
- *125 g (4 oz) onion, peeled and roughly chopped*
- *1 garlic clove, peeled and crushed*
- *15 ml (1 tbsp) Thai green curry paste or Indian curry paste*
- *225 g (8 oz) Thai fragrant rice or basmati rice*
- *600 ml (1 pint) fish stock*
- *150 ml (5 fl oz) coconut milk*
- *175 g (6 oz) cod fillet, skinned and cut into bite-sized pieces*
- *125 g (4 oz) sugar snap peas, blanched*
- *125 g (4 oz) cooked, peeled tiger prawns*
- *25 g (1 oz) toasted almonds*
- *15 ml (1 tbsp) lemon juice*
- *salt and pepper*
- *chopped fresh coriander, to garnish*

1 Heat the oil in a large, non-stick frying pan and fry the onion and garlic for 4-5 minutes or until golden. Stir in the curry paste and cook, stirring, for 1-2 minutes.
2 Add the rice, stock and coconut milk. Bring to the boil. Cover and simmer gently for about 15 minutes, stirring occasionally with a fork.
3 When the rice is tender and all the liquid has been absorbed, add the cod. Cook for a further 3-5 minutes or until the fish is cooked through.
4 Stir in the sugar snap peas, prawns, almonds and lemon juice. Season. Heat through for about 1 minute then serve immediately, garnished with coriander.

# SPICED FISH KEBABS WITH AVOCADO SALSA

PREPARATION TIME 15 minutes, plus marinating
COOKING TIME 6-8 minutes
FREEZING Not suitable

SERVES 4-6

- *700 g (1½ lb) monkfish fillets, skinned*
- *12 large raw tiger prawns*

MARINADE

- *2 garlic cloves, peeled and crushed*
- *5 ml (1 tsp) ground coriander*
- *5 ml (1 tsp) ground turmeric*
- *2.5 ml (½ tsp) ground cumin*
- *2.5 ml (½ tsp) sea salt*
- *2.5 ml (½ tsp) chilli powder*
- *1.25 ml (¼ tsp) ground cinnamon*

465-310 CALS/SERVING

- *juice of 1 lime*
- *15 ml (1 tbsp) tomato purée*
- *90 ml (6 tbsp) olive oil*

AVOCADO SALSA

- *1 small ripe avocado*
- *½ small red onion, peeled and finely chopped*
- *15 ml (1 tbsp) lime juice*
- *15 ml (1 tbsp) chopped fresh coriander*
- *1 garlic clove, peeled and crushed*
- *pinch of sugar*
- *salt and pepper*

1 Wash and dry the monkfish and cut into 12 large chunks. Peel the prawns, discarding the heads, then cut down the back of each prawn and remove the black intestinal vein. Wash and dry well. Thread the monkfish and prawns alternately onto 4 skewers. Set aside.

2 To make the marinade, combine all the ingredients in a small bowl. Brush the marinade over the kebabs, then transfer to a shallow non-metallic dish, cover and marinate overnight.

3 Remove the kebabs from the refrigerator at least 1 hour before cooking.

4 Just before cooking the kebabs, make the salsa. Stone, peel and dice the avocado, then mix with the onion, lime juice, coriander, garlic and sugar. Season to taste and set aside for 10 minutes.

5 Place the kebabs on an oiled grill pan and grill as close to the heat as possible for 6-8 minutes, turning and basting frequently with the marinade juices, until charred and cooked through. Serve immediately with the salsa.

**VARIATION** Use any firm fleshed fish for this dish, such as swordfish or tuna. Scallops also work well as an alternative to the prawns.

---

*TIP*
If using wooden skewers, soak them in water for 30 minutes before threading on the seafood.

# MIXED SEAFOOD GRATIN

PREPARATION TIME 10 minutes
COOKING TIME 20 minutes
FREEZING Not suitable

SERVES 4

- *50 g (2 oz) butter*
- *50 g (2 oz) onion, peeled and roughly chopped*
- *2 garlic cloves, peeled and crushed*
- *15 ml (1 tbsp) white plain flour*
- *125 ml (4 fl oz) white wine*
- *50 ml (2 fl oz) milk*
- *225 g (8 oz) cod or haddock fillet, skinned and cut into cubes*
- *150 ml (5 fl oz) double cream*

800 CALS/SERVING

- *175 g (6 oz) Emmental cheese, grated*
- *225 g (8 oz) packet cooked mixed seafood*
- *125 g (4 oz) watercress, finely chopped*
- *salt and pepper*
- *50 g (2 oz) fresh breadcrumbs*
- *125 g (4 oz) plain tortilla chips, crumbled*

**1** Melt the butter in a large saucepan, add the onion and garlic and sauté for 2-3 minutes. Add the flour and cook, stirring, for 1 minute. Pour in the wine and milk, and bring to the boil, stirring all the time.
**2** Add the cod and simmer for 5-6 minutes. Add the cream and take off the heat.
**3** Add 125 g (4 oz) grated cheese, the mixed seafood and watercress to the sauce. Season to taste. Place over a gentle heat and bring up to simmering point. Immediately, spoon into a shallow, ovenproof dish.
**4** Mix the breadcrumbs, remaining cheese and tortilla chips together. Sprinkle over the fish then grill until golden and bubbling.

## FRESH SEAFOOD STEW

PREPARATION TIME 30 minutes
COOKING TIME 40 minutes
FREEZING Not suitable
COLOUR INDEX Page 17
♡

| SERVES 6 | 335 CALS/SERVING |
|---|---|
| • *60 ml (4 tbsp) olive oil* | • *30 ml (2 tbsp) tomato purée* |
| • *900 g (2 lb) onions, peeled and finely sliced* | • *60 ml (4 tbsp) chopped fresh parsley* |
| • *450 g (1 lb) thick cod fillets, skinned and cut into 5 cm (2 inch) pieces* | • *30 ml (2 tbsp) chopped fresh marjoram or oregano* |
| • *225 g (8 oz) plaice fillets, skinned and quartered* | • *150 ml (5 fl oz) dry white wine* |
| • *175 g (6 oz) peeled raw tiger prawns* | • *225 g (8 oz) cooked mixed seafood* |
| • *salt and pepper* | • *oregano leaves, to garnish* |
| • *450 g (1 lb) plum tomatoes, skinned, deseeded and chopped* | |

1 Heat half the oil in a large flameproof casserole and cook the onions over a low heat for 5 minutes until softened. Using a slotted spoon, lift out about half of the onions and set aside.

2 Spread the remainder evenly over the base of the casserole, then cover with half the fish and prawns – do not add any of the mixed seafood yet. Season well with salt and pepper to taste.

3 Cover with half of the tomatoes and the tomato purée, then repeat the layers. Sprinkle the herbs on top and pour the wine over. Drizzle the remaining oil on top and cook, uncovered, over a very low heat for about 30 minutes or until the liquid has thickened slightly. Stir in the mixed seafood and heat through for 3-5 minutes. Serve garnished with oregano leaves.

## CHILLIED MEDITERRANEAN PRAWNS

PREPARATION TIME 10 minutes
COOKING TIME 5-10 minutes
FREEZING Not suitable
♡ ⏱

| SERVES 2 | 235 CALS/SERVING |
|---|---|
| • *15 ml (1 tbsp) olive oil* | • *few drops of Tabasco sauce* |
| • *1 garlic clove, peeled and crushed* | • *salt and pepper* |
| • *4 small tomatoes, skinned and chopped* | • *12 raw peeled tiger prawns* |
| • *1 fresh medium chilli, deseeded and chopped* | • *slices of lemon, to garnish* |

1 Heat the oil in a small frying pan and add the garlic, tomatoes, chilli, a few drops of Tabasco and salt and pepper. Cover and cook gently for about 5 minutes or until the tomatoes are reduced to a pulp.

2 Stir in the prawns and cook gently for about 3 minutes until the prawns are cooked. Garnish with lemon slices.

## GRILLED LOBSTER

PREPARATION TIME 20 minutes
COOKING TIME 5 minutes
FREEZING Not suitable
♡ ⏲

SERVES 4

305 CALS/SERVING

- *4 cooked lobsters, each weighing 450-550 g (1-1¼ lb)*
- *salt and pepper*
- *50 g (2 oz) butter, melted*
- *lemon slices and parsley sprigs, to garnish*

1 Twist off the lobster claws and pincers. Crack open the large claws using the back of a heavy knife, being careful not to crush the meat inside.
2 Put the lobster, back upwards, on a flat surface and using a sharp knife split the lobster cleanly in two, piercing through the 'cross' at the centre of the head.
3 Remove and discard the intestine which runs through the centre of the tail, the stomach (which lies near the head) and the spongy looking gills or 'dead man's fingers', which are inedible.
4 Sprinkle the flesh with salt and pepper to taste and brush with melted butter. Cook under a medium grill for about 5 minutes.
5 Transfer to a warmed platter. Add the claws and garnish with lemon slices and parsley.

## WARM SCALLOP AND BASIL SALAD

PREPARATION TIME 10 minutes
COOKING TIME 4-6 minutes
FREEZING Not suitable
COLOUR INDEX Page 17
⏲

SERVES 6

355 CALS/SERVING

- *50 g (2 oz) drained sun-dried tomatoes in olive oil*
- *1 small bunch fresh basil*
- *60 ml (4 tbsp) walnut oil*
- *30 ml (2 tbsp) sherry vinegar or red wine vinegar*
- *selection of salad leaves, such as lollo rosso, rocket, frisée or lamb's tongue lettuce*
- *60 ml (4 tbsp) olive oil*
- *700 g (1½ lb) scallops*
- *salt and pepper*

1 Roughly chop the dried tomatoes and the basil. Whisk together the walnut oil and vinegar in a bowl. Stir in the tomatoes and basil. Place the salad leaves in a large bowl.
2 Heat the olive oil in a large sauté pan and sauté the scallops in two batches until well browned – about 2-3 minutes. Take care not to overcook.
3 Off the heat, return all the scallops to the pan. Stir in the tomato and basil mixture, adjust the seasoning and immediately pour over the salad leaves. Toss and serve on individual salad plates.

# MUSSELS WITH GINGER, CHILLI AND CORIANDER

PREPARATION TIME 20 minutes
COOKING TIME 10 minutes
FREEZING Not suitable
COLOUR INDEX Page 18
♡ ◷

**SERVES 2**

- *1 kg (2¼ lb) mussels in their shells*
- *15 g (½ oz) fresh coriander sprigs*
- *1 bunch spring onions, trimmed and shredded*
- *2 garlic cloves, peeled and finely chopped*
- *2.5 cm (1 inch) piece fresh root ginger, peeled and finely chopped*

**348 CALS/SERVING**

- *1 small red chilli, deseeded and cut into slivers*
- *150 ml (5 fl oz) white wine*
- *40 g (1½ oz) butter*
- *coriander sprigs, to garnish*

1 Discard any mussels with damaged shells, or any that remain open when tapped smartly on the shell. Scrub the mussels thoroughly under cold running water, pulling away the coarse threads (beards) from the side of the shells.
2 Strip the leaves from the coriander and set aside; reserve the coriander stalks.
3 Put the spring onions, garlic, ginger, chilli and coriander stalks in a saucepan which is large enough to hold the mussels. Add the wine and 150 ml (5 fl oz) water. Bring to the boil and simmer for 2 minutes.
4 Add the mussels to the pan, cover with a tight-fitting lid and cook for 4-5 minutes over a moderate heat, shaking the pan occasionally, until the shells open. Turn the mussels into a colander set over a bowl. Discard the coriander stalks and any unopened mussels.
5 Pour the liquid from the bowl back into the pan. Place over a low heat and whisk in the butter, a piece at a time, then add the coriander leaves.
6 Transfer the mussels to individual serving dishes and pour over the sauce. Serve at once, garnished with coriander sprigs.

**VARIATION** Replace the wine with 150 ml (5 fl oz) coconut milk for an exotic sauce.

# OYSTERS AU GRATIN

PREPARATION TIME 20 minutes
COOKING TIME 10 minutes
FREEZING Not suitable
♡ ◷

**SERVES 4-6**

- *50 g (2 oz) streaky bacon, finely chopped*
- *75 g (3 oz) celery, finely chopped*
- *200 g (7 oz) can artichoke hearts, drained and finely chopped*

**220-150 CALS/SERVING**

- *12 large oysters*
- *200 g (7 oz) mozzarella cheese, thinly sliced*

1 In a small frying pan, fry the bacon until the fat begins to run. Add the celery and artichokes. Cook, stirring, for 2 minutes. Cool.
2 Scrub the oyster shells well. Open the oysters by inserting an oyster knife into the hinge linking the shells and cutting through the muscle. Prise the shells apart and discard the flatter ones.
3 Spoon a little of the bacon and artichoke mixture over each oyster. Top with cheese.
4 Cook under a medium grill for 10 minutes.

150 ml (5 fl oz) of the hot stock and cook, stirring constantly, until the liquid is absorbed by the rice. Continue adding stock in 150 ml (5 fl oz) quantities until you have used half of it. This should take about 10 minutes and the rice should be about half cooked.

**3** Stir in the seafood and cook for 2-3 minutes. Continue adding the stock as before, until the rice is tender but with a firm bite (you may not need to add all the stock). The rice should hold together in a creamy mass.

**4** Stir in the lemon rind, tomato paste and tarragon. Season with salt and pepper to taste and leave to stand for a few minutes before serving.

**NOTE** Arborio rice is the classic Italian risotto rice and produces a delicious creamy texture. Ready-prepared mixed seafood is sold in packets from most supermarkets.

**VARIATION** If preferred, make the risotto with one type of seafood only, such as prawns or mussels. You can also vary the herbs used.

## SEAFOOD RISOTTO

PREPARATION TIME 10 minutes
COOKING TIME 30 minutes
FREEZING Not suitable

SERVES 4                     420 CALS/SERVING

- 60 ml (4 tbsp) sunflower oil
- 1 onion, peeled and finely chopped
- 2 garlic cloves, peeled and crushed
- 225 g (8 oz) Arborio rice
- 100 ml (3½ fl oz) dry white wine
- 1.5-1.6 litres (2¼-2½ pints) hot fish stock

- 300 g (10 oz) prepared mixed seafood
- grated rind of 1 small lemon
- 30 ml (2 tbsp) sun-dried tomato paste
- 15 ml (1 tbsp) chopped fresh tarragon
- salt and pepper

**1** Heat the oil in a heavy-based pan, add the onion and garlic and cook until softened. Add the rice and cook, stirring, for about 1 minute.
**2** Add the wine and stir until it is absorbed. Add

## MUSSELS IN TOMATO SAUCE

PREPARATION TIME 5 minutes
COOKING TIME About 10 minutes
FREEZING Not suitable
COLOUR INDEX Page 18
♡ ⏲

SERVES 4                     260 CALS/SERVING

- 45 ml (3 tbsp) olive oil
- 1 onion, peeled and finely chopped
- 2 garlic cloves, peeled and crushed
- 700g (1½ lb) plum tomatoes, peeled, deseeded and chopped

- 5 ml (1 tsp) sugar
- 45 ml (3 tbsp) chopped fresh oregano
- salt and pepper
- 15 ml (1 tbsp) tomato purée
- 450 g (1 lb) shelled cooked mussels

**1** Heat the oil in a saucepan, add the onion and cook for 5 minutes until softened. Stir in the garlic, tomatoes, sugar and half the oregano. Season with salt and pepper to taste and simmer gently for 2-3 minutes until the tomatoes soften.
**2** Stir in the tomato purée, add the mussels and simmer for 1-2 minutes until heated through. Scatter the remaining oregano over and serve hot.

## STEAMED MUSSELS IN SAFFRON CREAM SAUCE

PREPARATION TIME 15 minutes
COOKING TIME 30 minutes
FREEZING Not suitable

**SERVES 4-6**

**400-265 CALS/SERVING**

- *1.4 kg (3 lb) fresh mussels*
- *25 g (1 oz) butter*
- *60 ml (4 tbsp) olive oil*
- *6 shallots, peeled and chopped*
- *3 garlic cloves, peeled and chopped*
- *2 leeks, trimmed and thinly sliced*
- *150 ml (5 fl oz) fish stock*
- *200 ml (7 fl oz) dry white wine*

- *good pinch of saffron strands*
- *150 ml (5 fl oz) single cream*
- *salt and pepper*
- *3 strips of lemon rind*
- *several coriander stalks*
- *30-45 ml (2-3 tbsp) mixed chopped fresh tarragon and coriander*
- *shredded leek to garnish (optional)*

**1** Scrub the mussels and pull off the coarse threads (beards) from the side of the shells. Thoroughly rinse.

**2** Heat the butter and half the oil in a frying pan and gently fry the shallots, garlic and leeks for 10 minutes, stirring occasionally.

**3** Add the stock, 150 ml (5 fl oz) wine and the saffron, bring to the boil, then cover and simmer gently for 10 minutes. Cool slightly and purée in a blender or food processor. Transfer the sauce to a saucepan and add the cream. Reheat gently and season with salt and pepper.

**4** Place the mussels in a large saucepan with the strips of lemon rind, coriander stalks, 45 ml (3 tbsp) water and remaining wine. Bring to the boil, cover and steam over a moderate heat for about 5 minutes or until the mussels have opened; shake the pan frequently during cooking.

**5** Remove from the heat and discard any mussels that remain closed. Place the mussels in 4 or 6 warmed serving dishes. Strain the juices in the saucepan and add to the sauce. Heat through and pour over the mussels.

**6** Scatter chopped herbs and shredded leek over the mussels and serve at once.

**VARIATION** Use onions rather than the leeks, if preferred. Although the mussels look attractive served in their shells, you may serve them 'shell-less' in the saffron flavoured liquor, if wished.

113

# DRESSED CRAB

PREPARATION TIME I hour
FREEZING Not suitable
COLOUR INDEX Page 18
♡

**SERVES 2-3**

- *1 cooked crab, about 900 g (2 lb)*
- *salt and pepper*
- *15 ml (1 tbsp) lemon juice*
- *30 ml (2 tbsp) fresh white breadcrumbs*

**195-130 CALS/SERVING**

- *1 egg, hard-boiled*
- *15 ml (1 tbsp) chopped fresh parsley*
- *frisée lettuce, to serve*

1 Twist off the legs and claws as close to the body as possible. Break each claw in half then crack with a rolling pin or hammer without crushing the flesh. If you are not using the legs for garnishing, break the shell on the legs with your hands. Using a slender skewer to get at any awkward bits, carefully extract the flesh.

2 Put the crab on its back with the tail flap pointing towards you. Holding the shell firmly, press the body section upwards with your thumbs and it should come away. If it won't move, use the point of a rigid knife to ease it away.

3 With a teaspoon, scoop out into a separate bowl the creamy brown meat and roe (if any) from the shell. Remove and discard the stomach bag which you will find between the eyes. (If this breaks make sure you remove all the greenish or grey-white matter.)

4 Pull away from the body and discard the inedible feathery gills or 'dead man's fingers'. Using a large heavy knife, cut the body in half. Using a skewer, remove the flesh from the tiny crevices.

5 Using two forks, flake all the white meat from the crab. Season and add 5 ml (1 tsp) lemon juice.

6 Pound the brown meat in a bowl with the breadcrumbs and remaining lemon juice. Season.

7 Using a small spoon, put the white meat in both ends of the cleaned crab shell, making sure that it is well piled up in the shell. Spoon the brown meat in a neat line down the centre between the two sections of white crab meat.

8 Chop the egg white and sieve the yolk. Hold a blunt knife between the white and brown crab meat, then carefully spoon lines of parsley, egg yolk and egg white across the crab, moving the knife as you go. Serve on a bed of frisée.

# MIXED SEAFOOD SALAD

PREPARATION TIME 20 minutes, plus chilling
COOKING TIME About 25 minutes
FREEZING Not suitable
COLOUR INDEX Page 18

**SERVES 6**

- *150 ml (5 fl oz) dry white wine*
- *1 bay leaf*
- *few peppercorns*
- *1 parsley sprig*
- *½ small onion, peeled and sliced*
- *350 g (12 oz) raw tiger prawns, thawed if frozen*
- *700 g (1½ lb) haddock fillet, skinned and cut into 2.5 cm (1 inch) chunks*
- *75 g (3 oz) mangetout, trimmed*
- *salt and pepper*

**455 CALS/SERVING**

- *450 g (1 lb) cooked mussels*
- *1 red pepper, deseeded and cut into strips*
- *2 carrots, peeled and cut into strips*
- *50 g (2 oz) pitted black olives*
- *150 ml (5 fl oz) olive oil*
- *45 ml (3 tbsp) white wine vinegar*
- *1-2 garlic cloves, peeled and crushed*
- *45 ml (3 tbsp) chopped fresh parsley*

1 Put the wine in a saucepan with 150 ml (5 fl oz) water. Add the bay leaf, peppercorns, parsley sprig and sliced onion. Bring to the boil. Add the tiger prawns and simmer for 5 minutes or until they turn pink. Lift out with a slotted spoon. Leave to cool.

2 Add the haddock to the wine mixture and simmer gently for about 5 minutes until the fish is cooked. Remove with a slotted spoon. Leave to cool.

3 Bring the wine mixture back to the boil and boil vigorously until reduced to about a quarter of its original volume. Leave to cool.

4 Cook the mangetout in boiling salted water for about 3 minutes, then drain.

5 Carefully peel the prawns. Put them in a bowl with the haddock and mussels. Add the mangetout, red pepper, carrots and olives.

6 Whisk together the oil, vinegar, garlic and chopped parsley. Strain the wine reduction and add to the dressing. Season, then pour over the salad and mix gently. Chill the salad in the refrigerator for 2 hours before serving.

## CHARRED SCALLOPS WITH FENNEL AND PERNOD

PREPARATION TIME 10 minutes
COOKING TIME 10-15 minutes
FREEZING Not suitable

SERVES 4      415 CALS/SERVING

- *1 large fennel bulb, about 225 g (8 oz)*
- *50 g (2 oz) butter*
- *4 shallots, peeled and chopped*
- *2 garlic cloves, peeled and crushed*
- *30 ml (2 tbsp) Pernod*
- *90 ml (3 fl oz) double cream*
- *oil for frying*
- *salt and pepper*
- *12-16 shelled scallops*

**1** Trim the green feathery tops from the fennel. Reserve a few tops for garnishing and chop the remainder – you need 15 ml (1 tbsp) chopped tops. Slice the fennel bulb.

**2** Heat the butter in a small saucepan, add the shallots and garlic and cook for 3 minutes until soft. Add the Pernod and cream and cook gently for 2-3 minutes. Stir in the chopped fennel tops.

**3** Heat a heavy-based ridged frying pan or griddle pan with a little oil until very hot and just smoking. Turn down the heat a little, then place the fennel slices on the frying pan or griddle and cook for a few minutes on each side until slightly charred. Transfer to a warmed serving plate and keep warm.

**4** Gently reheat the sauce and season with salt and pepper to taste.

**5** Meanwhile, place the scallops on the frying pan or griddle and cook for 1-2 minutes on each side until slightly charred. Transfer to the serving plate of cooked fennel, garnish with the reserved fennel tops and serve at once with the hot sauce.

> ### TIP
> Serve the cooked scallops and fennel in scrubbed scallop shells for an attractive presentation.

# POULTRY
# AND GAME

## ROASTED PECAN CHICKEN

PREPARATION TIME 25 minutes
COOKING TIME 1½ hours
FREEZING Not suitable

SERVES 4

430 CALS/SERVING

- *50 g (2 oz) creamy goats' cheese*
- *7.5 ml (1½ tsp) lemon juice*
- *75 g (3 oz) pecan nuts*
- *1 small garlic clove, peeled*
- *30 ml (2 tbsp) olive oil*
- *salt and pepper*

- *1.6 kg (3½ lb) oven-ready chicken*
- *lemon and onion slices*
- *150 ml (5 fl oz) dry white wine*
- *300 ml (10 fl oz) chicken stock*
- *about 10-15 ml (2-3 tsp) cornflour*

1 Place the first five ingredients in a food processor and season with black pepper only. Blend until the mixture forms a paste.
2 Loosen the skin around the chicken breast and spread the mixture underneath the skin to form an even layer. Try not to pierce or break the skin. Secure the skin with a cocktail stick and tie the chicken legs together.
3 Place the chicken in a roasting tin with the lemon and onion slices, wine and 150 ml (5 fl oz) stock. Cook at 200°C (400°F) mark 6 for about 1½ hours, basting occasionally. If necessary, cover with foil towards the end of the cooking time. Test the thickest part of the thigh with a fine skewer – when cooked, the juices run clear.
4 Keep the chicken warm. Discard the lemon and onion slices. Skim the fat from the juices and stir in the remaining 150 ml (5 fl oz) stock. Bring to the boil, scraping any sediment off the base of the pan. Mix the cornflour to a smooth paste with a little water. Off the heat, stir it into the pan juices. Return to the heat and bring to the boil, stirring all the time. Bubble for 2-3 minutes. Adjust the seasoning and serve with the chicken.

**VARIATIONS** Beat together 50 g (2 oz) butter with 30 ml (2 tbsp) pesto sauce. Spread this under the chicken-breast skin and over the legs and cook as above. Stir 45 ml (3 tbsp) fromage frais into the gravy just before serving.
- Beat together 45 ml (3 tbsp) olive oil with 30 ml (2 tbsp) sun-dried tomato paste. Spread underneath the chicken-breast skin. Cook as above. If

you can't find the paste, use 75 g (3 oz) sun-dried tomatoes in oil. Purée with a little olive oil.

• Beat together 50 g (2 oz) softened butter with 5 ml (1 tsp) dried tarragon and the grated rind of 1 lemon. Spread underneath the chicken-breast skin and over the legs and cook as before, using dry vermouth instead of the wine.

• Beat together 50 g (2 oz) softened butter with 5 ml (1 tsp) each of ground cumin, ground coriander and ground turmeric, 1.25 ml (¼ tsp) mild chilli powder and 1 crushed garlic clove. Spread underneath the chicken-breast skin and over the legs, and cook as before.

# CHICKEN HOTPOT WITH LEEKS

PREPARATION TIME 15 minutes
COOKING TIME 1 hour 35 minutes
FREEZING Not suitable
COLOUR INDEX Page 21
♡

SERVES 4
• *15 ml (1 tbsp) olive oil*
• *1 large garlic clove, peeled and crushed*
• *700 g (1½ lb) trimmed leeks, thickly sliced*
• *200 g (7 oz) reduced-fat soft cheese with garlic and herbs*
• *125 ml (4 fl oz) white wine*

350 CALS/SERVING
• *175 ml (6 fl oz) chicken stock*
• *10 ml (2 tsp) cornflour*
• *8 skinless, boneless chicken thighs, about 350 g (12 oz) total weight*
• *salt and pepper*
• *300 g (10 oz) potatoes, unpeeled and thinly sliced*

1 Heat the oil in a flameproof casserole. Add the garlic and leeks and cook for about 5 minutes or until beginning to soften.
2 Meanwhile, place the cheese, wine, stock and cornflour in a food processor and blend for about 30 seconds or until smooth.
3 Arrange the chicken thighs on top of the leeks, pour the cheese mixture over and season to taste. Layer the potatoes on top of the chicken. Place a lightly oiled sheet of greaseproof paper on top of the potatoes, then cover with a lid or foil.
4 Cook at 180°C (350°F) mark 4 for 1½ hours or until the potatoes are quite tender. Brown the potatoes under a hot grill before serving.

# CHICKEN IN SMOKY BACON SAUCE

PREPARATION TIME 10 minutes
COOKING TIME 20 minutes
FREEZING Not suitable
COLOUR INDEX Page 19
♡ ⏲

SERVES 4
• *30 ml (2 tbsp) vegetable oil*
• *125 g (4 oz) chopped bacon pieces*
• *4 skinless chicken breast fillets, each weighing about 150 g (5 oz)*
• *200 ml (7 fl oz) apple juice*
• *15 ml (1 tbsp) chopped fresh thyme or 5 ml (1 tsp) dried thyme*

350 CALS/SERVING
• *salt and pepper*
• *1 bunch spring onions, trimmed and roughly chopped*
• *225 g (8 oz) crisp red apples, thickly sliced*
• *60 ml (4 tbsp) crème fraîche*

1 Heat the oil in a large deep frying pan or sauté pan. Add the chopped bacon and chicken pieces and fry for a few minutes until golden, stirring and turning occasionally.
2 Stir in the apple juice and thyme, and season to taste. Bring to the boil, cover and simmer for 10 minutes.
3 Uncover, then add the spring onions. Tip the apples into the pan and cook over a high heat for about 5 minutes or until the liquid has reduced by half and the chicken is tender.
4 Reduce the heat to low and stir in the crème fraîche. Adjust the seasoning and serve.

**NOTE** Chopped bacon pieces are sold in most supermarkets, but if unavailable, simply buy thin-cut, smoked, streaky bacon and chop roughly yourself.

## SWEET GINGERED CHICKEN

PREPARATION TIME 10 minutes
COOKING TIME About 30 minutes
FREEZING Not suitable

SERVES 6

- *120 ml (8 tbsp) apricot jam*
- *75 ml (5 tbsp) light soy sauce*
- *120 ml (8 tbsp) dry sherry*
- *juice of 1 lemon*
- *2 garlic cloves, peeled and crushed*
- *2.5 cm (1 inch) piece fresh root ginger, peeled and finely grated*

435 CALS/SERVING

- *350 g (12 oz) aubergine, thinly sliced*
- *6 chicken breast fillets with skin, each weighing about 150 g (5 oz)*

1 Mix together the first four ingredients. Add the garlic and the ginger.
2 Line a large roasting tin with foil. Spread out the aubergine and chicken in the tin. Spoon the ginger mixture over the top.
3 Cook at 220°C (425°F) mark 7 for about 30-35 minutes, basting occasionally, until the chicken and aubergine are well browned and glazed. Add a little water, if necessary, towards the end of cooking.

## WINTER CHICKEN

PREPARATION TIME 20 minutes
COOKING TIME 45 minutes
FREEZING Not suitable
COLOUR INDEX Page 21
♡

SERVES 4

- *4 chicken leg portions, about 700 g (1½ lb) total weight*
- *salt and pepper*
- *15 ml (1 tbsp) white plain flour*
- *15 ml (1 tbsp) olive oil*
- *225 g (8 oz) onion, peeled and cut into small wedges*
- *450 g (1 lb) carrots, peeled and cut into chunks*
- *450 g (1 lb) celery, cut into chunks*

350 CALS/SERVING

- *50 g (2 oz) rindless lean back bacon, roughly chopped*
- *200 ml (7 fl oz) apple juice*
- *400 g (14 oz) can butter beans (300 g/10 oz drained weight)*
- *1 bunch watercress, roughly chopped*
- *15-30 ml (1-2 tbsp) lemon juice*

1 Skin the chicken portions and divide them into thighs and drumsticks. Toss the chicken in seasoned flour.
2 Heat the oil in a medium-size, flameproof casserole. Add the onion, carrots, celery and bacon and fry for 2-3 minutes. Mix in the apple juice, drained butter beans and the chicken.
3 Bring to the boil on the hob, cover and cook in the oven at 180°C (350°F) mark 4 for about 45 minutes or until all the ingredients are tender.
4 Stir the watercress into the casserole with the lemon juice and seasoning to taste before serving.

## MARINATED CHICKEN WITH PRUNES

PREPARATION TIME 10 minutes, plus marinating
COOKING TIME 50 minutes
FREEZING Not suitable

### SERVES 4
- *4 chicken quarters (breast or leg), about 900 g (2 lb) total weight*
- *4 garlic cloves, peeled and sliced*
- *10 ml (2 tsp) dried mixed herbs*
- *30 ml (2 tbsp) red wine vinegar*
- *125 ml (4 fl oz) vegetable oil*
- *225 g (8 oz) pitted no-soak prunes*
- *30 ml (2 tbsp) capers, drained*

### 570 CALS/SERVING
- *salt and pepper*
- *300 ml (10 fl oz) dry white wine*
- *25 g (1 oz) demerara sugar*
- *5 ml (1 tsp) cornflour*
- *150 ml (5 fl oz) chicken stock*
- *about 5 ml (1 tsp) lemon juice*
- *flat-leaf parsley, to garnish*

1 Place the chicken in a large non-metallic bowl with the garlic. Add the next five ingredients with plenty of seasoning and mix well. Cover and marinate in the refrigerator overnight.

2 Remove the chicken from the marinade and reserve the marinade. With a little oil from the marinade, brown the chicken in a flameproof casserole large enough to hold the chicken in a single layer. Pour the remaining marinade, with the prunes and capers, over the chicken. Pour over the wine and sprinkle with the sugar. Bring to the boil.

3 Cover and bake at 180°C (350°F) mark 4 for 30 minutes, then uncover and baste. Return to the oven, uncovered, for a further 20 minutes, or until the chicken quarters are cooked through.

4 Using slotted spoons, lift the chicken into a serving dish. Cover the chicken and keep it warm. Skim the juices. Mix the cornflour to a smooth paste with 15 ml (1 tbsp) water. Add to the pan juices with the stock and bring to the boil, stirring all the time. Cook for 1-2 minutes. Adjust the seasoning, add about 5 ml (1 tsp) lemon juice to taste, spoon over the chicken and serve, garnished with flat-leaf parsley.

# SPICY COCONUT CHICKEN

PREPARATION TIME 10 minutes
COOKING TIME 35 minutes
FREEZING Not suitable
COLOUR INDEX Page 20
♡

**SERVES 6**                    **270 CALS/SERVING**

- *6 chicken breast fillets with skin, about 700 g (1½ lb) total weight*
- *45 ml (3 tbsp) vegetable oil*
- *225 g (8 oz) onion, peeled and finely chopped*
- *1 garlic clove, peeled and crushed*
- *1 cm (½ inch) piece fresh root ginger, peeled and finely chopped*
- *2.5 ml (½ tsp) ground turmeric*
- *5 ml (1 tsp) each ground cumin, ground coriander and mild curry powder*
- *pinch hot chilli powder (optional)*
- *225 g (8 oz) can chopped tomatoes*
- *75 g (3 oz) creamed coconut, coarsely grated*
- *30 ml (2 tbsp) poppy seeds*
- *300 ml (10 fl oz) chicken stock*
- *salt and pepper*
- *30 ml (2 tbsp) Greek natural yogurt*
- *chopped fresh coriander, to garnish*

**1** Tuck the ends of the chicken breasts under to shape into neat rounds; tie with string.
**2** Heat the oil in a pan and sauté the chicken fillets until golden. Remove with a slotted spoon and drain on absorbent kitchen paper.
**3** Add the onion, garlic and ginger and cook, stirring, for 1-2 minutes. Add the spices. Cook for a further minute, then add the tomatoes, coconut and poppy seeds. Cook for a further minute, add the stock, then bring to the boil and simmer for 2-3 minutes.
**4** Replace the chicken, cover and simmer for about 20 minutes or until the chicken is cooked through.
**5** Skim off any excess oil and adjust the seasoning. Off the heat, stir in the yogurt. Serve garnished with fresh coriander.

# ORIENTAL CHICKEN PARCELS

PREPARATION TIME 20 minutes, plus marinating
COOKING TIME 35 minutes
FREEZING Not suitable
COLOUR INDEX Page 20
♡

**SERVES 4**                    **215 CALS/SERVING**

- *3 oranges*
- *juice of 1 lemon*
- *30 ml (2 tbsp) dark soy sauce*
- *30 ml (2 tbsp) yellow bean sauce*
- *15 ml (1 tbsp) dry sherry*
- *15 ml (1 tbsp) vegetable oil*
- *salt and pepper*
- *four 125 g (4 oz) skinless chicken breast fillets*
- *50 g (2 oz) stem ginger or 2.5 cm (1 inch) piece fresh root ginger, peeled and thinly sliced*
- *1 bunch spring onions, trimmed and shredded*
- *125 g (4 oz) carrots, peeled and shredded*

**1** In a bowl mix together the finely grated rind of one orange with 60 ml (4 tbsp) orange juice, the lemon juice, soy sauce, yellow bean sauce, sherry and oil. Season well with salt and pepper.
**2** Lightly slash the chicken breasts all over and stir into the marinade with the ginger, spring onions and carrot. Refrigerate overnight.
**3** The next day, segment the remaining oranges. Cut four 30 cm (12 inch) squares of foil and pull up the edges to make open purses. Divide the chicken and marinade among the foil pieces and top with orange segments. Pinch the corners of the foil together. Place the parcels in a roasting tin.
**4** Cook at 180°C (350°F) mark 4 for about 35 minutes or until the chicken is tender. Open the parcels into soup bowls to serve as there is quite a lot of juice.

# HERB MARINATED CHICKEN WITH SPRING VEGETABLES IN A WARM DRESSING

PREPARATION TIME 20 minutes, plus marinating
COOKING TIME 50-55 minutes
FREEZING Not suitable

## SERVES 4

- *60 ml (4 tbsp) extra-virgin olive oil*
- *25 g (1 oz) chopped mixed spring herbs*
- *1 garlic clove, peeled and crushed*
- *4 spring onions, chopped*
- *60 ml (4 tbsp) dry white wine*
- *4 large chicken breast fillets, with skin, each weighing about 150 g (5 oz)*
- *225 g (8 oz) baby new potatoes, scrubbed and halved if large*

## 510 CALS/SERVING

- *175 g (6 oz) baby carrots, scrubbed*
- *175 g (6 oz) mangetout, trimmed*

*DRESSING*
- *30 ml (2 tbsp) extra-virgin olive oil*
- *15 ml (1 tbsp) balsamic vinegar*
- *4 ripe tomatoes, skinned, deseeded and diced*
- *10 ml (2 tsp) sun-dried tomato paste*
- *salt and pepper*

1 Heat 45 ml (3 tbsp) oil in a small frying pan, add the herbs, garlic and spring onions and heat gently for 3 minutes. Do not allow the oil to get too hot and burn the herbs. Set aside until cold, then stir in the wine.

2 Wash and dry the chicken. Place in a shallow baking dish and pour over the cooled herb marinade. Cover and leave to marinate for 4 hours or overnight. Remove the chicken 1 hour before cooking.

3 Briskly fry the chicken breasts in the remaining oil for a few minutes to brown the skin.

4 Place the chicken in an ovenproof dish, cover with foil and bake in the oven at 180°C (350°F) mark 4 for 40-45 minutes.

5 Meanwhile, cook the potatoes in lightly salted boiling water for 10-12 minutes until just cooked, adding the carrots after 6 minutes and the mangetout after 8 minutes. Drain the vegetables and keep warm.

6 Remove the chicken from the oven, and strain off the cooking juices, reserving 30 ml (2 tbsp). Keep the chicken warm.

7 Place the dressing ingredients and reserved chicken juices in a small pan, heat gently until just boiling, then remove from the heat. Arrange the vegetables on serving plates, top with the chicken and spoon over the dressing. Serve at once.

## SPRING CHICKEN FRICASSEE

PREPARATION TIME 20 minutes
COOKING TIME 35 minutes
FREEZING Not suitable
COLOUR INDEX Page 20

SERVES 4      650 CALS/SERVING

- 225 g (8 oz) cauliflower florets
- 225 g (8 oz) broccoli florets
- salt and pepper
- 225 g (8 oz) full-fat soft cheese with garlic and herbs
- 8 chicken breast fillets with skin, about 800 g (1¾ lb) total weight
- 15 ml (1 tbsp) white plain flour
- about 30 ml (2 tbsp) vegetable oil
- 225 g (8 oz) baby carrots, cut into fingers
- 225 g (8 oz) button onions, peeled and halved
- 100 ml (3½ fl oz) dry vermouth
- 300 ml (10 fl oz) chicken stock
- 30 ml (2 tbsp) chopped fresh tarragon or 2.5 ml (½ tsp) dried
- 1 garlic clove, peeled and crushed
- 60 ml (4 tbsp) single cream
- carrot tops, to garnish

1 Blanch the cauliflower and broccoli in salted water for 1-2 minutes only, then drain.
2 Push a little of the soft cheese underneath the skin of each chicken breast and tuck the ends of the breast under to form small, neat rounds. Toss in the flour.
3 Heat the oil in a shallow flameproof casserole. Brown the chicken pieces a few at a time, adding more oil as necessary. Remove with a slotted spoon. Add the carrots and onions to the casserole and brown lightly.
4 Return the chicken to the pan and pour in the vermouth and stock. Bring to the boil, stirring in the tarragon, garlic and seasoning.
5 Cover tightly and simmer gently for about 10 minutes. Stir in the cauliflower and broccoli and cook for another 10 minutes or until the chicken is cooked through.
6 Stir in the cream and simmer for 1-2 minutes. Adjust the seasoning and serve garnished with carrot tops. Accompany with rice.

## COUNTRY CHICKEN CASSEROLE

PREPARATION TIME 10 minutes
COOKING TIME 1½ hours
FREEZING Suitable
COLOUR INDEX Page 21

❄

SERVES 4      405 CALS/SERVING

- about 30 ml (2 tbsp) vegetable oil
- 175 g (6 oz) lightly smoked streaky bacon, roughly chopped
- 4 chicken quarters, about 700 g (1½ lb) total weight
- 225 g (8 oz) button onions, peeled and halved if large
- 1 garlic clove, peeled and crushed
- 225 g (8 oz) brown-cap mushrooms, thickly sliced
- 20 g (¾ oz) white plain flour
- 300 ml (10 fl oz) chicken stock
- 300 ml (10 fl oz) white wine
- salt and pepper

1 Gently heat the oil in a large, shallow, flameproof casserole. Add the bacon and fry until golden. Drain on absorbent kitchen paper. Brown the chicken, adding a little more oil if necessary. Drain on absorbent kitchen paper.
2 Sauté the onions and garlic for 2-3 minutes, then add the mushrooms for a further 2 minutes. Stir in the flour until smooth.
3 Off the heat, stir in the stock and wine and season generously. Bring to the boil and replace the bacon and chicken. Cover and cook at 170°C (325°F) mark 3 for 1¼ hours or until tender.

## GARLIC CHICKEN WITH ROAST PEPPER PUREE

PREPARATION TIME 20 minutes, plus marinating
COOKING TIME 1 hour and 5 minutes
FREEZING Not suitable

**SERVES 6**

- *6 skinless chicken breast fillets*
- *4 garlic cloves, peeled and crushed*
- *15 ml (1 tbsp) chopped fresh thyme*
- *105 ml (7 tbsp) olive oil*
- *15 ml (1 tbsp) clear honey*
- *15 ml (1 tbsp) white wine vinegar*
- *salt and pepper*
- *4 red peppers, deseeded*

**420 CALS/SERVING**

- *2 yellow peppers, deseeded*
- *2 onions, peeled and sliced*
- *225 g (8 oz) plum tomatoes, skinned and halved*
- *10 ml (2 tsp) paprika*
- *15 ml (1 tbsp) tomato purée*
- *thyme sprigs, to garnish*

1 Cut several deep slits across each chicken breast and lay them in a large shallow dish. Scatter the garlic over the chicken with the chopped thyme. Mix 30 ml (2 tbsp) oil with the honey and wine vinegar. Season and pour over the chicken. Leave to marinate for several hours.

2 Drain the chicken, reserving the marinade juices. Heat 30 ml (2 tbsp) olive oil in a frying pan. Add the chicken, slit sides down, and fry quickly to sear. Turn the chicken and cook for a further minute. Transfer to a shallow baking dish with a slotted spoon.

3 Cut each pepper into 8 chunks. Place the onions, peppers and tomatoes in a large shallow ovenproof dish. Sprinkle with the paprika and pour over the remaining oil.

4 Bake the vegetables at 200°C (400°F) mark 6, near the top of the oven, for 1 hour, until lightly charred. Halfway through cooking, place the chicken on a lower shelf and bake for 30 minutes until cooked through.

5 Reserve 6 pieces of red pepper and 6 pieces of yellow pepper for garnish – cut into strips and keep warm. Place the remaining vegetable mixture in a food processor or blender and blend until almost smooth. Place in a saucepan and heat through, adding the tomato purée and seasoning to taste.

6 Spoon the pepper purée onto warmed serving plates and top with the chicken breasts and reserved peppers. Garnish with thyme sprigs and serve.

## SOUTHERN FRIED CHICKEN WITH CORN FRITTERS

PREPARATION TIME 15 minutes
COOKING TIME 20 minutes
FREEZING Not suitable
COLOUR INDEX Page 20

**SERVES 4-6**

- 6 allspice berries
- 10 black peppercorns
- 40 g (1½ oz) white plain flour
- 1 garlic clove, peeled and finely chopped
- 2.5 ml (½ tsp) dried thyme
- salt and pepper
- 8-12 chicken drumsticks, skinned
- 1 egg, beaten
- 125-175 g (4-6 oz) dried breadcrumbs
- vegetable oil for frying

CORN FRITTERS
- 75 g (3 oz) white plain flour
- 1 egg
- 75 ml (3 fl oz) milk

**660-440 CALS/SERVING**

- 200 g (7 oz) can sweetcorn, drained
- 2 spring onions, trimmed and finely chopped

TOMATO SALSA
- 6 ripe tomatoes, cored and finely chopped
- 1 red onion, peeled and finely chopped
- 1 spring onion, trimmed and finely chopped
- ¼ cucumber, finely chopped
- a little olive oil
- dash of wine vinegar
- chopped fresh chives, basil or coriander

1 First make the tomato salsa. Mix the tomatoes with the chopped onions and cucumber, moistening with a little olive oil and vinegar. Season liberally with salt and pepper. Add chopped herbs to taste.
2 For the chicken, crush the allspice berries and peppercorns together, using a pestle and mortar. Mix the flour with the allspice mixture, garlic, thyme and plenty of salt. Toss the chicken in the flour mixture to coat evenly.
3 Dip each chicken portion first in the beaten egg, and then in the breadcrumbs to coat. Arrange in a single layer on a plate and chill while making the corn fritters.
4 To make the corn fritters, put the flour and a large pinch of salt into a bowl and make a well in the centre. Add the egg and milk and beat thoroughly to make a smooth thick batter. Fold the sweetcorn and spring onion into the batter.
5 Heat a little oil in a frying pan and fry a few large spoonfuls of the sweetcorn batter mixture for 2-3 minutes each side until golden brown and

crisp. Drain on absorbent kitchen paper and keep warm in a hot oven while you cook the remainder. (There should be sufficient to make 12 fritters.)
6 Meanwhile heat the oil for deep frying in a deep-fat fryer to 170°C (325°F). Fry the chicken, in batches, for about 10 minutes until crisp and golden and cooked right through. Keep warm with the corn fritters.
7 Serve the chicken and corn fritters as soon as they are all cooked, with the salsa.

## CHICKEN BREASTS WITH APPLE AND THYME

PREPARATION TIME 15 minutes
COOKING TIME 1 hour
FREEZING Not suitable
COLOUR INDEX Page 19
♡

**SERVES 4**

- 50 g (2 oz) butter
- 175 g (6 oz) onion, peeled and chopped
- 2 crisp dessert apples
- 50 g (2 oz) mature Cheddar cheese
- 40 g (1½ oz) fresh breadcrumbs
- 30 ml (2 tbsp) chopped fresh thyme or 5 ml (1 tsp) dried
- salt and pepper

**330 CALS/SERVING**

- 4 chicken breast fillets with skin, about 700 g (1½ lb) total weight
- 75 ml (3 fl oz) apple juice
- 20 ml (4 tsp) cornflour
- 300 ml (10 fl oz) chicken stock
- 15 ml (1 tbsp) wholegrain mustard

1 Heat 25 g (1 oz) butter in a frying pan and sauté the onion until softened. Leave to cool. Grate the apples and cheese into the onion. Add the breadcrumbs, thyme and seasoning.
2 Loosen the skin of the chicken and push the stuffing underneath, pressing into place. Place in a roasting tin, dot with the remaining butter and season. Pour the apple juice over.
3 Cook at 190°C (375°F) mark 5 for about 50 minutes or until cooked through. Remove the chicken from the pan and keep warm.
4 Blend the cornflour with 30 ml (2 tbsp) cold water, add to the pan with the stock and mustard, bring to the boil, stirring, and cook for 2-3 minutes. Season and spoon over the chicken.

## CHICKEN AND APPLE CASSEROLE

PREPARATION TIME 20 minutes
COOKING TIME 1 hour 10 minutes
FREEZING Not suitable

SERVES 4      440 CALS/SERVING

- *30 ml (2 tbsp) olive oil*
- *4 chicken quarters, about 900 g (2 lb) total weight*
- *900 g (2 lb) mixed seasonal root vegetables, peeled and sliced*
- *350 g (12 oz) onion, peeled and roughly chopped*
- *125 g (4 oz) green lentils*
- *2 small eating apples, peeled, cored and sliced*
- *200 ml (7 fl oz) apple juice*
- *300 ml (10 fl oz) chicken stock*
- *salt and pepper*

**1** Heat the oil in a large flameproof casserole, add the chicken quarters and brown well. Remove from the pan with a slotted spoon and drain on absorbent kitchen paper.

**2** Add all the vegetables to the pan and sauté for 4-5 minutes or until beginning to colour. Add the lentils, sliced apples, apple juice and chicken stock and bring to the boil. Season well and replace the chicken quarters.

**3** Cover and cook at 190°C (375°F) mark 5 for about 50 minutes or until the chicken and lentils are tender and cooked through. Adjust the seasoning before serving.

**VARIATIONS** You can add any of your favourite seasonal root vegetables to this casserole – just keep the total weight the same. If you prefer a casserole with thicker juices, simply purée some of the vegetables and stir back in.

---

*TIP*
If you want to prepare the apples slightly in advance, place the slices in cold water mixed with lemon juice as you cut them up. This will stop the flesh from discolouring.

---

## SAVOURY CRUMBED CHICKEN

PREPARATION TIME 10 minutes
COOKING TIME 45 minutes
FREEZING Not suitable

**SERVES 4-6**
- *90 ml (6 tbsp) mayonnaise*
- *125 g (4 oz) spring onions, chopped*
- *45 ml (3 tbsp) chopped fresh thyme*
- *salt and pepper*
- *12 skinless chicken thighs, about 1.4 kg (3 lb) total weight, with bone*

**480-320 CALS/SERVING**
- *75 g (3 oz) dry white breadcrumbs*
- *50 g (2 oz) butter, melted*
- *fresh thyme sprigs, to garnish*

1 Mix together the mayonnaise, spring onions, thyme and seasoning. Spread over the chicken, then roll in the breadcrumbs.
2 Place in a single layer in an ovenproof dish. Spoon over the butter.
3 Cook at 200°C (400°F) mark 6 for 45 minutes. Serve immediately or drain and serve cold, garnished with thyme.

## HOT RED JUNGLE CURRY

PREPARATION TIME 10 minutes
COOKING TIME 15 minutes
FREEZING Not suitable
COLOUR INDEX Page 21
♡ ⏲

**SERVES 4**
- *15 ml (1 tbsp) vegetable oil*
- *350 g (12 oz) skinless chicken breast fillet, cut into strips*
- *30 ml (2 tbsp) red curry paste*
- *125 g (4 oz) aubergine, cut into bite-sized pieces*
- *125 g (4 oz) baby sweetcorn, halved lengthways*
- *75 g (3 oz) green beans*
- *75 g (3 oz) button or brown-cap mushrooms, halved if necessary*
- *2-3 Kaffir lime leaves (optional)*

**200 CALS/SERVING**
- *450 ml (15 fl oz) chicken stock*
- *2.5 cm (1 inch) piece fresh root ginger, peeled and finely sliced*
- *30 ml (2 tbsp) fish sauce*
- *grated rind of ½ lime*
- *5 ml (1 tsp) tomato purée*
- *15 ml (1 tbsp) soft brown sugar*
- *pared lime rind, to garnish*

1 Heat the oil in a wok or large sauté pan. Add the chicken and cook, stirring, for 5 minutes or until the chicken turns golden brown.
2 Stir in the red curry paste and cook for a further minute. Add the vegetables and lime leaves, if using, and stir until coated in the red curry paste.
3 Add all the remaining ingredients and bring to the boil. Simmer gently for 10-12 minutes or until the chicken and vegetables are just tender. Serve immediately, garnished with pared lime rind.

**VARIATION** Add a drained 227 g (8 oz) can of bamboo shoots with the other vegetables in stage 2 for extra texture.

# CHICKEN BREASTS WITH SPINACH AND RICOTTA

PREPARATION TIME 30 minutes
COOKING TIME 35-45 minutes
FREEZING Not suitable

**SERVES 4**

- *4 skinless chicken breast fillets*
- *50 g (2 oz) frozen chopped spinach, thawed*
- *175 g (6 oz) ricotta cheese*
- *60 ml (4 tbsp) freshly grated Parmesan cheese*
- *freshly grated nutmeg*

**400 CALS/SERVING**

- *salt and pepper*
- *8 large fresh spinach leaves*
- *150 ml (5 fl oz) dry white wine*
- *300 ml (10 fl oz) chicken stock*
- *50 g (2 oz) butter, chilled and diced*

1 Using a sharp knife, make a deep horizontal slit in each chicken breast through the thicker side, to make a pocket.

2 Squeeze the moisture out of the thawed spinach, then place in a bowl. Add the ricotta, Parmesan and plenty of nutmeg, salt and pepper. Mix well, then spoon the filling evenly into the chicken pockets.

3 Bring a saucepan of salted water to the boil and add the spinach leaves. Immediately remove with a slotted spoon and plunge into a bowl of cold water to set the colour and prevent further cooking. Wrap two spinach leaves around each chicken breast. Tie with thin cotton string to secure.

4 Lay the chicken breasts in a wide shallow pan or flameproof casserole and pour in the wine and stock. Bring to the boil, lower the heat, cover and simmer gently for 30-40 minutes until cooked. Remove from the pan with a slotted spoon and keep warm.

5 Boil the cooking liquid rapidly until reduced by half. Take off the heat and whisk in the diced butter. Adjust the seasoning.

6 To serve, slice the chicken breasts and arrange on warmed serving plates with a little sauce. Serve the remaining sauce separately.

**VARIATION** Another type of curd cheese or soft cream cheese can be used in place of the ricotta.

# POACHED CHICKEN IN WATERCRESS SAUCE

PREPARATION TIME 5 minutes
COOKING TIME 15 minutes
FREEZING Not suitable
COLOUR INDEX Page 19
♡ ⊙

**SERVES 4**
- *4 skinless chicken breast fillets, each weighing about 125 g (4 oz)*
- *4 thin slices of Parma ham*
- *90 ml (6 tbsp) dry white wine*
- *50 ml (2 fl oz) chicken stock*

**215 CALS/SERVING**
- *60 ml (4 tbsp) single cream*
- *90 ml (6 tbsp) chopped watercress*
- *ground black pepper*
- *flat-leaf parsley, to garnish*

1 Wrap each chicken breast in a slice of ham. Place in a saucepan just large enough to fit the chicken in one layer.
2 Pour the wine and stock over. Bring to the boil, cover and simmer for 10-12 minutes or until the chicken is tender. Remove to a serving dish.
3 Boil down the juices to about 75 ml (5 tbsp). Add the cream and bring to the boil. Remove from the heat and mix in the watercress. Season with pepper, pour over chicken and garnish.

## TIP
To serve cold, complete to the end of stage 2, then cool and thickly slice. Fold the watercress into 60 ml (4 tbsp) low-calorie mayonnaise and serve with the chicken.

# STIR-FRIED CHICKEN WITH COURGETTES

PREPARATION TIME 10 minutes
COOKING TIME 7-10 minutes FREEZING Not suitable
♡ ⊙

**SERVES 4**
- *30 ml (2 tbsp) oil*
- *1 garlic clove, peeled and crushed*
- *450 g (1 lb) skinless chicken breast fillets, sliced into strips*
- *450 g (1 lb) courgettes, sliced*

**250 CALS/SERVING**
- *1 red pepper, deseeded and cut into strips*
- *45 ml (3 tbsp) dry sherry*
- *15 ml (1 tbsp) light soy sauce*
- *pepper*

1 Heat the oil in a wok or a large frying pan and fry the garlic for 1 minute. Add the chicken and cook for 3-4 minutes, stirring continuously.
2 Add the courgettes and red pepper and continue to cook for 1-2 minutes, until the chicken is cooked and the vegetables are tender but still crisp.
3 Stir in the sherry and soy sauce and cook for 1 minute. Season to taste with pepper and serve.

# LIME-PEPPERED CHICKEN

PREPARATION TIME 15 minutes, plus marinating
COOKING TIME 10-12 minutes
FREEZING Not suitable
♡

**SERVES 6**

- *6 skinless chicken breast fillets*
- *2 small red or yellow chillies, thinly sliced*
- *10 ml (2 tsp) coarse-ground black peppercorns*
- *shredded rind and juice of 3 limes*
- *1 garlic clove, peeled and crushed*
- *30 ml (2 tbsp) clear honey*
- *small aubergines or wedges of courgette, onion or lemon, to finish*

**350 CALS/SERVING**

*DIPPING SAUCE*
- *60 ml (4 tbsp) mango chutney*
- *1 garlic clove, peeled and crushed*
- *1 green chilli, seeded*
- *2.5 cm (1 inch) piece fresh root ginger, peeled and grated*
- *10 ml (2 tsp) light soft brown sugar*
- *10 ml (2 tsp) white wine vinegar*
- *45 ml (3 tbsp) soy sauce*
- *few drops Tabasco*
- *90 ml (6 tbsp) oil*

1 Cut the chicken into bite-size pieces. Toss together the chicken, chillies and the next four ingredients. Cover and marinate in the refrigerator for at least 10 minutes.

2 Meanwhile, make the dipping sauce. Place all the ingredients in a food processor and blend for about 15 seconds or until well combined. Cover and refrigerate until required.

3 Thread the marinated chicken pieces onto metal or wooden skewers. Thread an aubergine half, a slice of courgette or a wedge of onion or lemon on to the end of each skewer.

4 Cook on the barbecue or under a hot grill for 10-12 minutes, turning frequently, basting with the reserved marinade. Serve immediately with the sauce for dipping.

**NOTE** Garnish the dip with a few small mixed chillies for added colour.

It's a good idea to wear rubber gloves when preparing chillies as they can irritate the skin. Remove the seeds to reduce the hotness.

131

## MEDITERRANEAN CHICKEN

PREPARATION TIME 40 minutes
COOKING TIME About 5 minutes
FREEZING Not suitable
COLOUR INDEX Page 22

**SERVES 6**                    **480 CALS/SERVING**

- *225 g (8 oz) courgettes*
- *olive oil*
- *10 sun-dried tomatoes in olive oil, drained, about 75 g (3 oz) total weight*
- *salt and pepper*
- *75 g (3 oz) young spinach leaves*
- *400 g (14 oz) crusty loaf*

- *350 g (12 oz) cooked skinned chicken breast fillet, thinly sliced*
- *340 g (12 oz) jar peperonata*
- *10 pitted black olives, halved*
- *300 g (10 oz) mozzarella cheese, thinly sliced*
- *10 fresh basil leaves*

1 Thinly slice the courgettes lengthways, brush lightly with olive oil and grill on each side for 3-4 minutes or until golden brown; drain and cool. Slice the sun-dried tomatoes.
2 Bring a large saucepan of salted water to the boil. Blanch the spinach leaves in batches for 10 seconds, remove with a slotted spoon and plunge into cold water. Drain well.
3 Cut away and remove the base of the loaf, leaving a border of about 2.5 cm (1 inch). Reserve the base. Hollow out the loaf so that the walls are about 1 cm (½ inch) thick. (Use the leftover bread to make breadcrumbs and freeze for use later.)
4 Drizzle the inside of the loaf with about 30 ml (2 tbsp) olive oil. Layer up the chicken, spinach, courgettes, peperonata, olives, sun-dried tomatoes, mozzarella and basil leaves, pressing well into the loaf. Season between layers.
5 When the loaf is full, replace the base. Press into shape and wrap tightly in clingfilm. Chill for at least 2 hours, preferably overnight.
6 Leave the loaf at room temperature for 1 hour before cutting into slices to serve.

**NOTE** Peperonata is a colourful Italian mixture of peppers, onions and tomatoes in a little oil. You'll find it with the pasta sauces in the supermarket, and in delicatessens. There's no need to drain the mixture, as the juice adds extra flavour and texture to the loaf.

## CHEESY CHICKEN AND BACON ROLLS

PREPARATION TIME 10 minutes
COOKING TIME 35 minutes
FREEZING Suitable (stage 2)
COLOUR INDEX Page 20

❊

**SERVES 4**                    **600 CALS/SERVING (WITHOUT DIP)**

- *12 boneless, skinless chicken thighs, about 700 g (1½ lb) total weight*
- *30 ml (2 tbsp) wholegrain mustard*
- *125 g (4 oz) Gruyère cheese*

- *12 slices lightly smoked streaky bacon, about 250 g (9 oz)*
- *Garlic Dip, to serve (see Tip)*

1 Unroll each chicken thigh and spread the inside with mustard. Cut the cheese into 12 fat sticks and place on top of the mustard. Roll up the chicken.
2 Gently stretch the bacon with the back of a knife and wrap one piece tightly around each thigh. Secure with wooden satay sticks.
3 Place the chicken rolls in a non-stick roasting tin and bake at 190°C (375°F) mark 5 for 30-35 minutes or until cooked through and golden brown. Serve immediately with Garlic Dip.

**VARIATION** Other types of cheese can be used inside these chicken pieces. Try Cheddar or Emmental.

---

*TIP*
For an instant Garlic Dip just beat equal quantities of fromage frais and mayonnaise with a little crushed garlic. Top with crispy grilled bacon and black pepper.

---

## CHICKEN WITH SPICED WHEAT

PREPARATION TIME 20 minutes, plus marinating and cooling
COOKING TIME 20-24 minutes
FREEZING Not suitable

♡

**SERVES 6**

- *15 ml (1 tbsp) mango chutney*
- *15 ml (1 tbsp) mild curry paste*
- *10 ml (2 tsp) ground turmeric*
- *50 ml (2 fl oz) olive oil*
- *4 skinless chicken breast fillets, 575 g (1¼ lb) total weight*
- *30 ml (2 tbsp) white wine vinegar*

**337 CALS/SERVING**

- *175 g (6 oz) bulghur wheat*
- *salt and pepper*
- *30 ml (2 tbsp) snipped fresh chives*
- *175 g (6 oz) cherry tomatoes*
- *1 bunch spring onions, roughly chopped*
- *marjoram leaves, to garnish (optional)*

1 Mix together the chutney, curry paste and turmeric. Stir in half the oil. Cut the chicken into bite-size pieces and toss into the mixture. Cover and marinate in the refrigerator for 30 minutes, or overnight.

2 Spread the chicken pieces over a foil-lined grill pan. Cook under a hot grill in batches for 10-12 minutes until the chicken is cooked through and golden brown. Transfer to a bowl with the pan juices and stir in the remaining oil and the vinegar. Leave to cool.

3 Meanwhile, place the bulghur wheat in a bowl and pour over enough boiling water to cover. Leave to soak for about 30 minutes until all of the water has been absorbed and the grains are soft. Stir once or twice and drain well. Season to taste. Stir in the chives.

4 Drain the oil mixture from the chicken and stir into the wheat. Spoon onto a platter.

5 Halve the tomatoes. Mix together with the spring onions and chicken and spoon over the wheat. Garnish with marjoram, if wished.

## WARM ASPARAGUS AND CHICKEN SALAD

PREPARATION TIME 15 minutes
COOKING TIME 10 minutes
FREEZING Not suitable

SERVES 4      420 CALS/SERVING
- *2 large chicken breast fillets, skinned*
- *225 g (8 oz) thin asparagus, trimmed*
- *slivers of fresh Parmesan cheese, to garnish*
- *DRESSING*
- *about 120 ml (8 tbsp) virgin olive oil*
- *20 ml (1½ tbsp) red or white wine vinegar*
- *2 sun-dried tomatoes, finely chopped*
- *15 ml (1 tbsp) capers, finely chopped*
- *about 8 pitted black olives, finely chopped*
- *1 small garlic clove, peeled and finely chopped*
- *large pinch of sugar*
- *salt and pepper*

**1** To make the dressing, whisk 105 ml (7 tbsp) of the olive oil with the wine vinegar to make a thick dressing. Stir in the rest of the dressing ingredients, seasoning to taste with pepper and a little salt.

**2** Beat the chicken breasts between two sheets of clingfilm to flatten thoroughly. Heat a heavy-based ridged frying pan or griddle pan and brush with olive oil. Cook the chicken for 3-4 minutes on each side until golden on the outside and cooked right through. Cut into neat serving pieces and set aside.

**3** Meanwhile, tie the asparagus in a bundle with string. Bring a 7.5 cm (3 inch) depth of salted water to the boil in a small saucepan. Stand the bundle of asparagus in the pan, tips uppermost, and cover with a piece of foil. Cook for 5 minutes or until the asparagus is just tender. Drain thoroughly.

**4** Arrange the asparagus and chicken on individual plates. Pour on the dressing and scatter with Parmesan. Serve while still warm.

**NOTE** This refreshing, warm salad makes an ideal light lunch dish, served with garlic bread. For a more substantial dinner party main course, double up the quantities.

## GRILLED CHICKEN SALAD

PREPARATION TIME 15 minutes, plus cooling
COOKING TIME 30 minutes
FREEZING Not suitable
COLOUR INDEX Page 22

SERVES 4      350 CALS/SERVING
- *175 g (6 oz) ripe tomatoes, halved*
- *30 ml (2 tbsp) tapenade (black olive paste)*
- *olive oil*
- *4 skinless chicken breast fillets, each weighing about 125 g (4 oz)*
- *DRESSING*
- *1 shallot, peeled and finely chopped*
- *45 ml (3 tbsp) olive oil*
- *15 ml (1 tbsp) walnut oil*
- *20 ml (4 tsp) white wine vinegar*
- *30 ml (2 tbsp) single cream*
- *15 ml (1 tbsp) chopped fresh basil*
- *salt and pepper*
- *mixed salad, to serve, such as green leaves, cherry tomatoes, olives, onions and cooked globe artichoke hearts*

## CINNAMON ROAST POUSSIN WITH COUSCOUS

PREPARATION TIME 30 minutes
COOKING TIME 50-55 minutes
FREEZING Not suitable

SERVES 4

720 CALS/SERVING

- 250 g (9 oz) couscous
- 4 small spatch-cocked poussins, each weighing about 400 g (14 oz)
- 5 ml (1 tsp) ground turmeric
- 5 ml (1 tsp) ground cinnamon
- 125 g (4 oz) butter ·
- salt and pepper
- about 60 ml (4 tbsp) clear honey
- large pinch of saffron strands

- 2 onions, peeled and sliced
- 1 garlic clove, peeled and chopped
- 50 g (2 oz) pistachio nuts
- grated rind and juice of 1 lemon
- chopped parsley, to garnish
- lemon wedges, to serve

1 Put the couscous in a bowl and pour over 350 ml (12 fl oz) cold water. Leave to soak for about 15 minutes or until all of the water has been absorbed.
2 Place the poussins in two roasting tins. Sprinkle with the turmeric and cinnamon. Melt 40 g (1½ oz) of the butter and brush over the poussins. Season with salt and pepper. Roast in the oven at 200°C (400°F) mark 6 for 20 minutes. Reduce the temperature to 190°C (375°F) mark 5 and cook

for a further 15 minutes. Brush with a little honey and cook for 15-20 minutes more or until cooked right through.
3 Meanwhile, add the saffron to a little boiling water, then mix with the soaked couscous. Spoon into a large muslin-lined metal sieve and steam over a pan of boiling water for about 35 minutes or until the grains are light and fluffy.
4 Remove the poussins from the roasting tins; cover with foil and keep warm. Tip all the juices into one pan, add the onions and garlic and cook quickly over a high heat until browned and softened. Add the nuts, lemon rind and juice and the remaining butter. Add the couscous and mix carefully with a fork. Season with salt and pepper.
5 Pile the couscous onto a large serving platter. Put the poussins on top and garnish with chopped parsley and lemon wedges.

**NOTE** For extra flavour, serve with Harissa sauce which is available in cans from larger supermarkets and delicatessens.

---

1 Grill the tomatoes skin-side up until black and charred. Purée in a blender or food processor with the olive paste and a little olive oil, if necessary, to give a thinnish paste.
2 Place the chicken skinned-side down on a foil-lined grill pan. Brush lightly with olive oil and grill for 7-8 minutes.
3 Turn the chicken skinned-side up and grill for 5 minutes. Spoon the tomato paste over the chicken and grill for a further 5-6 minutes or until the chicken is cooked through and the topping is well browned. Cool, cover, then refrigerate for at least 1 hour to firm up.
4 Meanwhile, make the dressing. Whisk the shallot with the olive oil, walnut oil, vinegar, cream, basil and salt and pepper to taste. Set aside.
5 Thickly slice the chicken and serve with a selection of salad ingredients. Spoon over the dressing.

## SMOKED CHICKEN WITH CUCUMBER AND MANGO

PREPARATION TIME 45 minutes, plus chilling
FREEZING Not suitable
COLOUR INDEX Page 21

SERVES 6

370 CALS/SERVING

- 1.1 kg (2½ lb) smoked chicken
- 1 small cucumber
- 1 large, ripe mango
- grated rind and juice of 2 limes
- 150 ml (5 fl oz) vegetable oil

- 30 ml (2 tbsp) chopped fresh coriander
- 1 bunch spring onions, trimmed and finely chopped
- salt and pepper

1 Slice the chicken flesh into 5 cm (2 inch) pieces, discarding skin and bone. You should end up with about 700 g (1½ lb) chicken flesh.
2 Halve the cucumber lengthways and remove the seeds with a teaspoon. Slice on the diagonal, then leave to drain on absorbent kitchen paper for about 30 minutes.
3 Cut down either side of the mango stone. Cut away the flesh from the skin and place in a blender or food processor, with the grated lime rind and strained lime juice. Process until smooth. Keep the processor running and add the oil in a slow, steady stream.
4 Pour the mango dressing into a large bowl and

mix in all the remaining ingredients, adding seasoning to taste. Cover and chill for up to a day before serving.

**NOTE** Smoked chicken is available from larger supermarkets. Alternatively, use 350 g (12 oz) smoked ham and 350 g (12 oz) cooked chicken.

## FRENCH ROAST CHICKEN

PREPARATION TIME 10 minutes
COOKING TIME About 1¼-1½ hours
FREEZING Not suitable
COLOUR INDEX Page 19

SERVES 4

470 CALS/SERVING

- 1.4 kg (3 lb) roasting chicken, with giblets
- 1 carrot, peeled
- 1 onion, peeled
- 1 bouquet garni
- 140 g (4½ oz) butter
- 2 fresh tarragon sprigs

- ½ lemon
- 6 garlic cloves
- salt and pepper
- 10 ml (2 tsp) white plain flour

1 Remove the giblets from the chicken and put them in a saucepan with the carrot, onion, bouquet garni and 600 ml (1 pint) water. Bring to the boil, then cover and simmer for 1 hour while the chicken is cooking.
2 Melt 125 g (4 oz) of the butter. Put the tarragon and lemon inside the chicken. Lay the bird on its side on a rack in a roasting tin. Brush the uppermost side with butter. Roast in the oven at 200°C (400°F) mark 6 for 20 minutes. Turn the chicken onto the other side, brush with more butter and roast for a further 20 minutes.
3 Turn the chicken again so that the breast is uppermost. Brush with more butter. Scatter the garlic cloves in the base of the roasting tin. Cook the chicken for a further 40 minutes, or until the juices run clear when pierced with a skewer. Rest the chicken for 10 minutes.
4 To make the gravy, skim off excess fat from the roasting tin. Lift out the garlic cloves, remove the skins and return to the tin; mash with a fork. Strain the giblet stock into the pan and bring to the boil.
5 Blend together the remaining butter and the flour. Whisk a small piece at a time into the gravy. Simmer for a few minutes, whisking. Season to taste. Serve the chicken accompanied by the gravy.

## GOOSE WITH PRUNE STUFFING

PREPARATION TIME 30 minutes
COOKING TIME 1¾-2¼ hours
FREEZING Not suitable

SERVES 10      480-600 CALS/SERVING
- *4-5 kg (9-11 lb) oven-ready goose, with giblets*
- *salt and pepper*
- *450 g (1 lb) prunes, soaked overnight*
- *300 ml (10 fl oz) dry white wine*
- *50 g (2 oz) butter*
- *1 small onion, peeled and finely chopped*
- *30 ml (2 tbsp) port*
- *125 g (4 oz) fresh breadcrumbs*
- *5 ml (1 tsp) white plain flour*
- *caramelized clementines and roasted onion wedges, to garnish*

1 Pull the inside fat out of the goose and reserve. Prick the skin of the goose with a fork in several places. Rub salt over the skin.
2 Drain the prunes and put in a saucepan with the wine. Bring to the boil and simmer for about 10 minutes or until tender. Remove the prunes from the liquid, discard the stones, chop the flesh and put in a bowl. Reserve the cooking liquid.
3 Melt 40 g (1½ oz) of the butter in another pan, add the onion and cook gently until soft but not coloured. Separate the goose liver from the giblets and chop finely. Add to the onion and cook gently for 2-3 minutes, then mix with the prunes.

4 Add the port to the pan and bubble for 1 minute, scraping the pan to dislodge any sediment. Pour the liquid into the prune mixture, add the breadcrumbs and mix well. Allow to cool for 10 minutes.
5 Spoon the stuffing into the neck cavity of the goose. Skewer the neck skin to the back of the bird, then truss and tie up the goose with string. Weigh the bird and calculate the cooking time, allowing 15 minutes per 450 g (1 lb) plus 15 minutes.
6 Put the goose on a wire rack in a roasting tin. Cover the breast with the reserved fat and foil. Roast in the oven at 200ºC (400ºF) mark 6, basting frequently. Remove the foil for the last 30 minutes to brown.
7 When the goose is cooked, transfer to a serving dish and keep warm in a low oven. Pour off all but 30 ml (2 tbsp) fat from the juices in the roasting tin. Transfer to the top of the cooker and blend in the flour. Cook for 1 minute until just colouring, then slowly add the reserved prune liquid, stirring well. Bring to the boil and simmer for 2-3 minutes. Season to taste and whisk in the remaining butter. Serve the sauce with the garnished goose.

**NOTE** For the clementine garnish, make a butter and brown sugar syrup, add the peeled fruit and coat well.

---

## LEMON AND GINGER POUSSIN WITH ONIONS

PREPARATION TIME 15 minutes, plus marinating
COOKING TIME 45 minutes
FREEZING Not suitable
COLOUR INDEX Page 22

SERVES 6      555 CALS/SERVING
- *grated rind and juice of 6 lemons*
- *5 cm (2 inch) piece fresh root ginger, peeled and finely chopped*
- *120 ml (8 tbsp) clear honey*
- *150 ml (5 fl oz) vegetable oil*
- *1 stalk lemon grass, split (optional)*
- *salt and pepper*
- *3 oven-ready poussins, each weighing about 450 g (1 lb)*
- *900 g (2 lb) onions, peeled and sliced*
- *75 g (3 oz) soft light brown sugar*
- *slices of lemon, to garnish*

1 Whisk together the lemon rind and juice, ginger, honey and oil. Add the split lemon grass if using. Season with salt and pepper. Halve the poussins lengthways and place in a non-metallic dish. Pour over the marinade, cover and refrigerate for at least 12 hours.
2 Place the poussins with half the marinade in a roasting tin, discard the lemon grass. Bake at 200ºC (400ºF) mark 6 for 45 minutes or until tender, basting occasionally.
3 Meanwhile, heat the remaining marinade in a sauté pan. Add the onions and sugar and bring to the boil, then simmer for about 35 minutes, stirring occasionally, until the onions soften and caramelize.
4 Lift the poussins into a serving dish, cover and keep warm. Bubble down the cooking juices to reduce them.
5 Serve the poussins on a bed of onions with the juices spooned over, and top with lemon slices.

## GUINEA FOWL WITH ROCKET SAUCE AND SPRING VEGETABLES

PREPARATION TIME 20 minutes
COOKING TIME 1¼-1½ hours
FREEZING Not suitable
COLOUR INDEX Page 23

SERVES 6      515 CALS/SERVING
- *75 g (3 oz) butter*
- *30 ml (2 tbsp) olive oil*
- *2 guinea fowl*
- *450 g (1 lb) very small new potatoes, scrubbed*
- *2 garlic cloves, peeled*
- *300 ml (10 fl oz) dry white wine*
- *8 baby leeks, about 125 g (4 oz) total weight*
- *225 g (8 oz) small new carrots*
- *125 g (4 oz) broad beans, skinned*
- *125 g (4 oz) peas*
- *50 g (2 oz) rocket leaves*
- *150 ml (5 fl oz) double cream*
- *salt and pepper*
- *chervil, to garnish*

1 Heat 50 g (2 oz) of the butter with the oil in a large frying pan and cook the guinea fowl until browned. Arrange the potatoes and garlic in a casserole. Put the guinea fowl on top. Pour in the wine and 450 ml (15 fl oz) water.
2 Cover with a tight-fitting lid and cook at 200ºC (400°F) mark 6 for 45 minutes. Add the leeks, carrots, broad beans and peas. Re-cover and cook for 30-45 minutes until the guinea fowl are cooked.
3 Remove the guinea fowl and vegetables from the casserole and keep warm. Skim off any excess fat from the cooking liquid, then pour into a measuring jug. Make up to 600 ml (1 pint) with stock or water if necessary. Put in a food processor with the rocket and cooked garlic cloves and process until smooth. Put the purée in the casserole.
4 Reheat the rocket purée, add the cream and season with salt and pepper to taste. Bring to the boil, then gradually whisk in the remaining butter a little at a time to make a thin, shiny sauce.
5 Carve the guinea fowl and serve with the vegetables and sauce.

**VARIATIONS** Replace the rocket with sorrel, but halve the quantity. Alternatively, make the sauce with watercress.

# PAN-FRIED TURKEY WITH LEMON AND HAZELNUTS

PREPARATION TIME 15 minutes
COOKING TIME About 10 minutes
FREEZING Not suitable

⏱

**SERVES 4**

- *8 turkey escalopes, each weighing about 75 g (3 oz)*
- *2 eggs, beaten*
- *175 g (6 oz) finely chopped hazelnuts*
- *75 g (3 oz) butter*
- *lemon wedges, to garnish*

*SAUCE*

- *125 ml (4 fl oz) dry white wine*

**790 CALS/SERVING**

- *30 ml (2 tbsp) lemon juice*
- *15 ml (1 tbsp) chopped fresh tarragon or parsley*
- *salt and pepper*
- *75 g (3 oz) butter, diced*

1 Place the turkey escalopes between two sheets of greaseproof paper, and beat with a rolling pin, until about half the original thickness.
2 Dip the escalopes in the beaten egg, then press into the hazelnuts, coating all sides.
3 Heat the butter in a large frying pan until foaming, add the turkey and fry for about 1½ minutes on each side, until golden brown. Remove from the pan and keep warm.
4 To make the sauce, add the wine to the hot pan and boil rapidly until reduced by half. Add the lemon juice and tarragon and season to taste. Remove from the heat and gradually whisk in the diced butter to thicken the sauce slightly. Adjust the seasoning and pour over the turkey. Serve immediately, garnished with lemon wedges.

**NOTE** Turkey escalopes are sold in larger supermarkets; if unavailable, use thin slices of breast meat.

## MUSTARD-ROASTED TURKEY

PREPARATION TIME 30 minutes, plus standing
COOKING TIME 3¾-4 hours
FREEZING Not suitable

SERVES 8

650 CALS/SERVING

- *oven-ready turkey, about 4.5 kg (10 lb)*
- *45 ml (3 tbsp) wholegrain or Dijon mustard*
- *butter or margarine*
- *salt and pepper*
- *about 450 ml (15 fl oz) turkey or chicken stock*
- *60 ml (4 tbsp) sherry (optional)*
- *grated rind and juice of 1 orange*
- *cornflour*
- *fresh rosemary and sage, to garnish*

*STUFFING*
- *450 g (1 lb) onions, peeled and finely chopped*
- *50 g (2 oz) butter*
- *45 ml (3 tbsp) chopped fresh sage, or 10 ml (2 tsp) dried sage*
- *225 g (8 oz) fresh breadcrumbs*
- *125 g (4 oz) medium oatmeal*
- *grated rind and juice of 1 orange*
- *salt and pepper*
- *1 egg, beaten*

1 To make the stuffing, sauté the onions in the butter for 6-7 minutes or until beginning to soften. Mix with the sage and breadcrumbs.

2 Toast the oatmeal under the grill and stir into the breadcrumb mixture with the grated orange rind and 30 ml (2 tbsp) orange juice. Season well and bind with beaten egg. Cool.

3 Spoon the stuffing into the neck end of the turkey only. Shape into a neat rounded end, then tuck the neck skin under the bird and secure firmly with a small skewer or wooden cocktail

stick. Place any remaining stuffing in a buttered ovenproof dish, dot with butter and cover with foil. Weigh the turkey and calculate the cooking time (see page 347).

4 Place the turkey on a large, strong sheet of foil, in a large roasting tin. Spread the breast and legs thinly with the mustard. Dot the turkey generously with butter and grind over some pepper. Fold the foil around the turkey to enclose it.

5 Cook at 180°C (350°F) mark 4 for about 3 hours. Fold the foil back, baste well and return to the oven for a further 45 minutes-1 hour. Put the stuffing in the oven to bake for about 1 hour. The turkey will be a rich golden brown.

6 Lift the turkey onto a warmed serving dish, cover with foil and leave to rest for 30 minutes to make carving easier.

7 Pour the cooking liquor into a saucepan and skim. Add the stock, sherry, grated orange rind and juice. Boil for 4-5 minutes to reduce slightly.

8 Mix about 60 ml (4 tbsp) cornflour to a smooth paste with a little water. Stir into the pan juices and bring to the boil. Simmer for 1-2 minutes or until slightly thickened. Adjust the seasoning. Garnish the turkey with sprigs of fresh rosemary and sage, and serve with the gravy.

## ORIENTAL TURKEY

PREPARATION TIME 20 minutes, plus standing
COOKING TIME 1 hour
FREEZING Ginger butter (stage 1)
COLOUR INDEX Page 22

❋

SERVES 6

765 CALS/SERVING

- *1.8 kg (4 lb) oven-ready turkey saddle or breast, bone in*
- *lychees and limes, to decorate*
- *apple and plum sauce, to serve (see Note)*

*GINGER BUTTER*
- *5 cm (2 inch) piece fresh root ginger, peeled and finely grated*
- *125 g (4 oz) butter, softened*

- *salt and pepper*
*GLAZE*
- *5 cm (2 inch) piece fresh root ginger, peeled and finely grated*
- *30 ml (2 tbsp) each light soy sauce and rice or distilled malt vinegar*
- *90 ml (6 tbsp) clear honey*
- *salt and pepper*

**1** To make the ginger butter, beat the ginger with the butter and season well.

**2** To make the glaze, mix all the ingedients together and season to taste.

**3** Carefully loosen the turkey skin and push the soft ginger butter evenly underneath.

**4** Place the turkey in a roasting tin and brush with the ginger glaze. Cover with foil and cook at 190°C (375°F) mark 5 for 15 minutes per 450 g (1 lb). Baste frequently with the glaze.

**5** Uncover the turkey for the last 15 minutes to brown the skin. At this stage baste the breast again with any remaining glaze.

**6** Rest the turkey for 15 minutes before carving. Serve with apple and plum sauce (see Note).

**NOTE** To make the accompanying apple and plum sauce, peel, core and chop 900 g (2 lb) apples and cook over a low heat with 30 ml (2 tbsp) caster sugar and 150 ml (5 fl oz) water until soft. Add the grated rind and juice of 1 lime and 50 ml (2 fl oz) oriental plum sauce. Work in a blender until smooth. Season. Reheat gently to serve hot or serve cold. Garnish with chopped chillies.

## TURKEY, APRICOT AND HAZELNUT PILAFF

PREPARATION TIME 20 minutes
COOKING TIME 45 minutes
FREEZING Not suitable

SERVES 4                540 CALS/SERVING

- *30 ml (2 tbsp) hazelnut or olive oil*
- *8 baby onions, peeled and halved*
- *2 garlic cloves, peeled and crushed*
- *15 ml (1 tbsp) medium curry powder*
- *10 ml (2 tsp) ground coriander*
- *5 ml (1 tsp) ground mixed spice*
- *2 celery sticks, thickly sliced*
- *125 g (4 oz) dried apricots, halved*

- *225 g (8 oz) easy-cook brown rice*
- *750 ml (1¼ pints) chicken stock*
- *350 g (12 oz) cold cooked turkey, shredded*
- *125 g (4 oz) French beans, trimmed and halved*
- *50 g (2 oz) hazelnuts, toasted*
- *30 ml (2 tbsp) chopped fresh parsley*
- *salt and pepper*

**1** Heat the oil in a heavy-based saucepan, add the onions, garlic, spices and celery and fry for 10 minutes until browned. Add the apricots and rice and stir-fry for 1 minute until all the grains are glossy.

**2** Pour in the stock, stir well and bring to the boil. Cover and simmer gently for 20 minutes. Stir in all the remaining ingredients, and cook for a further 10 minutes. Remove from the heat and leave undisturbed for 5 minutes. Season to taste and serve at once.

**VARIATION** This dish can be adapted to serve cold as part of a salad spread. Chop an onion and fry in the oil with the garlic and spices for 5 minutes. Leave until cold and fold into 150 ml (5 fl oz) bought mayonnaise. In a large bowl, combine the turkey with 350 g (12 oz) cooked brown rice and the sliced raw celery, French beans, chopped dried apricots, toasted hazelnuts and parsley. Toss in the mayonnaise and serve.

# DUCKLING BREASTS
# WITH ARMAGNAC

PREPARATION TIME 5 minutes, plus marinating
COOKING TIME 25 minutes
FREEZING Not suitable
COLOUR INDEX Page 23
♡

SERVES 6                    240 CALS/SERVING
- *6 duckling breast*       - *75 ml (5 tbsp)*
  *fillets, each weighing*    *Armagnac*
  *about 175 g (6 oz)*      - *sprigs of fresh thyme*
- *salt and pepper*         - *bay leaves*
- *2 shallots or small*     - *sprigs of fresh herbs,*
  *onions, peeled and*        *to garnish*
  *finely chopped*
- *2 garlic cloves,*
  *peeled and crushed*

1 Score the duckling skin and rub with salt. Place the breasts side by side in a shallow non-metallic dish.
2 Mix the shallots or onions with the garlic and Armagnac and spoon over the duckling breasts. Add sprigs of fresh thyme, bay leaves and plenty of black pepper. Turn the duckling in the marinade, cover and marinate at room temperature for about 1 hour.
3 Place the duckling breasts on a wire rack standing over a roasting tin. Baste with marinade.
4 Roast at 230°C (450°F) mark 8 for 10 minutes, then lower the temperature to 200°C (400°F) mark 6 for a further 10-15 minutes.
5 Serve thickly sliced, garnished with sprigs of fresh herbs.

# ROAST DUCKLING
# WITH SHERRY VINEGAR

PREPARATION TIME 15 minutes
COOKING TIME 50 minutes
FREEZING Not suitable
COLOUR INDEX Page 23

SERVES 6                    390 CALS/SERVING
- *salt and pepper*         - *225 g (8 oz) turnips,*
- *6 duckling breast*         *peeled and roughly*
  *fillets, each weighing*    *chopped*
  *about 175 g (6 oz)*      - *40 g (1½ oz)*
- *125 g (4 oz) sugar*        *butter*
- *60 ml (4 tbsp) each*     - *125 g (4 oz)*
  *dry sherry and white*      *spring onions,*
  *wine vinegar or 120*       *trimmed and roughly*
  *ml (8 tbsp) sherry*        *chopped*
  *vinegar*                 - *125 g (4 oz)*
- *900 ml (1½ pints)*         *mangetout, trimmed*
  *chicken stock*           - *lemon juice*
- *350 g (12 oz)*
  *carrots, peeled and*
  *roughly chopped*

1 Season the duckling breast fillets and place in a roasting tin. Cook at 230°C (450°F) mark 8 for 10 minutes, then reduce the temperature to 200°C (400°F) mark 6 for about a further 20 minutes.
2 Meanwhile, place the sugar, the dry sherry and white wine vinegar in a heavy-based pan and cook over a gentle heat until the sugar dissolves and caramelizes to a deep golden colour. Add the chicken stock and bring to the boil, stirring. Boil to reduce by half, then set aside.
3 Place the carrots and turnips in a saucepan with 150 ml (5 fl oz) water, 25 g (1 oz) butter and a pinch each of salt, pepper and sugar. Bring to the boil, then cover and simmer for about 15 minutes until the vegetables are just tender and the liquid has evaporated to leave the vegetables glazed and shiny. Boil off excess liquid if necessary.
4 Blanch the spring onions and mangetout in boiling salted water for 1-2 minutes. Drain.
5 To finish, leave the duckling to rest in a warm place for about 10 minutes, then carve into thick slices. Bring the sauce to a simmer, whisk in the remaining butter and sharpen with lemon juice. Adjust the seasoning.
6 Reheat the vegetables in the sauce. Arrange the duckling and vegetables on a large serving platter and serve.

## WARM DUCK SALAD

PREPARATION TIME 20 minutes
COOKING TIME 15-20 minutes
FREEZING Not suitable

♡

SERVES 8
- *8 boned duckling breasts, each weighing about 125 g (4 oz)*
- *30 ml (2 tbsp) ground coriander*
- *10 ml (2 tsp) ground ginger*
- *10 ml (2 tsp) ground mace*
- *1 garlic clove, peeled and crushed*
- *75 ml (3 fl oz) fresh orange juice*

325 CALS/SERVING
- *75 ml (3 fl oz) olive oil*
- *salt and pepper*
- *7.5 ml (1½ tsp) clear honey*
- *15 ml (1 tbsp) red wine vinegar*
- *7.5 ml (1½ tsp) Dijon mustard*
- *selection of mixed salad leaves, to line the dish*
- *about 20 pitted black olives*

1 Remove the skin from the duck. Mix together the coriander, ginger, mace and garlic with 30 ml (2 tbsp) each of orange juice and oil. Season with salt and pepper.

2 Spread the spice mixture on both sides of the duck breasts and place in a shallow ovenproof dish. Roast at 200°C (400°F) mark 6 for 15-20 minutes until the duckling is tender and the top has browned.

3 Meanwhile, whisk together the honey, vinegar, mustard and remaining orange juice and oil. Season to taste. Wash the salad leaves, dry them and arrange on a shallow platter.

4 Lift the duck breasts out of the pan juices, slice neatly and arrange on the salad leaves. Scatter the olives over the top and spoon over the dressing.

**VARIATION** If wished, the duck can be cooked in advance and served cold.

# CRISPY CHINESE DUCK WITH ORIENTAL VEGETABLES

PREPARATION TIME 10 minutes
COOKING TIME 20 minutes
FREEZING Not suitable
COLOUR INDEX Page 23

SERVES 6

- 6 duckling breasts, each weighing about 175 g (6 oz)
- salt and pepper
- 45 ml (3 tbsp) vegetable oil
- 30 ml (2 tbsp) sesame oil
- 90 ml (6 tbsp) yellow bean sauce
- 45 ml (3 tbsp) caster sugar
- 2 garlic cloves, peeled and crushed
- 1 cm (½ inch) piece fresh root ginger, peeled and finely chopped
- 15 ml (1 tbsp) sesame seeds

410 CALS/SERVING

- 125 g (4 oz) cabbage, cut into fine strips
- 125 g (4 oz) carrots, peeled and cut into fine strips
- 1 red pepper, deseeded and cut into fine strips
- 75 g (3 oz) baby corn, quartered
- 5 cm (2 inch) piece cucumber, cut into fine strips
- 6 spring onions, cut into fine strips

1 Prick the skin of the duck breasts well with a fork and rub with salt and pepper. Place on a baking sheet on the top shelf of the oven and cook at 230°C (450°F) mark 8 for about 15-20 minutes or until the duck is just cooked, but still pink.
2 Meanwhile, heat 15 ml (1 tbsp) of each oil in a frying pan, add the yellow bean sauce, sugar and 30 ml (2 tbsp) water, and cook for 1 minute. Remove and leave to cool.
3 Heat both remaining oils in the rinsed and dried frying pan. Add the garlic, ginger and sesame seeds and stir for about 1 minute or until golden brown. Add the cabbage, carrots, pepper and baby corn and stir-fry briskly for 2-3 minutes. Remove from the heat and stir in the cucumber and spring onions.
4 Carve the duck into slices and arrange on top of the vegetables. Serve immediately with the sauce.

**VARIATION** Use chicken breast pieces instead of duckling.

# CHRISTMAS PHEASANT

PREPARATION TIME 30 minutes
COOKING TIME 2¼ hours
FREEZING Suitable (stage 4)
COLOUR INDEX Page 24

SERVES 6

- 2 oven-ready pheasants
- salt and pepper
- 30 ml (2 tbsp) vegetable oil
- 50 g (2 oz) butter
- 225 g (8 oz) shallots or small onions, peeled
- 225 g (8 oz) streaky bacon, chopped
- 2 garlic cloves, peeled and crushed
- 300 ml (10 fl oz) Madeira
- 600 ml (1 pint) beef stock

490 CALS/SERVING

- sprig of fresh thyme or pinch of dried
- 2 bay leaves
- 6 juniper berries
- pared rind and juice of 1 orange
- 90 ml (6 tbsp) redcurrant jelly
- 225 g (8 oz) fresh cranberries
- 225 g (8 oz) cooked chestnuts
- fresh thyme, to garnish

1 Joint both pheasants into four, discarding backbone and knuckles. Season to taste.
2 Heat the oil and butter in a large, flameproof casserole and brown the shallots and bacon. Remove and set aside. Add the pheasant, half at a time, and fry for 5-6 minutes or until golden. Remove the pheasant from the casserole.
3 Stir in the garlic, half the Madeira, the stock, thyme, bay leaves, juniper berries and pared orange rind. Bring to the boil and add the pheasant. Cover and cook at 170°C (325°F) mark 3 for 1 hour.
4 Add the shallots, bacon and redcurrant jelly. Re-cover and return to the oven for 45 minutes or until the pheasant is quite tender.
5 Meanwhile, marinate the cranberries and chestnuts in the remaining Madeira and the orange juice for 30 minutes.
6 Remove the pheasant, vegetables and bacon from the liquid, cover and keep warm. Bubble the sauce for about 5 minutes to reduce to a syrupy consistency. Add the cranberry and chestnut mixture and simmer for a further 5 minutes. Adjust the seasoning and spoon the sauce over the pheasant. Serve garnished with fresh thyme.

## POT-ROASTED PHEASANT WITH RED CABBAGE

PREPARATION TIME 20 minutes
COOKING TIME 40 minutes
FREEZING Not suitable

SERVES 4                          505 CALS/SERVING
- *25 g (1 oz) butter*            - *30 ml (2 tbsp)*
- *15 ml (1 tbsp)*                  *redcurrant jelly*
  *vegetable oil*                 - *15 ml (1 tbsp)*
- *2 oven-ready*                    *balsamic vinegar*
  *pheasants, halved*             - *salt and pepper*
- *2 onions, peeled and*          - *4 rashers smoked*
  *sliced*                          *streaky bacon,*
- *450 g (1 lb) red*                *halved*
  *cabbage, finely*               - *flat-leaf parsley and*
  *shredded*                        *bay leaves, to*
- *5 ml (1 tsp) cornflour*          *garnish*
- *250 ml (8 fl oz) red*
  *wine*

**1** Melt the butter with the oil in a large flameproof casserole. Add the pheasant halves, and brown on all sides. Remove the pheasant and add the onions and red cabbage to the casserole. Fry for 5 minutes until softened.

**2** Blend the cornflour with a little water. Add to the pan with the red wine, redcurrant jelly, vinegar and seasoning. Bring to the boil, stirring.
**3** Arrange the pheasant halves, skin-side up, on top of the cabbage. Place the halved bacon rashers on top of the pheasant. Cover with a lid and bake at 200°C (400°F) mark 6 for 30 minutes until tender. Lift out the pheasant halves and keep warm. Using a slotted spoon, divide the cabbage between warmed serving plates. Arrange the pheasant on top and garnish with parsley and bay leaves. Serve any juices in a sauceboat.

**VARIATION** Pigeon can also be cooked in this way. Use 4 oven-ready pigeons and place a quarter of an onion inside each bird before browning for extra flavour. Tuck the parsley and bay leaf garnish into the cavities for an attractive finish.

# CASSEROLE OF GROUSE WITH RED WINE

PREPARATION TIME 10 minutes
COOKING TIME 1¼ hours
FREEZING Suitable
COLOUR INDEX Page 24
♡ ✳

**SERVES 4**
- *2 brace of grouse*
- *about 45 ml (3 tbsp) vegetable oil*
- *450 g (1 lb) shallots or button onions, peeled*
- *4 large celery sticks, sliced*
- *200 ml (7 fl oz) red wine*

**300 CALS/SERVING**
- *2 bay leaves*
- *salt and pepper*
- *200 ml (7 fl oz) stock*
- *15 ml (1 tbsp) arrowroot*
- *15 ml (1 tbsp) lemon juice*
- *chopped parsley, to garnish*

1 Wipe the grouse, trim the feet and remove any feather ends. Heat the oil in a flameproof casserole and brown the birds well, in batches if necessary. Lift out of the casserole using a slotted spoon.
2 Add the shallots and celery to the casserole with a little extra oil, if necessary, and brown lightly.
3 Pour in the wine and bring to the boil. Add the bay leaves and seasoning and return the grouse to the casserole.
4 Cover tightly and cook at 170°C (325°F) mark 3 for about 50 minutes or until the grouse are just tender. Lift the birds out of the casserole, cover and keep warm.
5 Add the stock to the casserole and warm slightly. Mix the arrowroot to a smooth paste with a little water and stir into the casserole. Bring to the boil, stirring, and cook until slightly thickened. Stir in the lemon juice, adjust the seasoning and spoon over the birds. Garnish with parsley to serve.

# FRENCH ROAST PHEASANT WITH GRAPES AND NUTS

PREPARATION TIME 25 minutes
COOKING TIME 1 hour
FREEZING Not suitable
COLOUR INDEX Page 24

**SERVES 6**
- *6 clementines*
- *700 g (1½ lb) white or red grapes*
- *15 ml (1 tbsp) green tea (Gunpowder or Darjeeling)*
- *200 ml (7 fl oz) Madeira or sweet sherry*
- *2 young oven-ready pheasants*

**635 CALS/SERVING**
- *softened butter, for basting*
- *salt and pepper*
- *10 ml (2 tsp) balsamic or sherry vinegar*
- *15 ml (1 tbsp) dark soy sauce*
- *225 g (8 oz) walnut halves*
- *grapes, to garnish*

1 Grate the rind from 2 clementines and squeeze the juice from all six; place in a bowl. Reserve the ungrated squeezed halves. Chop the grapes roughly in a food processor and pour into the clementine juice. Pour 300 ml (10 fl oz) boiling water over the green tea, leave to steep for 5 minutes, then strain and reserve.
2 Pour half the clementine and grape juice into a roasting tin, adding the Madeira and any giblets (except the liver). Place the reserved clementine halves inside the pheasant cavities. Smear the pheasants with butter and season with salt and pepper.
3 Place the birds in the roasting tin on one side. Roast at 200°C (400°F) mark 6 for 45 minutes, turning and basting every 15 minutes until cooked. Test by pushing a skewer into the meatiest part of the thigh; the juices should run clear. Transfer the pheasants to a warmed serving platter and keep warm.
4 Pour the reserved clementine and grape juice into the roasting tin. Stir in the tea, balsamic vinegar and soy sauce. Bring to the boil, scraping up any sediment from the bottom of the pan. Boil for 1-2 minutes, then strain into a saucepan. Stir in the walnuts, bring to the boil and reduce to 450 ml (15 fl oz). Adjust the seasoning. The sauce should be slightly syrupy; if not, reduce a little more. Spoon the walnuts around the pheasant and pour the sauce into a warmed sauceboat. Garnish with extra grapes.

**NOTE** If your butcher is preparing the birds, ask him to keep the giblets. Or use chicken or turkey giblets.

146

# RAISED GAME PIE

PREPARATION TIME 1¼ hours, plus resting and chilling
COOKING TIME 1 hour 55 minutes
FREEZING Suitable (stage 9)

❅

**SERVES 8-10**

HOT WATER CRUST
PASTRY
- *300 g (10 oz) white plain flour*
- *1.25 ml (¼ tsp) salt*
- *65 g (2½ oz) white vegetable fat*

PIE FILLING
- *225 g (8 oz) rabbit joints, skinned*
- *225 g (8 oz) shoulder venison*
- *1.1 litres (2 pints) brown stock*
- *225 g (8 oz) pork sausagemeat*
- *½ onion, peeled and finely chopped*
- *2 garlic cloves, peeled and crushed*

**440-355 CALS/SERVING**
- *60 ml (4 tbsp) Madeira*
- *2.5 ml (½ tsp) ground mace*
- *salt and pepper*
- *125 g (4 oz) no-soak dried apricots*
- *4 no-soak prunes*
- *2 pheasant or chicken breasts, boned and skinned, about 225 g (8 oz) total weight*
- *8 large sage leaves or 5 ml (1 tsp) dried sage*
- *beaten egg, to glaze*
- *5 ml (1 tsp) powdered gelatine*

**1** For the filling, remove the flesh from the rabbit joints. Cut the rabbit and venison into small pieces. Place in a saucepan and cover with the stock. Bring to the boil, cover and simmer for 25 minutes, or until tender; drain and cool. Reduce the stock by boiling to 150 ml (5 fl oz).

**2** Base-line a 25 x 7.5 cm (10 x 3 inch) loose-sided pie mould with non-stick baking parchment. Mix the cooled meats, sausagemeat, onion, garlic, Madeira, mace and seasoning. Cover and chill.

**3** To prepare the hot water crust pastry, sift the flour and salt into a bowl and make a well in the centre. Heat the fat and 125-150 ml (4-5 fl oz) water gently together until the fat melts, then bring to the boil and pour into the well.

**4** Gradually lap the flour into the liquid, then beat together. Lightly knead against the side of the bowl until smooth. Immediately wrap the pastry in a tea towel. (If exposed to the air, it will become dry and impossible to use.) Leave for up to 30 minutes; no longer. Use warm.

**5** On a lightly floured surface, roll out three quarters of the pastry to an oblong 20 x 35 cm (8 x 14 inches), turning to keep an even shape and thickness.

Use the rolling pin to help lift pastry over the tin. (Keep the remaining pastry covered on a plate placed over warm water.)

**6** Ease the pastry into the corners and press evenly up the sides of the tin. Trim off excess pastry. Line with baking parchment and beans and bake blind at 200°C (400°F) mark 6 for 15-20 minutes, until golden brown and set. Remove paper and beans. Allow to cool.

**7** Spoon half the meat mixture into the pastry case. Scissor-snip half the apricots and 2 prunes into the tin. Place the pheasant or chicken breasts end to end over the fruit. Place the sage leaves on top. Repeat the fruit and meat layers.

**8** Roll out the remaining pastry to a 28 x 10 cm (11 x 4 inch) oblong and use to top the pie. Seal well, then trim and flute the edges. Make a small hole in the centre of the pie, and two more near the edge. Shape the pastry trimmings into leaf and berry shapes. Arrange on top of the pie, half covering the holes.

**9** Place the pie on a baking tray and glaze with egg. Bake at 200°C (400°F) mark 6 for 20 minutes, then reduce the temperature to 180°C (350°F) mark 4 and cook for a further 1¼ hours, covering the top lightly with foil if necessary. Ease away the sides of the tin and bake the pie for a further 20 minutes to brown the sides. Cool.

**10** Soak the gelatine in 20 ml (4 tsp) water, then dissolve in the stock. Chill until beginning to set. Place the pie on a large edged plate, easing off the base gently. Gradually pour in the stock through the holes. Cover loosely, then refrigerate overnight.

# MEAT

# BEEF RENDANG

PREPARATION TIME 15 minutes
COOKING TIME About 2 hours 10 minutes
FREEZING Suitable
COLOUR INDEX Page 25
✳

| SERVES 6 | 955 CALS/SERVING |
|---|---|
| • *1 large onion, peeled and quartered* | • *5 ml (1 tsp) turmeric* |
| • *6 garlic cloves, peeled* | • *45 ml (3 tbsp) vegetable oil* |
| • *5 cm (2 inch) piece fresh root ginger, peeled* | • *1.1 kg (2½ lb) stewing or braising beef, cut into large cubes* |
| • *1 red pepper, deseeded and chopped* | • *1.7 litres (3 pints) coconut milk* |
| • *4 dried hot chillies* | • *1 lemon grass stalk, bruised* |
| • *10 ml (2 tsp) ground coriander* | • *salt* |
| • *10 ml (2 tsp) ground cinnamon* | • *finely shredded lime leaves, to garnish (optional)* |
| • *5 ml (1 tsp) ground cloves* | |

1 Put the first nine ingredients in a food processor or blender with 15 ml (1 tbsp) water. Process until smooth.
2 Heat the oil in a large, wide flameproof casserole dish or a saucepan. Add the spice paste and cook over a moderate heat for 3-5 minutes, stirring all the time.
3 Add the meat and cook for 2-3 minutes, stirring to coat in the spice mixture.
4 Add the coconut milk and bring to the boil, stirring all the time. Add the lemon grass and about 5 ml (1 tsp) salt. Reduce the heat and simmer very gently, uncovered, for about 2 hours, stirring from time to time. The beef is ready when it is really tender and almost falling apart; the sauce should be well reduced and quite thick.
5 If the sauce is too thin, transfer the meat to a warmed serving dish, using a slotted spoon; keep warm. Bring the sauce to the boil and boil vigorously, stirring frequently, until sufficiently reduced. Pour over the meat. Check the seasoning before serving, garnished with shredded lime leaves, if available.

# GRILLED STEAKS WITH SHALLOTS AND WINE

PREPARATION TIME 10 minutes
COOKING TIME 15–25 minutes
FREEZING Not suitable
COLOUR INDEX Page 25
🕑

| SERVES 4 | 555 CALS/SERVING |
|---|---|
| • *50 g (2 oz) chilled butter* | • *salt and pepper* |
| • *225 g (8 oz) shallots, peeled and chopped* | • *8 slices French bread* |
| • *350 ml (12 fl oz) red Bordeaux wine* | • *10-15 ml (2-3 tsp) Dijon mustard* |
| • *4 sirloin steaks, each weighing about 175-200 g (6-7 oz)* | • *30 ml (2 tbsp) chopped fresh parsley* |
| • *30 ml (2 tbsp) vegetable oil* | • *parsley sprigs, to garnish* |

1 Melt 15 g (½ oz) of the butter in a saucepan. Add the shallots and sauté for a few minutes until slightly softened. Add the wine and bring to the boil. Simmer, uncovered, until the wine is reduced by half and the shallots are soft.
2 Smear the steaks on both sides with the oil and arrange on the grill rack. Cook, as close to the heat as possible, turning the steaks every 2 minutes. Allow 4 minutes (one turn) for very rare steaks; 8 minutes (three turns) for medium. For well-done steaks allow 12 minutes, increasing the time between turns to 3 minutes. Season the steaks with salt and pepper as you make the final turn.
3 Meanwhile, cut the remaining butter into 6 cubes and beat one at a time into the shallot sauce.
4 Transfer the steaks to warmed serving plates and keep warm. Press the bread slices onto the grill pan to soak up the juices, then spread each lightly with Dijon mustard. Put 2 slices beside each steak. Pour the sauce over the steaks, sprinkle with chopped parsley and serve garnished with sprigs of parsley.

**VARIATIONS** Use rump rather than sirloin steaks. Use a hot griddle pan to cook the steaks, rather than grill them.

## SPICED RIB OF BEEF

PREPARATION TIME 15 minutes, plus resting
COOKING TIME 2 hours
FREEZING Not suitable

**SERVES 6**

- *2.3 kg (5 lb) rib of beef or 1.8 kg (4 lb) boned and rolled rib of beef*
- *75 g (3 oz) softened butter*
- *salt and pepper*
- *30 ml (2 tbsp) soft brown sugar*
- *5 ml (1 tsp) ground allspice*
- *2.5 ml (½ tsp) each ground mace and ground cloves*

**725 CALS/SERVING**

- *30 ml (2 tbsp) wholegrain mustard*
- *45 ml (3 tbsp) chopped fresh parsley*
- *2 garlic cloves, peeled and crushed*

*GRAVY*

- *45 ml (3 tbsp) white plain flour*
- *750 ml (1½ pints) beef stock or vegetable water*

**1** Wipe the rib of beef and place fat side up in a roasting tin that is just large enough to hold it. Spread 25 g (1 oz) butter over the surface of the beef and season well.

**2** Roast at 230°C (450°F) mark 8 for 30 minutes, then baste well. Lower the oven to 200°C (400°F) mark 6 and return the meat for a further 1 hour, basting the beef occasionally.

**3** Mix together the remaining 50 g (2 oz) butter with the sugar, spices, mustard, parsley, garlic and plenty of seasoning.

**4** Remove most of the fat from the roasting tin. Spread the spiced mixture evenly over the meat fat and return to the oven for a further 30 minutes, basting occasionally. Cover loosely with foil if the meat begins to overbrown.

**5** Place the meat on a carving dish, loosely cover with foil and leave to rest for 15 minutes.

**6** Meanwhile, prepare the gravy. Skim off the excess fat to leave 60 ml (4 tbsp) in the tin. Sprinkle in the flour and whisk over a low heat until the mixture begins to brown and is a smooth paste.

**7** Gradually whisk in the stock, scraping all the sediment off the bottom of the pan. Bring to the boil, then simmer gently for 2-3 minutes, adjust the seasoning and serve with the beef.

153

# BEEF MEDALLIONS WITH STILTON MOUSSE

PREPARATION TIME 15 minutes
COOKING TIME 15 minutes
FREEZING Not suitable
COLOUR INDEX Page 25

**SERVES 6**

**630 CALS/SERVING**

- *225 g (8 oz) skinless chicken breast fillets, chilled*
- *300 ml (10 fl oz) double cream, chilled*
- *225 g (8 oz) crumbled Stilton cheese*
- *salt and pepper*
- *25 g (1 oz) butter*
- *300 g (10 oz) celery, cut into matchsticks*

- *six 150 g (5 oz) fillet steaks*
- *15 ml (1 tbsp) chopped fresh parsley*
- *squeeze of lemon juice*
- *extra Stilton, to crumble (optional)*

1 Blend the chicken in a food processor until smooth. Add the cream and pulse for 2-3 seconds or until the cream is just combined. Add the Stilton cheese to the chicken in the same way. Season and refrigerate for 10 minutes.
2 Meanwhile, melt the butter in a medium saucepan, add the celery and cook gently, covered, for about 5 minutes or until just tender. Keep warm.
3 Heat a non-stick frying pan. Fry the steaks on both sides for about 3 minutes for rare (5 minutes for medium; 6-7 minutes for well done). Be careful to time your steaks accurately. Place on a hot baking sheet.
4 Divide the chilled Stilton mixture among the medallions and spread evenly over the top of each one. Grill for about 6 minutes or until the mousse turns golden brown and is firm and cooked through.
5 Add the chopped parsley and lemon juice to the celery and serve alongside the beef medallions. Crumble a little extra Stilton over the steaks, if wished.

# FESTIVE BEEF CASSEROLE

PREPARATION TIME 30 minutes, plus soaking
COOKING TIME 2 hours 25 minutes
FREEZING Suitable (stage 3)
COLOUR INDEX Page 25
♡ ❄

**SERVES 8**

**275 CALS/SERVING**

- *150 g (5 oz) each no-soak pitted prunes and apricots*
- *125 g (4 oz) raisins*
- *finely grated rind and juice of 1 orange*
- *200 ml (7 fl oz) orange juice*
- *150 ml (5 fl oz) dry sherry*
- *450 g (1 lb) stewing beef, cut into 4 cm (1½ inch) cubes*
- *450 g (1 lb) venison, cut into 4 cm (1½ inch) cubes*
- *5 ml (1 tsp) salt*
- *30 ml (2 tbsp) vegetable oil*

- *450 g (1 lb) onions, peeled and finely sliced*
- *2.5 ml (½ tsp) each ground mace and ground cinnamon*
- *5 ml (1 tsp) black peppercorns, crushed*
- *pinch of allspice*
- *10 ml (2 tsp) coriander seeds, crushed*
- *15 ml (1 tbsp) white plain flour*
- *450 ml (15 fl oz) beef stock*
- *30 ml (2 tbsp) balsamic vinegar*

1 Soak the dried fruit in the combined orange juices and the sherry. Cover and leave for 1 hour or overnight. Season the meat with salt.
2 Heat the oil in a large, flameproof casserole and brown the meat in small batches. Ensure it is well browned so that the casserole juices will have a rich, dark colour. Add a little more oil if necessary and fry the onions until they are golden. Return all the meat to the pan with the spices, orange rind and flour. Cook, stirring, for 3 minutes. Add the beef stock and bring to the boil. Add the vinegar. Cover and cook at 150°C (300°F) mark 2 for 1 hour.
3 Remove the casserole from the oven. Strain the fruit and reserve. Add the soaking liquid to the casserole, re-cover and cook for a further 1 hour 10 minutes or until the meat is very tender. Stir in the reserved fruits and return to the oven for 5 minutes to heat through before serving.

## COUNTRY BEEF WITH BARLEY

PREPARATION TIME 15 minutes
COOKING TIME About 2¼ hours
FREEZING Suitable

♡ ❄

**SERVES 4**

- *450 g (1 lb) braising steak, cubed*
- *salt and pepper*
- *25 g (1 oz) plain flour*
- *15 ml (1 tbsp) vegetable oil*
- *350 g (12 oz) carrots, peeled and chopped*
- *575 g (1¼ lb) swede, peeled and chopped*
- *4 sticks celery, chopped*
- *225 g (8 oz) button onions, peeled*

**330 CALS/SERVING**

- *1 garlic clove, peeled and crushed*
- *50 g (2 oz) pearl barley*
- *pared rind and juice of 1 orange*
- *150 ml (5 fl oz) red wine*
- *2 large rosemary sprigs or 10 ml (2 tsp) dried*
- *450-600 ml (16-20 fl oz) beef stock*
- *fresh rosemary, to garnish*

1 Toss the beef in seasoned flour until evenly coated. Heat the oil in a 4.2 litre (7 pint) flameproof casserole and brown the beef in batches. Remove with a slotted spoon and drain on absorbent kitchen paper.

2 Lower the heat, add the carrots, swede, celery, onions and garlic, with a little more oil, if necessary. Sauté for 4-5 minutes, stirring occasionally. Return all the beef to the casserole with the pearl barley, orange rind and juice, wine, rosemary and enough stock to cover.

3 Bring to the boil, stir well, cover and cook in the oven at 170°C (325°F) mark 3 for about 2 hours or until the meat is tender. Adjust the seasoning. Serve garnished with fresh rosemary.

# BABOTEE

PREPARATION TIME 20 minutes, plus soaking
COOKING TIME 1 hour
FREEZING Not suitable

SERVES 4      695 CALS/SERVING

- 2 slices of bread
- 450 ml (15 fl oz) milk and single cream, mixed
- 30 ml (2 tbsp) vegetable oil
- 225 g (8 oz) onion, peeled and chopped
- 2 eating apples, peeled and grated
- 5 ml (1 tsp) chilli seasoning
- 5 ml (1 tsp) ground coriander
- 2 garlic cloves, peeled and crushed
- 450 g (1 lb) lean minced beef
- salt and pepper
- 30 ml (2 tbsp) white plain flour
- 25 g (1 oz) flaked almonds
- 25 g (1 oz) no-soak dried apricots, roughly chopped
- 15 ml (1 tbsp) tomato purée
- 10 ml (2 tsp) balsamic vinegar
- 3 eggs
- 5 ml (1 tsp) ground turmeric
- about 125 g (4 oz) grated Cheddar cheese

1 Break up the bread and leave to soak in the milk and cream for 30 minutes.

2 Heat the oil in a saucepan and stir in the onion and apples. Add the chilli seasoning, coriander and garlic. Cook, stirring, for 2 minutes. Add the meat and seasoning and fry until it changes colour and is lump-free, stirring occasionally. Mix in the flour, almonds, apricots, tomato purée and balsamic vinegar.

3 Squeeze the milk out of the bread, reserving the milk. Beat the bread into the meat mixture and season well. Whisk the eggs and turmeric with the reserved milk and seasoning.

4 Spread the meat into a 2.8 litre (5 pint) shallow ovenproof dish. Pour over the milk and egg mixture and sprinkle over 75 g (3 oz) Cheddar cheese.

5 Cook at 180°C (350°F) mark 4 for about 50 minutes or until light golden and piping hot. To serve, sprinkle with more grated cheese if wished.

## ITALIAN MEATLOAF

PREPARATION TIME 20 minutes
COOKING TIME 1 hour
FREEZING Suitable (stage 4)
Freeze crumb mixture separately
COLOUR INDEX Page 26
❄

**SERVES 8**
- *vegetable oil*
- *125 g (4 oz) chorizo or Italian sausage, finely diced*
- *175 g (6 oz) red onion, peeled and finely diced*
- *450 g (1 lb) lean minced beef*
- *2 garlic cloves, peeled and crushed*
- *75 ml (5 tbsp) chopped fresh parsley*
- *150 g (5 oz) fresh white breadcrumbs*

**420 CALS/SERVING**
- *2 eggs and 1 egg yolk*
- *150 ml (5 fl oz) passata*
- *salt and pepper*
- *75 g (3 oz) Cheddar cheese, grated*
- *50 g (2 oz) Roquefort cheese or any other soft blue cheese, crumbled*
- *150 ml (5 fl oz) single cream*
- *125 g (4 oz) sliced white bread, crusts removed, diced*

1 Mark a rectangle measuring 43 x 35.5 cm (17 x 14 inches) on a piece of foil and brush with oil.
2 Add the sausage and onion to the mince with the garlic, 60 ml (4 tbsp) parsley, 125 g (4 oz) breadcrumbs, the whole eggs, passata and seasoning. Knead well until the mixture is quite smooth. Spread over the foil, leaving a 2.5 cm (1 inch) border.
3 Mix the Cheddar cheese into the crumbled Roquefort. Set aside 25 g (1 oz) cheese and mix with the remaining 25 g (1 oz) breadcrumbs and 15 ml (1 tbsp) parsley for the topping.
4 Bring the cream to the boil and pour over the bread. Add the Cheddar and Roquefort and the egg yolk, and beat with a fork until well mixed. Spread over the meat. Roll up from the shorter side, using the foil as an aid. Place seam-side down on a lightly oiled non-stick, edged baking sheet or roasting tin; remove foil.
5 Bake at 180°C (350°F) mark 4 for about 1 hour. Sprinkle the reserved cheese and crumb mixture over the top and return to the oven for about a further 15 minutes or until the topping is well browned. Allow the meatloaf to sit for 5 minutes before cutting into thick slices, then serve immediately.

## SPICY BURGERS

PREPARATION TIME 15 minutes
COOKING TIME 10 minutes
FREEZING Suitable (stage 1)
♡ ⏱ ❄

**SERVES 4**
- *3 spring onions, chopped*
- *450 g (1 lb) lean minced beef*
- *1 garlic clove, peeled and crushed*
- *15 ml (1 tbsp) ground coriander*
- *15 ml (1 tbsp) ground cumin*
- *1 egg, beaten*
- *30 ml (2 tbsp) chopped fresh parsley*

**230 CALS/SERVING**
- *30 ml (2 tbsp) chopped fresh coriander*
- *15 ml (1 tbsp) Tabasco or chilli sauce*
- *salt and pepper*
- *vegetable oil for brushing*
- *pitta bread, fried onions, roast peppers, cucumber slices and mint leaves, to serve*

1 Mix together the first ten ingredients, beating well. Divide into 8 burgers.
2 Brush lightly with oil and grill or fry for about 5 minutes on each side or until cooked through. Serve in pitta bread with fried onions, roast peppers, cucumber slices and mint leaves.

1 Place the diced lamb in a bowl, add the next 5 ingredients and stir well. Pour the orange juice and 45 ml (3 tbsp) olive oil over. Stir. Cover the bowl and leave the lamb to marinate in the refrigerator for 3-8 hours.

2 Mix the dried apricots and raisins with the saffron, sherry and vinegar. Cover and leave to marinate at room temperature for at least 3 hours or overnight, stirring the mixture occasionally.

3 Heat the remaining olive oil in a large, flameproof casserole. Lift the meat from the marinade and brown in batches on a high heat. Lower the heat and return all the meat to the casserole dish. Add the flour and stir well. Add the marinade, soaked fruit and its liquid and lamb stock. Season, stir well and bring to the boil.

4 Cover the casserole with a tight-fitting lid and cook at 180°C (350°F) mark 4 for about 1¼ hours or until the meat is very tender. Serve the lamb with saffron rice.

## FRUITY LAMB CASSEROLE WITH SPICES

PREPARATION TIME 30 minutes, plus marinating
COOKING TIME 1½ hours
FREEZING Suitable (stage 4)
❄

**SERVES 8**

- 1.4 kg (3 lb) diced shoulder of lamb
- 10 ml (2 tsp) ground cumin
- 2.5 ml (½ tsp) ground cloves
- 10 ml (2 tsp) dried coriander
- 10 ml (2 tsp) dried thyme
- 4 garlic cloves, peeled and crushed
- 175 ml (6 fl oz) fresh orange juice
- 60 ml (4 tbsp) olive oil
- 175 g (6 oz) no-soak dried apricots

**540 CALS/SERVING**

- 75 g (3 oz) raisins
- 5 ml (1 tsp) saffron strands
- 300 ml (10 fl oz) sherry
- 75 ml (3 fl oz) vinegar, preferably sherry vinegar
- 60 ml (4 tbsp) white plain flour
- 600 ml (1 pint) stock, preferably lamb stock
- salt and pepper
- saffron rice, to serve

## HONEYED LEG OF LAMB WITH WINTER VEGETABLES

PREPARATION TIME 20 minutes
COOKING TIME 1½ hours
FREEZING Not suitable
COLOUR INDEX Page 27

**SERVES 4**

- 1 orange
- four 10 cm (4 inch) sprigs rosemary
- 1 small half leg of lamb, weighing about 1.1 kg (2½ lb)
- 30-60 ml (2-4 tbsp) vegetable oil
- 225 g (8 oz) carrots, peeled and cut into large chunks
- 225 g (8 oz) parsnips, peeled and cut into large chunks

**600 CALS/SERVING**

- 450 g (1 lb) potatoes, peeled and cut into large chunks
- 75 g (3 oz) turnip, peeled and cut into large chunks
- 6 shallots, peeled
- 300 ml (10 fl oz) white wine
- 15 ml (1 tbsp) honey
- salt and pepper

1 Pare the rind from half the orange and cut into strips about 5 mm (¼ inch) wide and 2.5 cm (1 inch) long. Squeeze the juice from the orange and reserve. Divide the rosemary into 2.5 cm (1 inch) pieces.

2 Place the lamb and 30 ml (2 tbsp) oil in a large

roasting tin and, over a high heat, brown the lamb all over. Remove from the tin using slotted spoons. Add the vegetables to the pan, adding more oil if necessary, and sauté for 4-5 minutes or until golden, stirring occasionally.

3 Meanwhile, make 10-12 incisions in the lamb and insert a piece of rosemary and orange rind in each.

4 Sprinkle the extra pieces of orange rind and rosemary over the vegetables. Top with the lamb. Mix together the white wine, juice of the orange, the honey and seasoning. Pour over the lamb.

5 Roast at 200°C (400°F) mark 6 for about 1¼ hours; for well done meat, roast for about 30 minutes longer. Serve the lamb accompanied by the vegetables with any juices spooned over.

## LAMB AND LENTIL BAKE

PREPARATION TIME 20 minutes, plus cooling
COOKING TIME 1¼ hours
FREEZING Suitable (stage 4)

❄

**SERVES 4**
- *30 ml (2 tbsp) vegetable oil*
- *125 g (4 oz) onion, peeled and finely chopped*
- *2.5 cm (1 inch) piece fresh root ginger, peeled and finely chopped*
- *1 garlic clove, peeled and crushed*
- *2.5 ml (½ tsp) chilli seasoning*
- *2.5 ml (½ tsp) paprika*
- *2.5 ml (½ tsp) dried marjoram*

**520 CALS/SERVING**
- *225 g (8 oz) minced lamb*
- *175 g (6 oz) red lentils*
- *30 ml (2 tbsp) tomato purée*
- *30 ml (2 tbsp) lemon juice*
- *50 g (2 oz) raisins*
- *600 ml (1 pint) chicken stock*
- *salt and pepper*
- *50 g (2 oz) butter*
- *about 125 g (4 oz) filo pastry*
- *poppy seeds*

1 Heat the oil in a saucepan. Fry the onions until translucent, about 4-5 minutes. Stir in the ginger, garlic, chilli seasoning, paprika and marjoram. Cook, stirring, for 1 minute. Add the mince and stir until it changes colour and is free of lumps.

2 Mix in the lentils, tomato purée, lemon juice, raisins and stock. Cover and cook over a low heat for 20-25 minutes or until the lentils and mince are tender and most of the liquid is absorbed.

Uncover and bubble off any excess liquid, stirring occasionally. Adjust the seasoning then turn into a bowl and allow to cool completely.

3 Melt the butter and lightly grease a 23 cm (9 inch) base measurement, 3 cm (1¼ inch) deep, loose-based fluted flan tin. Line with sheets of filo pastry, brushing with butter between the layers and overlapping them in a random manner. There should be no gaps in the pastry and the excess pastry should hang over the sides of the tin.

4 Spoon the cold filling into the flan case. Wrap over the pastry to enclose the filling. Brush with butter and garnish with crumpled up pastry trimmings. Brush with butter again, and sprinkle with poppy seeds.

5 Cook at 190°C (375°F) mark 5 for about 50-55 minutes, covering lightly with foil after about 30-35 minutes. Cool for 10 minutes before serving.

### *TIP*

Filo pastry sheets come in all sizes. You'll need about 125 g (4 oz) pastry sheets to line and cover the flan. Cut or trim the sheets as required so that they easily fit into the tin; use a little extra pastry if necessary. Whilst lining the tin, always keep the pastry covered with clingfilm or a tea towel as once it's exposed to air it quickly dries and becomes impossible to handle as it often breaks into pieces.

# MOUSSAKA

PREPARATION TIME 30 minutes
COOKING TIME 1½ hours
FREEZING Suitable (stage 4)

✲

SERVES 6
- *45 ml (3 tbsp) vegetable oil*
- *175 g (6 oz) onion, peeled and chopped*
- *450 g (1 lb) lean minced lamb*
- *400 g (14 oz) can chopped tomatoes*
- *1.25 ml (¼ tsp) ground cinnamon*
- *5 ml (1 tsp) dried oregano*
- *salt and pepper*

490 CALS/SERVING
- *900 g (2 lb) aubergines, sliced*
- *75 g (3 oz) butter*
- *75 g (3 oz) white plain flour*
- *568 ml (1 pint) warm milk*
- *25 g (1 oz) grated Parmesan cheese*
- *1 egg yolk*
- *30 ml (2 tbsp) fresh breadcrumbs*

**1** Heat 30 ml (2 tbsp) oil in a large, heavy-based frying pan, and fry the onion until soft. Stir in the meat and fry until it changes colour. Add the next 3 ingredients, then season to taste. Cover and cook for 20 minutes or until all liquid has evaporated.
**2** Brush the aubergine slices with oil and grill

until golden on both sides. Drain on absorbent kitchen paper and season.
**3** Melt the butter in a saucepan, stir in the flour, remove from the heat and whisk in the milk. Return to the heat and keep whisking for about 3-4 minutes or until it forms a thick sauce. Remove from the heat, cool slightly, then beat in half the cheese and the egg yolk. Season to taste.
**4** Place the seasoned aubergines in a 2.8 litre (5 pint) shallow, ovenproof dish. Spread the meat mixture on top and cover with the sauce. Sprinkle over the remaining cheese and the breadcrumbs.
**5** Cook at 180°C (350°F) mark 4 for about 1 hour or until golden.

**VARIATION** This classic Greek dish is also delicious made with lean minced beef instead of lamb.

# LAMB CHOPS WITH LEEKS AND LENTILS

PREPARATION TIME 20 minutes, plus marinating
COOKING TIME 30 minutes
FREEZING Not suitable
COLOUR INDEX Page 27

**SERVES 4**

- *4 loin lamb chops, each weighing about 125 g (4 oz)*
- *1 small onion, peeled and finely chopped*
- *125 ml (4 fl oz) fresh orange juice*
- *salt and pepper*
- *15 ml (1 tbsp) vegetable oil*
- *450 g (1 lb) leeks, washed, trimmed and cut into 1 cm (½ inch) slices*

**420 CALS/SERVING**

- *125 g (4 oz) split red lentils, boiled rapidly for 10 minutes, then drained*
- *5 ml (1 tsp) paprika*
- *300 ml (10 fl oz) lamb stock*
- *fresh coriander, to garnish*

1 Trim the chops of fat and place in a non-metallic dish. Sprinkle onion and orange juice over the lamb and season with pepper. Cover and refrigerate for at least 12 hours, turning once.
2 Lift the chops out of the marinade and pat dry on absorbent kitchen paper. Heat the oil in a medium-sized frying pan and brown the chops on both sides. Drain on absorbent kitchen paper.
3 Add the leeks, lentils and paprika to the pan and stir over a moderate heat for 1 minute. Place the chops on the lentils. Pour in the marinade and stock and bring to the boil.
4 Cover and simmer for 20 minutes or until the chops are cooked. Adjust the seasoning. Serve garnished with coriander.

> *TIP*
> Fast-boiling pulses for 10 minutes before cooking ensures that any harmful toxins present are destroyed.

# SPICED LAMB HOT POT

PREPARATION TIME 30 minutes
COOKING TIME 2½ hours
FREEZING Suitable

❄

**SERVES 6**

- *about 45 ml (3 tbsp) vegetable oil*
- *900 g (2 lb) boned leg of lamb, trimmed and cut into 5 cm (2 inch) cubes*
- *350 g (12 oz) onion, peeled and roughly chopped*
- *4 garlic cloves, peeled and sliced*
- *2 red peppers, deseeded and roughly chopped*
- *700 g (1½ lb) potatoes, peeled and cut into large chunks*

**560 CALS/SERVING**

- *10 ml (2 tsp) ground ginger*
- *1 cinnamon stick, broken in two halves*
- *50 g (2 oz) pearl barley*
- *600 ml (1 pint) beef stock*
- *30 ml (2 tbsp) Worcestershire sauce*
- *salt and pepper*
- *lemon wedges and marjoram sprigs, to garnish*

1 Heat 45 ml (3 tbsp) oil in a large flameproof casserole and brown the meat in batches, adding a little more oil if necessary. Drain on absorbent kitchen paper.
2 Sauté onions and garlic until well browned. Add the peppers, potatoes, ginger, cinnamon and pearl barley; sauté for 2 minutes. Stir in the stock, Worcestershire sauce and plenty of seasoning. Bring to the boil and replace the meat.
3 Cover and cook at 170°C (325°F) mark 3 for about 2 hours or until the lamb is tender. Adjust the seasoning and garnish with lemon wedges and marjoram sprigs to serve.

169

## MOROCCAN LAMB PIE WITH
## SPINACH AND SULTANAS

PREPARATION TIME 20 minutes
COOKING TIME 1¼ hours
FREEZING Suitable (stage 3)

❊

**SERVES 4**
- *15 ml (1 tbsp) oil*
- *175 g (6 oz) onion, peeled and finely chopped*
- *450 g (1 lb) minced lamb*
- *2 garlic cloves, peeled and crushed*
- *5 ml (1 tsp) ground cinnamon*
- *2.5 ml (½ tsp) ground cloves*
- *10 ml (2 tsp) ground cumin*
- *2.5 ml (½ tsp) mild curry powder*
- *45 ml (3 tbsp) Worcestershire sauce*
- *30 ml (2 tbsp) red wine*

**580 CALS/SERVING**
- *15 ml (1 tbsp) tomato purée*
- *50 g (2 oz) sultanas*
- *150 ml (5 fl oz) light stock*
- *225 g (8 oz) frozen leaf spinach, thawed, drained and finely chopped*
- *30 ml (2 tbsp) orange marmalade*
- *30 ml (2 tbsp) chopped fresh parsley*
- *salt and pepper*
- *50 g (2 oz) butter, melted*
- *275 g (10 oz) filo pastry*

**1** Heat the oil in a heavy-based flameproof casserole. Sauté the onion, stirring, until it begins to soften and brown. Add the minced lamb and brown thoroughly over high heat, breaking up any lumps of meat.

**2** Stir in the garlic with the next seven ingredients and cook for 5 minutes, stirring frequently. Add the sultanas and the stock and bring to the boil.

**3** Cover tightly and cook gently for about 20 minutes or until the lamb is tender. Stir once or twice during cooking.

**4** Stir the spinach into the casserole with the marmalade and parsley. Adjust the seasoning and leave to cool.

**5** Lightly grease a 1.4-1.7 litre (2½-3 pint) shallow ovenproof dish with melted butter. Line with the pastry, buttering between the layers, leaving the edges hanging over the dish. Reserve three or four sheets of pastry. Add the mince mixture. Top with the remaining pastry, brushing with butter, and bring the pastry edges over the top, arranging them randomly. Brush over the remaining butter.

**6** Bake at 200°C (400°F) mark 6 for 25 minutes or until golden brown. Cover loosely with foil and cook for a further 15 minutes or until the filling is piping hot.

## KIDNEYS IN SHERRY SAUCE

PREPARATION TIME 15 minutes
COOKING TIME About 25 minutes
FREEZING Not suitable
COLOUR INDEX Page 28

SERVES 4

445 CALS/SERVING

- *16 lambs' kidneys, about 900 g (2 lb) total weight*
- *salt and pepper*
- *30 ml (2 tbsp) olive oil*
- *2 onions, peeled and finely chopped*
- *2 garlic cloves, peeled and crushed*
- *30 ml (2 tbsp) chopped fresh parsley*

- *45 ml (3 tbsp) white plain flour*
- *350 ml (12 fl oz) dry sherry*
- *350 ml (12 fl oz) beef stock*
- *chopped fresh parsley, to garnish*

1 Cut the kidneys in half. Remove the cores and fat, then cut each in half again. Sprinkle with salt and pepper.
2 Heat the oil in a large frying pan and fry the kidneys over a high heat for 1 minute. Transfer to a warm dish. Using the same pan, add the onion, garlic and parsley and gently fry until soft. Stir in the flour and cook for 1 minute. Add the sherry and stock, stirring continuously until thickened and smooth. Cover and simmer gently for 10 minutes.
3 Return the kidneys to the pan and simmer for a further 5-10 minutes. Serve hot, garnished with chopped parsley.

### TIP
Be careful not to overcook the kidneys or they will become tough. The insides should be just pale pink. If you prefer a smooth sauce, sieve the sauce before returning the kidneys to the pan in stage 3.

## SAUTEED LIVER WITH ORANGE AND SAGE

PREPARATION TIME 10 minutes
COOKING TIME 10-15 minutes
FREEZING Not suitable
♡ ⏲

SERVES 4

310 CALS/SERVING

- *450 g (1 lb) lamb's liver, cut into 5 cm (2 inch) strips*
- *25 g (1 oz) seasoned flour*
- *10 ml (2 tsp) chopped fresh sage or 5 ml (1 tsp) dried*

- *3 large oranges*
- *15 ml (1 tbsp) vegetable oil*
- *225 g (8 oz) onion, peeled and roughly chopped*
- *chopped fresh sage or parsley, to garnish*

1 Toss the liver in the seasoned flour and sage mixed together. Using a serrated knife, peel, halve and thickly slice one orange.
2 Heat the oil in a frying pan, add the onion and cook, stirring, for about 3-4 minutes. Add the liver and toss over a high heat for a further 5-7 minutes until browned and just cooked.
3 Reduce the heat, stir in the grated rind and juice of the remaining 2 oranges and allow to heat through. Garnish with the orange slices and herbs.

3 Add the mustards, Worcestershire sauce and anchovy paste to the pan. Cook over moderate heat, stirring, for 1-2 minutes. Stir in the cream and bring to the boil. Return the kidneys and mushrooms to the pan. Stir to coat with the sauce and simmer for 5 minutes. Season to taste and transfer to a warm serving dish. Sprinkle with plenty of chopped parsley.

**VARIATION** Brown cap or oyster mushrooms are equally delicious with these kidneys as chanterelles.

## GRILLED PORK WITH SPICED BUTTER

PREPARATION TIME 5 minutes
COOKING TIME 20 minutes
FREEZING Not suitable
COLOUR INDEX Page 29

## AUTUMN SPICED KIDNEYS

PREPARATION TIME 10 minutes
COOKING TIME About 20 minutes
FREEZING Not suitable

SERVES 4        595 CALS/SERVING
- 50 g (2 oz) unsalted butter
- 700 g (1½ lb) lamb's kidneys, skinned, halved and cored
- 225 g (8 oz) chanterelle mushrooms, thickly sliced
- 30 ml (2 tbsp) green peppercorn mustard (Maille)
- 15 ml (1 tbsp) wholegrain mustard

- dash of Worcester-shire sauce
- 5 ml (1 tsp) anchovy paste or essence
- 300 ml (10 fl oz) double cream
- salt and pepper
- plenty of roughly chopped fresh parsley, to garnish

1 Heat the butter in a frying pan until foaming. Add the kidneys in batches and cook briskly until brown. Remove from the pan with a slotted spoon and transfer to a sieve to drain out the bitter juices.
2 Fry the mushrooms in the same pan, stirring occasionally until just tender, and remove to the sieve.

SERVES 4        455 CALS/SERVING
- 300 ml (10 fl oz) cider
- 30 ml (2 tbsp) mixed peppercorns, crushed
- 60 ml (4 tbsp) brown sugar
- 60 ml (4 tbsp) wholegrain mustard

- 50 g (2 oz) butter
- salt and pepper
- 4 pork chops, each weighing about 175 g (6 oz)

1 Place the cider in a small saucepan and boil for 15 minutes.
2 Meanwhile, combine the peppercorns with the sugar, mustard and butter.
3 Season the chops and cook under a grill for 5 minutes on one side. Turn over, spread each chop with the butter, then cook for a further 5 minutes or until golden and cooked through.
4 Pour the grill pan juices into the cider and heat for 2-3 minutes. Pour over the pork chops and serve.

## ROAST PORK WITH APPLE GRAVY

PREPARATION TIME 15 minutes, plus marinating
COOKING TIME 1½-1¾ hours
FREEZING Not suitable

**SERVES 6**

- *4 garlic cloves, peeled and finely chopped*
- *5 long sprigs rosemary, finely chopped*
- *about 90 ml (6 tbsp) olive oil*
- *rock salt and pepper*
- *1.7-1.8 kg (3½-4 lb) boneless leg, loin or shoulder of pork*

**515 CALS/SERVING**
*GRAVY*

- *1 shallot, peeled and finely chopped*
- *1 small eating apple, peeled, cored and finely chopped*
- *600 ml (1 pint) unsweetened apple juice*
- *300 ml (10 fl oz) dry cider*
- *½ onion stock cube*

**1** Mix the garlic and rosemary with 30 ml (2 tbsp) olive oil to form a very rough paste. Season.

**2** Place the meat, rind-side down, in a non-metallic dish. Spread the garlic paste all over the meat (not the rind). Cover and refrigerate for about 6 hours or overnight.

**3** Place the pork in a roasting tin, rind-side up. Score the rind, then pour about 45 ml (3 tbsp) olive oil over. Rub rock salt into the rind. Cook at 230°C (450°F) mark 8 for 15 minutes, then reduce the heat to 200°C (400°F) mark 6 for 25 minutes per 450 g (1 lb), basting occasionally.

**4** Meanwhile, sauté the shallot and apple in about 15 ml (1 tbsp) olive oil for about 3 minutes until beginning to soften. Pour in the apple juice, cider and 600 ml (1 pint) stock made with the half stock cube. Bring to the boil and boil rapidly for about 15 minutes to reduce by half. Remove from the heat.

**5** Place the meat on a serving dish. Keep warm, uncovered. Pour away excess fat from the tin, then add the gravy mixture. Bring to the boil, scraping any sediment from the bottom. Season. Serve the meat, thickly sliced, with the gravy.

## HARVEST PORK CASSEROLE

PREPARATION TIME 20 minutes
COOKING TIME 2 hours
FREEZING Suitable

❋

SERVES 4-6
- *45 ml (3 tbsp) oil*
- *700 g (1½ lb) boneless leg of pork, cut into pieces*
- *225 g (8 oz) onion, peeled and chopped*
- *1 garlic clove, peeled and crushed*
- *450 g (1 lb) parsnips, peeled and sliced*
- *15 ml (1 tbsp) ground coriander*
- *5 ml (1 tsp) cumin seeds or 15 ml (1 tbsp) ground cumin*

530-355 CALS/SERVING
- *30 ml (2 tbsp) white plain flour*
- *300 ml (10 fl oz) beef stock*
- *300 ml (10 fl oz) apple juice or cider*
- *salt and pepper*
- *2 small, crisp, red eating apples, roughly chopped*
- *snipped chives, to garnish*

**1** Heat the oil in a flameproof casserole, add the meat and brown well. Remove with a slotted spoon and drain on absorbent kitchen paper.

**2** Add the onion and garlic to the casserole and sauté for 2-3 minutes. Add the parsnips, coriander and cumin and sauté for 2 minutes. Stir in the flour. Off the heat, gradually add the stock, apple juice and seasoning.

**3** Bring to the boil and replace the meat. Cover and cook at 170°C (325°F) mark 3 for 1¼ hours or until the pork is almost tender.

**4** Stir the apple into the pork, cover and cook for a further 15-20 minutes or until tender. Season to taste and garnish with snipped chives.

**NOTE** Do not peel the apples, as the red skin adds colour and texture to the dish.

# HOMEMADE SAUSAGES WITH ROCKET PESTO

PREPARATION TIME 20 minutes, plus chilling
COOKING TIME 10-12 minutes
FREEZING Suitable (stage 2)
COLOUR INDEX Page 30
❄

**SERVES 6**

- *125 g (4 oz) rindless smoked streaky bacon, finely chopped*
- *450 g (1 lb) lean minced pork*
- *225 g (8 oz) pork sausagemeat*
- *1 small red chilli, deseeded and finely chopped*
- *2 garlic cloves, peeled and crushed*
- *25 g (1 oz) fresh white breadcrumbs*
- *salt and pepper*
- *1 egg plus 1 egg yolk*

**495 CALS/SERVING**
*ROCKET PESTO*

- *75 g (3 oz) goats' cheese or low-fat soft cheese*
- *25 g (1 oz) Gruyère or Emmental cheese, grated*
- *200 ml (7 fl oz) olive oil*
- *25 g (1 oz) shelled pistachio nuts*
- *1 garlic clove, peeled*
- *2.5 ml (½ tsp) salt*
- *75 g (3 oz) rocket leaves or watercress*

1 Mix together the bacon, minced pork, sausagemeat, chilli, garlic and breadcrumbs. Season with salt and pepper, then beat in the egg and egg yolk.
2 Shape the mixture into about 18 sausages. Cover and chill for at least 15 minutes and preferably overnight.
3 Cook the sausages on the barbecue for about 10-12 minutes or until cooked through.
4 To make the rocket pesto, blend all the ingredients in a blender or food processor until smooth.
5 Serve the sausages with the rocket pesto as a dip.

**VARIATION** To oven-cook the sausages, heat 60 ml (4 tbsp) olive oil in a large roasting tin on the hob. Add the sausages in batches and brown on all sides. Return the sausages to the tin and cook in the oven at 200°C (400°F) mark 6 for 20-25 minutes or until cooked through.

# CHINESE-STYLE SPARE RIBS

PREPARATION TIME 5 minutes
COOKING TIME 60-70 minutes
FREEZING Not suitable
♡

**SERVES 4-6**

- *900 g (2 lb) lean pork ribs*
- *30 ml (2 tbsp) vegetable oil*
- *salt*
- *spring onion and orange rind strips, to garnish*

*SAUCE*

- *2.5 cm (1 inch) piece fresh root ginger, peeled and finely chopped*

**295-195 CALS/SERVING**

- *1 garlic clove, peeled and chopped*
- *60 ml (4 tbsp) clear honey*
- *30 ml (2 tbsp) dark soy sauce*
- *30 ml (2 tbsp) tomato ketchup*
- *2 good pinches of five-spice powder*
- *150 ml (5 fl oz) unsweetened orange juice*

1 Cut the ribs into smaller pieces, if wished. Heat the oil in a large frying pan, add the ribs and season well with salt. Fry the ribs over a moderate heat for about 10 minutes, turning frequently.
2 Mix together all the sauce ingredients and pour over the ribs. Cover the pan and cook gently for 50-60 minutes or until the meat is tender and the sauce is reduced to a sticky syrup, turning the ribs occasionally.
3 Arrange the ribs on a hot serving plate and garnish with spring onion and orange rind strips.

# CHEESE AND EGGS

# FOUR-CHEESE PIZZA

PREPARATION TIME 30 minutes, plus rising
COOKING TIME 40-50 minutes
FREEZING Suitable
COLOUR INDEX Page 31
♡ ✻

**SERVES 6**

- *5 ml (1 tsp) sugar*
- *5 ml (1 tsp) dried yeast*
- *125 g (4 oz) white plain flour*
- *125 g (4 oz) strong white plain flour*
- *5 ml (1 tsp) salt*
- *10 ml (2 tsp) olive oil*
- *400 g (14 oz) can chopped tomatoes*
- *5 ml (1 tsp) dried oregano*
- *15 ml (1 tbsp) tomato purée*
- *black pepper*

**300 CALS/SERVING**
*CHEESE TOPPING*

- *125 g (4 oz) mozzarella cheese, thinly sliced*
- *50 g (2 oz) Dolcelatte cheese, chopped*
- *125 g (4 oz) ricotta cheese, crumbled*
- *30 ml (2 tbsp) freshly grated Parmesan cheese*
- *a few olives*
- *fresh basil leaves, to garnish*

**1** To make the dough, dissolve the sugar in 150 ml (5 fl oz) tepid water. Sprinkle over the yeast. Leave in a warm place for 15 minutes or until frothy.
**2** Mix the flours and salt in a bowl. Add the yeast liquid and oil. Mix to a soft dough. Turn the dough onto a floured surface and knead for 5 minutes. Return the dough to the bowl and cover. Leave to rise in a warm place for 30 minutes or until doubled in size.
**3** Place the tomatoes, oregano and tomato purée in a saucepan, adding pepper to taste, and bring to the boil. Reduce the heat and simmer, uncovered, for 15-20 minutes or until thick and pulpy. Remove from the heat and leave to cool.
**4** Quickly knead the risen dough, then roll out to a 25 cm (10 inch) round and place on a lightly greased baking tray. Fold up the edges of the dough slightly to form a rim.
**5** Spread the sauce over the dough to within 1 cm (½ inch) of the edge. Arrange the cheeses evenly over the sauce. Finish with a topping of Parmesan cheese. Decorate with the olives.
**6** Bake in the oven at 200°C (400°F) mark 6 for 25-30 minutes or until the cheese has melted and the dough is golden. Serve the pizza piping hot, garnished with basil leaves.

# DEEP-FRIED CAMEMBERT WITH RHUBARB SAUCE

PREPARATION TIME 25 minutes
COOKING TIME About 15 minutes
FREEZING Not suitable
COLOUR INDEX Page 31

**SERVES 4**

- *8 Camembert cheese portions*
- *1 large egg (size 1)*
- *125 g (4 oz) fine fresh breadcrumbs*
- *sunflower oil, for deep-frying*
- *green salad leaves, to garnish*

**510 CALS/SERVING**
*SAUCE*

- *225 g (8 oz) rhubarb, trimmed and cut into pieces*
- *40 g (1½ oz) sugar*
- *1.25 ml (¼ tsp) ground ginger*
- *salt and pepper*

**1** To make the sauce, place the rhubarb and sugar in a saucepan with 15 ml (1 tbsp) water. Cover the pan and cook over a low heat for 10 minutes until the rhubarb is very soft.
**2** Remove the pan from the heat and blend the rhubarb and liquid in a food processor until smooth. Stir in the ginger and add salt and pepper to taste, then return to the pan and heat through gently.
**3** Meanwhile, trim off the rind from the Camembert portions. Beat the egg with salt and pepper to taste and pour onto a large plate. Spread out the breadcrumbs on another plate. Dip the Camembert portions first in egg, then in breadcrumbs. Repeat the process, dipping them carefully a second time.
**4** Heat the oil in a deep-fat fryer to 190°C (375°F). Fry the Camembert portions, four at a time, for about 2 minutes until crisp and golden. Drain on absorbent kitchen paper and serve at once with the sauce. Garnish with salad leaves.

# AUBERGINE AND PEPPER
## PARMIGIANA

PREPARATION TIME 15 minutes
COOKING TIME 1¼ hours
FREEZING Suitable (stage 4)

✳

**SERVES 6**

- *two 400 g (14 oz) cans chopped tomatoes*
- *30 ml (2 tbsp) olive oil*
- *2 garlic cloves, peeled and crushed*
- *30 ml (2 tbsp) chopped fresh basil*
- *5 ml (1 tsp) grated lemon rind*
- *pinch of sugar*

**360 CALS/SERVING**

- *salt and pepper*
- *4 large red peppers, deseeded and quartered*
- *3 aubergines*
- *225 g (8 oz) Cheddar cheese, grated*
- *50 g (2 oz) freshly grated Parmesan cheese*

**1** Start by making the tomato sauce. Place the chopped tomatoes in a saucepan and add half the oil, the garlic, basil, lemon rind, sugar and seasoning. Bring to the boil, cover and simmer gently for 30 minutes. Remove the lid and cook for a further 15 minutes. Allow to cool.
**2** Meanwhile, place the pepper quarters on the grill pan, brush with a little oil and grill for 5-6 minutes on each side until charred and tender. Transfer to a plastic bag and leave to cool.
**3** Cut the aubergines lengthways into thick slices, place on the grill pan and brush with oil. Grill for 6-8 minutes on each side, then leave to cool. Peel the cooled peppers.
**4** Spoon a little sauce into the base of a large greased dish and top with a layer of aubergines and peppers. Sprinkle over a little of the Cheddar cheese. Continue to add layers of sauce, vegetables and cheese, finishing with a layer of Cheddar cheese. Sprinkle over the Parmesan.
**5** Bake in the oven at 200°C (400°F) mark 6 for 30-40 minutes until bubbling and golden. Serve at once.

buttered 2 litre (3½ pint) ovenproof dish. Cover with half of the bread and sprinkle over two-thirds of the Gruyère. Add the remaining spinach, then top with the remaining bread. Pour over the egg and milk mixture. Press the bread gently into the milk.

**4** Sprinkle over the remaining Gruyère and Parmesan and allow to stand for at least 30 minutes to absorb most of the liquid.

**5** Place the dish in a roasting tin and pour in enough boiling water to come halfway up the sides of the dish. Bake at 220°C (425°F) mark 7 for about 30 minutes or until puffed, lightly set and well browned, covering loosely with foil if necessary.

# STILTON, WALNUT AND BACON FLAN

PREPARATION TIME 10 minutes, plus pastry and chilling
COOKING TIME 50 minutes
FREEZING Suitable
COLOUR INDEX Page 31

✽

SERVES 4-6
- *Walnut Shortcrust Pastry, made with 175 g (6 oz) white plain flour (see page 369)*

FILLING
- *125 g (4 oz) rindless back bacon, diced*
- *10 ml (2 tsp) olive oil*

610-405 CALS/SERVING
- *2 sticks of celery, chopped*
- *75 g (3 oz) Stilton cheese, crumbled*
- *1 egg*
- *1 egg yolk*
- *150 ml (5 fl oz) single cream*
- *salt and pepper*

**1** Roll out the pastry on a lightly floured surface and use to line a 20 cm (8 inch) flan tin. Prick the bottom with a fork and chill for 20 minutes.
**2** Bake the flan blind (see page 368) at 200°C (400°F) mark 6 until pale golden.
**3** Dry fry the bacon for 5 minutes to release the fat. Add the oil to the pan with the celery and fry for 2 minutes. Scatter the bacon, celery and Stilton over the base of the flan.
**4** Beat the egg and egg yolk into the cream, and season with salt and pepper. Pour the cream mixture into the pastry case, and bake the flan for 30 minutes, until just set and golden. Serve warm or cold.

# GOLDEN CHEESE AND SPINACH PUDDING

PREPARATION TIME 20 minutes, plus standing
COOKING TIME 35 minutes
FREEZING Not suitable

SERVES 4
- *450 g (1 lb) spinach leaves*
- *600 ml (1 pint) milk*
- *3 eggs*
- *60 ml (4 tbsp) freshly grated Parmesan cheese*
- *2.5 ml (½ tsp) chilli seasoning (not powder)*

625 CALS/SERVING
- *freshly grated nutmeg*
- *salt and pepper*
- *5 large thick slices white crusty bread, about 225 g (8 oz) total weight*
- *butter for greasing*
- *225 g (8 oz) Gruyère cheese, grated*

**1** Cook the spinach with just the water clinging to the leaves after washing, for about 4-5 minutes or until wilted. Drain thoroughly, squeezing out as much of the liquid as possible. Chop the spinach.
**2** Whisk together the milk, eggs, 45 ml (3 tbsp) Parmesan, the chilli seasoning and nutmeg. Season with salt and pepper. Halve the bread slices if large.
**3** Place half the spinach in the base of a well

## FETA AND OREGANO TARTS

PREPARATION TIME 20 minutes, plus chilling
COOKING TIME 45 minutes
FREEZING Suitable (stage 1)

❋

**MAKES 6**
- *Shortcrust Pastry, made with 225 g (8 oz) white plain flour (see page 369)*
- *300 g (10 oz) tomatoes, skinned*
- *175 g (6 oz) feta cheese, roughly chopped*

**435 CALS/TART**
- *45 ml (3 tbsp) chopped fresh oregano*
- *2 eggs, beaten*
- *150 ml (5 fl oz) single cream*
- *pepper*

**1** Roll out the pastry and use to line six 9 cm (3½ inch) flan tins about 2.5 cm (1 inch) deep. Chill for about 30 minutes then bake the pastry blind (see page 368) for 20 minutes or until golden.

**2** Cut each tomato into 6-8 pieces, discarding the seeds. Place the feta cheese in a bowl. Stir in the oregano, eggs and cream.

**3** Fill each tart case with a little of the mixture to come to within 5 mm (¼ inch) of the top of the pastry. Arrange the tomato pieces over the top of each flan.

**4** Bake at 180°C (350°F) mark 4 for about 25 minutes or until just set and beginning to brown. Cool for 10 minutes. Grind over pepper and serve.

**NOTE** These tarts can be made a day in advance. Store them in the refrigerator and serve at room temperature.

> *TIP*
> These individual tarts are ideal for picnics. Allow to cool completely and wrap each one in foil before packing in a rigid container.

5 When the omelette is just set but still moist, tip the filling into the middle and fold the four sides over the top to encase, like a parcel. Invert a warmed plate over the wok or pan then turn out the filled omelette. Serve immediately.

**VARIATIONS** Substitute minced beef for the pork. For a vegetarian option, omit the meat altogether and replace with another vegetable, such as beansprouts.

## STUFFED THAI OMELETTE

PREPARATION TIME 10 minutes
COOKING TIME About 15 minutes
FREEZING Not suitable

**SERVES 2**
- *3 eggs*
- *salt and pepper*
- *45 ml (3 tbsp) vegetable oil*
- *125 g (4 oz) minced pork*
- *1 large garlic clove, peeled and crushed*
- *2.5 cm (1 inch) piece fresh root ginger, peeled and grated*
- *1 carrot, peeled and grated*
- *1 small leek, trimmed and shredded*

**460 CALS/SERVING**
- *1 tomato, skinned and finely chopped*
- *5 ml (1 tsp) soft brown sugar*
- *15 ml (1 tbsp) nam pla (Thai fish sauce) (optional)*
- *10-15 ml (2-3 tsp) soy sauce*
- *5-15 ml (1-3 tsp) rice vinegar or cider vinegar*

1 In a bowl, beat the eggs together lightly, and season with salt and pepper.
2 Heat half of the oil in a wok or frying pan. Add the pork with the garlic and ginger and stir-fry until the pork is cooked through.
3 Add the carrot and leek and stir-fry for 1 minute, then add the tomato, sugar, fish sauce if using, soy sauce and vinegar. Season generously with pepper and stir-fry for 2-3 minutes. Transfer to a warmed dish and keep warm.
4 Wipe out the wok or frying pan, place over a moderate heat and add the remaining oil; swirl to distribute evenly. Pour in the beaten eggs.

## CARAMELIZED ONION AND GRUYERE FRITTATA

PREPARATION TIME 10 minutes
COOKING TIME 40 minutes
FREEZING Not suitable
COLOUR INDEX Page 32
♡

**SERVES 4**
- *30 ml (2 tbsp) vegetable oil*
- *700 g (1½ lb) onions, peeled and sliced*
- *1 garlic clove, peeled and sliced*
- *4 eggs*
- *15 ml (1 tbsp) each chopped fresh chives and parsley*

**330 CALS/SERVING**
- *salt and pepper*
- *125 g (4 oz) fresh spinach, roughly chopped*
- *75 g (3 oz) each Gruyère and Edam cheese, cut into 1 cm (½ inch) cubes*

1 Heat the oil in a small 9 cm (7½ inch) non-stick frying pan. Cook the onions and the garlic, covered, for 25-30 minutes or until caramelized and golden brown, stirring occasionally.
2 Beat together the eggs and herbs with plenty of seasoning.
3 Remove the onions from the pan and add the spinach. Stir over a low heat until wilted and all the excess moisture has evaporated. Return the onions to the pan with the cheese and stir until the mixture is thoroughly combined.
4 Pour in the egg mixture and allow to run through the onions. Cook over a medium heat, loosening the edge with a spatula, for about 3-4 minutes or until the base and edge of the mixture are set. Cover the pan handle with foil and place under a hot grill for a further 3-4 minutes or until the top is set and golden brown.

## SWEET POTATO AND LEEK TORTILLA

PREPARATION TIME 10 minutes
COOKING TIME About 20 minutes
FREEZING Not suitable

**SERVES 4**

**525 CALS/SERVING**

- *450 g (1 lb) sweet potato*
- *salt and pepper*
- *60 ml (4 tbsp) olive oil*
- *3 leeks, trimmed, washed and thinly sliced*
- *4 eggs*
- *125 ml (4 fl oz) single cream or milk*
- *125 g (4 oz) Gruyère or mature Cheddar cheese, grated*
- *30 ml (2 tbsp) chopped fresh parsley*

**1** Peel the sweet potato, and cut into 2.5 cm (1 inch) chunks. Cook in boiling salted water for about 5-8 minutes, until just tender. Drain.
**2** Heat the oil in a large frying pan, add the leeks and cook until softened. Add the sweet potato, and cook, stirring occasionally, until the potato is just beginning to colour.
**3** Meanwhile, beat the eggs with the cream. Season with salt and pepper, then pour into the frying pan. Add the grated cheese, and stir a little until the cheese is evenly distributed. Cook gently until set on the bottom.
**4** Place the omelette under the grill, and cook until puffed up and golden. Serve straight from the pan, sprinkled with the parsley.

**VARIATION** Use carrots instead of sweet potato.

*TIP*
This variation of a Spanish tortilla can be served as a tapas-style snack with drinks – allow to cool and cut into neat chunks.

# COURGETTE AND BACON FRITTATA

PREPARATION TIME 10 minutes
COOKING TIME 6-10 minutes
FREEZING Not suitable
♡ ⏲

**SERVES 4**      **160 CALS/SERVING**

- *15 ml (1 tbsp) vegetable oil*
- *450 g (1 lb) courgettes, thickly sliced*
- *125 g (4 oz) rindless smoked streaky bacon, chopped*
- *50 g (2 oz) onion, peeled and chopped*
- *30 ml (2 tbsp) chopped fresh thyme*
- *15 ml (1 tbsp) chopped fresh rosemary*
- *2 eggs*
- *salt and pepper*
- *chopped fresh herbs, to garnish*

1 Heat the oil in a non-stick 20-25 cm (8-10 inch) frying pan. Sauté the courgettes, bacon and onion together for 4-5 minutes, stirring continuously, until just beginning to soften and turn golden brown.
2 Whisk together the thyme, rosemary and eggs. Season with salt and pepper. Pour over the courgette mixture and leave to set over a low heat for 2-3 minutes. Serve immediately, cut into wedges and sprinkled with chopped fresh herbs.

# VEGETABLE EGG NESTS

PREPARATION TIME 15 minutes
COOKING TIME 15 minutes
FREEZING Not suitable
COLOUR INDEX Page 32
♡ ⏲

**SERVES 4**      **240 CALS/SERVING**

- *450 g (1 lb) trimmed leeks, sliced*
- *550 g (1¼ lb) courgettes, sliced*
- *225 g (8 oz) asparagus tips*
- *125 g (4 oz) peas*
- *50 g (2 oz) low-fat spread*
- *30 ml (2 tbsp) chopped fresh parsley*
- *1 garlic clove, peeled and crushed*
- *salt and pepper*
- *4 eggs*
- *8 anchovy fillets*

1 Steam the leeks, courgettes and asparagus for about 12-15 minutes or until tender, adding the peas for the last 5 minutes of cooking time.
2 Meanwhile, mix together the low-fat spread, parsley and garlic. Season well.
3 Poach the eggs in gently simmering water for 4-5 minutes or until just set.
4 Divide the hot vegetables among four individual dishes. Make a well in the centre and place an egg in each. Season each egg with pepper and cross two anchovy fillets on top. Top the vegetables with a little herb mixture to serve.

**NOTE** Many people believe that brown eggs are more nutritious than white, but this is not the case – the only difference is the colour of the shell.

**VARIATION** Vary the vegetables according to what is available – steamed baby sweetcorn, baby carrots and small broccoli florets will also work well in this dish.

## POACHED EGGS ON SMOKED HADDOCK WITH HOT CAPER DRESSING

PREPARATION TIME 10 minutes, plus soaking
COOKING TIME 12-15 minutes
FREEZING Not suitable

**SERVES 4**

- *50 g (2 oz) baby French capers in salt*
- *4 thick slices rustic bread*
- *oil for frying*
- *4 smoked haddock fillets, each weighing about 125 g (4 oz)*
- *600 ml (1 pint) fish stock or water*
- *4 eggs*

**550 CALS/SERVING**

- *75 ml (3 fl oz) olive oil*
- *15 ml (1 tbsp) lemon juice*
- *15 ml (1 tbsp) balsamic vinegar*
- *salt and pepper*
- *125 g (4 oz) baby spinach leaves*

1 Wash the salted capers and place in a small bowl. Cover with cold water and set aside to soak for 30 minutes. Drain, wash well and pat dry.
2 Cut the bread into bite-sized pieces. Heat a shallow layer of oil in a large, non-stick frying pan. When hot, add the bread and stir-fry for 4-5 minutes until crisp and golden. Drain on absorbent kitchen paper and set aside.
3 Place the haddock in a small saucepan with the fish stock or water. Bring to the boil and poach gently for 4-5 minutes until the fish is firm and cooked through. Remove from the pan with a slotted spoon, cover with foil and keep warm.
4 Poach the eggs in the fish liquid for 3 minutes; 5 minutes for harder-set eggs.
5 Meanwhile, place the olive oil in a small saucepan, with the lemon juice, vinegar and capers. Season and heat until almost boiling.
6 Arrange the fish on individual plates. Top with an egg, garnish with spinach and croûtons, and pour over caper dressing. Serve at once.

### TIP
French capers are small and come packed in salt, unlike the larger capers which are kept in brine. French capers have a firmer texture and superior flavour to the larger capers. They are available from good delicatessens – normal capers can be used instead, but should also be soaked to remove the brine flavour.

# PASTA AND NOODLES

# NOODLES WITH MEATBALLS AND SHALLOTS

PREPARATION TIME 25 minutes
COOKING TIME 15 minutes
FREEZING Not suitable
♡

**SERVES 4**
- *300 g (10 oz) shallots, peeled*
- *30 ml (2 tbsp) olive oil*
- *225 g (8 oz) lean minced beef*
- *30 ml (2 tbsp) chopped fresh parsley*

**335 CALS/SERVING**
- *salt and pepper*
- *25 g (1 oz) pitted black olives*
- *30 ml (2 tbsp) chopped chives*
- *30 ml (2 tbsp) pesto sauce*
- *125 g (4 oz) dried noodles*

1 Chop 50 g (2 oz) shallots and sauté in 15 ml (1 tbsp) oil until golden. Cool, then mix with the beef mince, parsley and seasoning. Shape into 8 small patties. Fry in a non-stick pan for about 5-7 minutes each side or until cooked through.
2 Meanwhile, thinly slice the remaining shallots. Cook in the remaining oil in a covered pan for about 8-10 minutes until golden. Stir in the olives, chives and pesto, warm through and season.
3 Cook the noodles in boiling salted water until just tender, then drain well.
4 Toss the noodles with the shallot mixture and serve immediately accompanied by the meatballs.

# SEAFOOD SPAGHETTI WITH PEPPER AND ALMOND SAUCE

PREPARATION TIME 20 minutes
COOKING TIME 20 minutes
FREEZING Not suitable
COLOUR INDEX Page 33
♡

**SERVES 4**
- *1 small red pepper, about 150 g (5 oz)*
- *1 fresh red chilli*
- *50 g (2 oz) toasted, blanched almonds*
- *2-3 garlic cloves, peeled and crushed*
- *30 ml (2 tbsp) red wine vinegar*
- *350 ml (12 fl oz) tomato juice*
- *60 ml (4 tbsp) chopped fresh parsley*

**305 CALS/SERVING**
- *salt and pepper*
- *125 g (4 oz) dried spaghetti*
- *450 g (1 lb) cooked mixed seafood, such as prawns, mussels and squid*
- *chopped fresh chilli, to garnish*

1 Place the pepper and chilli under the grill and cook, turning occasionally, until the skins char and blacken. Cool slightly, then pull off the skins. Halve, discard the seeds, then put the flesh into a large food processor bowl.
2 Add the nuts, garlic, vinegar, tomato juice, half the parsley and seasoning. Blend until almost smooth. Transfer to a pan.
3 Cook the pasta in boiling salted water until just tender (*al dente*). Drain and toss in the rest of the fresh parsley. Season to taste and cover.
4 Meanwhile, gently heat the sauce until it simmers, then add the seafood. Simmer for 3-5 minutes or until heated through, stirring frequently. Adjust the seasoning and serve immediately over the spaghetti. Garnish with chopped fresh chilli.

> *TIPS*
> Remember to wear rubber gloves when handling chillies to prevent skin irritation. You can buy fresh or frozen mixed cooked seafood in supermarkets. If you can't find it, put together your own selection of prepared cooked seafood.

# GINGERED CHICKEN AND NOODLES

PREPARATION TIME 5 minutes
COOKING TIME 20-25 minutes
FREEZING Not suitable
COLOUR INDEX Page 33
♡ ⏲

SERVES 4

- *15 ml (1 tbsp) vegetable oil*
- *1 bunch spring onions, sliced*
- *2.5 cm (1 inch) piece fresh root ginger, peeled and grated*
- *1 garlic clove, peeled and crushed*
- *275 g (10 oz) skinless chicken breast fillet, cut into bite-sized pieces*
- *30 ml (2 tbsp) mild curry paste or 15 ml (1 tbsp) Thai hot curry paste*

310 CALS/SERVING

- *300 ml (10 fl oz) coconut milk*
- *about 300 ml (10 fl oz) chicken stock*
- *salt and pepper*
- *125 g (4 oz) Chinese egg noodles*
- *10 ml (2 tsp) lemon or lime juice*

1 Heat the oil in a large, non-stick sauté pan and fry the spring onions, ginger and garlic until just beginning to soften. Add the chicken pieces and curry paste and cook for a further 3-4 minutes or until golden brown.
2 Stir in the coconut milk, stock and seasoning. Bring to the boil. Break the noodles in half and add to the pan. Cover and simmer for about 5-10 minutes or until the noodles are just tender, stirring occasionally. Add a little more stock if the mixture becomes too dry.
3 Add the lemon or lime juice, season to taste and serve immediately, stirring well to mix.

## TIP
Coconut milk: use canned coconut milk or roughly chop a 50 g (2 oz) block of creamed coconut and make up to 300 ml (10 fl oz) with boiling water. Stir well to mix.

# CHILLI PORK WITH NOODLES

PREPARATION TIME 10 minutes
COOKING TIME 15 minutes
FREEZING Not suitable
♡ ⏲

SERVES 4

- *30 ml (2 tbsp) vegetable oil*
- *350 g (12 oz) pork fillet, cut into thin slices*
- *1 yellow pepper, deseeded and cut into thin slices*
- *225 g (8 oz) broccoli, divided into small florets*
- *1 onion, peeled and roughly chopped*
- *2.5 ml (1/2 tsp) mild chilli powder or few drops Tabasco sauce*

285 CALS/SERVING

- *5 ml (1 tsp) dried oregano or dried mixed herbs*
- *50 g (2 oz) rice noodles or dried pasta*
- *30 ml (2 tbsp) sherry or medium white wine*
- *450 ml (15 fl oz) beef stock*
- *15 ml (1 tbsp) soy sauce*
- *pepper*

1 Heat the oil in a large non-stick sauté pan or wok and brown the pork well for about 2-3 minutes. Remove with a slotted spoon and drain on absorbent kitchen paper. Add the yellow pepper, broccoli and onion. Stir in the chilli powder and herbs and sauté, stirring, for 1-2 minutes.
2 Mix in the pork, noodles, sherry, stock and soy sauce. Bring to the boil, cover and simmer for about 7 minutes or until all the ingredients are tender. Add pepper to taste and serve.

## ITALIAN SEAFOOD PASTA SALAD

PREPARATION TIME 15 minutes, plus marinating
COOKING TIME 15-20 minutes
FREEZING Not suitable

**SERVES 6**

- *225 g (8 oz) dried pasta twists*
- *1 small red pepper, quartered and deseeded*
- *two 225 g (8 oz) packets cooked mixed seafood*
- *6 each black and green olives, pitted and quartered*
- *flat-leaf parsley sprigs, to garnish*

**440 CALS/SERVING**
*DRESSING*

- *60 ml (4 tbsp) balsamic or white wine vinegar*
- *150 ml (5 fl oz) olive oil*
- *2 garlic cloves, peeled and crushed*
- *45 ml (3 tbsp) chopped fresh parsley*
- *salt and pepper*

1 Bring a large pan of salted water to the boil, add the pasta and cook for 10-12 minutes until just tender (*al dente*). Drain, rinse in cold water and drain again, then leave to cool.
2 Meanwhile, grill the pepper, skin-side up, for 5-8 minutes until the skin is blistering and beginning to blacken. Place the pepper quarters in a polythene bag, seal tightly and leave to cool.
3 Place the mixed seafood in a large bowl, add the olives and set aside.
4 To make the dressing, whisk together the vinegar, olive oil, garlic and parsley and season with salt and pepper. Pour over the seafood mixture and leave to marinate at room temperature for 20 minutes.

5 When the pepper is cool, peel off the skin, rinse the pepper under cold water and pat dry with absorbent kitchen paper. Shred finely and add to the seafood with the pasta. Toss lightly to mix, garnish with flat-leaf parsley sprigs and serve.

## PASTA WITH WALNUT AND BASIL SAUCE

PREPARATION TIME 15 minutes
COOKING TIME 12 minutes
FREEZING Not suitable
COLOUR INDEX Page 35
🕐

**SERVES 4**

- *2 large garlic cloves, peeled*
- *40 g (1½ oz) fresh basil leaves (a large bunch)*
- *50 g (2 oz) freshly grated Parmesan cheese*
- *1 small tomato, skinned and deseeded*
- *60 ml (4 tbsp) olive oil*
- *salt and pepper*

**480 CALS/SERVING**

- *350 g (12 oz) fresh pasta or 225 g (8 oz) dried*
- *45 ml (3 tbsp) single cream*
- *50 g (2 oz) walnut pieces, chopped*
- *basil sprigs*
- *freshly grated Parmesan, to serve*

1 Place the garlic, basil leaves, Parmesan cheese and tomato flesh in a blender or food processor and work to a smooth paste.
2 Gradually add the olive oil, drop by drop, as if making mayonnaise. Season the mixture with salt and pepper to taste.
3 Cook the pasta in plenty of boiling, salted water until it is just tender (*al dente*). Drain well. Toss in a warmed serving bowl with the cream, basil sauce and walnuts. Serve immediately with fresh basil sprigs and freshly grated Parmesan cheese.

## LINGUINE WITH PARMA HAM AND SUN-DRIED TOMATOES

PREPARATION TIME 5 minutes
COOKING TIME 11 minutes
FREEZING Not suitable

SERVES 4

- *400 g (14 oz) dried linguine (or fettucini)*
- *salt and pepper*
- *30 ml (2 tbsp) olive oil*
- *125 g (4 oz) Parma ham (about 6 thin slices), cut into thin strips*
- *65 g (2½ oz) butter*
- *1 large onion, peeled and chopped*
- *2 garlic cloves, peeled and crushed*
- *50 g (2 oz) sun-dried tomatoes, drained and cut into strips*

1020 CALS/SERVING

- *150 ml (5 fl oz) double cream*
- *150 g (5 oz) mascarpone cheese*
- *small bunch of marjoram or oregano sprigs, leaves pulled from stalks*
- *30-45 ml (2-3 tbsp) toasted pine nuts (optional)*

1 Cook the pasta in a large saucepan of boiling, salted water for 10 minutes or until almost tender *(al dente)*.

2 Meanwhile, heat the oil in a frying pan, add the strips of Parma ham and fry quickly for about 1 minute or until frazzled. Using a slotted spoon, remove the ham from the pan and reserve.

3 Add the butter to the frying pan and gently fry the onion, garlic and sun-dried tomatoes for 2 minutes. Drain the pasta, and while still hot, add to the frying pan. With a fork in each hand, lift the pasta strands a few times, so the buttery mixture coats and separates them.

4 In a saucepan, gently heat the cream with the mascarpone, stirring until smooth. Season with salt and pepper, add to the pasta mixture and toss with half the Parma ham and half the marjoram or oregano leaves.

5 Transfer the mixture to a warm serving bowl and scatter with the remaining Parma ham, herbs and toasted pine nuts, if using. Serve at once.

**VARIATIONS** Use strips of pancetta or smoked streaky bacon instead of Parma ham and cook in the same way. Sautéed sliced mushrooms or asparagus tips also make tasty additions.

## CREAMY PASTA BAKE

PREPARATION TIME 15 minutes
COOKING TIME 45 minutes
FREEZING Not suitable

SERVES 4     550 CALS/SERVING

- *175 g (6 oz) dried pasta shapes, such as penne*
- *salt and pepper*
- *olive oil*
- *125 g (4 oz) onion, peeled and finely chopped*
- *1 garlic clove, peeled and crushed*
- *300 ml (10 fl oz) single cream*
- *2 eggs*
- *175 g (6 oz) Gruyère cheese, coarsely grated*

1 Cook the pasta in boiling, salted water until just tender *(al dente)*. Drain well and toss in a little oil.
2 Meanwhile, heat 15 ml (1 tbsp) oil in a small frying pan and add the onion and garlic. Fry for a few minutes until the mixture is beginning to soften.
3 In a large bowl, whisk together the single cream and the eggs; then season generously. Stir in the cheese, the onion mixture and the cooked pasta.
4 Spoon into a 1.1 litre (2 pint) ovenproof dish. Stand the dish on a baking sheet and bake at 190°C (375 °F) mark 5 for 35-40 minutes or until the top is golden brown.

## ROASTED VEGETABLE AND PASTA GRATIN

PREPARATION TIME 35 minutes
COOKING TIME 1½ hours
FREEZING Suitable (stage 4)
COLOUR INDEX Page 34

❄

SERVES 8     585 CALS/SERVING

- *450 g (1 lb) aubergines, cut into bite-sized pieces*
- *700 g (1½ lb) mixed peppers, deseeded and cut into bite-sized pieces*
- *450 g (1 lb) squash, such as butternut or pumpkin, peeled and cut into bite-sized pieces*
- *90 ml (6 tbsp) olive oil*
- *225 g (8 oz) dried pasta shapes*
- *50 g (2 oz) butter*
- *50 g (2 oz) white plain flour*
- *900 ml (1½ pints) milk*
- *30 ml (2 tbsp) wholegrain mustard*
- *150 g (5 oz) soft cheese with garlic and herbs*
- *225 g (8 oz) mature Cheddar cheese, grated*
- *salt and pepper*
- *450 g (1 lb) frozen leaf spinach, thawed and drained*

1 Put the aubergines, mixed peppers and squash into two roasting tins with the oil. Roast at 220°C (425°F) mark 7 for 45 minutes or until tender and charred.

2 Meanwhile, cook the pasta shapes in boiling salted water until just tender *(al dente)*. Drain them thoroughly.

3 Melt the butter in a pan and then stir in the flour. Cook, stirring, for 1 minute before adding the milk. Bring to the boil, stirring all the time. Simmer for 2-3 minutes or until the sauce thickens. Off the heat, add the mustard, soft cheese and all but 50 g (2 oz) of the Cheddar. Stir thoroughly until smooth. Season well.

4 Mix the pasta, spinach and roasted vegetables with the sauce. Spoon the vegetable and pasta gratin into a large, shallow ovenproof dish and sprinkle over the remaining Cheddar cheese.

5 Stand the dish on a baking sheet and cook at 200°C (400°F) mark 6 for about 40 minutes or until hot and golden brown, covering with foil, if necessary, to prevent over browning.

**VARIATIONS** This dish is a great way of using up leftovers. You can add cooked ham, chicken or spicy sausage. Any variety of cheese can be used; for a special vegetarian meal, add goats' cheese or Stilton.

# PAD THAI NOODLES

PREPARATION TIME 15 minutes
COOKING TIME 5 minutes
FREEZING Not suitable
⏲

SERVES 4

- *250 g (9 oz) flat, thin rice or egg noodles*
- *30 ml (2 tbsp) sesame oil*
- *125 g (4 oz) turnip, diced*
- *2 garlic cloves, peeled and crushed*
- *2.5 ml (½ tsp) hot paprika*
- *60-75 ml (4-5 tbsp) fish sauce*
- *juice of 1 lime*
- *15 ml (1 tbsp) tomato purée*

615 CALS/SERVING

- *125 g (4 oz) tofu, diced*
- *50 g (2 oz) roasted peanuts, finely chopped*
- *125 g (4 oz) cooked, peeled prawns*
- *175 g (6 oz) beansprouts*
- *2 eggs, beaten*
- *chopped peanuts, to serve*
- *whole cooked prawns and basil, to garnish*

1 Cook the noodles according to the packet instructions. Heat the oil in a wok or large non-stick sauté pan. Add the noodles, turnip, garlic and paprika and sauté for 1-2 minutes, stirring to prevent the noodles from sticking. Add the fish sauce, lime juice and tomato purée and cook for a further 1 minute, stirring continuously.

2 Stir in the tofu, peanuts, prawns and beansprouts. Lower the heat, add the eggs and stir for about 1 minute or until the noodles are coated in lightly cooked egg. Serve sprinkled with chopped peanuts and garnished with prawns and basil.

*TIP*
Work quickly and merely toss the ingredients in the pan to heat them through and lightly cook the egg.

# CRUNCHY COURGETTE PASTA

PREPARATION TIME 15 minutes
COOKING TIME 15 minutes
FREEZING Not suitable
♡ ⏰

| SERVES 4 | 260 CALS/SERVING |
|---|---|
| • 175 g (6 oz) dried pasta | • 225 g (8 oz) tomatoes, diced |
| • salt and pepper | • 225 g (8 oz) courgettes, diced |
| • 15 ml (1 tbsp) vegetable oil | • 350 ml (12 fl oz) tomato juice |
| • 125 g (4 oz) onion, peeled and finely chopped | • 15 ml (1 tbsp) red wine vinegar |
| • 1 garlic clove, peeled and crushed | • 30 ml (2 tbsp) chopped fresh parsley |
| • 1.25 ml (¼ tsp) mild chilli powder | • 20 ml (4 tsp) freshly grated Parmesan cheese |
| • 1 red pepper, halved, deseeded and chopped | |

1 Cook the pasta in boiling, salted water until just tender (*al dente*), then drain.
2 Meanwhile, heat the oil in a non-stick frying pan and cook the onion and garlic for about 3 minutes or until beginning to soften. Stir in the chilli powder and cook for a further minute.
3 Add the red pepper, tomatoes and courgettes to the frying pan and cook over a medium heat for about 5 minutes or until hot but still crunchy. Stir in the tomato juice and vinegar with plenty of

seasoning. Bring to the boil and simmer for 2-3 minutes or until piping hot.
4 Spoon the sauce over the cooked pasta and serve immediately, sprinkled with the chopped parsley and Parmesan cheese.

# TOMATO AND MOZZARELLA NOODLES

PREPARATION TIME 10 minutes
COOKING TIME 10 minutes
FREEZING Not suitable
COLOUR INDEX Page 35
⏰

| SERVES 4 | 410 CALS/SERVING |
|---|---|
| • 225 g (8 oz) mozzarella cheese | • salt and pepper |
| • 450 g (1 lb) tomatoes, deseeded and roughly chopped | • 225 g (8 oz) dried pasta noodles, such as pappardelle |
| • grated rind of 1 lemon | • 15 ml (1 tbsp) olive oil |
| • 45 ml (3 tbsp) balsamic vinegar | • 15 ml (1 tbsp) chopped fresh thyme |

1 Dice the mozzarella cheese and set aside. Place the tomatoes in a saucepan with the lemon rind and balsamic vinegar and season with salt and pepper.
2 Meanwhile, cook the pasta in boiling, salted water until just tender (*al dente*). Drain well. Toss in the olive oil with the fresh thyme.
3 Warm the tomato mixture for 2-3 minutes and spoon it over the pasta. Top with mozzarella cheese and serve immediately.

**VARIATION** Try cubes of dolcelatta cheese instead of the mozzarella.

If you like garlic, sauté 2 crushed garlic cloves in a little olive oil and add to the tomato mixture at stage 3.

## CRESPOLINE

PREPARATION TIME 20 minutes, plus standing
COOKING TIME 40-50 minutes
FREEZING Not suitable

♡

**SERVES 4**
- *225 g (8 oz) leaf spinach*
- *175 g (6 oz) ricotta cheese*
- *pinch of freshly grated nutmeg*
- *1 garlic clove, peeled and crushed*
- *8 dried pasta cannelloni tubes, about 75 g (3 oz) total weight*
- *300 ml (10 fl oz) Classic Tomato Sauce (see page 212) or passata*

**345 CALS/SERVING**
*PARMESAN SAUCE*
- *40 g (1½ oz) butter or margarine*
- *25 g (1 oz) white plain flour*
- *450 ml (15 fl oz) milk*
- *40 g (1½ oz) freshly grated Parmesan cheese*
- *salt and pepper*

**1** To make the Parmesan sauce, melt the butter in a small saucepan over a low heat. Stir in the flour and cook for a few seconds, stirring. Remove from the heat and gradually add the milk, whisking until smooth. Slowly bring to the boil, stirring. Simmer gently for 4-5 minutes, whisking again if necessary. Stir in the Parmesan cheese and season with salt and pepper.

**2** Wash the spinach and cook in a large saucepan with just the water clinging to the leaves for 3-4 minutes or until wilted. Drain well, then cool and roughly chop.

**3** Mix the spinach with the ricotta, nutmeg and garlic, and season with salt and pepper. Fill the pasta tubes with the mixture.

**4** Pour the tomato sauce or passata into an ovenproof dish and place the stuffed cannelloni on top in a single layer. Pour the Parmesan sauce over the top. Leave to stand for 30 minutes.

**5** Cook at 190°C (375°F) mark 5 for 30-40 minutes or until piping hot and golden brown.

**NOTE** Most cannelloni does not need any pre-cooking, but it is worth checking the packet instructions first.

If the cheese sauce gets too hot it may separate slightly around the edges, but it is still delicious.

## CLASSIC TOMATO SAUCE

PREPARATION TIME 10 minutes
COOKING TIME 40 minutes
FREEZING Suitable (stage 2)

♡ ❄

SERVES 4
- *15 ml (1 tbsp) olive oil*
- *75 g (3 oz) onion, peeled and diced*
- *75 g (3 oz) carrots, peeled and diced*
- *75 g (3 oz) celery, trimmed and diced*
- *1 garlic clove, peeled and crushed*
- *two 400 g (14 oz) cans chopped tomatoes*
- *30 ml (2 tbsp) tomato purée*

150 CALS/SERVING OF SAUCE (WITHOUT PASTA)
- *150 ml (5 fl oz) light stock*
- *125 ml (4 fl oz) red wine*
- *salt and pepper*
- *50 g (2 oz) sun-dried tomatoes, in olive oil, drained and finely chopped*
- *freshly pared Parmesan cheese, to serve*

1 Heat the olive oil in a large saucepan. Add the diced vegetables and garlic. Cook, stirring continuously, for 5 minutes or until beginning to soften but not colour.
2 Stir in the canned tomatoes, tomato purée, stock, wine and seasoning. Simmer, covered, for about 30 minutes, stirring occasionally. Purée in a food processor, then stir in the sun-dried tomatoes.
3 Adjust the seasoning and reheat to serve before tossing into hot pasta. Top with Parmesan.

## PASTA PRIMAVERA

PREPARATION TIME 15 minutes
COOKING TIME 35-40 minutes
FREEZING Not suitable
COLOUR INDEX Page 35

SERVES 4-6
- *175 g (6 oz) fine asparagus*
- *125 g (4 oz) sugar snap peas, topped and tailed*
- *1 red pepper*
- *50 g (2 oz) butter*
- *1 small onion, peeled and chopped*
- *2 celery stalks, diced*
- *2 courgettes, diced*
- *225 g (8 oz) baby carrots*
- *6-8 spring onions, white parts only, diced*
- *400 g (14 oz) dried tagliatelle*

950-635 CALS/SERVING
- *300 ml (10 fl oz) double cream*
- *60 ml (4 tbsp) freshly grated Parmesan cheese*
- *salt and pepper*
- *15 ml (1 tbsp) vegetable oil*
- *20 ml (4 tsp) snipped chives*
- *20 ml (4 tsp) chopped fresh chervil*
- *20 ml (4 tsp) chopped fresh dill*

1 Halve the asparagus spears and cook in boiling salted water for 3-4 minutes, adding the sugar snaps after 2 minutes so that both are cooked until just tender. Drain and refresh with cold water, then drain again; set aside.
2 Using a potato peeler, thinly pare the skin from the red pepper and discard, along with the core and seeds. Dice the red pepper.
3 Melt the butter in a large frying pan. Add the onion and sauté for 7-8 minutes until soft and golden. Add the red pepper and celery and cook for 5 minutes. Stir in the courgettes, carrots and spring onions and cook for 12-15 minutes, stirring frequently, until the vegetables are tender and beginning to colour.
4 Cook the pasta in boiling salted water until just tender *(al dente)*.
5 Meanwhile, stir the cream into the vegetables and bring to a gentle boil. Allow to bubble, stirring frequently, for a few minutes until it reduces by about one third. Stir in the asparagus and sugar snaps. Add the Parmesan and heat gently. Season to taste.
6 Drain the pasta thoroughly, toss with the oil and pour the sauce over. Sprinkle with the herbs, toss well and serve at once.

## JAPANESE NOODLES WITH PAK CHOI AND MOOLI

PREPARATION TIME 15 minutes
COOKING TIME 30 minutes
FREEZING Not suitable
♡

**SERVES 4**
- *125 g (4 oz) flat rice or egg noodles*
- *30 ml (2 tbsp) sunflower oil*
- *1 garlic clove, peeled and sliced*
- *5 ml (1 tsp) freshly grated root ginger*
- *pinch of sugar*
- *3 pak choi, about 350 g (12 oz) total weight, roughly chopped*
- *1.1 litres (2 pints) vegetable stock*

**215 CALS/SERVING**
- *30 ml (2 tbsp) miso*
- *15 ml (1 tbsp) lemon juice*
- *15 ml (1 tbsp) light soy sauce*
- *125 g (4 oz) mooli, sliced*
- *1 packet mustard and cress, cut*
- *15 ml (1 tbsp) chopped fresh coriander*

**1** Cook the noodles according to the packet instructions. Drain, refresh under cold water and drain again. Set aside.
**2** Heat the oil in a saucepan and fry the garlic, ginger and sugar over a low heat for 2 minutes. Add the pak choi, in a single layer if possible, cover and cook over a low heat for 5 minutes. Add the stock, miso, lemon juice, soy sauce and mooli, bring to the boil, cover and simmer for 15 minutes.
**3** Stir in the noodles, mustard and cress and coriander. Heat through for 1 minute and serve at once.

**NOTE** Miso is a thick paste made from fermented soya beans and is fermented together with either barley or rice. It is used to flavour soups, sauces, stews etc. Miso is available from good health food stores.

**VARIATION** Use another Chinese cabbage in place of pak choi. Mooli (related to the radish) is a popular Japanese ingredient and gives this dish a distinctive oriental flavour, but if it is unavailable use thinly sliced turnip instead.

# PUMPKIN RAVIOLI WITH HERBS

PREPARATION TIME About 45 minutes
COOKING TIME 1¼ hours
FREEZING Suitable (stage 4)
COLOUR INDEX Page 34

❄

SERVES 4        490 CALS/SERVING
- *200 g (7 oz) '00' pasta flour*
- *2 eggs (size 3)*
FILLING
- *450 g (1 lb) wedge pumpkin*
- *30 ml (2 tbsp) olive oil*
- *75 g (3 oz) prosciutto or Parma ham, finely chopped*
- *50 g (2 oz) Parmesan cheese, finely grated*

- *20 ml (1½ tbsp) chopped fresh basil*
- *20 ml (1½ tbsp) chopped fresh parsley*
- *1 egg yolk*
- *freshly grated nutmeg, to taste*
- *30 ml (2 tbsp) double cream*
- *salt and pepper*
- *melted butter and chopped fresh herbs, to serve*

1 Brush the pumpkin flesh with the oil and bake in the oven at 190°C (375°F) mark 5 for about 1 hour until soft. Scrape out the flesh and mash until smooth. Add all the other filling ingredients.
2 To make the pasta, heap the flour on a work surface and make a well in the centre. Break the eggs into the well and work the flour into the eggs with your fingers to form a dough. Knead lightly for about 5 minutes. Wrap in clingfilm and leave to rest for 15 minutes.
3 Roll out the pasta dough as thinly as possible on an unfloured surface. Keep covered with clingfilm to prevent drying out.
4 Take a strip of pasta 10-12 cm (4-5 inches) wide. Spoon on heaped teaspoonfuls of stuffing at 6 cm (2½ inch) intervals. Brush the edges and between the stuffing with a little water. Cover with another sheet of pasta and press along the edges and between the stuffing to seal. Cut between the stuffing at 6 cm (2½ inch) intervals and cut neatly along the long edges. Repeat to use all of the pasta and stuffing, to make 20-24 ravioli.
5 Cook the ravioli in batches in boiling water for about 3 minutes until the sealed edges are just tender (*al dente*). Drain and serve tossed in melted butter and chopped herbs.

# CALABRIAN PASTA

PREPARATION TIME 10 minutes
COOKING TIME 12-15 minutes
FREEZING Not suitable
COLOUR INDEX Page 35

🕐

SERVES 4-6        695-465 CALS/SERVING
- *50 g (2 oz) sultanas*
- *150 g (5 oz) broccoli, cut into small florets*
- *300-350 g (10-12 oz) long fusilli or spaghetti*
- *salt and pepper*
- *125 ml (4 fl oz) olive oil*
- *75 g (3 oz) white breadcrumbs*

- *2 garlic cloves, peeled and finely chopped*
- *25 g (1 oz) pine nuts*
- *10 ml (2 tsp) anchovy essence or anchovy paste*
- *45 ml (3 tbsp) chopped fresh parsley*
- *cayenne pepper, to taste*

1 Bring about 600 ml (1 pint) water to the boil. Put the sultanas in a bowl, pour on a little of the boiling water and leave to soak. Pour the rest of the boiling water over the broccoli in a pan and simmer for 30 seconds; drain.
2 Cook the pasta in a large pan of boiling salted water until just tender (*al dente*).
3 Meanwhile, heat the oil in a frying pan and add the breadcrumbs. Fry, stirring, until they begin to crisp, then add the garlic and pine nuts. Continue to fry, stirring until the pine nuts begin to colour, then add the broccoli to heat through.
4 Drain the pasta, setting it back on top of the saucepan to catch the last 15 ml (1 tbsp) cooking water. Stir the anchovy essence or paste and drained sultanas into this liquid, then return the pasta to the pan. Toss with a generous grinding of black pepper and half of the chopped parsley. Transfer to a heated serving bowl.
5 Mix the remaining parsley into the crumb mixture and sprinkle over the pasta. Sprinkle with cayenne pepper and toss at the table.

*TIP*
It's an Italian trick to toss the pasta with a little of its cooking water. This helps to keep the pasta hot, as well as preventing it from drying out before serving.

# PASTA WITH GRILLED ASPARAGUS AND BROAD BEANS

PREPARATION TIME 20 minutes
COOKING TIME 12-15 minutes
FREEZING Not suitable

**SERVES 4**                    **665 CALS/SERVING**

- *225 g (8 oz) shelled broad beans*
- *salt and pepper*
- *350 g (12 oz) dried pasta*
- *450 g (1 lb) asparagus, trimmed and halved crossways*
- *90 ml (6 tbsp) extra-virgin olive oil*
- *2 garlic cloves, peeled and crushed*
- *grated rind and juice of 1 lemon*
- *45 ml (3 tbsp) chopped fresh mint*
- *60 ml (4 tbsp) single cream*
- *60 ml (4 tbsp) grated Pecorino or Parmesan cheese*

1 Blanch the beans in a large saucepan of lightly salted water for 2 minutes, then strain the water into a clean pan and reserve. Refresh the beans under cold running water and carefully remove the hard outer skin. Reserve the beans.
2 Return the bean water to a rolling boil, add the pasta, return to the boil and cook for 10 minutes until just tender (*al dente*).
3 Meanwhile, place the asparagus on the grill pan, brush with a little oil and grill for 3-4 minutes on each side until charred and tender.
4 While the asparagus is cooking, heat 30 ml (2 tbsp) of the oil in a pan, add the garlic and lemon rind and fry gently for 3 minutes until almost golden. Add the beans, mint and cream and heat gently.
5 Drain the pasta and immediately toss with the remaining oil, transfer to a warmed bowl and stir in the asparagus and the bean sauce. Stir in the cheese and lemon juice, then season to taste. Serve at once.

**VARIATION** Fresh peas also combine well with asparagus and mint and can be used instead of the broad beans if wished.

# VEGETARIAN DISHES

# STUFFED PEPPERS WITH PINE NUTS

PREPARATION TIME 20 minutes
COOKING TIME 30-35 minutes
FREEZING Not suitable
COLOUR INDEX Page 37

♡

### SERVES 4
- *2 large orange or red peppers*
- *2 large yellow peppers*
  FILLING
- *45 ml (3 tbsp) extra-virgin olive oil*
- *1 large onion, peeled and finely chopped*
- *2-3 garlic cloves, peeled and finely chopped*
- *450 g (1 lb) tomatoes, skinned and roughly chopped*
- *30 ml (2 tbsp) tomato purée*

### 315 CALS SERVING
- *5 ml (1 tsp) light muscovado sugar*
- *salt and pepper*
- *50 g (2 oz) mushrooms, thickly sliced*
- *50 g (2 oz) pine nuts*
- *15 ml (1 tbsp) fresh marjoram leaves, roughly torn*
- *50 g (2 oz) black olives*
- *25-50 g (1-2 oz) freshly grated Parmesan cheese*

1 Halve the peppers lengthways, then remove the core and seeds. Place cut-side down on a baking sheet and roast at 200°C (400°F) mark 6 for 15 minutes, turning frequently.
2 Meanwhile, make the sauce. Heat 30 ml (2 tbsp) oil in a saucepan, add the onion and garlic and fry gently until softened and lightly coloured. Add the tomatoes, tomato purée, sugar, salt and pepper. Cook, uncovered, for 15-20 minutes until reduced to a thick sauce. Check the seasoning.
3 Heat the remaining 15 ml (1 tbsp) oil in a pan and sauté the mushroom slices until softened.
4 Place the peppers, cut-side up, in an ovenproof dish. Transfer two thirds of the tomato mixture to a bowl and stir in the mushrooms, nuts, marjoram and olives. Fill the peppers with the mixture and top with the grated Parmesan cheese. Bake in the oven for 15-20 minutes until thoroughly heated through.

**NOTE** Use any remaining sauce to make a tasty accompaniment. Spread thick slices of crusty bread with the tomato mixture and sprinkle with sesame seeds. Warm through in the oven.

# VEGETABLE PITHIVIER

PREPARATION TIME 1 hour, plus cooling
COOKING TIME About 1½ hours
FREEZING Not suitable
COLOUR INDEX Page 36

### SERVES 6
- *4 red peppers*
- *50 g (2 oz) butter*
- *125 g (4 oz) shallots, peeled and finely diced*
- *125 g (4 oz) mushrooms, sliced*
- *75 ml (3 fl oz) double cream or crème fraîche*
- *15 ml (1 tbsp) freshly grated Parmesan cheese*

### 585 CALS/SERVING
- *225 g (8 oz) ricotta cheese*
- *salt and pepper*
- *125 g (4 oz) goats' cheese*
- *450 g (1 lb) fresh spinach, washed*
- *freshly grated nutmeg*
- *450 g (1 lb) Puff Pastry (see page 370)*
- *1 egg, beaten*

1 Roast the peppers in the oven at 200°C (400°F) mark 6 for 30-40 minutes. Remove their skins and slice the flesh into strips.
2 Meanwhile, melt 40 g (1½ oz) of the butter in a frying pan, add the shallots and sauté until soft. Add the mushrooms to the pan and cook until the liquid has evaporated. Pour in the cream and allow to bubble until the mushrooms are just coated in the cream. Cool. Stir in the Parmesan and half the ricotta. Add salt and pepper.
3 Crumble the rest of the ricotta and the goats' cheese. Set aside.
4 Melt the remaining butter in a large saucepan. Add the spinach and sauté until the leaves wilt. Drain and press out any excess moisture; roughly chop. Season with salt, pepper and nutmeg.
5 Roll out 175 g (6 oz) of the pastry into a rectangle 15 x 30 cm (6 x 12 inch). Place on a baking sheet, prick with a fork and bake at 200°C (400°F) mark 6 for about 15 minutes. Cool.
6 Place the cooked pastry on a baking sheet. Top with the pepper strips, crumbled ricotta, goat's cheese then the spinach, making an indentation along the centre. Fill with the mushroom mixture.
7 Thinly roll out 225 g (8 oz) pastry, large enough to wrap around the filling with some to tuck under the base. Brush with egg. Use the remaining pastry and trimmings for a lattice pattern over the top. Glaze with egg and chill until ready to cook.
8 Bake at 220°C (425°F) mark 7 for about 35-40 minutes.

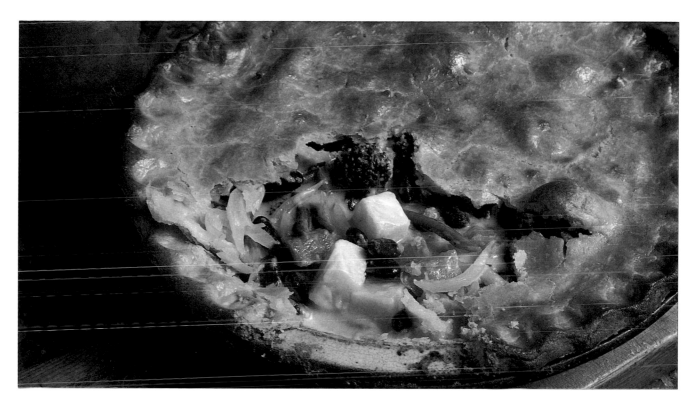

## VEGETABLE CHEESE PIE WITH POTATO CRUST

PREPARATION TIME 55 minutes, plus cooling
COOKING TIME 1 hour 10 minutes
FREEZING Suitable

❄

**SERVES 4**

- *225 g (8 oz) white plain flour*
- *salt and pepper*
- *100 g (3½ oz) butter, diced*
- *175 g (6 oz) mashed potato*

*FILLING*

- *25 g (1 oz) butter*
- *2 large onions, peeled and sliced*
- *4 garlic cloves, peeled and crushed*
- *350 g (12 oz) celeriac, peeled and cut into chunks*
- *50 g (2 oz) white plain flour*
- *300 ml (10 fl oz) vegetable stock*

**645 CALS/SERVING**

- *300 ml (10 fl oz) milk*
- *175 g (6 oz) broccoli, cut into small florets*
- *125 g (4 oz) French beans, trimmed and cut into 2.5 cm (1 inch) lengths*
- *2 large carrots, peeled and cut into chunks*
- *grated nutmeg*
- *400 g (14 oz) can pinto or red kidney beans, drained*
- *225 g (8 oz) Cheddar cheese, grated*
- *egg yolk, to glaze*

**1** To make the pastry, sift the flour and salt into a bowl. Add the butter, and rub in with the fingertips. Add the mashed potato and about 20-25 ml (4-5 tsp) cold water. Mix to a firm dough and knead lightly. Chill while making the filling.
**2** To make the filling, melt the butter in a large saucepan. Add the onions and garlic and fry gently for 5 minutes. Add the celeriac and fry for a further 10 minutes. Stir in the flour and cook for 1 minute. Gradually stir in the stock and milk and bring just to the boil, stirring.
**3** Add the broccoli, French beans and carrots. Season with nutmeg and salt and pepper. Cover and cook gently for 15 minutes. Cool slightly, then stir in the canned beans and cheese. Turn the filling into a pie dish.
**4** Roll out the pastry on a lightly floured surface until 5 cm (2 inches) larger than the diameter of the dish. Cut off a 2.5 cm (1 inch) strip of pastry from around the edges.
**5** Moisten the rim of the pie dish with water and position the strip on the rim. Dampen the pastry strip and position the pastry lid, pressing the edges firmly together to seal. Flute the edge and make a hole in the top of the pie to allow the steam to escape. If wished, decorate with pastry trimmings.
**6** Brush the pie with beaten egg to glaze and sprinkle with a little nutmeg. Bake at 200°C (400°F) mark 6 for 30-35 minutes until the pastry is golden.

# VEGETABLES AND SALADS

## RED CABBAGE WITH PINE NUTS

PREPARATION TIME 10 minutes
COOKING TIME About 25 minutes
FREEZING Not suitable

♡

**SERVES 8**

- *25 ml (1 fl oz) olive oil*
- *900 g (2 lb) red cabbage, finely shredded*
- *2.5 cm (1 inch) piece fresh root ginger, peeled and grated (optional)*
- *150 ml (5 fl oz) light stock*

**135 CALS/SERVING**

- *salt and pepper*
- *40 g (1½ oz) butter*
- *30 ml (2 tbsp) balsamic vinegar or red wine vinegar plus 10 ml (2 tsp) muscovado sugar*
- *50 g (2 oz) toasted pine nuts*

**1** Heat the oil in a large saucepan and sauté the cabbage with the ginger, if using, over a high heat for 3-4 minutes or until reduced in bulk, stirring occasionally.

**2** Add the stock and seasoning, bring to the boil, then cover and cook over a low heat for about 20 minutes. Stir occasionally.

**3** When the cabbage is just tender, uncover and bubble down any excess liquid. Off the heat, stir in the butter, balsamic vinegar and pine nuts. Adjust the seasoning and serve.

## CITRUS LEEKS WITH SUGAR SNAP PEAS

PREPARATION TIME 15 minutes
COOKING TIME 10-15 minutes
FREEZING Not suitable
COLOUR INDEX Page 39

♡ 🕐

**SERVES 6**

- *20-30 ml (1½-2 tbsp) olive oil*
- *700 g (1½ lb) trimmed leeks, cut into 1 cm (½ inch) slices*
- *450 g (1 lb) sugar snap peas or mangetouts, topped and tailed*
- *salt and pepper*
*DRESSING*
- *45 ml (3 tbsp) olive oil*

**150 CALS/SERVING**

- *15 ml (1 tbsp) balsamic vinegar*
- *2.5 ml (½ tsp) soft light brown sugar*
- *10-15 ml (2-3 tsp) lemon juice*
- *2.5 ml (½ tsp) Dijon mustard*
- *grated rind and juice of ½ orange*

1 Heat the oil in a large sauté pan. Add the leeks and sauté gently for 5-6 minutes or until just tender. Cook the sugar snap peas in boiling salted water for 5 minutes. Drain, then mix with the leeks.
2 Mix together all the dressing ingredients and season with salt and pepper to taste. Stir into the hot vegetables and serve at once.

---

### TIP
This dish can also be served cold as a tangy salad accompaniment to cold turkey.

---

## CHESTNUT AND SPROUT SAUTE

PREPARATION TIME 15-25 minutes
COOKING TIMF 15-45 minutes
FREEZING Not suitable

**SERVES 8**

- *900 g (2 lb) fresh chestnuts or 875 g (1 lb 15 oz) can whole chestnuts*
- *600 ml (1 pint) chicken stock*
- *900 g (2 lb) Brussels sprouts, trimmed*
- *salt and pepper*

**350 CALS/SERVING**

- *450 g (1 lb) onions*
- *125 g (4 oz) butter*
- *225 g (8 oz) celery, cut into 2.5 cm (1 inch) pieces*
- *grated rind of 1 lemon*
- *chopped fresh parsley, to garnish*

1 If using fresh chestnuts, nick the brown outer skins with a sharp knife. Cook in boiling water for 10 minutes. Drain, cool and peel off the shells and inner skins. Cover with the stock and simmer for 20 minutes or until tender. Drain the chestnuts well.
2 Cook the sprouts in boiling, salted water for 3-4 minutes only, then drain well. Peel the onions, then quarter them and separate the layers.
3 Melt the butter in a large sauté or frying pan. Sauté the celery and onions with the lemon rind until beginning to soften.
4 Add the cooked chestnuts, Brussels sprouts and seasoning. Sauté over a high heat for a further 2-3 minutes or until piping hot, stirring frequently. Cover and keep warm until ready to serve, then sprinkle with chopped parsley to garnish.

## SWEET AND HOT GREEN BEANS WITH PEANUTS

PREPARATION TIME 15 minutes
COOKING TIME About 10 minutes
FREEZING Not suitable
♡ ⏲

SERVES 4-6
- *450 g (1 lb) French beans, topped*
- *30 ml (2 tbsp) vegetable oil*
- *1 onion, peeled, halved and cut into thin slivers*
- *6 dried red chillies, finely chopped*

200-135 CALS/SERVING
- *2 garlic cloves, peeled and crushed*
- *15 ml (1 tbsp) dark soy sauce*
- *30 ml (2 tbsp) clear honey*
- *50 g (2 oz) unsalted roasted peanuts*

1 Blanch the beans in a pan of boiling water for 2 minutes. Drain and refresh the beans under cold water, then drain well again.
2 Heat the oil in a wok or large frying pan, add the beans, onion, chillies and garlic and stir-fry for 2 minutes. Add the soy sauce and the honey, reduce the heat, cover and cook for 3 minutes.
3 Uncover and cook until the liquid thickens, turning the beans to coat them in the honey and soy mixture. Sprinkle with the nuts and serve.

## SPICY MUSHROOMS

PREPARATION TIME 10 minutes
COOKING TIME 45 minutes
FREEZING Not suitable
COLOUR INDEX Page 39
♡

SERVES 6
- *oil for frying*
- *1 large aubergine, about 350 g (12 oz), cut into chunks*
- *3 garlic cloves, peeled and crushed*
- *2 large onions, about 450 g (1 lb), peeled and finely sliced*
- *5 cm (2 inch) piece fresh root ginger, peeled and coarsely grated*
- *10 ml (2 tsp) hot chilli powder*

180 CALS/SERVING
- *5 ml (1 tsp) turmeric*
- *5 ml (1 tsp) garam masala*
- *5 ml (1 tsp) cumin*
- *two 400 g (14 oz) cans chopped tomatoes*
- *salt and pepper*
- *350 g (12 oz) button mushrooms, halved*
- *225 g (8 oz) frozen peas*

1 Heat about 60 ml (4 tbsp) oil in a large, non-stick frying pan. Fry the aubergine pieces until golden brown, adding more oil if necessary. Remove the aubergine from the pan and drain on absorbent kitchen paper. Add a little more oil to the pan if necessary then add the garlic, onions and ginger. Cook until golden, stirring occasionally. Mix in the spices and cook for 1 minute, stirring all the time.
2 Return the aubergine to the pan with the tomatoes. Adjust the seasoning then bring to the boil, cover and simmer for about 20 minutes or until the aubergines are tender.
3 Stir in the mushrooms and frozen peas and cook for about a further 10 minutes, adding a little water if necessary to thin down slightly. Transfer to a heated serving dish.

*TIP*
Hot chilli powder is a blend of chilli, cumin, salt, garlic and oregano. It can be found on the spice racks in supermarkets. Don't be tempted to use pure ground chillies as they are too hot for this recipe.

## BROAD BEANS IN HERBED LEMON CREAM

PREPARATION TIME 20 minutes
COOKING TIME About 20 minutes
FREEZING Not suitable

**SERVES 4-6**

- *50 g (2 oz) butter*
- *2 garlic cloves, peeled and chopped*
- *4 shallots, peeled and finely chopped*
- *450 g (1 lb) fresh baby broad beans, shelled*
- *150 ml (5 fl oz) vegetable stock*
- *200 ml (7 fl oz) double cream*

**385-260 CALS/SERVING**

- *30 ml (2 tbsp) chopped fresh chervil or chives*
- *30 ml (2 tbsp) chopped fresh parsley*
- *grated rind of 1 lemon*
- *salt and pepper*

**1** Melt the butter in a saucepan, add the garlic and shallots and cook gently for 3 minutes. Stir in the beans and stock. Bring to the boil, cover and simmer gently for 12-15 minutes, until the beans are tender.
**2** Strain, reserving the liquid. Place the cooking liquid in a blender or food processor with 90 ml (4 tbsp) beans and blend to a purée, gradually adding the cream to make a smooth sauce.
**3** Return the mixture to the pan. Add the beans, herbs and lemon rind and season with salt and pepper to taste. Reheat gently and serve hot.

**VARIATION** Omit the lemon rind and sprinkle with crisp, crumbled bacon just before serving.

> *TIP*
> Tender, fresh baby broad beans are best for this dish, or use frozen baby beans and skin them, if necessary, before cooking.

## MARROW WITH TOMATO AND ONION

PREPARATION TIME 20 minutes
COOKING TIME 30 minutes
FREEZING Not suitable
♡

SERVES 4-6
- *1 marrow*
- *25 g (1 oz) butter or margarine*
- *2 onions, peeled and chopped*
- *1 garlic clove, peeled and crushed*
- *6 large tomatoes, skinned and chopped*

100-65 CALS/SERVING
- *30 ml (2 tbsp) tomato purée*
- *30 ml (2 tbsp) chopped mixed herbs or 10 ml (2 tsp) dried*
- *salt and pepper*
- *parsley sprigs, to garnish*

1 Peel the marrow, cut in half lengthways and scoop out the seeds. Cut the flesh into 2.5 cm (1 inch) cubes.
2 Melt the butter in a large saucepan and gently fry the onions and garlic for 5 minutes, until soft. Add the marrow and cook for a further 5 minutes.
3 Stir in the tomatoes, tomato purée and herbs. Cover and simmer for 20 minutes, until the vegetables are tender. Season to taste. Serve at once, garnished with parsley.

## MIXED ONION CASSEROLE WITH JUNIPER

PREPARATION TIME 15 minutes
COOKING TIME 1¾ hours
FREEZING Not suitable
COLOUR INDEX Page 40

SERVES 4
- *6 onions*
- *1 bunch of spring onions*
- *8 juniper berries*
- *50 g (2 oz) butter*
- *5 garlic cloves, peeled and finely sliced*
- *approximately 600 ml (1 pint) vegetable stock*
- *coarse sea salt and pepper*

460 CALS/SERVING
- *6-8 shallots, peeled*
- *6 slices French bread, 1 cm (¹/₂ inch) thick*
- *125 g (4 oz) coarsely grated vegetarian mature Cheddar cheese*
- *15 ml (1 tbsp) snipped chives, to garnish*

1 Peel four of the onions, taking care to trim the minimum from the tops and bases. Cut each one crosswise into quarters, leaving the root end intact to ensure the onions do not fall apart during cooking.
2 Peel, halve and slice the remaining two ordinary onions. Trim the spring onions, then slice both the white and green parts. Crush the juniper berries, using a pestle and mortar.
3 Melt the butter in a saucepan, add the sliced ordinary onions, garlic and juniper berries and fry gently until golden. Add 300 ml (10 fl oz) of the vegetable stock and bring to the boil. Season with salt and pepper.
4 Stand the quarter-cut onions upright in a 1.2 litre (2 pint) casserole and add the shallots and sliced spring onions. Spoon the sautéed onion and garlic mixture on top. Cook, uncovered, in the oven at 180°C (350°F) mark 4 for 1½ hours, checking occasionally that the liquid hasn't dried out. Top up with more stock as necessary. At the end of the cooking time the liquid should be thick and syrupy.
5 About 15 minutes before the end of the cooking time, butter the slices of French bread and arrange butter-side up on top of the onion mixture. Sprinkle with the grated cheese and return to the oven to crisp and brown. (If, by the end of the cooking time, the cheese has not browned, flash

the dish under a hot grill for 1-2 minutes.) Sprinkle with the snipped chives to garnish and serve immediately, directly from the casserole.

**NOTE** The temperature isn't crucial for this dish, so if you are cooking a main course at a higher temperature, simply position the casserole lower in the oven.

## SPICED PUMPKIN FRITTERS

PREPARATION TIME 15 minutes
COOKING TIME About 15 minutes
FREEZING Not suitable

**SERVES 4**

- *700 g (1½ lb) pumpkin flesh, deseeded*
- *175 g (6 oz) wholemeal plain flour*
- *2.5-5 ml (½-1 tsp) salt*
- *1.25 ml (¼ tsp) baking powder*
- *5 ml (1 tsp) cumin seeds*
- *2.5 ml (½ tsp) ground cumin*
- *1 egg, separated*

**355 CALS/SERVING**

- *1 small onion, peeled and finely chopped*
- *1-2 garlic cloves, peeled and crushed*
- *7.5 ml (1½ tsp) chilli sauce*
- *30 ml (2 tbsp) chopped fresh coriander*
- *vegetable oil for frying*
- *coarse salt, to serve*

**1** Cut the pumpkin flesh into thick slices about 10 cm (5 inches) long and 1 cm (½ inch) wide. Steam for 8-10 minutes or until only just tender. Remove from the steamer and cool.

**2** Place the flour, salt, baking powder, cumin seeds and ground cumin in a bowl and mix well. Make a well in the centre, add the egg yolk and gradually stir in 175 ml (6 fl oz) water to form a smooth batter, adding a little extra if necessary. Stir in the onion, garlic, chilli sauce and chopped coriander. Stiffly whisk the egg white and fold lightly into the batter.

**3** One-third fill a deep-fat fryer with oil and heat to 180°C (350°F) or until hot enough to brown a cube of bread in 30 seconds. Using two forks, dip a few slices of pumpkin into the batter to coat evenly and place in the hot oil. Fry for 1-1½ minutes, turning frequently, until the fritters are crisp, golden brown and cooked through.

**4** Drain on crumpled absorbent kitchen paper and keep warm while cooking the remaining pumpkin in the same way. Serve hot, sprinkled with coarse salt.

**VARIATION** Button mushrooms are also extremely good cooked this way.

**NOTE** This is an excellent way of using up the flesh scooped out of a pumpkin lantern.

## SQUASH WITH NUTTY GINGERED CRUMBS

PREPARATION TIME 15 minutes
COOKING TIME 15 minutes
FREEZING Not suitable

SERVES 4

- *1.4 kg (3 lb) butternut squash, peeled and cut into large chunks*
- *125 g (4 oz) butter*
- *125 g (4 oz) fresh breadcrumbs*
- *5 cm (2 inch) piece fresh root ginger, peeled and chopped*

550 CALS/SERVING

- *2 garlic cloves, peeled and crushed*
- *50 g (2 oz) pine nuts*
- *60 ml (4 tbsp) chopped fresh parsley*
- *salt and pepper*

1 Boil the squash pieces in water until just tender. Drain well and keep warm.
2 Meanwhile, heat the butter in a frying pan, add the breadcrumbs with the ginger, garlic and pine nuts and fry for about 5 minutes until golden. Add the parsley and season to taste. Stir the breadcrumb mixture into the squash and serve.

## PARSNIP AND CARROT AU GRATIN

PREPARATION TIME 15 minutes
COOKING TIME 25 minutes
FREEZING Not suitable
COLOUR INDEX Page 40
♡

SERVES 4-6

- *450 g (1 lb) parsnips, peeled and coarsely chopped*
- *450 g (1 lb) carrots, peeled and coarsely chopped*
- *600 ml (1 pint) chicken stock*

195-130 CALS/SERVING

- *salt and pepper*
- *25 g (1 oz) butter*
- *50 g (2 oz) fresh breadcrumbs*
- *chopped fresh parsley, to garnish*

1 Put the parsnips and carrots in a saucepan with the stock and season with salt and pepper to taste. Bring to the boil, cover and simmer the vegetables gently for 15-20 minutes until they are well cooked. Drain and cool slightly.
2 Purée the vegetables in a blender or rub through a sieve. Add the butter and place in a flameproof dish. Sprinkle the breadcrumbs over the surface and cook under a hot grill until the top turns golden brown. Garnish with parsley.

# CAULIFLOWER IN CURRY SAUCE

PREPARATION TIME 15 minutes
COOKING TIME About 20 minutes
FREEZING Not suitable
COLOUR INDEX Page 39

**SERVES 4**
- *1 large cauliflower*
- *90 ml (6 tbsp) ghee or vegetable oil*
- *5 ml (1 tsp) black mustard seeds*
- *5 ml (1 tsp) cumin seeds*
- *2.5 cm (1 inch) piece fresh root ginger, peeled and finely chopped*
- *1 small onion, peeled and finely chopped*
- *5 ml (1 tsp) salt*

**260 CALS/SERVING**
- *5 ml (1 tsp) ground turmeric*
- *3 tomatoes, skinned and finely chopped*
- *1 small green chilli, deseeded and finely chopped*
- *2.5 ml (½ tsp) sugar*
- *30 ml (2 tbsp) chopped fresh coriander*

1 Divide the cauliflower into small florets, discarding the green leaves and tough stalks. Wash well and dry on absorbent kitchen paper.
2 Heat the ghee or oil in a heavy-based saucepan or flameproof casserole. Add the mustard seeds and, when they begin to pop, stir in the cumin seeds, ginger, onion, salt and turmeric. Fry for 2-3 minutes, stirring constantly.
3 Add the cauliflower and mix well to coat with the spice mixture. Stir in the tomatoes, chopped green chilli, sugar and half of the chopped coriander. Cover the pan tightly with a lid and cook gently for 15 minutes or until the cauliflower is tender but not mushy.
4 Uncover the pan and boil rapidly for 1-2 minutes to thicken the sauce. Transfer to a warmed serving dish and sprinkle with the remaining chopped coriander. Serve immediately.

**NOTE** This spicy dish makes an excellent addition to an Indian meal. Alternatively serve on its own accompanied by chapatis, as a quick and tasty supper dish.

# SWEDE AND ORANGE PUREE

PREPARATION TIME 15 minutes
COOKING TIME 30 minutes
FREEZING Suitable (stage 2)

**SERVES 4**
- *1.1 kg (2½ lb) swede, peeled and sliced quite thinly*
- *salt and pepper*
- *25 g (1 oz) butter or margarine*
- *finely grated rind of 1 orange*

**100 CALS/SERVING**
- *30 ml (2 tbsp) orange juice*
- *45 ml (3 tbsp) soured cream*
- *parsley, to garnish*

1 Put the swede into a saucepan, cover with cold salted water and bring to the boil. Cook for about 20 minutes, until quite tender. Allow to drain thoroughly in a colander for several minutes.
2 Mash the swede, then add the butter, seasoning and grated orange rind. Stir over a moderate heat for several minutes until thoroughly hot and all excess moisture has been driven off.
3 Stir in the orange juice and the soured cream. Reheat gently, stirring all the time to prevent the purée sticking to the pan. Sprinkle with pepper and garnish with parsley.

## AROMATIC SWEDE AND CARROTS

PREPARATION TIME 20 minutes
COOKING TIME 15 minutes
FREEZING Not suitable
COLOUR INDEX Page 40

♡

SERVES 4     105 CALS/SERVING

- *450 g (1 lb) swede, peeled and diced*
- *450 g (1 lb) carrots, peeled and thinly sliced*
- *salt and pepper*
- *25 g (1 oz) butter*
- *5 ml (1 tsp) black mustard seeds*
- *2 pieces preserved stem ginger in syrup, drained*
- *parsley or chervil sprigs, to garnish*

1 Cook the vegetables separately in boiling salted water until tender.
2 Meanwhile, melt the butter in a small heavy-based saucepan. Add the mustard seeds and heat gently until the seeds begin to pop. Add the chopped ginger and cook for 1 minute over a low heat.
3 Drain the cooked swede and carrots thoroughly, then mash together using a potato masher or vegetable mill. Season generously with pepper and stir in half of the mustard and ginger mixture.
4 Transfer the mashed swede and carrots to a warmed serving dish and drizzle the remaining mustard and ginger mixture over the top. Garnish with parsley or chervil and serve at once.

## POTATO AND CELERIAC GALETTE

PREPARATION TIME 25 minutes
COOKING TIME 1¼ hours
FREEZING Not suitable
COLOUR INDEX Page 41

♡

SERVES 4     150 CALS/SERVING

- *450 g (1 lb) old potatoes, peeled*
- *450 g (1 lb) celeriac, peeled*
- *1 garlic clove, peeled and crushed*
- *freshly grated nutmeg*
- *salt and pepper*
- *25 g (1 oz) butter, melted*
- *chopped fresh parsley, to garnish*

1 Grease and base-line a 20 cm (8 inch) sandwich tin with non-stick baking parchment.
2 Very thinly slice the potatoes and celeriac, preferably in a food processor.
3 Layer up the vegetables with the garlic, nutmeg and seasoning, pressing down firmly as you go. Pour the melted butter over the vegetables.
4 Cover with foil and bake at 230°C (450°F) mark 8 for 1¼ hours or until the vegetables are quite tender. Test with a skewer.
5 Turn the galette out onto a serving plate and garnish with parsley.

## GOLDEN POTATOES

PREPARATION TIME 5 minutes
COOKING TIME 1½ hours
FREEZING Not suitable
COLOUR INDEX Page 41

SERVES 6     230 CALS/SERVING

- *1.1 kg (2½ lb) old potatoes*
- *salt and pepper*
- *2 sprigs rosemary*
- *6 garlic cloves (optional)*
- *45 ml (3 tbsp) olive oil*

1 Wash the potatoes and cut into large chunks, but do not peel. Place in cold, salted water, bring to the boil and simmer for 3 minutes. Drain the potatoes well. Strip the spiky rosemary leaves off the sprigs.
2 Place the potatoes in a roasting tin with the unpeeled garlic cloves, if using, rosemary and olive oil.
3 Roast at 200°C (400°F) mark 6 for 1½ hours.

## PARSNIPS IN A LIME GLAZE

PREPARATION TIME 5 minutes
COOKING TIME 17 minutes
FREEZING Not suitable

⏱

SERVES 4

- *700 g (1½ lb) parsnips, peeled*
- *salt and pepper*
- *1 lime*
- *50 g (2 oz) butter*

225 CALS/SERVING

- *25 g (1 oz) light muscovado sugar*
- *thyme sprigs, to garnish*

**1** Cut the parsnips in half lengthways. (If using older, tougher parsnips, cut into quarters and remove the woody cores.) Add to a pan of boiling salted water and cook for 5 minutes.
**2** Meanwhile, using a vegetable peeler, pare thin slivers of rind from the lime, then set aside for the garnish. Halve the lime and squeeze out the juice.
**3** Melt the butter in a large saucepan together with the sugar. Add the lime juice and heat gently,

stirring, to dissolve the sugar.
**4** Drain the parsnips, then add to the lime mixture in the pan. Toss in the buttery lime mixture and cook over a moderate heat, shaking the pan frequently, for about 10 minutes until golden brown.
**5** Transfer to a warmed serving dish and garnish with the slivers of lime rind and thyme sprigs.

**VARIATIONS** The sharp glaze can be used with any sweet root vegetable to excellent effect – try it with sweet potatoes or carrots. A handful of walnuts tossed in towards the end of the cooking time adds a delicious crunch.

## NEW POTATOES WITH CREAMY MINT BUTTER

PREPARATION TIME 5 minutes
COOKING TIME 15 minutes
FREEZING Not suitable

SERVES 4

240 CALS/SERVING

- *25 g (1 oz) butter, softened*
- *10 ml (2 tsp) chopped fresh mint*
- *575 g (1¼ lb) small new potatoes*
- *salt*

- *15 ml (1 tbsp) vegetable oil*
- *45 ml (3 tbsp) crème fraîche or double cream*
- *mint sprigs, to garnish*

1 Beat together the butter and mint. Spoon on to greaseproof paper and shape into a neat round. Chill.
2 Boil the potatoes in salted water until almost tender. Drain well.
3 Heat the oil in a large non-stick frying pan. Sauté the potatoes over a high heat until golden brown.
4 Lower the heat and add the crème fraîche and chilled mint butter. Garnish and serve immediately.

## SPRING GREEN SAUTE

PREPARATION TIME 5 minutes
COOKING TIME 5 minutes
FREEZING Not suitable
COLOUR INDEX Page 39
♡ ⏲

SERVES 6

90 CALS/SERVING

- *700 g (1½ lb) spring greens*
- *30 ml (2 tbsp) olive oil*
- *25 g (1 oz) butter*
- *1 garlic clove, peeled and crushed*

- *15 ml (1 tbsp) lemon juice*
- *salt and pepper*
- *toasted pine nuts, to garnish*

1 Coarsely shred the spring greens, discarding any thick stalks.
2 Heat the oil and butter in a large wok or sauté pan. Add the spring greens and garlic and stir-fry over a high heat for about 4-5 minutes until just tender. Add the lemon juice and season with salt and pepper.
3 Serve immediately, sprinkled with pine nuts.

## CRISPY CHINESE GREENS

PREPARATION TIME 15 minutes
COOKING TIME 2 minutes
FREEZING Not suitable
COLOUR INDEX Page 39
⏲

SERVES 4

540 CALS/SERVING

- *700 g (1½ lb) spring greens*
- *about 600 ml (1 pint) sunflower oil*
- *7.5 ml (1½ tsp) caster sugar*

- *salt*
- *25 g (1 oz) natural roasted peanuts, halved*

1 Discard the thick stems from the spring greens and wash the leaves. Dry thoroughly, then roll the leaves together tightly, a few at a time, and shred them very finely with a sharp knife. Spread out on absorbent kitchen paper and pat dry with more paper (the shreds must be completely dry before frying).
2 Heat the oil in a wok or large, deep pan until just smoking, then remove from the heat and add the spring greens. Stir well, return the pan to the

heat and fry for about 2 minutes, stirring.
3 Using a slotted spoon, carefully remove the
fried greens to a plate lined with absorbent
kitchen paper and drain for a few moments.
4 Turn the greens onto a warm plate and sprinkle
with the sugar, salt to taste and nuts.

**NOTE** These crispy-fried shreds of spring greens
make an excellent addition to a Chinese-style
meal. The dish is particularly good served as a
starter, accompanied by sesame prawn toasts and
a crisp dry white wine.

**VARIATION** Use cashew nuts or sunflower seeds
instead of the peanuts.

## CARROTS IN SPICED DRESSING

PREPARATION TIME 5 minutes
COOKING TIME 5-7 minutes
FREEZING Not suitable
♡ ⏱

SERVES 4
- *450 g (1 lb) young carrots, scrubbed*
- *salt and pepper*
- *50 g (2 oz) butter or margarine*
- *25 g (1 oz) flaked almonds*
- *5 ml (1 tsp) ground cumin*

170 CALS/SERVING
- *10 ml (2 tsp) ground coriander*
- *5 ml (1 tsp) honey*
- *30 ml (2 tbsp) roughly chopped chives*
- *5 ml (1 tsp) lemon juice*

1 Steam the carrots or cook in boiling salted
water for 4-5 minutes or until just tender. Drain.
2 Melt the butter or margarine in a large frying
pan and stir in the almonds and spices. Cook,
stirring, for 1-2 minutes or until the almonds are
golden brown. Toss in the carrots, honey, chives
and lemon juice. Stir over a high heat until well
mixed, then season and serve.

## OKRA WITH APRICOTS

PREPARATION TIME 10 minutes
COOKING TIME 35-40 minutes
FREEZING Not suitable
COLOUR INDEX Page 42

SERVES 4                                    250 CALS/SERVING
- *450 g (1 lb) small okra*
- *juice of ½ orange*
- *60 ml (4 tbsp) olive oil*
- *1 onion, peeled and thinly sliced*
- *400 g (14 oz) can tomatoes*
- *30 ml (2 tbsp) tomato purée*
- *125 g (4 oz) no-soak dried apricots, cut into thick shreds*
- *salt and pepper*
- *30 ml (2 tbsp) chopped fresh basil*
- *orange rind strips and orange slices, to garnish*

1 Place the okra in a bowl, pour over the orange juice, toss lightly and set aside.
2 Heat the oil in a large saucepan, add the onion and cook for 5 minutes until softened. Add the okra and orange juice, then add the tomatoes and break up slightly with a wooden spoon.
3 Stir in the tomato purée and the apricots and season with salt and pepper to taste. Cover the pan and cook gently for 30-35 minutes until the okra and apricots are tender and the sauce thickened.
4 Stir in the basil and serve hot, garnished with orange rind strips and orange slices.

## BAKED ARTICHOKES

PREPARATION TIME 10 minutes
COOKING TIME 45-50 minutes
FREEZING Not suitable
COLOUR INDEX Page 41
♡

SERVES 6                                    110 CALS/SERVING
- *6 small globe artichokes*
- *salt and pepper*
- *90 ml (6 tbsp) extra-virgin olive oil*
- *lemon slices and chervil or parsley sprigs, to garnish*

1 Trim the artichoke stalks close to the base. Bring a large saucepan of salted water to the boil.
2 Add the artichokes. Simmer, covered, for 30

minutes or until you can pull away a base leaf easily.
3 Drain the artichokes and refresh under cold water, then halve them lengthways. With a small spoon, remove the 'hairy' choke.
4 Place the artichokes cut side uppermost on a baking sheet. Drizzle with olive oil and season with salt and pepper. Bake at 200°C (400°F) mark 6 for about 15-20 minutes. Serve garnished with lemon slices and herbs.

**VARIATION** The artichokes can be grilled instead of baked. Grill for 20 minutes, basting occasionally with olive oil.

## PAN-FRIED TOMATOES

PREPARATION TIME 8 minutes
COOKING TIME 3 minutes
FREEZING Not suitable
COLOUR INDEX Page 41
🕐

SERVES 4                                    240 CALS/SERVING
- *450 g (1 lb) plum tomatoes, thickly sliced*
- *rock salt and pepper*
- *100 ml (3½ fl oz) olive oil*
- *2 garlic cloves, peeled and sliced*
- *30 ml (2 tbsp) capers, drained and rinsed*
- *30 ml (2 tbsp) chopped fresh parsley*

1 Season the tomatoes with salt and pepper.
2 Heat the olive oil with the garlic in a large sauté pan. Fry the tomatoes for 1 minute only on each side. Using draining spoons, remove to a shallow serving dish.
3 Add the capers and parsley to the pan. Heat for 1 minute, stirring, then pour the contents of the pan over the tomatoes. Serve at once.

*TIP*
This dish also makes a refreshing starter served warm or cold with toasted ciabatta bread and goats' cheese.

# VEGETABLE AND APPLE STIR-FRY

PREPARATION TIME 15 minutes
COOKING TIME 15 minutes
FREEZING Not suitable

### SERVES 4

- *60 ml (4 tbsp) vegetable oil*
- *1 garlic clove, peeled and crushed*
- *350 g (12 oz) small leeks, trimmed and sliced*
- *4 sticks green celery, sliced*
- *225 g (8 oz) courgettes, sliced*
- *1 red pepper, deseeded and chopped*

### 285 CALS/SERVING

- *30 ml (2 tbsp) medium curry paste*
- *5 ml (1 tsp) ground ginger*
- *15 ml (1 tbsp) clear honey*
- *2 crisp, green eating apples*
- *50 g (2 oz) unsalted cashew nuts*
- *salt and pepper*
- *juice of 1 lemon*
- *flat-leaf parsley, to garnish*

**1** Heat the oil in a non-stick sauté pan and cook the garlic for a few seconds. Stir in the vegetables and cook over a high heat for 10 minutes, stirring occasionally.

**2** Add the curry paste, ginger, honey and 45 ml (3 tbsp) water and stir until smooth.

**3** Roughly chop the apples. Add to the pan with the cashew nuts and plenty of seasoning. Cook for a further 5 minutes or until the vegetables are just tender but retain some bite. Squeeze lemon juice over to serve. Garnish with flat-leaf parsley.

### TIP

When stir-frying, always make sure that the oil is sizzling before you add the ingredients. Keep the food on the move to ensure even cooking.

# DESSERTS

5 Cover the pudding with a saucer, that fits just inside the top of the pudding basin, then set a 2 kg (4 lb) weight on the saucer. Chill overnight.
6 To serve the pudding, invert onto a serving plate, spoon the reserved juice over the pudding and decorate with redcurrant sprigs and lemon balm or mint sprigs.

**NOTE** Choose a good quality close-textured large white loaf, preferably one-day old.

## RASPBERRY FOOL

PREPARATION TIME 10 minutes, plus chilling
FREEZING Not suitable
COLOUR INDEX Page 44
♡

| SERVES 4 | 95 CALS/SERVING |
|---|---|
| • *450 g (1 lb) raspberries* | • *raspberry leaves, to decorate (optional)* |
| • *25 g (1 oz) caster sugar* | |
| • *300 ml (10 fl oz) very low-fat fromage frais* | |

1 Reserve a few raspberries for decoration. Put the rest with the sugar in a blender or food processor and process to form a purée.
2 Turn the raspberry purée into a bowl, then gently swirl in the fromage frais to make a marbled effect. Divide the mixture between 4 individual serving dishes.
3 Chill in the refrigerator for about 2 hours before serving. Serve decorated with the reserved raspberries and raspberry leaves, if wished.

**NOTE** Using low-fat fromage frais makes this delicious fool surprisingly light in calories.

**VARIATIONS** Strawberry fool can be made in exactly the same way as the above recipe, simply substituting strawberries for the raspberries. For a mixed soft fruit fool, use an equal weight of raspberries and strawberries. Don't forget to reserve a little of the fruit for decoration.

## SUMMER PUDDING

PREPARATION TIME 35 minutes, plus chilling
COOKING TIME 5 minutes
FREEZING Suitable
♡ ❄

| SERVES 6-8 | 180-135 CALS/SERVING |
|---|---|
| • *450 g (1 lb) raspberries* | • *8 large slices white bread, 5 mm (¼ inch) thick* |
| • *225 g (8 oz) redcurrants, prepared* | • *redcurrant sprigs and lemon balm or mint leaves, to decorate* |
| • *225 g (8 oz) blackcurrants, prepared* | |
| • *75 g (3 oz) caster sugar* | |

1 Place the raspberries in a saucepan, with the red and black currants, sugar and 45 ml (3 tbsp) water. Bring to a gentle simmer over a low heat, then cook gently for 3-4 minutes until the juices begin to run. Set aside.
2 Remove the crusts from the bread slices, then cut a round of bread from one slice to fit the base of a 1.5 litre (2½ pint) pudding basin. Cut the remaining slices in half lengthways.
3 Arrange the bread slices around the side of the pudding basin, overlapping them slightly at the bottom, so they fit neatly and tightly together. Position the round of bread to cover the base.
4 Spoon 100 ml (3½ fl oz) of the fruit juice into a jug. Spoon the remaining fruit and its juice into the bread-lined basin. Cover completely with the remaining bread slices, trimming to fit.

# BERRY COMPOTE

PREPARATION TIME 15 minutes
COOKING TIME 5 minutes
FREEZING Not suitable
COLOUR INDEX Page 44
♡ ⏲

**SERVES 6**                     **95 CALS/SERVING**

- *50 g (2 oz) granulated sugar*
- *225 g (8 oz) blackcurrants, prepared*
- *450 g (1 lb) redcurrants, prepared*
- *pared rind and juice of 1 orange*
- *30 ml (2 tbsp) clear honey*
- *350 g (12 oz) strawberries, hulled*

1 Dissolve the sugar in 150 ml (5 fl oz) water. Bring to the boil and bubble for 1 minute.
2 Add the prepared currants with the pared orange rind and simmer for about 1 minute only until the fruits are just beginning to soften. Immediately remove from the heat and pour into a heatproof bowl. Stir in the honey and leave to cool.
3 Mix in the strained orange juice, cover the bowl and chill well in the refrigerator.
4 Just before serving, thinly slice the strawberries and stir gently into the compote.

**NOTE** With 50 g (2 oz) sugar the compote will be quite tart – add more sugar to taste.

# STRAWBERRY MILLE FEUILLES

PREPARATION TIME 1 hour, plus chilling and cooling
COOKING TIME 15 minutes
FREEZING Suitable for the pastry
COLOUR INDEX Page 44
❄

**SERVES 6-8**                  **425-320 CALS/SERVING**

- *225 g (8 oz) Puff Pastry (see page 370)*
- *50 g (2 oz) raspberries*
- *30 ml (2 tbsp) redcurrant jelly*
- *350 g (12 oz) strawberries, hulled and halved*
- *150 ml (5 fl oz) double cream, whipped*
- *strawberry leaves, to decorate*
- *CREME PATISSIERE*
- *300 ml (10 fl oz) milk*
- *1 vanilla pod, split*
- *3 egg yolks*
- *75 g (3 oz) caster sugar*
- *30 ml (2 tbsp) cornflour*
- *15 g (½ oz) butter*

1 Roll out the pastry to a 23 x 30 cm (9 x 12 inch) rectangle. Transfer to a dampened baking tray, prick the pastry all over with a fork and chill for 15 minutes. Bake at 220°C (425°F) mark 7 for 10-12 minutes until golden brown. Trim the edges, then cut widthways into three equal strips. Turn the strips over, return to the oven and bake for 5 minutes more. Cool on a wire rack.
2 To make the crème pâtissière, heat the milk with the vanilla pod in a heavy-based saucepan until almost boiling, then remove from the heat and leave to infuse for 30 minutes.
3 Whisk together the egg yolks and sugar until frothy, then whisk in the cornflour. Strain in the milk and whisk again. Return this mixture to the pan and cook over a low heat, stirring all the time, until boiling and thickened. Remove from the heat and beat in the butter. Cover the surface of the sauce with clingfilm and leave to cool.
4 Meanwhile, purée the raspberries in a blender and place in a saucepan with the redcurrant jelly. Place over a low heat and stir until the jelly has melted. Leave to cool, stirring occasionally, then stir in one third of the strawberries. When the crème pâtissière is cold, fold in the cream.
5 When ready to serve, spread the crème pâtissière over two strips of the pastry and carefully arrange half of the plain strawberries on top of each. Lay one strip on top of the other, then top with the final layer of pastry and spoon the fruit mixture on top. Decorate and serve at once.

# STRAWBERRY CHEESECAKE

PREPARATION TIME 25 minutes, plus cooling
COOKING TIME 50 minutes
FREEZING Suitable (stage 3)
❅

**SERVES 8**

- *50 g (2 oz) butter or margarine*
- *75 g (3 oz) plain flour*
- *25 g (1 oz) porridge oats*
- *75 g (3 oz) caster sugar*
- *700 g (1½ lb) natural cottage cheese*
- *2 eggs*

**245 CALS/SERVING**

- *grated rind of 1 lemon*
- *60 ml (4 tbsp) natural yogurt*
- *225 g (8 oz) fresh strawberries, hulled*

1 Grease and base-line a 20 cm (8 inch) loose-based round cake tin. Put the fat in a saucepan and heat until melted, then stir in the flour, oats and 25 g (1 oz) of the sugar. Stir until well mixed, then press into the base of the cake tin. Bake at 180°C (350°F) mark 4 for 10 minutes.

2 Meanwhile, rub the cottage cheese through a sieve into a bowl. Beat the eggs, then beat into the cottage cheese. Add the lemon rind and the remaining 50 g (2 oz) caster sugar and mix well together.

3 Pour the mixture into the cake tin. Return to the oven and bake for 20 minutes. Spoon the yogurt over the cheesecake and bake for a further 20 minutes. Leave to cool in the tin for 3-4 hours.

4 When cold, carefully remove the cheesecake from the tin. Slice most of the strawberries and arrange, with the remaining whole berries, on top of the cheesecake before serving.

---

*TIP*
The texture of a cooked cheesecake almost seems to improve with standing. Make and cook the day before and store, undecorated, in the refrigerator overnight. Remove from the refrigerator an hour before serving, to allow the cheesecake to return to room temperature.

## CHERRY BRULEES

PREPARATION TIME 15 minutes, plus chilling
COOKING TIME 40-45 minutes
FREEZING Not suitable
COLOUR INDEX Page 44

**SERVES 8**

**395 CALS/SERVING**

- *350 g (12 oz) fresh cherries*
- *15 ml (1 tbsp) kirsch*
- *4 egg yolks*
- *50 g (2 oz) caster sugar*
- *450 ml (15 fl oz) double cream*
- *125 g (4 oz) granulated sugar*

1 Stone the cherries, reserving eight with stems for decoration. Pour the kirsch over the remaining pitted cherries.
2 Whisk together the egg yolks and caster sugar until they have thickened and lightened in colour. Pour in the cream, stirring. Place in a heavy-based saucepan. Cook over a low heat, stirring continuously, until the mixture thickens to the consistency of double cream. This will take about 10 minutes. Do not boil.
3 Divide the soaked cherries among 8 ramekins or heatproof cups. Strain over the custard mixture.
4 Bake at 150°C (300°F) mark 2 for 30-35 minutes or until very lightly set. Cool and refrigerate until firm.
5 Place the granulated sugar in a small, heavy-based saucepan. Heat gently until the sugar dissolves and turns a golden caramel colour. Place a reserved cherry on each ramekin. Pour a thin layer of the caramel over each one. Chill, uncovered, for about 1 hour but not more than 6 hours before serving.

### TIP
Cherry stoners are available from all good kitchen equipment shops. This inexpensive tool not only saves time but removes the stone with very little damage.

## GOOSEBERRY MOUSSE

PREPARATION TIME 25 minutes, plus setting
COOKING TIME 15 minutes
FREEZING Not suitable
♡

**SERVES 4**

**130 CALS/SERVING**

- *15 ml (1 tbsp) powdered gelatine*
- *450 g (1 lb) gooseberries, trimmed*
- *50 g (2 oz) caster sugar*
- *150 ml (5 fl oz) natural yogurt*
- *a few drops of green food colouring (optional)*
- *fresh mint sprigs, to decorate*

1 In a small bowl, sprinkle the gelatine over 60 ml (4 tbsp) cold water. Put the gooseberries in a saucepan with 30 ml (2 tbsp) water. Bring to the boil, reduce the heat, cover and simmer for 15 minutes until the fruit is tender. If very juicy, drain off the cooking liquid and reserve. Stir in the sponged gelatine and stir well. Cool slightly.
2 Put the gooseberries and sugar in a blender or food processor and process to form a purée.
3 Push the purée through a nylon sieve into a measuring jug to remove the seeds. If necessary, make up to 450 ml (15 fl oz) with reserved juice.
4 When the gooseberry mixture is beginning to set, fold in the yogurt. Add a few drops of green food colouring if wished.
5 Pour the mousse into 4 individual serving dishes or one large dish. Put in the refrigerator to set. Serve decorated with sprigs of fresh mint.

# POACHED APRICOTS

PREPARATION TIME 10 minutes, plus chilling
COOKING TIME 10 minutes
FREEZING Not suitable
COLOUR INDEX Page 44
♡

**SERVES 6**
- *18 apricots, about 700 g (1½ lb) total weight*
- *1 cinnamon stick*
- *50 g (2 oz) caster sugar*

**100 CALS/SERVING**
- *300 ml (10 fl oz) white wine*
- *1 vanilla pod*
- *15 ml (1 tbsp) brandy*

**1** Halve and stone the apricots, if wished.
**2** Cut the cinnamon stick lengthways and place in a saucepan with the sugar, wine, vanilla pod and 225 ml (8 fl oz) water.
**3** Heat gently until the sugar dissolves. Bring to the boil and bubble for 2-3 minutes. Add the apricots and brandy and reduce to gentle simmer. Poach the fruit for 5-6 minutes or until just tender.
**4** Pour into a heatproof glass bowl and leave to cool completely. Cover and chill in the refrigerator before serving.

**NOTE** When chilling the dish, make sure that the apricots are covered in syrup so that they don't

### TIP
This recipe makes plenty of syrup for the apricots; if you don't serve it all, freeze the remainder and use as a base for a fruit salad.

# GOLDEN NECTARINE TART

PREPARATION TIME 20 minutes, plus cooling
COOKING TIME 1 hour 20 minutes
FREEZING Suitable (stage 2)
COLOUR INDEX Page 47
❈

**SERVES 8**
PATE SUCREE
- *125 g (4 oz) butter*
- *225 g (8 oz) white plain flour*
- *125 g (4 oz) caster sugar*
- *1 whole egg plus 1 egg yolk, beaten together*

FILLING
- *15 g (½ oz) fresh white breadcrumbs*
- *6 ripe nectarines or peaches, about 700 g (1½ lb) total weight*

**500 CALS/SERVING**
- *2 whole eggs plus 1 egg yolk*
- *200 ml (7 fl oz) double cream*
- *40 g (1½ oz) icing sugar*
- *30 ml (2 tbsp) brandy*
- *1.25 ml (¼ tsp) freshly grated nutmeg*
- *90 ml (6 tbsp) apricot jam*

**1** Make the pâte sucrée following the instructions on page 371.
**2** Roll out the pâte sucrée carefully and use to line a 2.5 cm (1 inch) deep, 27.5 x 19.5 cm (10¾ x 7¾ inch) loose-based flan tin. Bake blind (see page 368) until set and lightly browned, then leave to cool.
**3** Scatter the breadcrumbs evenly over the pastry base. Halve and stone the nectarines and arrange cut side down in the flan case.
**4** Whisk together the two eggs, egg yolk, double cream, icing sugar, brandy and nutmeg. Pour the mixture around the nectarines.
**5** Bake at 180°C (350°F) mark 4 for about 50 minutes or until just set. Flash under a hot grill to brown, then set aside to cool.
**6** Warm the jam with 15 ml (1 tbsp) water to make a glaze. Sieve, then brush the glaze over the flan. Leave to set. Store in a cool place until ready to serve – not more than 6 hours.

**VARIATION** For an alternative dessert with fewer calories (215 per serving), simply place the nectarines in a shallow ovenproof dish. Pour the whisked egg mixture over and bake as above. Peaches can also be used but remove the skin first as it can be tough when cooked.

## GRILLED PEACHES WITH CHOCOLATE AND MARZIPAN

PREPARATION TIME 10 minutes
COOKING TIME 5 minutes
FREEZING Not suitable

**SERVES 4**

- *4 ripe peaches*
- *150 ml (5 fl oz) double cream*
- *125 g (4 oz) plain chocolate, broken into pieces*
- *1 lime*
- *50 g (2 oz) marzipan, chopped into small pieces*

**445 CALS/SERVING**

- *30 ml (2 tbsp) icing sugar*
- *pouring cream, to serve*
- *mint sprigs, to decorate*

1 Halve the peaches and remove the stones. Arrange the peaches, cut-side up, in a shallow flameproof dish.
2 Pour the cream into a saucepan. Bring just to the boil, then add the chocolate and stir until smooth.
3 Pare thin strips of rind from the lime using a citrus zester; set aside. Squeeze 10 ml (2 tsp) juice from the lime and add to the chocolate sauce. Sprinkle a further 10 ml (2 tsp) over the peaches.
4 Divide the marzipan between the peach halves. Drizzle a little of the chocolate sauce over the peaches and pour the remainder into the dish.
5 Sift the icing sugar over the peaches and grill for about 5 minutes until the peaches and marzipan are lightly coloured.
6 Transfer to warmed serving plates and scatter with the pared lime rind. Pour a little cream onto the sauce. Serve decorated with mint sprigs and accompanied by pouring cream.

**VARIATION** Use ripe nectarines or pears in place of the peaches. You may need to take a thin slice off the rounded sides of the pears so they sit flat.

## APPLE AND FIG STRUDEL

PREPARATION TIME 25 minutes
COOKING TIME 30 minutes
FREEZING Suitable
COLOUR INDEX Page 46
♡ ❋

**SERVES 6**

- *125 g (4 oz) no-soak dried figs, roughly chopped*
- *grated rind and juice of 1 lemon*
- *25 g (1 oz) fresh white breadcrumbs*
- *450 g (1 lb) cooking apples*

**160 CALS/SERVING**

- *4 sheets filo pastry, about 125 g (4 oz) total weight*
- *25 g (1 oz) low-fat spread*
- *5 ml (1 tsp) caster sugar*
- *icing sugar, to dust*

1 Place the figs in a large bowl with the lemon rind and juice and the breadcrumbs.
2 Peel, quarter, core and thinly slice the apples. Mix the apples with the figs.
3 Lay two pieces of filo pastry side by side on a clean tea towel, overlapping the longest edges by about 5 cm (2 inches). Brush with a little melted low-fat spread. Top with the other two sheets of pastry and brush again.
4 Place the apple mixture along the longest edge and roll up, using the tea towel to help you. Roll onto a non-stick baking sheet, curling it slightly to fit the sheet. Brush with the remaining fat and sprinkle the sugar over.
5 Bake at 190°C (375°F) mark 5 for 30-35 minutes or until the pastry is golden brown and the apple is quite soft. Cover with foil if necessary. Serve hot, dusted lightly with icing sugar.

**NOTE** Using low-fat spread reduces the calorie content slightly, helping to make this delicious strudel a surprisingly healthy dessert.

**VARIATION** *Apple, Apricot and Almond Strudel*
Replace the figs with 125 g (4 oz) no-soak dried apricots. Add 30 ml (2 tbsp) ground almonds and 2.5 ml (½ tsp) ground cinnamon to the filling. Sprinkle 15 g (½ oz) flaked almonds over before baking.

## BRAMLEY APPLES WITH GINGER

PREPARATION TIME 15 minutes, plus soaking
COOKING TIME 50 minutes
FREEZING Not suitable
COLOUR INDEX Page 45

**SERVES 4**

- *175 g (6 oz) no-soak dried prunes*
- *150 ml (5 fl oz) apple juice*
- *15 g (½ oz) stem ginger, finely chopped and 15 ml (1 tbsp) syrup from the stem ginger jar*

**275 CALS/SERVING**

- *grated rind and juice of 1 lemon*
- *about 150 g (5 oz) soft light brown sugar*
- *4 small Bramley apples, about 225 g (8 oz) each*

1 Snip the prunes into the apple juice and leave to soak for 30 minutes.
2 Mix the stem ginger with the ginger syrup, lemon rind and juice and 125 g (4 oz) sugar. Strain the prunes, reserving the juice, and add the prunes to the ginger mixture.
3 Wash and core the apples. Cut the skin at the centre of the apple to stop the fruit bursting in the oven. Place in an ovenproof dish.
4 Fill the centre of each apple with the prune mixture, sprinkling any extra over the top. Pour the reserved apple juice over and sprinkle with a little sugar. Cover loosely.
5 Bake at 200°C (400°F) mark 6 for about 50 minutes. Serve with the juices spooned over.

*TIP*
If you don't have stem ginger in your store-cupboard, use 2.5 ml (½ tsp) ground ginger and omit the ginger syrup.

## ALMOND TARTE TATIN

PREPARATION TIME 15 minutes, plus chilling
COOKING TIME 35 minutes
FREEZING Not suitable

**SERVES 6**

- *125 g (4 oz) white plain flour*
- *pinch of salt*
- *25 g (1 oz) ground almonds*
- *50 g (2 oz) caster sugar*
- *125 g (4 oz) butter*
- *2 egg yolks*
- *few drops almond essence*

**380 CALS/SERVING**

- *125 g (4 oz) soft light brown sugar*
- *5 Cox's Orange Pippins, about 700 g (1½ lb) total weight*
- *50 g (2 oz) toasted flaked almonds*

1 Put the flour, salt, ground almonds, caster sugar and 50 g (2 oz) of the butter in a food processor and process until the mixture resembles fine breadcrumbs. Add the egg yolks and almond essence and process until the mixture just comes together. Knead to a smooth dough on a floured surface. Wrap and chill for about 1 hour.
2 Peel, quarter and core the apples. Melt the remaining butter in a non-stick frying pan, add

the brown sugar and slowly dissolve. Increase the heat slightly and stir for about 1 minute or until the mixture becomes smooth and thick.
3 Add the apples and flaked almonds and cook over a medium heat, stirring occasionally, for 10 minutes or until the apples soften slightly and the sugar mixture caramelizes. Pour into a 2.5 cm (1 inch) deep, 20 cm (8 inch) round non-stick sandwich tin. Leave to cool.
4 Roll out the chilled dough to a round slightly larger than the sandwich tin. Place on top of the apples, tucking the edges down the sides of the tin.
5 Bake at 190°C (375°F) mark 5 for about 20 minutes or until the pastry is golden brown. Leave to cool for 10 minutes. Invert on to a serving plate and serve.

**NOTE** The cake tin must be non-stick or the metal may taint the apples.

# APPLE AND BLACKBERRY UPSIDE-DOWN PUDDING

PREPARATION TIME 20 minutes
COOKING TIME 1 hour
FREEZING Suitable

❄

SERVES 8
TOPPING
- *90 ml (6 tbsp) raspberry jam*
- *350 g (12 oz) blackberries or loganberries*
- *1 large eating apple, peeled, cored and chopped*
CAKE
- *75 g (3 oz) white self-raising flour*
- *75 g (3 oz) wholemeal self-raising flour*

225 CALS/SERVING
- *5 ml (1 tsp) baking powder*
- *large pinch of salt*
- *1 egg*
- *finely grated rind and juice of 1 large orange*
- *30 ml (2 tbsp) milk*
- *75 g (3 oz) butter or margarine*
- *75 g (3 oz) caster sugar*

1 To make the topping, gently heat the jam in a small saucepan and pour into a greased 23 cm (9 inch) round spring-release cake tin. Wash the blackberries and arrange with the apple evenly over the base of the cake tin.
2 To make the cake, put all the ingredients into a large bowl and beat until smooth and glossy. Carefully spread over the fruit
3 Bake in the oven at 190°C (375°F) mark 5 for about 1 hour until the pudding is well risen and

firm to the touch. Cover the top with a double sheet of greaseproof paper after 40 minutes to prevent overbrowning.
4 Leave the pudding to cool in the tin for 5 minutes, then turn out and serve.

# PLUM CUSTARD BAKE

PREPARATION TIME 10 minutes
COOKING TIME 40 minutes
FREEZING Not suitable
COLOUR INDEX Page 45

♡

SERVES 6
- *450 g (1 lb) plums*
- *75 g (3 oz) caster sugar*
- *3 eggs*
- *300 ml (10 fl oz) milk*
- *grated zest of ½ lemon*

175 CALS/SERVING
- *5 ml (1 tsp) ground ginger*
- *5 ml (1 tsp) vanilla essence*
- *45 ml (3 tbsp) clear honey*

1 Halve and stone the plums, then arrange, cut-side down, in a round, shallow 1.1 litre (2 pint) ovenproof dish. Sprinkle with 30 ml (2 tbsp) of the sugar.
2 Whisk the eggs with all the remaining ingredients except the honey to make a smooth custard. Pour over the fruit.
3 Place the dish in a roasting tin filled with enough hot water to reach halfway up the side of the dish. Cook at 150°C (300°F) mark 2 for 40 minutes or until just set. Serve immediately, drizzled with warmed clear honey.

**VARIATION** Use greengages instead of plums and replace the ginger with grated nutmeg to taste.

## POACHED PEARS WITH APRICOTS

PREPARATION TIME 8 minutes
COOKING TIME 5-10 minutes
FREEZING Not suitable
COLOUR INDEX Page 44
♡ ⏱

SERVES 4
- *25 g (1 oz) butter or margarine*
- *25 g (1 oz) soft brown sugar*
- *15 ml (1 tbsp) lemon juice*
- *700 g (1½ lb) ripe but firm pears*
- *50 g (2 oz) no-soak dried apricots*

195 CALS/SERVING
- *15 ml (1 tbsp) Grand Marnier or brandy*
- *chopped nuts, to decorate*
- *ice cream, to serve*

1 Put the butter, sugar and lemon juice in a saucepan with 150 ml (5 fl oz) water and warm together.
2 Peel, quarter and core the pears. Halve each quarter again if large. Snip the apricots into shreds.
3 Add the pears and apricots to the syrup, cover and simmer for 5-10 minutes or until the pears are just tender. Stir in the Grand Marnier.
4 Serve hot, sprinkled with chopped nuts and topped with ice cream.

## CRISPY PEAR CLAFOUTIS

PREPARATION TIME 15 minutes, plus standing
COOKING TIME 50 minutes
FREEZING Not suitable

SERVES 6
- *3 eggs*
- *50 g (2 oz) white self-raising flour*
- *150 g (5 oz) white plain flour*
- *large pinch of salt*
- *5 ml (1 tsp) ground cinnamon*
- *200 ml (7 fl oz) milk*

270 CALS/SERVING
- *30 ml (2 tbsp) Armagnac*
- *50 g (2 oz) butter*
- *350 g (12 oz) ripe dessert pears*
- *caster and icing sugar, to serve*

1 Whisk the eggs, flours, salt and cinnamon with 150 ml (5 fl oz) milk until smooth. Whisk in the remaining milk with the Armagnac. Cover and leave to stand for 2 hours.
2 Using half the butter, grease a 23 cm (9 inch) spring-release cake tin. Stand the tin on a baking sheet. Thinly slice the pears. Whisk the batter again and pour into the prepared tin. Lay the pear slices on top. Dot with the remaining butter.
3 Bake at 240°C (475°F) mark 9 for 15-20 minutes or until well risen, then lower the temperature to 220°C (425°F) mark 7 for a further 35 minutes or until risen and well browned. Dust with a mixture of caster and icing sugar to serve.

## PINEAPPLE AND DATE SALAD
## WITH KUMQUATS

PREPARATION TIME 35 minutes, plus chilling
COOKING TIME 15 minutes
FREEZING Not suitable

SERVES 6                    330 CALS/SERVING
- *75 ml (5 tbsp) acacia*     - *2 oranges, peeled*
  *honey*                    - *1 medium pineapple*
- *50 g (2 oz) soft*          - *12 fresh or dried*
  *brown sugar*                *dates, halved and*
- *300 ml (10 fl oz)*          *stoned*
  *Earl Grey tea,*           - *125 g (4 oz) walnut*
  *strained*                   *halves*
- *225 g (8 oz)*
  *kumquats, halved*

**1** First make the syrup. Place the honey, sugar and tea in a saucepan and bring to the boil. Boil for 1 minute. Place the kumquats in the syrup. Simmer, uncovered, for about 10 minutes until the kumquats are tender. Leave to cool in the syrup.
**2** Slice the oranges crosswise and place in a bowl. Using a sharp knife, cut the top and bottom off the pineapple and cut away the skin. Quarter the pineapple lengthways and cut out the core. Cut the flesh into large chunks. Carefully mix with the oranges.
**3** Stir the dates into the fruit mixture with the walnuts. Drain the kumquats and set aside; strain

the syrup and pour over the fruit in the bowl. Cover and chill for 1 hour.
**4** Spoon the fruit salad into a serving dish or individual glass bowls and scatter the kumquats on top. Serve with whipped cream.

**NOTE** Kumquats are readily available at Christmas and have a sharp perfumed flavour. Some stores sell crystallized kumquats which are ideal for decorating desserts and cakes.

**VARIATION** Substitute 4 ripe pears for the pineapple and cook the kumquats in a syrup flavoured with jasmine tea rather than Earl Grey.

## CLEMENTINES IN BRANDY

PREPARATION TIME 10-15 minutes
FREEZING Not suitable
COLOUR INDEX Page 45
♡ ⏱

SERVES 6                    140 CALS/SERVING
- *10 clementines or*         - *30 ml (2 tbsp) caster*
  *other seedless 'easy*       *sugar*
  *peelers'*                 - *60 ml (4 tbsp)*
- *12 pitted dates or no-*     *brandy*
  *soak prunes*
- *juice of 1 lemon*

**1** Peel the clementines. Remove as much pith as possible then thickly slice into a bowl. Roughly slice the dates or prunes and stir into the clementines.
**2** Stir the lemon juice, sugar and brandy into the fruit. Cover and chill until required.

## FRAGRANT FRUIT SALAD

PREPARATION TIME 20-30 minutes, plus chilling
FREEZING Not suitable
COLOUR INDEX Page 45
♡

SERVES 6

- *50 g ( 2 oz) caster sugar*
- *grated rind and juice of 1 lemon*
- *2 pieces of preserved stem ginger in syrup, finely chopped*
- *60 ml (4 tbsp) ginger wine*
- *700 g (1½ lb) lychees*

175 CALS/SERVING

- *3 ripe mangoes*
- *450 g (1 lb) fresh or canned pineapple in natural juice*
- *4 kiwi fruit*
- *50 g (2 oz) Cape gooseberries, to decorate*

1 Put the sugar in a pan with 150 ml (5 fl oz) water and the lemon rind and juice. Heat gently until the sugar dissolves, then bring to the boil and simmer for 1 minute. Remove from the heat.

2 Stir the ginger into the sugar syrup with the wine. Leave to cool while preparing the fruit.

3 Peel the lychees, cut in half and remove the shiny stones. Peel the mangoes and cut the flesh away from the stones. Cut the flesh into cubes.

4 If using fresh pineapple, peel, slice and remove the tough centre core from each slice. If using canned pineapple, drain well. Cut the pineapple slices into cubes. Peel and thinly slice the kiwi fruit. Cut the slices in half.

5 Place the fruit in a serving dish, pour over the syrup and toss lightly to mix. Cover with clingfilm and chill for several hours to allow the flavours to develop.

6 To decorate, peel back the calyx from each Cape gooseberry to form a 'flower'. Wipe the orange berry with a damp cloth. Arrange on top of he fruit salad to serve.

**VARIATION** Replace one mango with 1-2 oranges, according to size. Pare the rind thinly and set aside. Remove the pith and segment the fruit. Cut the rind into very thin strips, blanch in boiling water for 1 minute and use to decorate the fruit salad if wished, in place of the Cape gooseberries.

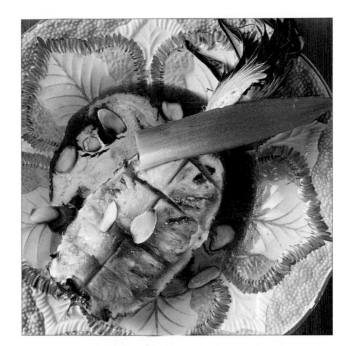

## FLAMBEED PINEAPPLE

PREPARATION TIME 20 minutes
COOKING TIME 50 minutes
FREEZING Not suitable
♡

SERVES 4

- *1 pineapple, weighing about 900 g (2 lb)*
- *30 ml (2 tbsp) clear honey*

175 CALS/SERVING

- *125 ml (4 fl oz) brandy*
- *toasted flaked almonds, to decorate*
- *cream, to serve*

1 Trim about 1 cm (½ inch) from each end of the pineapple, reserving a few green leaves. Cut in quarters lengthways. Carefully trim the core away, then cut along the base of each quarter so that the flesh is separated from the skin. Cut the flesh in half lengthways, then four times across to give bite-sized pieces of pineapple.

2 Lay the pineapple shell and flesh in an ovenproof dish and spoon the honey over. Cook at 190°C (375°F) mark 5 for 45 minutes, basting occasionally.

3 When the pineapple is golden, remove from the oven. Gently heat the brandy in a small saucepan, then pour over the pineapple and ignite. Once the flames have died down, pour the cooking juice over. Decorate with toasted flaked almonds and the reserved green leaves. Serve the pineapple with cream.

## LIGHT CHRISTMAS PUDDINGS

PREPARATION TIME 40 minutes, plus steeping and drying
COOKING TIME 2½ hours
FREEZING Suitable (stage 5)
❄

SERVES 8          445 CALS/PUDDING

- *225 g (8 oz) sultanas, roughly chopped*
- *150 g (5 oz) raisins, roughly chopped*
- *50 g (2 oz) stoned dates, chopped*
- *50 g (2 oz) currants, roughly chopped*
- *25 g (1 oz) no-soak dried apricots, roughly chopped*
- *1 small eating apple (preferably Granny Smith), peeled and coarsely grated*
- *grated rind of 1 lemon*
- *50 ml (2 fl oz) brandy*

- *125 g (4 oz) butter, softened*
- *125 g (4 oz) soft dark brown sugar*
- *2 small eggs, beaten*
- *125 g (4 oz) fresh white breadcrumbs*
- *40 g (1½ oz) white plain flour*
- *1.25 ml (¼ tsp) each of ground nutmeg and ground cinnamon*
- *2.5 ml (½ tsp) bicarbonate of soda*
- *frosted holly leaves, to decorate*
- *brandy sauce, to serve*

**1** Mix the dried fruit with the apple, lemon rind and brandy. Cover and leave in a cool place for two days.
**2** Beat the butter and sugar until light and fluffy, then gradually beat in the eggs. Add the fruit mixture with the remaining ingredients and mix.
**3** Divide the mixture among eight 25 cm (10 inch) squares of well-floured muslin. Draw up the edges

of muslin and tie with string, allowing room for expansion.
**4** Tie the puddings onto skewers and hang them over a large pan of boiling water. Tightly cover the pan with foil and steam for about 1½ hours, topping the pan up with more boiling water, if necessary.
**5** While the puddings are warm, mould into neat rounds. Hang in a cool place until quite dry. Overwrap in foil and refrigerate for up to a week.
**6** To serve, remove the foil and steam, as above, for about 1 hour. Decorate with frosted holly leaves and serve with brandy sauce.

## BREAD AND BUTTER PUDDING WITH PRUNES

PREPARATION TIME 10 minutes, plus soaking
COOKING TIME 1-1¼ hours
FREEZING Not suitable
COLOUR INDEX Page 46

SERVES 6          285 CALS/SERVING

- *25 g (1 oz) butter*
- *4 slices brown bread, about 150 g (5 oz)*
- *3 eggs*
- *25 g (1 oz) caster sugar*
- *150 ml (5 fl oz) single cream*
- *450 ml (15 fl oz) skimmed milk*

- *15 ml (1 tbsp) brandy*
- *125 g (4 oz) pitted no-soak prunes, finely chopped*
- *1.25 ml (¼ tsp) ground cinnamon*
- *25 g (1 oz) demerara sugar*

**1** Lightly butter a 7.5 cm (3 inches) deep 1.1 litre (2 pint) ovenproof dish. Spread one side of the bread with the remaining butter. Cut into 2.5 cm (1 inch) squares. Whisk together the eggs, sugar, cream, milk and brandy.
**2** Scatter the bread and prunes into the prepared dish. Pour the egg mixture over. Leave to soak for about 20 minutes, lightly pressing the bread into the egg mixture. Sprinkle with the cinnamon and demerara sugar.
**3** Place the dish in a roasting tin with enough warm water to come about 2.5 cm (1 inch) up the side of the dish. Cook at 170°C (325°F) mark 3 for about 1 hour-1¼ hours or until the pudding is lightly set. Serve immediately.

## STICKY FUDGE AND WALNUT PUDDING

PREPARATION TIME 15 minutes
COOKING TIME 50 minutes
FREEZING Not suitable

**SERVES 6**

**660 CALS/SERVING**

- *150 g (5 oz) butter, plus extra for greasing*
- *175 g (6 oz) soft light brown sugar*
- *300 ml (10 fl oz) double cream*
- *125 g (4 oz) chopped dates*

- *2.5 ml (½ tsp) bicarbonate of soda*
- *1 egg, beaten*
- *125 g (4 oz) white self-raising flour*
- *50 g (2 oz) chopped walnuts*

**1** Butter a 1.1 litre (2 pint) deep, ovenproof dish. In a saucepan gently warm 75 g (3 oz) butter, 125 g (4 oz) soft light brown sugar and the double cream. Bring the mixture up to a vigorous boil and bubble for about 3 minutes. Pour a little of the fudge sauce into the prepared dish just to cover the base.

**2** Put the dates in a small bowl and pour over 125 ml (4 fl oz) boiling water, add the bicarbonate of soda and leave to stand for 10 minutes.

**3** In a bowl, beat the remaining sugar with 50 g (2 oz) butter until light and fluffy. Beat in the egg with the date mixture – it will look slightly curdled. Stir in the flour and nuts. Pour into the dish.

**4** Bake at 180°C (350°F) mark 4 for about 50 minutes or until firm to the touch. Cool for 5 minutes, run a palette knife around the edge of the dish, then turn out. Warm the remaining fudge sauce and pour over the pudding.

## GOOEY CHOCOLATE PUDDING

PREPARATION TIME 15 minutes
COOKING TIME 1 hour 10 minutes
FREEZING Not suitable

**SERVES 4**

- *200 g (7 oz) milk chocolate*
- *200 ml (7 fl oz) milk*
- *50 g (2 oz) butter, softened*
- *75 g (3 oz) caster sugar*
- *2 eggs, separated*

**570 CALS/SERVING**

- *50 g (2 oz) white self-raising flour*
- *25 g (1 oz) cocoa powder*
- *extra cocoa powder, to decorate*
- *vanilla ice cream, to serve*

1 Break the chocolate into small pieces, place in a saucepan with the milk and heat very slowly until all the chocolate has melted. Stir until smooth.
2 Cream together the butter and sugar until light and fluffy. Keep beating and gradually add the egg yolks, chocolate mixture, flour and cocoa powder.
3 In a separate bowl, whisk the egg whites until they hold their shape. Gently fold into the chocolate with a metal spoon.

***TIP***
The egg whites should stand in soft peaks so that the tips of the peaks flop over gently when held up by the whisk. Overbeaten egg whites will be difficult to fold in evenly.

4 Pour into a deep 1.1 litre (2 pint) ovenproof dish. Place in a roasting tin filled with hot water and bake at 180°C (350°F) mark 4 for about 1 hour or until the pudding is very firm to the touch, but still slightly runny underneath. Cover loosely with foil after about 40 minutes to prevent overbrowning, if necessary. Dust with cocoa powder to decorate and serve with ice cream.

## APPLE AND WALNUT FILO PIE

PREPARATION TIME 25 minutes
COOKING TIME 50 minutes
FREEZING Not suitable
COLOUR INDEX Page 47

**SERVES 6**

- *50 g (2 oz) walnut pieces*
- *125 g (4 oz) butter, softened*
- *50 g (2 oz) caster sugar, plus 30 ml (2 tbsp)*
- *finely grated rind and juice of 1 lemon*
- *1 egg*

**425 CALS/SERVING**

- *25 g (1 oz) white self-raising flour*
- *2.5 ml (½ tsp) ground cinnamon*
- *700 g (1½ lb) crisp eating apples, peeled and sliced*
- *300 g (10 oz) packet filo pastry*
- *icing sugar, to dust*

1 Toast the walnuts. Allow to cool, then finely chop in a food processor.
2 Beat half the butter with 50 g (2 oz) caster sugar, the lemon rind, egg, flour, half the cinnamon and the chopped walnuts.
3 Mix the apples together with 30 ml (2 tbsp) caster sugar, 15 ml (1 tbsp) lemon juice and the remaining cinnamon.
4 Melt the remaining butter and grease a 25 cm (10 inch) loose-based, fluted flan tin. Use about three-quarters of the pastry to line the tin, buttering well after each piece of pastry and allowing about 7.5 cm (3 inches) of pastry to hang over the sides of the tin.
5 Spread the nut mixture over the pastry base and top with the apples. Fold the pastry edges over the filling and top with a little more pastry to cover the filling completely. Butter between the pastry layers as before. Crumple up any remaining pastry and scatter over the pie. Drizzle with butter.
6 Stand the tin on a baking sheet and bake at 190°C (375°F) mark 5 for about 50 minutes, covering loosely with foil when well browned.
7 Serve warm, dusted with icing sugar.

# RHUBARB AND CINNAMON COBBLER

PREPARATION TIME 15 minutes
COOKING TIME 50 minutes
FREEZING Suitable
COLOUR INDEX Page 46
❋

**SERVES 4**

- *175 g (6 oz) white plain flour*
- *125 g (4 oz) butter*
- *150 g (5 oz) caster sugar*
- *700 g (1½ lb) rhubarb, trimmed and cut into bite-sized chunks*

**565 CALS/SERVING**

- *30 ml (2 tbsp) cornflour*
- *2.5 ml (½ tsp) ground cinnamon*
- *a little milk and sugar for glazing*
- *vanilla ice cream, to accompany*

1 Place the flour, butter and 25 g (1 oz) sugar in a food processor and blend until it has the texture of fine breadcrumbs. Add 45 ml (3 tbsp) cold water and blend until the pastry comes together to form a ball. If it is slightly sticky roll in some flour and chill for 20 minutes or until it is firm enough to handle.
2 Roll out the pastry into a large circle, making sure you leave the edges ragged and uneven. It should be large enough to line a 23 cm (9 inch) round, greased, ovenproof dish with sides at least 5 cm (2 inches) deep, and to allow the edge of the pastry to drape over the sides of the dish.
3 Toss the rhubarb in the remaining sugar, cornflour and cinnamon. Spoon into the dish. Bring the pastry edges up and over the fruit, leaving a gap in the centre to reveal the filling. Glaze with milk and sprinkle with sugar.
4 Place on a baking sheet and bake at 200°C (400°F) mark 6 for about 50 minutes or until the pastry is golden brown and the juice is bubbling up around the pastry. Serve hot with ice cream.

# BANOFFI FUDGE PIE

PREPARATION TIME 30 minutes, plus chilling
COOKING TIME About 30 minutes
FREEZING Not suitable
COLOUR INDEX Page 46

**SERVES 6**

- *Shortcrust Pastry, made with 225 g (8 oz) white plain flour (see page 369)*
- *75 g (3 oz) butter*
- *50 g (2 oz) light soft brown sugar*
- *30 ml (2 tbsp) milk*

**560 CALS/SERVING**

- *218 g (8 oz) can condensed milk*
- *5 bananas*
- *300 ml (10 fl oz) double cream*
- *lemon juice*
- *50 g (2 oz) caster sugar*

1 Use the pastry to line a 23 cm (9 inch) round, 2.5 cm (1 inch) deep, loose-based flan tin and bake blind (see page 368) at 200°C (400°F) mark 6 for 15 minutes until light golden.
2 Meanwhile, place the butter and the brown sugar in a small, heavy-based saucepan. Heat gently until the butter melts and the sugar dissolves. Bring to the boil and bubble for 1 minute only, stirring frequently. Off the heat, add the milk and condensed milk, bring to the boil and bubble for 2 minutes only or until the mixture thickens to the consistency of a very thick sauce and turns golden. Stir constantly or the mixture will burn. Keep warm.
3 Meanwhile, thickly slice four of the bananas and place in the pastry case. Spoon the warm fudge thinly but evenly over the bananas to cover completely. Leave to cool, then chill for about 45 minutes until set.
4 Whisk the cream until it just holds its shape. Pile the cream in the centre of the pie. Refrigerate for at least 1 hour until chilled, so that the caramel sets immediately on it.
5 Slice the remaining banana and coat with lemon juice. Pile on top of the cream.
6 Place the caster sugar in a small, heavy-based saucepan. Heat gently until the sugar melts and turns a golden caramel colour. Cool for about 1 minute or until the caramel thickens and darkens slightly, then spoon over the banana. (The caramel will run through the cream.) Chill immediately to set. The pie will hold up in the refrigerator for 2-3 hours. Leave at room temperature for 30 minutes before serving.

## SAFFRON MERINGUES WITH BLUEBERRY SAUCE

PREPARATION TIME 25 minutes
COOKING TIME 2 hours
FREEZING Suitable

❄

SERVES 6

*MERINGUES*
- *small pinch of saffron strands (optional)*
- *2 egg whites*
- *125 g (4 oz) caster sugar*
- *200 ml (7 fl oz) crème fraîche*

260 CALS/SERVING

*BLUEBERRY SAUCE*
- *450 g (1 lb) blueberries*
- *40 g (1½ oz) caster sugar*
- *30 ml (2 tbsp) chopped fresh mint*

1 Line two baking sheets with non-stick baking parchment. Put the saffron (if using) in a small bowl and pour on 15 ml (1 tbsp) boiling water. Whisk the egg whites in a large bowl until holding soft peaks. Whisk in 30 ml (2 tbsp) of the sugar, then strain in the saffron liquid and whisk again until the meringue is stiff. Fold in the remaining sugar.

2 Using two large spoons, shape the meringue mixture into 12 oval mounds on the prepared baking sheets. Bake in the oven at 110°C (225°F) mark ¼ for about 2 hours until the meringues are well dried out. Carefully peel the meringues off the paper and leave to cool on a wire rack.

3 To make the sauce, place the blueberries in a saucepan with the sugar and 45 ml (3 tbsp) water and cook over a low heat for 5-7 minutes until they are just tender, but still holding their shape. Using a slotted spoon, remove about one quarter of the blueberries and press through a fine sieve into a large bowl. Stir in the rest of the blueberries with the chopped mint and leave to cool, stirring occasionally.

4 About 1 hour before serving, sandwich the meringues together with the crème fraîche. Pile on to one or two serving dishes, cover and chill until ready to serve. Pour the sauce into a jug and serve with the meringues.

**VARIATION** *Cinnamon Meringues with Red Sauce* Omit the saffron, and add 5 ml (1 tsp) ground cinnamon to the egg whites with the sugar. Replace the blueberries with 450 g (1 lb) cherries, raspberries or strawberries.

## CHOCOLATE TRUFFLE CAKE

PREPARATION TIME 25 minutes, plus setting
COOKING TIME 20 minutes
FREEZING Suitable
COLOUR INDEX Page 47

❄

SERVES 16
- *150 g (5 oz) sugar*
- *90 g (3½ oz) blanched whole almonds, toasted*
- *23 cm (9 inch) round chocolate sponge*
- *90 ml (6 tbsp) Tia Maria*

580 CALS/SERVING
- *600 g (1 lb 6 oz) plain chocolate*
- *600 ml (1 pint) double cream*
- *3 egg yolks*
- *40 g (1½ oz) caster sugar*

1 Melt the sugar in a heavy-based saucepan over a gentle heat. Add the almonds and cook until dark golden. Carefully pour onto an oiled baking sheet – the pan and caramel will be very hot. Set aside to cool.

2 Line the sides of a 23 cm (9 inch) spring-release cake tin with non-stick baking parchment. Carefully slice a thin circle of chocolate sponge, about 5 mm (¼ inch) deep. Place cut side up in

the base of the tin. Push down firmly and use pieces of sponge to patch up any holes (any remaining sponge can be frozen). Drizzle 30 ml (2 tbsp) Tia Maria over and set aside.

**3** Break the chocolate into a heatproof bowl and add 150 ml (5 fl oz) cream. Melt the chocolate over a pan of gently simmering water. Do not stir.

**4** Meanwhile, using an electric whisk, whisk together the egg yolks and caster sugar in a bowl for 10 minutes or until pale, thick and creamy.

**5** Break the almond caramel into small pieces. Process in a blender or food processor until it resembles coarse breadcrumbs.

**6** With a metal spoon, fold the melted chocolate into the egg mixture and mix well. Fold in the almond caramel and the remaining Tia Maria.

**7** Lightly whip the remaining double cream until it just holds its shape, then fold it into the chocolate mixture. Pour into the cake tin. Set in the refrigerator overnight.

**8** To serve, remove from the tin, discarding the lining paper, and cut with a sharp, hot knife.

**NOTE** For an autumnal decoration, melt 50 g (2 oz) dark, milk and white chocolate in separate bowls. Coat about 10 opened cape gooseberries in chocolate. Heat 50 g (2 oz) sugar and melt until golden brown. Coat about 5 cape gooseberries in the caramel. Decorate the cake with coated and fresh cape gooseberries. Fix greaseproof paper around the base, then tie raffia over it.

# HONEY-TOASTED RICE

PREPARATION TIME 10 minutes
COOKING TIME 3 hours
FREEZING Not suitable

**SERVES 4**

**435 CALS/SERVING**

- *600 ml (1 pint) milk*
- *300 ml (10 fl oz) single cream*
- *75 g (3 oz) pudding rice*
- *knob of butter*
- *30 ml (2 tbsp) caster sugar*
- *1.25 ml (¼ tsp) vanilla essence*
- *large pinch of grated nutmeg*
- *50 g (2 oz) flaked or shredded almonds, roughly chopped or cut into thin shreds*
- *45 ml (3 tbsp) clear honey*
- *15 ml (1 tbsp) lemon juice*

**1** Mix together the first seven ingredients. Pour into a 5 cm (2 inch) deep 1.4 litre (2½ pint) ovenproof dish. Place in a roasting tin with enough warm water to come halfway up the side of the dish.

**2** Cook at 150°C (300°F) mark 2 for about 2½-3 hours or until lightly set and golden. Turn off the oven and leave the pudding inside for about 20 minutes.

**3** Scatter the almonds over the pudding. Mix together the honey and lemon juice and drizzle over the nuts. Place under a hot grill until a golden brown colour. Serve hot or cold.

*TIP*
Keep a whole nutmeg for grating in your store-cupboard, rather than a tub of ready-grated nutmeg. The flavour is fresh and cleaner and a single nutmeg will last for years.

# WHITE CHOCOLATE TORTE

PREPARATION TIME 20 minutes, plus chilling
COOKING TIME 10 minutes
FREEZING Suitable

✳

**SERVES 12**
- *75 g (3 oz) butter*
- *225 g (8 oz) ginger biscuits, finely crushed*
- *700 g (1½ lb) white chocolate*
- *600 ml (1 pint) double cream*

**785 CALS/SERVING**
- *icing sugar and cocoa powder, to decorate*
CHOCOLATE STARS
- *225 g (8 oz) white, plain or milk chocolate*
- *25 g (1 oz) butter*

**1** To make the chocolate stars, roughly chop the chocolate and melt with the butter in a bowl set over a pan of simmering water. Spread thinly on two baking sheets lined with non-stick baking parchment and refrigerate to set. Soften at room temperature for a few seconds and stamp out star shapes. Place the star shapes in the refrigerator as you make them. When the chocolate gets too soft to handle, chill again. Freeze the complete batch interleaved with non-stick baking parchment.
**2** Line the base of a 23 cm (9 inch) round, 6.5 cm (2½ inches) deep, spring-release tin with non-stick

baking parchment or greaseproof paper.
**3** Melt the butter and stir into the biscuit crumbs. Press into the prepared tin and chill for 15 minutes.
**4** Break up the chocolate and put it in a medium-size saucepan with half the cream. Heat very gently, stirring occasionally, until almost smooth. Pour into a bowl and cool for 15 minutes or until just beginning to thicken. Stir occasionally.
**5** Whip the remainder of the cream until it forms soft peaks. Fold into the cool chocolate mixture. Pour over the biscuit base and chill for at least 3 hours, preferably overnight.
**6** Serve chilled. Remove from the tin, decorate with the frozen chocolate stars and dust with icing sugar and cocoa.

**NOTE** Chocolate should be barely warm but still liquid before adding the whipped cream at stage 5. If the chocolate is allowed to reach too high a temperature it becomes a solid mass, but if it's too cold it won't combine with the cream.

# WHISKY MOCHA FLAN

PREPARATION TIME I hour, plus chilling
COOKING TIME 20 minutes
FREEZING Not suitable

**SERVES 6-8**
- *Pâte Sucrée, made with 225 g (8 oz) flour (see page 371)*
- *75 g (3 oz) plain chocolate*
*FILLING*
- *10 ml (2 tsp) powdered gelatine*
- *150 ml (5 fl oz) milk*
- *15 ml (1 tbsp) instant coffee granules*
- *3 egg yolks*

**640-480 CALS/SERVING**
- *15 ml (1 tbsp) caster sugar*
- *150 ml (5 fl oz) double cream*
*TOPPING*
- *200 ml (7 fl oz) double cream*
- *15-30 ml (1-2 tbsp) whisky*
- *15 ml (1 tbsp) caster sugar*
- *chocolate caraque, to decorate*

1 Roll out the pastry on a lightly floured surface and use to line a 23 cm (9 inch) heart-shaped tin. Bake blind (see page 368) at 200°C (400°F) mark 6 for 15 minutes, then remove the paper and beans, reduce the oven temperature to 190°C (375°F) mark 5 and bake for 5 minutes. Cool on a wire rack.

2 Melt the chocolate. Place the pastry case, upside-down, on a sheet of greaseproof paper. Using a pastry brush, brush half of the melted chocolate evenly all over the outside of the pastry case. Leave in a cool place until the chocolate sets. Turn the flan case over and brush the inside with the remaining chocolate. Leave in a cool place to set.

3 To make the filling, sprinkle the gelatine over 30 ml (2 tbsp) water in a small heatproof bowl and leave to soak for 2-3 minutes. Place the bowl over a saucepan of simmering water and stir until the gelatine has dissolved.

4 Put the milk and coffee granules into a small saucepan. Heat gently until the coffee dissolves completely and the milk comes almost to the boil. Very lightly whisk the egg yolks and sugar together in a heatproof bowl. Pour in the coffee-flavoured milk and mix well.

5 Place the bowl over a pan of hot water and cook the custard, stirring continuously, until thick enough to coat the back of the spoon. As soon as the custard thickens, strain it through a nylon sieve into a clean bowl. Stir in the dissolved gelatine. Leave the custard to cool, stirring

frequently to prevent a skin forming.

6 Whip the cream until it will just hold soft peaks, then gently fold it into the coffee custard. Place the chocolate-coated flan case on a flat serving plate and fill it with the coffee cream mixture. Chill until set.

7 To make the topping, whip the cream with the whisky and sugar until it will just hold soft peaks. Spread an even layer of cream over the top of the flan. Whip the remaining cream until thick enough to pipe and fill a piping bag fitted with a medium star nozzle. Pipe whirls of cream around the top of the flan, then decorate with chocolate caraque. Chill before serving.

---

*TIP*
To make chocolate caraque spread melted chocolate in a thin layer on a marble slab or clean, smooth work surface. When the chocolate is only just set, draw a fine-bladed knife across the chocolate at an angle of 45°.

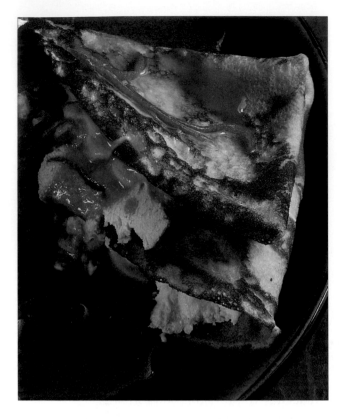

# CREPES WITH ORANGE ICE

PREPARATION TIME 30 minutes, plus freezing
COOKING TIME About 20 minutes
FREEZING Suitable, except sauce

❋

SERVES 6

- *125 g (4 oz) white plain flour*
- *pinch of salt*
- *2 eggs, beaten*
- *300 ml (10 fl oz) milk*
- *25 g (1 oz) butter, melted*
- *15 ml (1 tbsp) Grand Marnier*

ORANGE ICE CREAM

- *50 g (2 oz) sugar*
- *finely pared rind and juice of 1 orange*
- *225 g (8 oz) mascarpone cheese*

505 CALS/SERVING

- *200 g (7 oz) fromage frais*
- *30 ml (2 tbsp) Grand Marnier*

SAUCE

- *25 g (1 oz) unsalted butter*
- *50 g (2 oz) caster sugar*
- *juice of 2 oranges, strained*
- *juice of 1/2 lemon, strained*
- *30-45 ml (2-3 tbsp) Grand Marnier, warmed*

1 First make the ice cream. Put the sugar in a saucepan with 150 ml (5 fl oz) water and heat gently until the sugar has dissolved. Add the pared orange rind and boil rapidly until reduced

by about half. Remove the orange rind with a slotted spoon, cut into strips and set aside. Add the orange juice to the syrup. Allow to cool.

2 Mix the mascarpone and fromage frais together in a bowl. Gradually work in the cooled orange syrup and liqueur. Turn into a freezerproof container, cover and freeze until firm, whisking occasionally during freezing. Transfer to the refrigerator to soften 30 minutes before serving.

3 To make the crêpe batter, place the flour, salt, eggs, milk, melted butter and Grand Marnier in a blender or food processor and work until smooth.

4 Heat a crêpe pan until very hot and wipe with a little oil. When a light haze forms, pour in just enough batter to thinly coat the base of the pan, tilting the pan to get an even coating. Cook over a fairly high heat until the upper surface looks set and the edges begin to curl. Turn the crêpe over and cook the other side. Transfer to a warmed plate and repeat to make 12 pancakes, interleaving the cooked ones with greaseproof paper.

5 To make the sauce, melt the butter in a large frying pan, add the sugar and heat gently until dissolved, then cook to a golden brown caramel. Carefully add the orange and lemon juices and stir until the caramel has dissolved.

6 To serve, place a spoonful or two of ice cream on each crêpe and fold to enclose the filling. Arrange the crêpes in the large frying pan and spoon the sauce over to warm them through. Sprinkle with the orange rind strips. Pour on the liqueur and set alight, shaking the pan gently. Serve immediately.

**NOTE** This is an ideal dinner party dish because most of the preparation can be done in advance; at the last minute you only need to assemble the dish, heat it through and flambé!

**VARIATION** Use any orange-flavoured liqueur instead of the Grand Marnier.

# MELON ICE

PREPARATION TIME 20 minutes, plus marinating and freezing
FREEZING Suitable (stage 3)

❄

### SERVES 6-8
- *450 ml (16 fl oz) double cream*
- *75 g (3 oz) caster sugar*
- *700 g (1½ lb) ripe orange-fleshed melon, such as charentais or cantaloupe, halved and deseeded*
- *250 ml (9 fl oz) sweet wine, such as Moscatel de Valencia, or a light sugar syrup*

### 465-350 CALS/SERVING
- *1 ripe ogen or galia melon, halved and deseeded*
- *ginger biscuits, to serve*
- *fresh mint sprigs, to decorate*

1 Gently heat the cream and sugar until the sugar dissolves, stirring, then set aside to cool.
2 Place the 700 g (1½ lb) melon flesh in a blender or food processor with half the wine. Blend until smooth, then sieve to remove any coarse fibres.
3 Mix the sweetened cream with the purée. Pour into a freezerproof container. Freeze for 2½-3 hours, then stir to break down any ice crystals. Repeat this process twice, then leave to freeze for at least 2 hours until firm.
4 Scoop out the ogen or galia melon flesh with a melon baller and place in serving bowls. Pour a little of the remaining wine over each serving. Marinate in the refrigerator for about 1 hour.
5 To serve, scoop the melon ice into balls and serve with the marinated melon and ginger biscuits. Decorate with mint sprigs.

---

*TIP*
Although any freezerproof container is suitable for holding water ices or ice creams, a shallow one speeds up the freezing process.

## ICED ORANGE AND LEMON TERRINE WITH BURNT SUGAR SAUCE

PREPARATION TIME 25 minutes, plus chilling and freezing
COOKING TIME 8 minutes (sauce)
FREEZING Suitable (stage 3)

❄

### SERVES 6

- *4 egg yolks*
- *30 ml (2 tbsp) caster sugar*
- *300 ml (10 fl oz) whipping cream*
- *finely grated rind and juice of 1 large orange*
- *finely grated rind and juice of 1 lemon*

### 375 CALS/SERVING

- *mandarin or orange segments, to decorate*
- *SAUCE*
- *125 g (4 oz) caster sugar*
- *juice of ½ lemon*
- *pinch of salt*
- *150 ml (5 fl oz) single cream*

1 Using an electric whisk, whisk together the egg yolks and sugar for 5 minutes or until pale and thick.

2 Lightly whip the cream until it just holds its shape. Fold it into the egg mixture, along with all the orange and lemon juice and rind. The mixture will become quite liquid.

3 Line a 1.1 litre (2 pint) terrine or loaf tin with clingfilm. Pour in the mixture and freeze for 3 hours or overnight.

4 To make the sauce, put the sugar, plus 100 ml (3½ fl oz) water and the lemon juice in a heavy-based saucepan. Place over a medium heat for

about 3 minutes, until the sugar has dissolved. Do not stir. Increase the heat and cook for 5 minutes, until the sugar is a light caramel colour. Add the salt and, off the heat, stir in the cream. Chill for 3 hours or overnight.

5 Briefly dip the tin in hot water, then invert the terrine onto a serving plate. Remove the clingfilm and slice the terrine with a hot knife. Serve with the burnt sugar sauce and decorate with mandarin segments.

**NOTE** The young, the elderly, pregnant women and people with immune-deficiency diseases should not eat raw eggs, due to the possible risk of salmonella.

## FROZEN STRAWBERRY ICE

PREPARATION TIME 10 minutes, plus freezing
FREEZING Suitable
COLOUR INDEX Page 48

♡ ❄

### SERVES 6

- *450 g (1 lb) strawberries, hulled*
- *150 ml (5 fl oz) low-fat or low-calorie ice cream, slightly softened*
- *150 ml (5 fl oz) low-fat bio natural yogurt*

### 110 CALS/SERVING

- *15 ml (1 tbsp) framboise or cassis liqueur*
- *2 egg whites*
- *2 oranges*
- *strawberry leaves, to decorate*

1 In a blender or food processor, blend 225 g (8 oz) of the strawberries, the ice cream, yogurt and liqueur until smooth.

2 In a clean, dry bowl, whisk the egg whites until they just form soft peaks. Fold them into the strawberry mixture. Divide the mixture among 6 individual ramekins and freeze for at least 4 hours, or preferably overnight.

3 Slice the remaining strawberries into a bowl. Add the juice of the oranges, cover and marinate for about 1 hour.

4 To serve, dip the outside of the ramekins into warm water for a few seconds and turn out onto serving plates. Leave at room temperature for about 10 minutes to soften a little before serving with the marinated strawberries. Decorate with strawberry leaves.

# LIME AND CRANBERRY ICE

PREPARATION TIME 15 minutes, plus freezing
COOKING TIME 5-10 minutes
FREEZING Suitable
COLOUR INDEX Page 48

❄

**SERVES 8**
- *550 g (1¼ lb) cranberries*
- *8 egg yolks*
- *225 g (8 oz) caster sugar*
- *450 ml (15 fl oz) milk*

**270 CALS/SERVING**
- *2 limes*
- *500 g (1 lb 2 oz) carton bio natural yogurt*
- *juice of 1 orange*

1 Place the cranberries in a saucepan with a little water and heat gently until slightly softened. Drain well.
2 Whisk together the egg yolks and 175 g (6 oz) sugar until thick and pale. Bring the milk to just below boiling point, then pour it onto the egg mixture, whisking continuously. Rinse out the saucepan.
3 Return the mixture to the pan and heat gently, stirring, until the custard thickens slightly and just coats the spoon. Do not boil or the custard will curdle. Strain into a large bowl. Leave to cool.
4 Finely grate the rind of both limes and squeeze out 30 ml (2 tbsp) lime juice. Add the yogurt to the custard with 350 g (12 oz) cranberries and the lime rind and juice. Blend in batches in a food processor until almost smooth.
5 Pour into a freezer container to a depth of about 5 cm (2 inches). Freeze for about 4 hours until mushy, then beat well to break down the ice crystals. Freeze again until firm, for at least 8 hours. (If using an ice-cream maker, churn the mixture in the usual way.)
6 Place the remaining cranberries in a pan with the remaining sugar and the orange juice. Place over a gentle heat until the sugar dissolves and the cranberries are heated through. Pour into a bowl and leave to cool. Cover and chill.
7 About 1½ hours before serving, transfer the ice cream to the refrigerator to soften. Serve scoops with the cranberries in syrup.

# VANILLA ICE WITH ESPRESSO

PREPARATION TIME 5 minutes
FREEZING Not suitable

🕐

**SERVES 6**
- *espresso coffee*
- *vanilla or a 'nutty' luxury ice cream*

**260 CALS/SERVING**
- *chocolate-covered coffee beans or tiny chocolates, to serve*

1 Make up the espresso coffee according to the instructions on your machine.
2 Scoop the ice cream into glasses and pour about 45-60 ml (3-4 tbsp) hot espresso over each serving.
3 Serve with some chocolate-covered coffee beans or tiny chocolates.

*TIP*
If you don't have an espresso machine, use very strong black coffee or the sachets or jars of instant espresso coffee that can be found in most supermarkets.

# BAKING

# HAZELNUT VACHERIN
# WITH APRICOTS

PREPARATION TIME 35 minutes, plus cooling
COOKING TIME 55-65 minutes
FREEZING Not suitable

**SERVES 6**                    **400 CALS/SERVING**

- 125 g (4 oz) hazelnuts
- 3 egg whites
- 175 g (6 oz) caster sugar
- 2.5 ml (½ tsp) vanilla essence
- 50 g (2 oz) granulated sugar

- 225 g (8 oz) fresh apricots, halved and stoned
- grated rind of 1 lemon
- 150 ml (5 fl oz) double cream
- mint sprigs and fresh apricots, to decorate

**1** Spread out the hazelnuts on a baking tray and grill, shaking frequently, until browned. Leave to cool completely, then finely chop with a sharp knife. (Do not chop in the food processor as this will make the meringue too oily.)

**2** Whisk the egg whites until holding soft peaks, then whisk in half of the caster sugar, one spoonful at a time. Whisk for about 30 seconds until holding quite stiff peaks, then fold in the remaining caster sugar. Carefully fold in the hazelnuts with the vanilla essence.

**3** Spoon the mixture into a large piping bag fitted with a 5 mm (¼ inch) plain nozzle. Line 2 baking trays with non-stick baking parchment and draw a 23 cm (9 inch) circle on each.

**4** Pipe the meringue in a spiral to make a complete round on each piece of paper.

**5** Bake the meringue in the oven at 150°C (300°F) mark 2 for 40-45 minutes until dry and crisp. Leave to cool on the baking trays, then carefully peel off the paper.

**6** While the meringues are cooling, place the granulated sugar in a saucepan with 150 ml (5 fl oz) water and place over a low heat. Stir until the sugar has dissolved, then add the apricots and lemon rind and simmer for 10 minutes until the apricots are just tender, yet still holding their shape.

**7** Remove half of the apricots from the pan and set aside. Cook the rest for 5 minutes more until very soft, then drain (reserving the syrup) and push through a sieve to remove the skins. Allow to cool.

**8** When ready to serve, spread half of the apricot purée over one meringue. Whip the cream to soft peak stage and carefully spread over the apricot purée. Arrange the reserved apricot halves on the cream, and place the remaining meringue round on top. Stir 45 ml (3 tbsp) of the reserved syrup into the remaining apricot purée and serve as a sauce with the vacherin. Decorate the vacherin with sprigs of mint and fresh apricots.

**VARIATION** If wished, the apricot purée can be folded into the whipped cream to make a simple fool filling.

# RASPBERRY MOUSSE GATEAU

PREPARATION TIME 1½ hours, plus chilling
COOKING TIME 30-35 minutes
FREEZING Suitable (stage 6)
COLOUR INDEX Page 50

❄

**SERVES 6-8**

- *175 g (6 oz) shelled hazelnuts*
- *4 eggs*
- *125 g (4 oz) light muscovado sugar*
- *125 g (4 oz) white plain flour*
- *2.5 ml (½ tsp) baking powder*
- *25 g (1 oz) butter, melted and cooled*

**845-630 CALS/SERVING**
*FILLING*

- *450 g (1 lb) raspberries*
- *1 egg, separated*
- *25 g (1 oz) caster sugar*
- *7.5 ml (1½ tsp) powdered gelatine*
- *450 ml (15 fl oz) double cream*
- *150 ml (5 fl oz) Greek-style yogurt*

1 Grease and base-line a 20 cm (8 inch) round cake tin. Spread out the hazelnuts on a baking sheet and grill until browned. Leave to cool, then roughly chop 25 g (1 oz) and set aside. Finely grind the remaining nuts.
2 Whisk the eggs and muscovado sugar in a large bowl over a saucepan of barely simmering water until the mixture is thick and pale and will hold a trail. Remove the bowl from the heat and whisk for a further 3 minutes. Sift the flour and baking powder together and fold into the mixture alternately with the ground hazelnuts and butter.
3 Spread the mixture in the prepared tin and bake at 180°C (350°F) mark 4 for 30-35 minutes until risen and firm to the touch. Turn out, remove the paper and cool on a wire rack.
4 To make the mousse filling, rub half the raspberries through a sieve. Whisk the egg yolk, sugar and raspberry purée in a large bowl over a pan of barely simmering water until the mixture is thick and foamy and will hold a trail. Remove the bowl from the heat and whisk until cold.
5 Sprinkle the gelatine over 30 ml (2 tbsp) water in a small heatproof bowl and leave to soak, then stand the bowl in a pan of hot water until the gelatine is dissolved. Whip 50 ml (2 fl oz) cream and fold into the raspberry mixture. Gently stir in the gelatine. Whisk the egg white until holding soft peaks, then fold into the mixture.
6 Line a 20 cm (8 inch) spring-release cake tin with clingfilm. Cut the hazelnut cake into three

rounds and trim to a 20 cm (8 inch) diameter. Place one sponge round in the base of the tin. Whip 150 ml (5 fl oz) cream and fold in the yogurt, then spread over the cake. Scatter over one third of the reserved raspberries and cover with a second sponge round. Spoon on the mousse, scatter over another third of the raspberries and cover with the remaining sponge. Press down gently. Chill for 2 hours or until set.
7 Transfer to a plate. Whip the remaining cream and spoon mounds onto the cake. Scatter raspberries and chopped nuts in the middle.

# CHOCOLATE ROULADE

PREPARATION TIME 30 minutes, plus cooling
COOKING TIME 25 minutes
FREEZING Suitable (undecorated)
COLOUR INDEX Page 49

❄

**SERVES 6-8**

- *60 ml (4 tbsp) cocoa powder*
- *150 ml (5 fl oz) milk*
- *4 eggs, separated*
- *125 g (4 oz) caster sugar*
- *150 ml (5 fl oz) double cream*

**330-250 CALS/SERVING**

- *150 ml (5 fl oz) Greek yogurt*
- *strawberries and grated chocolate, to decorate*

1 Grease and line a 20 x 30 cm (8 x 12 inch) Swiss roll tin. Mix the cocoa powder and milk in a small saucepan and heat gently until the cocoa powder has dissolved. Leave to cool.
2 Whisk the egg yolks and sugar together until pale and fluffy. Whisk the cooled milk mixture into the egg yolk mixture.
3 Whisk the egg whites until stiff, then fold into the cocoa mixture. Spread the mixture evenly into the prepared tin and bake in the oven at 180°C (350°F) mark 4 for about 20 minutes until the sponge has risen and is just firm to the touch.
4 Turn out onto a sheet of greaseproof paper and cover with a warm, damp tea towel to prevent the sponge from drying out. Leave for 20 minutes.
5 Meanwhile, whip the cream until quite stiff, then stir in the yogurt. Spread over the sponge, reserving half for decorating, and then roll it up carefully. Do not roll it up too tightly and do not worry if it cracks slightly. Decorate with cream, strawberries and chocolate. Serve chilled.

## RICH CHRISTMAS CAKE

PREPARATION TIME 30 minutes, plus storing and icing
COOKING TIME 2½-3 hours
FREEZING Not suitable

**SERVES 12-16**
- *150 g (5 oz) each glacé cherries, dried figs, apricots, dates, raisins, sultanas*
- *50 g (2 oz) mixed peel*
- *175 ml (6 fl oz) dark rum*
- *175 g (6 oz) skinned, roasted hazelnuts*
- *225 g (8 oz) butter, softened*
- *grated rind of 1 lemon*
- *225 g (8 oz) soft dark brown sugar*
- *4 eggs, beaten*

**610-460 CALS/SERVING**
- *30 ml (2 tbsp) black treacle*
- *225 g (8 oz) white plain flour*
- *10 ml (2 tsp) ground mixed spice*

TO COVER
- *60-90 ml (4-6 tbsp) honey or apricot jam*
- *350 g (12 oz) white marzipan*
- *450 g (1 lb) ready-to-roll fondant icing*

TO DECORATE
- *gold ribbon*
- *red and gold berries*
- *gold fir cones*

1 Line a 20 cm (8 inch) round deep cake tin with a double thickness of greaseproof paper.
2 Rinse the glacé cherries to remove all the syrup.

Drain and dry on absorbent kitchen paper. Very roughly chop the cherries, figs, apricots and dates. Mix all the fruit and the mixed peel with 125 ml (4 fl oz) rum and soak for 3-4 hours.
3 Place 50 g (2 oz) hazelnuts in a blender or food processor and blend until finely chopped. Roughly chop the remainder.
4 Beat the butter with the lemon rind until soft and pale in colour. Gradually beat in the sugar until well mixed. Beat in the eggs a little at a time. Beat in the treacle until evenly blended.
5 Sift the flour and spice together and fold half into the creamed ingredients. Stir in all the hazelnuts. Gently fold in all the fruit, followed by the remaining flour. Spoon into the prepared cake tin, then level off the surface. Tie a band of brown paper around the outside of the tin.
6 Bake at 150°C (300°F) mark 2 for 2½-3 hours or until a fine skewer inserted into the centre comes out clean.
7 Pierce the surface with a fine skewer and spoon over the remaining rum. Leave the cake in the tin for 1 hour, then turn out. Cool on a wire rack. Remove all the lining paper and wrap tightly in fresh greaseproof paper and foil. Store in a cool, dry place for at least a week and up to 2 months.
8 To marzipan the cake, warm half the honey or apricot jam with 15 ml (1 tbsp) water in a pan

and brush over the cake. On a surface lightly dusted with icing sugar, roll out the marzipan in a circle, large enough to cover the top and sides of the cake – about 10 cm (4 inches) bigger than the cake top. Place over the cake, press gently around the sides, then trim the edges. Dry for 2 days.

9 To fondant-ice, warm the remaining honey or sieved apricot jam with 15 ml (1 tbsp) water in a pan. Lightly brush over the cake. Sprinkle a work surface and rolling pin with cornflour. Roll out the fondant icing until it is about 10 cm (4 inches) larger than the cake top. Cover the cake. Leave to dry in a cool place for 2 days, covered, then decorate with ribbon, berries and cones.

# STOLLEN

PREPARATION TIME 40 minutes, plus rising
COOKING TIME About 40 minutes
FREEZING Suitable
COLOUR INDEX Page 50
❋

**SERVES 10**
- *15 g (½ oz) fresh yeast or 7 g (¼ oz) sachet fast-action dried yeast*
- *about 175 ml (6 fl oz) tepid milk*
- *350 g (12 oz) strong white plain flour*
- *5 ml (1 tsp) salt*
- *3.75 ml (¾ tsp) ground mixed spice*
- *50 g (2 oz) butter*
- *finely grated rind of 1 lemon*
- *25 g (1 oz) caster sugar*

**325 CALS/SERVING**
- *50 g (2 oz) currants*
- *75 g (3 oz) raisins or sultanas*
- *25 g (1 oz) chopped mixed peel*
- *40 g (1½ oz) flaked almonds*
- *1 egg, beaten*
- *melted butter, for brushing*
- *175 g (6 oz) almond paste or white marzipan*
- *icing sugar for dusting*

1 If using fresh yeast, blend with the milk. Sift the flour, salt and spice into a bowl and rub in the butter. Stir in the lemon rind, sugar, currants, raisins, mixed peel, almonds and fast-action dried yeast, if using. Make a well in the centre of the dry ingredients and add the yeast liquid or milk and egg. Beat to form a soft dough, adding a little more milk if necessary.

2 Turn out the dough onto a floured surface and, with floured hands, knead for 8-10 minutes until the dough is elastic and almost smooth. Place in

an oiled bowl. Cover with oiled clingfilm and leave in a warm place for 1½-2 hours until doubled in size.

3 Using floured hands, knock down the dough, then place on a lightly floured work surface and knead for 1-2 minutes only. Roll out the dough to a 25 cm (10 inch) square. Brush lightly with melted butter. Knead and roll out the almond paste to a strip about 23 x 10 cm (9 x 4 inches) and place down the centre of the dough. Fold the dough over the almond paste and seal well.

4 Pinch the ends together to enclose the almond paste. Place, seam-side down, on a buttered baking sheet. Make a few slits across the top. Cover and leave in a warm place for 30-45 minutes until doubled in size.

5 Bake at 190°C (375°F) mark 5 for 40 minutes or until sounding hollow when tapped. Cool on a wire rack. Dust with icing sugar.

# MINCE PIES

PREPARATION TIME 1 hour
COOKING TIME About 25 minutes
FREEZING Suitable
COLOUR INDEX Page 51
❋

**MAKES ABOUT 24**
- *Shortcrust Pastry, made with 225 g (8 oz) flour (see page 369)*
- *about 225 g (8 oz) Apricot Mincemeat (see page 314)*

**105 CALS/MINCE PIE**
- *1 egg white, lightly beaten*
- *caster sugar*
- *cream, to serve*

1 Roll out the pastry thinly and cut out about 48 5.5 cm (2¼ inch) rounds, re-rolling as necessary.

2 Place half the rounds on baking sheets and spoon mincemeat onto the centre of each. Moisten the pastry edges. Cover with the remaining pastry rounds, sealing the edges well; flute, if wished. Make a hole in the top to allow steam to escape.

3 Bake at 200°C (400°F) mark 6 for about 15 minutes or until just set but not browned.

4 Take out of the oven and brush with lightly beaten egg white and dredge with caster sugar. Return to the oven for a further 8-10 minutes or until well browned. Serve the mince pies warm with cream.

# HONEY AND YOGURT MUFFINS

PREPARATION TIME 15 minutes
COOKING TIME 17-20 minutes
FREEZING Suitable
COLOUR INDEX Page 51
♡ ⏱ ❄

MAKES 12
- *225 g (8 oz) white plain flour*
- *7.5 ml (1½ tsp) baking powder*
- *5 ml (1 tsp) bicarbonate of soda*
- *pinch of salt*
- *2.5 ml (½ tsp) ground mixed spice*
- *1.25 ml (¼ tsp) ground nutmeg*
- *50 g (2 oz) medium oatmeal*

180 CALS/MUFFIN
- *50 g (2 oz) light muscovado sugar*
- *50 g (2 oz) butter*
- *225 g (8 oz) Greek yogurt*
- *125 ml (4 fl oz) milk*
- *1 egg*
- *60 ml (4 tbsp) clear honey*
- *oatmeal, for dusting*

1 Line 12 deep bun tins or muffin tins with paper muffin cases. Sift the flour, baking powder, bicarbonate of soda, salt, mixed spice and nutmeg into a bowl. Stir in the oatmeal and sugar.
2 Melt the butter and leave to cool slightly. Mix the yogurt and milk together in a bowl, then beat in the egg, butter and honey.
3 Pour over the dry ingredients and stir in quickly until only just blended; do not over-mix.
4 Divide the mixture equally between the paper cases. Sprinkle with oatmeal and bake at 200°C (400°F) mark 6 for 17-20 minutes until well risen and just firm to the touch. Remove from the oven and leave in the tins for 5 minutes, then transfer to a wire rack. Serve warm or cold, with a little butter if desired.

**VARIATION** *Chocolate Banana Muffins* Omit the honey. Mash 1 small ripe banana and mix with 125 g (4 oz) melted plain chocolate. Add to the muffin mixture after the liquids, blending until rippled with colour.

# BERRY SCONES

PREPARATION TIME 20 minutes
COOKING TIME 10 minutes
FREEZING Suitable
COLOUR INDEX Page 51
♡ ⏱ ❄

MAKES ABOUT 16
- *450 g (1 lb) white self-raising flour*
- *2.5 ml (½ tsp) salt*
- *10 ml (2 tsp) baking powder*
- *75 g (3 oz) butter, diced*
- *75 g (3 oz) caster sugar*

160 CALS/SERVING
- *225 g (8 oz) blackberries*
- *about 200 ml (7 fl oz) semi-skimmed milk*
- *1 egg, beaten*

1 Sift the dry ingredients together in a large bowl. Rub in the butter until the mixture resembles breadcrumbs. Stir in the sugar and the berries.
2 Stir in enough milk to form a firm dough. Knead very lightly and roll out on a floured surface until about 2.5 cm (1 inch) thick. Using a 6 cm (2½ inch) plain cutter, stamp out rounds, taking care to avoid cutting through the berries. Knead and carefully re-roll as necessary.
3 Place the scones on a greased baking tray and brush the tops with beaten egg. Bake at 220°C (425°F) mark 7 for about 10 minutes until well risen and golden.

**NOTE** Frozen blackberries also work very successfully in this recipe – just add them straight from the freezer.

**VARIATION** For traditional fruit scones, use 125g (4 oz) currants, sultanas, or raisins instead of the blackberries. Omit the sugar.

# SIMNEL CAKE

PREPARATION TIME 40 minutes, plus cooling
COOKING TIME About 2½ hours
FREEZING Suitable (stage 6)
❊

**SERVES 20**

- *175 g (6 oz) butter or block margarine, softened*
- *175 g (6 oz) caster sugar*
- *3 eggs, lightly beaten*
- *225 g (8 oz) white plain flour*
- *pinch of salt*
- *2.5 ml (½ tsp) ground cinnamon*
- *2.5 ml (½ tsp) grated nutmeg*
- *125 g (4 oz) glacé cherries, washed, dried and cut into quarters*

**345 CALS/SERVING**

- *50 g (2 oz) chopped mixed peel*
- *250 g (9 oz) currants*
- *125 g (4 oz) sultanas*
- *finely grated rind of 1 lemon*
- *15-30 ml (1-2 tbsp) milk (if necessary)*
- *450 g (1 lb) white almond paste or marzipan*
- *1 egg white, lightly beaten*
- *ribbon and fresh or fondant flowers, to decorate*

1 Line and grease an 18 cm (7 inch) round cake tin. Cream the butter and sugar together until pale and fluffy. Gradually beat in the eggs.
2 Sift in the flour, salt and spices and fold into the mixture. Add all the fruit and the lemon rind, folding in to give a smooth dropping consistency. If too firm add 15-30 ml (1-2 tbsp) milk.
3 Divide the almond paste in half. Lightly dust a surface with icing sugar and roll out one half to a 16 cm (6½ inch) circle.
4 Spoon half of the cake mixture into the prepared tin. Place the round of almond paste on top and cover with the remaining cake mixture.
5 Tie a double thickness of brown paper around the outside of the tin. Bake at 150°C (300°F) mark 2 for about 2½ hours. When cooked the cake should be a rich brown colour, and firm to touch.
6 Cool in the tin for about 1 hour, then turn out and leave to cool completely on a wire rack.
7 Divide the remaining almond paste in two. Roll out one half to a 19 cm (7½ inch) circle and the rest into 11 small balls. Brush the top of the cake with egg white. Place the circle of almond paste on top, crimp the edges and, with a little egg white, fix the balls around the top edge of the cake.
8 Brush the almond paste with the remaining egg white and place under a hot grill for 1-2 minutes until the paste is well browned. Tie ribbon around the cake and decorate with flowers.

**VARIATION** Before grilling, apply a rope edging of almond paste around the top edge of the cake. When cool, cover the top of the cake with white glacé icing (see page 304).

with floured hands, knead for about 8-10 minutes or until the dough is elastic and almost smooth. Place in a large, lightly oiled bowl. Cover with oiled clingfilm and leave in a warm place until doubled in size; this usually takes 1½-2 hours.
3 Knock down the dough and knead lightly for 1-2 minutes. Divide the dough into about 25 equal-sized pieces and knead each one into a small ball. Place on buttered baking sheets, seam-side down, and flatten slightly with the heel of your hand.
4 Roll out the pastry and cut into narrow strips. Brush the buns with egg to glaze and top each one with a pastry cross. Glaze again. Leave in a warm place until doubled in size; about 30 minutes. Bake at 190°C (375°F) mark 5 for 15-18 minutes until they sound hollow when tapped. Cool on wire racks.

## MINI HOT CROSS BUNS

PREPARATION TIME 30 minutes, plus rising
COOKING TIME 15-18 minutes
FREEZING Suitable
❋

**MAKES 25**
- 15 g (½ oz) fresh yeast or 7 g sachet fast-action dried yeast
- about 175 ml (6 fl oz) tepid milk
- 350 g (12 oz) strong white plain flour
- 5 ml (1 tsp) salt
- 5 ml (1 tsp) ground mixed spice
- 5 ml (1 tsp) ground cinnamon
- 5 ml (1 tsp) freshly grated nutmeg

**95 CALS/BUN**
- 50 g (2 oz) butter
- finely grated rind of 1 lemon
- 25 g (1 oz) caster sugar
- 75 g (3 oz) currants
- 25 g (1 oz) chopped mixed peel
- 1 egg, beaten
- 75 g (3 oz) ready-made shortcrust pastry
- beaten egg, to glaze

1 If using fresh yeast, blend with the milk. Sift the flour, salt and spices into a bowl and rub in the butter. Stir in the lemon rind, sugar, currants, mixed peel and fast-action dried yeast if using. Make a well in the centre; add yeast liquid or milk and egg. Beat to form a soft dough, adding a little more milk if necessary.
2 Turn out the dough onto a floured surface and,

## EASTER BISCUITS

PREPARATION TIME 20 minutes
COOKING TIME 15 minutes
FREEZING Suitable
COLOUR INDEX Page 52
❋

**MAKES 30**
- 125 g (4 oz) butter, softened
- 75 g (3 oz) caster sugar
- 1 egg, separated
- 200 g (7 oz) white plain flour
- pinch of salt
- 2.5 ml (½ tsp) ground mixed spice

**65 CALS/BISCUIT**
- 2.5 ml (½ tsp) ground cinnamon
- 50 g (2 oz) currants
- 15 ml (1 tbsp) chopped mixed peel
- 15-30 ml (1-2 tbsp) brandy or milk
- caster sugar, for sprinkling

1 Cream the butter and sugar together in a bowl until pale and fluffy, then beat in the egg yolk. Sift the flour, salt and spices together over the mixture. Stir well, then add the fruit and mixed peel, with enough brandy or milk to give a fairly soft dough.
2 Knead lightly on a lightly floured surface and roll out to a 5 mm (¼ inch) thickness. Cut into 5 cm (2 inch) rounds using a fluted cutter. Place on lightly greased baking sheets.
3 Bake at 200°C (400°F) mark 6 for 10 minutes, then brush with the lightly beaten egg white and sprinkle with a little caster sugar. Return to the oven for a further 5 minutes, or until golden brown. Transfer to wire racks to cool.

## STICKY ORANGE FLAPJACKS

PREPARATION TIME 10 minutes
COOKING TIME 25-30 minutes
FREEZING Suitable

✳

**MAKES 18**
- *2 small oranges*
- *250 g (9 oz) unsalted butter, diced*
- *250 g (9 oz) caster sugar*
- *175 g (6 oz) golden syrup*

**300 CALS/FLAPJACK**
- *425 g (15 oz) porridge oats*
- *30 ml (2 tbsp) sunflower seeds*
- *45 ml (3 tbsp) fine-shred orange marmalade*

1 Grease a baking tin measuring about 22 x 9 cm (8½ x 11½ inches) across the top and 19 x 27 cm (7½ x 10½ inches) across the base.
2 Using a citrus zester, finely pare the rind from the oranges in strips. Place in a heavy-based saucepan. Add the butter with the sugar and syrup. Cook over a moderate heat, stirring until the butter has melted. Remove from the heat and stir in the oats, until evenly coated in syrup.
3 Turn the mixture into the prepared tin and level the surface. Sprinkle with the sunflower seeds. Bake at 180°C (350°F) mark 4 for 25-30 minutes until turning deep golden around the edges; the

mixture will still be very soft in the centre. Leave in the tin until almost cold.
4 Heat the marmalade in a small saucepan with 15 ml (1 tbsp) water until syrupy. Brush evenly over the flapjack. Turn out onto a board and cut into 18 bars. Store in an airtight container for up to 1 week.

**NOTE** To weigh syrup, first measure out the sugar quantity and leave it in the scales' bowl, making a small well in the centre. Add additional weights for the required quantity of syrup and spoon the syrup into the well. Both sugar and syrup will then slide cleanly into the saucepan.

**VARIATION** *Fruit and Nut Flapjacks* Omit the orange rind, sunflower seeds and marmalade. Add 125 g (4 oz) luxury mixed dried fruit and 75 g (3 oz) chopped and toasted mixed nuts with the oats.
*Pear and Cinnamon Flapjacks* Omit the orange rind, sunflower seeds and marmalade. Add 5 ml (1 tsp) ground cinnamon with the sugar, and 150 g (5 oz) roughly chopped dried pears with the oats.

# ALMOND SQUARES

PREPARATION TIME 25 minutes
COOKING TIME 35 minutes
FREEZING Suitable

❋

MAKES ABOUT 12
- *Sweet Flan Pastry, made with 125 g (4 oz) white plain flour (see page 371)*
FILLING
- *45 ml (3 tbsp) raspberry jam*
- *1 egg white*

140 CALS/SERVING
- *45 ml (3 tbsp) ground almonds*
- *50 g (2 oz) caster sugar*
- *few drops of almond flavouring*
- *45 ml (3 tbsp) flaked almonds*

1 Roll out the pastry on a lightly floured surface to an 18 cm (7 inch) square and use to line the base of a greased shallow 18 cm (7 inch) square cake tin. Spread the pastry with the jam, almost to the edges.
2 Whisk the egg white until stiff. Fold in the ground almonds, sugar and a few drops of almond flavouring. Spread the mixture over the jam on the pastry.

3 Sprinkle with flaked almonds and bake at 180°C (350°F) mark 4 for about 35 minutes until crisp and golden. Cool in the tin, then cut into squares to serve.

**VARIATION** *Glacé Icing Topping* For an indulgent treat, drizzle the top of the cooled baked mixture with glacé icing. To make the icing, simply sift 125 g (4 oz) icing sugar into a bowl, then gradually mix in 15 ml (1 tbsp) warm water until the icing is thick enough to coat the back of a spoon. If you would like to flavour the icing with orange or lemon, substitute 15 ml (1 tbsp) strained orange or lemon juice for the water.

## HONEY WAFERS

PREPARATION TIME 20 minutes, plus cooling
COOKING TIME 20-30 minutes
FREEZING Suitable
COLOUR INDEX Page 52

❋

**MAKES 24**                    **50 CALS/WAFER**
- *50 g (2 oz) unsalted butter (at room temperature)*
- *75 g (3 oz) icing sugar*
- *60 ml (4 tbsp) clear honey*
- *75 g (3 oz) white plain flour*
- *5 ml (1 tsp) ground cinnamon*
- *1 egg white, lightly beaten*

1 Line 2 large baking sheets with non-stick baking parchment. Beat the butter until very soft, then beat in the icing sugar and honey. Sift together the flour and cinnamon and stir into the mixture with the egg white to make a smooth batter.
2 Drop 4-6 heaped teaspoonfuls of the mixture onto the baking sheets, spacing well apart, and spread out to 7.5 cm (3 inch) rounds with the back of the spoon.
3 Bake at 220°C (425°F) mark 7 for 5-7 minutes until golden, then carefully lift off the baking sheet with a palette knife and transfer to a wire rack to cool and crisp. Use the remaining mixture to make at least 24 wafers in all.

**NOTE** Don't overcrowd the baking sheets, when making the wafers. Spread them on the baking sheet, keeping them well-spaced apart, so they cook to an even golden colour. It is important that the baking parchment is flat and smooth, not creased, otherwise the wafers will form odd shapes.

**VARIATIONS** These crisp wafers can be layered with raspberries, cream and yogurt to make a delicious dessert. Whip 300 ml (10 fl oz) double cream until holding soft peaks. Fold in 150 ml (5 fl oz) Greek-style yogurt, 30 ml (2 tbsp) icing sugar, and 30 ml (2 tbsp) framboise or kirsch if liked. Layer up the wafers in threes, sandwiching them together with the cream and 350-450 g (12 oz-1lb) raspberries. Dust generously with icing sugar and serve at once, decorated with mint sprigs. Alternatively use 225 g (8 oz) strawberries, sliced, and 2 oranges, peeled and segmented, in place of the raspberries. Use Grand Marnier or other orange-flavoured liqueur rather than framboise.

## ORANGE FLOWER BISCUITS

PREPARATION TIME 10 minutes, plus chilling
COOKING TIME 8 minutes
FREEZING Not suitable

**MAKES 20-24**                 **65 CALS/BISCUIT**
- *125 g (4 oz) white plain flour*
- *15 g (½ oz) cornflour*
- *100 g (3½ oz) firm, lightly salted butter, diced*
- *50 g (2 oz) icing sugar*
- *20 ml (4 tsp) orange flower water*
- *icing sugar, for dusting*

1 Sift the flour and cornflour and place in a food processor. Add the butter and blend until combined. (Alternatively sift the flours into a bowl and rub in the butter.)
2 Add the icing sugar and orange flower water and blend until the mixture binds together. Knead lightly and chill for 30 minutes.
3 Thinly roll out the paste on a lightly floured surface and cut out rounds using a 6.5 cm (2½ inch) cutter, re-rolling trimmings to make more biscuits.
4 Place on a lightly greased baking sheet and bake at 200°C (400°F) mark 6 for about 8 minutes until beginning to colour around the edges.
5 Transfer to a wire rack and leave to cool. Dust generously with icing sugar to serve.

**VARIATION** Use rosewater instead of the orange flower water, or add the finely grated rind of 1 orange or lemon.

# BUCHE DE NOEL

PREPARATION TIME I hour
COOKING TIME About 10 minutes
FREEZING Suitable (stage 7)

❄

**SERVES 8-10**
- *3 eggs*
- *125 g (4 oz) caster sugar*
- *75 g (3 oz) white plain flour*
- *30 ml (2 tbsp) cocoa powder*
- *440 g (15½ oz) can sweetened chestnut purée*
- *icing sugar for dusting*

**720-575 CALS/SERVING**
- *holly sprigs, to decorate*

*BUTTER CREAM*
- *225 g (8 oz) unsalted butter*
- *50 g (2 oz) plain chocolate*
- *450 g (1 lb) icing sugar*

1 To make the cake, grease a 33 x 23 cm (13 x 9 inch) Swiss roll tin. Line with greaseproof paper and grease the paper. Dredge with a little caster sugar, then with a little flour, knocking out any excess.

2 Put the eggs and sugar in a deep heatproof bowl and stand it over a saucepan of simmering water. Whisk until thick enough to leave a trail on the surface when the whisk is lifted.

---

### TIP
For an attractive additional decoration, make meringue mushrooms; bake 'caps' and 'stalks' separately and stick together with butter cream.

---

3 Take the bowl off the saucepan and continue whisking the mixture for 5 minutes or until cool. Sift in the flour and cocoa and gently fold into the mixture. Fold in 15 ml (1 tbsp) hot water.

4 Pour the mixture gently into the prepared tin and lightly level the surface. Bake in the oven at 200°C (400°F) mark 6 for about 10 minutes or until slightly shrunk away from the sides of the tin.

5 Meanwhile, place a sheet of greaseproof paper on top of a tea towel. Dredge the paper with caster sugar and turn the cake out onto it. Trim off the crusty edges with a sharp knife. Roll up the cake with the paper inside. Transfer to a wire rack, seam side down, and leave to cool for 20 minutes.

6 To make the butter cream, beat the butter until soft. Put the chocolate with 15 ml (1 tbsp) water in a heatproof bowl over hot water. Melt, then leave to cool slightly. Gradually sift and beat the icing sugar into the softened butter, then add the melted chocolate.

7 Unroll the cold Swiss roll. Remove the paper and spread the chestnut purée over the cake. Roll up again and place on a cake board or plate.

8 Cut a thick diagonal slice off one end of the Swiss roll and attach with butter cream to the side of the roll.

9 Using a piping bag and a large star nozzle, pipe thin lines of butter cream over the log. Pipe one or two swirls of butter cream to represent knots in the wood. Decorate the log with sprigs of holly and dust lightly with icing sugar.

# FLORENTINES

PREPARATION TIME 20 minutes, plus cooling
COOKING TIME About 15 minutes
FREEZING Not suitable
COLOUR INDEX Page 52

**MAKES ABOUT 30**
- *100 g (3½ oz) butter*
- *125 g (4 oz) caster sugar*
- *125 g (4 oz) flaked almonds, roughly chopped*
- *25 g (1 oz) sultanas*
- *5 glacé cherries, chopped*

**120 CALS/SERVING**
- *25 g (1 oz) chopped mixed peel*
- *15 ml (1 tbsp) single cream or milk*
- *300 g (10 oz) plain chocolate*

1 Line 4 baking sheets with non-stick baking parchment. Melt the butter in a saucepan over a low heat, add the sugar and boil the mixture for 1 minute.

2 Remove the pan from the heat and add all the remaining ingredients, except the chocolate, stirring well to mix.

3 Drop the mixture into small heaps onto the prepared baking sheets, allowing space between each for the mixture to spread.

4 Bake in the oven at 180°C (350°F) mark 4 for 10-15 minutes or until golden brown.

5 Remove from the oven and press around the edges of the biscuits with the blade of a knife to neaten the shape. Leave on the baking sheets for 5 minutes or until beginning to firm, then cool on a wire rack.

6 When the biscuits are cool, melt the chocolate and leave it to cool for about 10-15 minutes or until it coats the back of a spoon and is just beginning to set.

7 Spread the chocolate over the backs of the biscuits. Mark wavy lines in the chocolate with a fork and leave to set.

**VARIATION** To make more elaborate florentines, for serving as petits fours, make them slightly smaller than here. Coat half with plain and half with milk chocolate, then pipe with contrasting lines of chocolate to decorate.

# SHORTBREAD

PREPARATION TIME 20 minutes, plus chilling
COOKING TIME 20 minutes
FREEZING Not suitable

MAKES 24-36
- *450 g (1 lb) butter*
- *225 g (8 oz) caster sugar*
- *450 g (1 lb) white plain flour*
- *225 g (8 oz) rice flour or ground rice*

270-180 CALS/BISCUIT
- *pinch of salt*
- *golden or coloured granulated sugar, for coating*
- *caster sugar, for sprinkling*

1 Line 2 baking sheets with greaseproof paper. Cream the butter and sugar together in a bowl until pale and fluffy. Sift the flour, rice flour and salt together and stir into the creamed mixture until it resembles breadcrumbs.

2 Gather the dough together with your hand and

turn onto a clean work surface. Knead lightly until it forms a ball, then lightly roll into a sausage, about 5-7.5 cm (2-3 inches) thick. Wrap in clingfilm and chill until firm.

3 Unwrap the roll and slice into discs, about 7-10 mm (1/3-1/2 inch) thick. Pour golden or coloured granulated sugar onto a plate and roll the edge of each disc in the sugar. Place the biscuits, cut-side up, on the baking sheets.

4 Bake at 190°C (375°F) mark 5 for about 15-25 minutes, until very pale golden. Remove from the oven and sprinkle with caster sugar. Allow to cool on the baking sheet for 10 minutes, then transfer to a wire rack to cool.

**VARIATIONS** *Spiced Shortbread:* Sift 15 ml (1 tbsp) ground mixed spice with the flours.
*Ginger Shortbread*: Sift 5 ml (1 tsp) ground ginger with the flours. Add 50 g (2 oz) chopped crystallized ginger to the dough.
*Chocolate Chip Shortbread*: Knead 50 g (2 oz) chocolate chips into the dough.

## OAT AND SESAME BISCUITS

PREPARATION TIME 30 minutes
COOKING TIME 12-15 minutes
FREEZING Suitable

❄

MAKES 50
- *125 g (4 oz) wholemeal self-raising flour*
- *125 g (4 oz) white self-raising flour*
- *2.5 ml (½ tsp) salt*
- *5 ml (1 tsp) mustard powder*
- *150 g (5 oz) butter, diced*

60 CALS/BISCUIT
- *5 ml (1 tsp) caster sugar*
- *225 g (8 oz) medium oatmeal*
- *50 g (2 oz) sesame seeds*
- *50 ml (2 fl oz) milk*
- *oil for greasing*

1 Place the first five ingredients in a bowl. Rub the butter into the flour until the mixture resembles fine breadcrumbs.
2 Stir in the sugar, oatmeal and sesame seeds. Add the milk with 25 ml (1 fl oz) water. Knead the mixture together to form a dough. Turn out onto a lightly floured surface.
3 Thinly roll out half the dough and cut into small biscuits, about 4 x 6.5 cm (1½ x 2½ inches) each. Repeat with the remaining dough to make about 50 biscuits. Place the biscuits on lightly oiled baking sheets, spacing them well.
4 Bake at 180°C (350°F) mark 4 for 12-15 minutes or until golden and cooked through. Cool on wire racks.

## COTTAGE CHEESE AND BRAZIL NUT TEABREAD

PREPARATION TIME 10 minutes
COOKING TIME 50-60 minutes
FREEZING Suitable
COLOUR INDEX Page 52

♡ ❄

MAKES ABOUT 12 SLICES
- *225 g (8 oz) cottage cheese*
- *75 g (3 oz) light muscovado sugar*
- *125 g (4 oz) wholemeal self-raising flour*
- *125 g (4 oz) white self-raising flour*
- *finely grated rind and juice of 1 lemon*
- *2 eggs, beaten*
- *75 ml (5 tbsp) milk*

190 CALS/SLICE
- *75 g (3 oz) stoned dates, rinsed and roughly chopped*
- *75 g (3 oz) brazil nuts, chopped*
- *6 whole brazil nuts, to decorate*
- *15 ml (1 tbsp) clear honey, to glaze*

1 Grease and line a 1.1 litre (2 pint) loaf tin.
2 Put all the ingredients, except the whole brazil nuts and honey, in a bowl and beat well until the mixture has a soft dropping consistency.
3 Spoon into the prepared loaf tin and level the surface. Lightly press the whole brazil nuts in a line down the centre of the mixture to decorate.
4 Bake at 180°C (350°F) mark 4 for 50-60 minutes until risen and golden. Cover with foil if the teabread browns too quickly. Turn out and brush with the honey while still warm. Cool on a wire rack. Serve sliced, spread with butter.

*TIP*
Oat and Sesame Biscuits are delicious served with rich blue cheeses. Try dolcelatte, a quite mild Italian Gorgonzola-type cheese with a soft, creamy texture, or Cambazola, a blue-Brie type German cheese that is creamy white with blue-green veining.

## OLIVE AND WALNUT BREAD

PREPARATION TIME 20 minutes, plus rising
COOKING TIME 37 minutes
FREEZING Suitable

♡ ❄

**MAKES TWO LOAVES**
**(12 SLICES EACH)**
- *125 g (4 oz) pitted black olives, roughly chopped*
- *75 g (3 oz) walnuts, finely chopped*
- *600 g (1 lb 5 oz) white strong plain flour*

**125 CALS/SLICE**
- *10 ml (2 tsp) salt*
- *7 g (¼ oz) sachet fast-action dried yeast*
- *75 ml (5 tbsp) chopped fresh parsley*
- *45 ml (3 tbsp) olive oil*

**1** Mix the olives and walnuts together with the flour, salt, yeast and parsley.
**2** Make a well in the centre of the dry ingredients and add 375 ml (12 fl oz) tepid water mixed with 45 ml (3 tbsp) oil. Stir together to form a soft dough, adding a little more water if necessary.
**3** Turn the dough onto a well-floured surface and knead well for about 10 minutes, or until it is smooth and elastic.
**4** Divide the dough in half and shape each piece into a roll 18-20 cm (7-8 inches) long. Place rolls of dough on separate oiled baking sheets and cover loosely with lightly oiled clingfilm.
**5** Leave the dough in a warm place for 30-40 minutes or until doubled in size. Lightly slash the top of each loaf.
**6** Bake at 220°C (425°F) mark 7 for 12 minutes. Lower the temperature to 180°C (350°F) mark 4 for a further 25 minutes or until well browned and sounding hollow when tapped. Leave to cool for a few minutes on wire racks.
**7** Serve warm, thickly sliced.

# CONFECTIONERY, PRESERVES AND DRINKS

# MENU PLANNER

# Basic Techniques and Information

## Boning Whole Round Fish

Small round fish like herrings are often cooked whole because they are fiddly to fillet. Sometimes you may need to bone a large round fish for cooking whole.

1 Scale and gut the fish in the usual way (see page 334). Cut off the head and tail or leave them on if preferred. Extend the cut along the belly (used for gutting) so that it goes right to the tail.

2 Open the fish out, then lay it on its side on a board. Carefully cut the rib bones free from the flesh on the upper-side.

3 Turn the fish over and repeat on the other side, working through to the backbone, being careful not to cut through the flesh.

4 With a pair of kitchen scissors, cut through the backbone as close to the head as possible. Hold the backbone at the head end and carefully pull it free. Snip it at the tail end so that it can be removed completely.

5 Check the flesh for any remaining bones, removing any small bones with tweezers.

NOTE If it is a small fish, simply open it out, then lay it on a board cut side down. Press firmly along the backbone with your fingers to loosen it. Turn the fish over and you should now be able to pull the backbone away with the ribs attached. Remove any fine bones that don't come away, using tweezers.

## COOKING FISH

Because white fish is lacking in fat, it is easily dried out during cooking. If you're cooking fish by a 'dry' method such as grilling or barbecuing then it's important to baste frequently with butter, oil or marinade. For moist methods of cooking like poaching it's vital to cook the fish gently; if the cooking liquid boils vigorously the fish will disintegrate during cooking.

Choose a cooking method that's appropriate to the fish. Chunky steaks of firm or oily fish or sturdy whole fish can withstand fierce treatments which would ruin less robust fillets. Here are a few basic methods of cooking.

### Deep-frying

Coat the prepared fish with seasoned flour, batter or egg and breadcrumbs. Half fill a deep saucepan or deep-fat fryer with vegetable oil and heat to 190°C (375°F). Fry the fish, a few pieces at a time, until golden brown. Test whether it is cooked by cutting a piece open and trying it. Drain on kitchen paper.

### Shallow-frying

Coat the fish in seasoned flour or egg and bread-crumbs and fry in vegetable oil or a mixture of vegetable oil and butter.

### Grilling

Before you start cooking, line the grill pan with foil to prevent lingering fish smells. If cooking whole fish or thick fillets with skin on, slash the skin so that the heat can penetrate. Brush generously with melted butter, oil or a marinade, and cook under a preheated hot grill until the flesh looks opaque. Turn large fillets or fish occasionally.

### Baking

Put the fish in a shallow dish with a few herbs, seasoning and a splash of wine, fish stock or milk. Cover and bake at 180°C (350°F) mark 4. Alternatively, bake wrapped in a foil or greaseproof paper parcel.

### Poaching

Heat a well-flavoured court bouillon or fish stock or some dry white wine or milk flavoured with parsley, onion, bay and a few peppercorns. Add the fish and simmer gently until the fish is just opaque.

### Steaming

Season thoroughly before cooking and sprinkle with a few herbs, a squeeze of lemon juice or a knob of butter. Wrap in foil and steam over boiling water until the fish is opaque. Takes about 10 minutes.

# SHELLFISH

Fresh, perfectly cooked shellfish is prized the world over for its delicate flavour and stunning appearance. There's nothing that quite compares with a plateful of juicy prawns; a bowl of steaming mussels; or a magnificent plate of fruits de mer. Shellfish can be divided into three types: crustaceans, molluscs and cephalopods. Crustaceans include the prized lobster, crabs, shrimps, prawns and freshwater crayfish. They have hard external skeletons which are segmented to allow for movement. Molluscs live inside one or two hard shells (valves). The bivalves include oysters, mussels, clams and scallops. Cephalopods, namely squid, octopus and cuttlefish, belong to the mollusc family but have no shells.

All shellfish is highly perishable, so freshness should be the main consideration. Get to know a good local fishmonger – look for a shop with a fast turnover and a clean, well presented display.

### Choosing Shellfish
Look for tightly closed, undamaged shells. Lobsters and crabs should feel heavy for their size. Fresh shellfish has a clean, unnoticeable smell – don't buy if it has a strong smell of any kind. Prawns develop a strong chlorine-like smell if past their best.

When buying frozen shellfish, choose firm, thoroughly frozen and undamaged packets. Buy more than the recipe calls for to allow for weight loss after thawing. Cook quickly once thawed.

Refrigerate shellfish as soon as possible after purchase. It will deteriorate rapidly if stored in warm conditions. All shellfish really should be eaten on the day of purchase, particularly oysters, mussels and prawns, but if this is impractical, it can be stored in the refrigerator for up to 1 day. Frozen shellfish will deteriorate and lose its flavour after 2-3 months.

### *LOBSTER*
There is much controversy surrounding the cooking of live lobsters. If you have the choice it is preferable to get your fishmonger to cook the lobster for you. If you haven't, here is our method.

Weigh the lobster. Take a large saucepan with a tightly fitting lid; fill with water and flavourings such as onion, carrot, celery, bouquet garni and peppercorns. Bring the water to a rapid boil then holding the lobster by its back lower it in. Cover, reduce the heat and boil gently for 10 minutes for the first 450 g (1 lb) and 5 minutes for each additional 450 g (1 lb).

Leave to cool in the liquid.

Some classic lobster dishes call for raw, cut-up pieces of lobster. This is another job that's best left to your fishmonger.

### To Prepare Cooked Lobster

**1** Twist off the claws and pincers. Crack open the large claws using the back of a heavy knife, being careful not to crush the meat inside. Reserve the smaller claws for garnishing.

**2** Put the lobster, back upwards, on a flat surface and using a sharp knife split the lobster cleanly in two, piercing through the 'cross' at the centre of the head.

**3** Remove and discard the intestine which runs through the centre of the tail, the stomach (which lies near the head) and the spongy looking gills or 'dead man's fingers', which are inedible.

**4** Using a teaspoon, scoop out the edible soft grey liver (tomalley) and red roe (if any). Carefully lift the tail meat from the shell, pulling it out neatly and in one piece if you can. Cut into thick slices or as required.

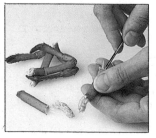

**5** Using a skewer, carefully remove the meat from each rear leg, in a whole piece.

## CRAB

There are numerous varieties of this crustacean which is particularly prized for its delicate white leg and claw meat. All crabs have a hard shell which is shed periodically to allow the crab to grow. Some species, caught when in this soft shell state, are cooked and eaten whole – claws and all.

Like lobsters the cooking of live crabs in controversial. The RSPCA recommends a humane method to de-sensitise crabs before cooking, but this is not for the squeamish. Therefore it's best to leave the cooking of crabs in the experienced hands of your fishmonger. Should you wish to cook a crab at home, here is our method:

Weigh the crab. Take a large saucepan with a tightly fitting lid; fill with water and flavouring ingredients such as bay leaves, onion, celery leaves and peppercorns. Bring to the boil. Lower the crab into the water. Reduce the heat, cover and boil gently for 15 minutes for the first 450 g (1 lb) and 5 minutes for each additional 450 g (1 lb). Leave to cool in the liquid.

### To Prepare Cooked Crab

Extracting the meat from a cooked crab is a fiddly, time-consuming job – but it's well worth the effort. Aim to keep separate the brown body meat, which is mostly liver, the flaky white meat and the creamy body meat.

1 Twist off the legs and claws as close to the body as possible. Break each claw in half then crack with a rolling pin or hammer without crushing the flesh. Break the shell on the legs with your hands. Using a slender skewer to get at any awkward bits, carefully extract the flesh.

2 Put the crab on its back with the tail flap pointing towards you. Holding the shell firmly, press the body section upwards with your thumbs and it should come away. If it won't move, use the point of a rigid knife to ease it away.

3 With a teaspoon scoop out into separate bowls the creamy meat and roe (if any) from the shell. Remove and discard the stomach bag which you will find between the eyes. (If it breaks make sure you remove all the greenish or grey-white matter.)

4 Pull away from the body and discard the inedible feathery gills or 'dead man's fingers'. Using a large heavy knife, cut the body in half. Using a skewer, remove the flesh from the tiny crevices.

## PRAWNS AND SHRIMPS

Prawns and shrimps are possibly the most popular members of the crustacean family. Good fishmongers and supermarkets now stock a multitude of prawns from the ubiquitous common prawn to the jumbo Mediterranean prawn. Shrimps are tiny prawn-like creatures which are often peeled and mixed with melted butter to make potted shrimps. To make things confusing, what we call prawns are known as shrimps by the Americans. And Dublin Bay prawns are not prawns at all, but belong to the lobster family. To make matters even more confusing, their peeled tail meat is known as scampi!

Until recently, prawns were generally sold ready-cooked; now raw prawns are increasingly available – fresh and frozen. These tend to have more flavour and 'bite' than ready-cooked prawns, so they're well worth looking out for, particularly for barbecues and Chinese-style dishes. Prawns need gentle cooking, or they will be tough. Simmer pre-cooked prawns briefly until heated through; cook raw prawns for a couple of minutes until they look opaque.

### To Peel Raw or Cooked Prawns

1 Grip head between thumb and forefinger. Gently pull until it comes off, holding tail shell with the other hand.

**2** Peel off the body shell and the legs.

**3** Large prawns have a bitter tasting intestinal vein running down their back. Remove this with a sharp knife and discard before cooking.

### SCALLOPS

Scallops are best bought live in the shell. However, they are kept tightly closed by a strong muscle which makes them really difficult to prise out – especially if you aren't practised at it. It's advisable to get your fishmonger to open them because it can be very frustrating! Don't forget to ask for the shells for serving.

Large scallops are usually sliced for cooking, while smaller ones are left whole. Like prawns they need only brief cooking or they will be tough. The really delicate orange coral takes a matter of seconds to cook so this is usually separated and added last.

**To Prepare Scallops in the Shell**
To open them yourself, follow the method below, but if they still refuse to open, heat them in a low oven for about 10 minutes. Don't leave them in the oven for too long or the delicate flesh will be overcooked.

**1** Scrub the shells under cold running water to remove as much sand as possible. Give any that are open a sharp tap with the back of a knife. Discard any that do not close.

**2** Put a scallop flat side up on a board or hold it level in the palm of your hand. Insert the point of a strong 10 cm (4 inch) long knife between the shells at about 45° to the hinge. It probably won't go straight in but be patient and continue twisting until it does.

**3** When the shells have opened slightly, slide your finger in between (wear a sturdy glove for this) then with the knife in your other hand quickly cut round the top shell to detach the muscle and part the shells.

**4** Push the top shell backwards until the hinge at the back snaps. Rinse the scallop (still attached to the lower shell) under cold running water to remove any sand.

**5** Using a small knife and being careful not to tear the flesh, cut away all the grey coloured beard-like fringe.

**6** Slide the knife point under the black thread on the side. Gently pull it off with the attached intestinal bag. Ease the scallop from the bottom shell.

### MUSSELS

Mussels are usually sold live in the shell although they are also available ready-cooked and frozen in 450 g (1 lb) bags (which is roughly equivalent to 900 g (2 lb) mussels in the shell).

The process of cleaning and preparing mussels puts a lot of people off, but it's very straightforward. Once prepared, they take only minutes to cook.

**To Prepare Mussels in the Shell**

**1** Put the mussels in the sink and under cold running water scrape off any mud or barnacles with a small sharp knife. Pull away the hair-like beard that protrudes from the shell.

2 Tap any mussels that remain open with the back of the knife. If they refuse to close, throw them away. Rinse again in cold water until there is no trace of sand.

## OYSTERS

The delicately flavoured oyster is praised the world over. To be appreciated fully they are best eaten raw from the half shell seasoned simply with lemon juice or black pepper, so freshness is of utmost importance. Choose oysters with tightly closed shells and refrigerate quickly after purchase, covered with a damp cloth. Always eat oysters on the day you buy them.

### To Open Oysters

1 Put the oyster, wrapped in a clean tea towel, on a firm surface with the flattest shell uppermost and the hinge pointing towards you. Gripping the oyster firmly, insert an oyster knife into the small gap in the hinge and twist to snap the shells apart.

2 Slide the blade of the knife along the inside of the upper shell to sever the muscle that keeps the shells together.

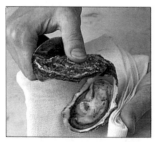

3 Lift off the top shell, being careful not to spill any juice. Clean away any bits of broken shell from the lower shell.

4 Run the blade of the knife under the oyster to loosen it from the shell.

## SQUID

In this country squid enjoys an undeserved reputation for being tough and rubbery. This is invariably due to bad cooking; squid should be cooked very quickly or very slowly to make it tender. Cooked properly, it is delicious and amazingly versatile. Try it deep-fried, stuffed and baked, or stewed in its own ink.

Squid is not difficult to prepare, but you may find the procedure slightly unpleasant. Look out for ready-prepared squid in the fishmongers or follow these instructions. It's best to do the whole operation in the sink under cold running water.

### To Prepare Squid

1 Holding the body firmly in one hand, grip the head and tentacles with the other hand, pull gently and they will come away along with the contents of the body.

2 Cut off the tentacles, just in front of the eyes. Remove the ink sac from the head if required for the recipe, otherwise throw the head and body contents away. Remove and discard the squid's beak which can be found where the tentacles are joined.

3 Peel off the thin layer of skin that covers the body and discard.

4 Pull out the plastic-like quill, then turn the body inside out and wash thoroughly.

# MEAT

The current desire for a healthier, lower-fat diet means that our consumption of meat is decreasing. Thankfully, meat producers are gradually responding to this and producing new leaner cuts. The increased demand for fast food means that they're also developing new tender cuts which cook quickly. In fact meat is highly nutritious, and for a lot of people it's still their major source of protein, B vitamins and iron. If you are worried about your fat consumption, or on a diet, choose the lean cuts without too much visible fat. Alternatively, make a small amount of meat go further by serving it with lots of vegetables or by mixing it with pulses in casseroles and stews.

### Choosing Meat

Meat should look and smell fresh. As for colour, a lurid red doesn't necessarily indicate freshness. Instead look for a good clear colour; the colour of meat will darken naturally on exposure to the air. A greyish tinge is certainly a bad sign. Any fat should be creamy white; if it's yellow – except for some specialist breeds such as Jersey and Guernsey beef – the meat is probably past its prime. Look for a smooth outer layer of fat, if appropriate to the cut, and a fair amount of 'marbled' fat distributed throughout the meat; this will keep it moist during cooking and add flavour.

Always look for a neat, generally well trimmed piece of meat. Splinters of bone and ragged edges indicate poor butchery. Cuts should be trimmed of sinew. Joints and steaks should be of uniform thickness so that they cook evenly. Offal should look fresh and moist, and it should not smell.

A good butcher is invaluable; a shop run by helpful knowledgeable staff inevitably means that they care about their meat and will have treated it properly. It is also likely that they will be able to advise you about cooking times and methods as well as prepare joints, steaks and the like to your specific requirements.

### Storing Meat

All meat should be stored loosely wrapped in the coldest part of the refrigerator. It's advisable to remove meat from its original wrapping and place, freshly wrapped, on a plate to prevent any blood dripping through the refrigerator shelves. Always store raw meat well away from cooked foods.

Offal, minced meat and small cuts of veal are best eaten on the day of purchase. Larger joints, chops and steaks will keep for 2-3 days. Lean cuts will keep for longer than fatty cuts since the fat turns rancid first. 'Off' or bad meat will have an unpleasant smell, slimy surface and possibly even a greenish tinge. Because of the possibility of food poisoning it's not worth taking a risk with meat that you suspect of being past its best.

### Marinades

A good marinade will make all the difference to the taste and texture of a piece of meat. Usually based on oil or wine or something acidic, like fruit juice or yogurt, it will tenderise tough cuts and lend a subtle aroma and flavour. Oil and wine based marinades tend to soak into the meat adding moisture to dry cuts while yogurt will tenderise and form a soft crust on the food as it cooks. Aromatics like lemon rind, bay leaves, thyme, garlic and onion add fragrance as well as flavour.

Put the food in a shallow non-metallic dish and pour over the marinade. Leave in a cool place for at least 1 hour but preferably overnight. When ready to cook, brush or strain off excess marinade and cook as directed in the recipe. If you're cooking on a barbecue or under the grill baste the meat frequently with the marinade as it cooks. Any remaining marinade can be brought to the boil in a small pan, strained if necessary, and poured over accompanying vegetables or salad leaves. The exception to this is any yogurt based marinade which would curdle.

## COOKING METHODS

To get the most from a cut or joint of meat it is vital to cook it appropriately. Lean, fine-grained cuts respond well to quick cooking while tougher cuts with more connective tissue need long, slow cooking to make them tender.

### Roasting

Only good quality tender joints are suitable for roasting. Opinions differ about roasting times and temperatures because there is a great deal of variation in the way people like their meat cooked. We found that high temperature roasting, at 230° C (450° F) mark 8, was only suitable for really top quality cuts, such as beef fillet.

However you decide to cook your roast, it's important to weigh the joint and bring it to room temperature before cooking. Put the meat, fat side up, on a roasting rack and smear with mustard or stud with slivers of garlic. Pork should be rubbed with oil and salt to make a nice crisp crackling. With the exception of pork with crackling, baste all roasts frequently during cooking to keep them moist; if the joint is very lean add moisture in the form of dripping or oil. Refer to the chart below for roasting times.

To determine accurately whether the meat is cooked, insert a meat thermometer into the thickest part to ascertain the internal temperature. Alternatively and much less accurately, push a skewer right into the middle of the joint. If the juices run clear the meat is thoroughly cooked; if they run pink, the meat is medium; if bloody, it's rare or under-cooked.

### Stewing and Casseroling

These cooking methods are almost identical except one is cooked on the hob and the other in the oven. For a good colour, brown the meat thoroughly, in

### ROASTING MEAT

| | COOKING TIME AT 180°C (350°F) MARK 4 | INTERNAL TEMPERATURE |
|---|---|---|
| **BEEF** | | |
| Rare | 20 mins per 450 g (1 lb) plus 20 mins | 60°C (140°F) |
| Medium | 25 mins per 450 g (1lb) plus 25 mins | 70°C (160°F) |
| Well done | 30 mins per 450 g (1 lb) plus 30 mins | 80°C (175°F) |
| **VEAL** | | |
| Well done | 25 mins per 450 g (1 lb) plus 25 mins | 70°C (160°F) |
| **LAMB** | | |
| Medium | 25 mins per 450 g (1 lb) plus 25 mins | 70-75°C (160-170°F) |
| Well done | 30 mins per 450 g (1 lb) plus 30 mins | 75-80°C (170-175°F) |
| **PORK** | | |
| Well done | 35 mins per 450 g (1 lb) plus 35 mins | 80-85°C (175-180°F) |

batches if necessary, before adding any liquid. If you are reducing your fat intake the fat can be skimmed off the stew or casserole before serving. The best way of removing fat is to prepare the dish ahead and allow it to cool completely until the fat solidifies on the surface; it can then be removed easily.

Choose a good heavy-based saucepan or casserole to prevent the contents burning or sticking to the bottom and make sure that it has a tightly fitting lid so that the liquid will not evaporate too rapidly. Keep the liquid at a gentle simmer just below boiling point; if it boils the meat is likely to be tough. All the less tender, more economical cuts of meat can be used. Any meat labelled 'stewing' will take longer to cook than meat labelled 'braising'. If you're making stews or casseroles for the freezer, add flavourings such as garlic sparingly.

### Braising

Braising is similar to the above methods although, generally speaking, it tends to involve less liquid. The browned meat is set on a bed of vegetables with sufficient liquid to create steam, covered tightly and cooked very gently. Slightly tenderer cuts are used. Read the labels in the supermarket or ask your butcher for advice on suitable cuts for braising.

### Frying, Grilling and Barbecuing

These methods are only suitable for tender cuts. Marinating the meat before cooking helps to add flavour and keeps it moist. Ensure that the frying pan, grill or barbecue is hot before you begin cooking so that the meat is sealed and browned. If cooking thicker pieces, or pork or sausages which must be cooked right through, reduce the heat once the meat has browned or if barbecuing move it away from the heat source.

If frying, use a good heavy-based pan and a fat that can withstand the high temperature: olive or vegetable oil; clarified butter rather than pure butter; dripping; some vegetable margarines (avoid low fat brands which contain water and therefore splatter).

For stir-frying, cut the meat into small evenly sized pieces across the grain. A marinade of soy sauce, garlic and a dash of dry sherry will ensure that the meat is tasty and tender if nothing is suggested in your recipe. Heat the wok and a little vegetable oil until very hot. Add the meat, drained of marinade if necessary, and keep turning and stirring as it cooks.
• COOKING STEAKS Professional chefs determine when a steak is cooked as required by pressing it with their fingertips – they can tell by the degree of resistance. For inexperienced cooks this is impractical. In

fact cooking steaks to perfection is difficult. The only really reliable way is to cut the steak open and look at it. The timing depends on the thickness rather than the size of the piece of meat. As a rough guide, a 2 cm (3/4 inch) thick steak will take about 2 minutes' grilling or frying each side for rare; 3-4 minutes each side for medium; and 6-7 minutes to be cooked through.

### Boiling

This is a misnomer since boiling produces tough and tasteless meat. Meat for boiling is usually salted, so it should be soaked overnight in several changes of cold water before cooking. Cover the meat with fresh water and a tightly fitting lid and simmer gently for about 25 minutes per 450 g (1 lb) plus 30 minutes for large joints and about 1 1/2 hours minimum for small joints; do not boil. Add vegetables, spices and herbs to the cooking liquid if you intend using it as stock. Pressure cookers greatly reduce the cooking time. Refer to the manufacturer's handbook but in general allow about two thirds of the cooking time.

### Carving Meat

Regardless of the cut or type of meat here are a few golden rules which make carving much easier.
• A decent-sized, really sharp knife is essential. It's worth keeping a knife sharpener to hand to re-sharpen the knife half way through.
• A proper carving fork with two long prongs and a finger guard helps keep the meat firmly in place.
• Leave the joint to stand on an edged dish in a warm place for 5-15 minutes before you start. This allows the meat to 'relax' and makes carving much easier. Pour off any juices that collect in the dish and add them to the gravy.
• Always put the joint on a firm, flat, non-slip surface. A board is ideal, but some people prefer to use a spiked metal dish.
• Remove any string or skewers which will get in the way as you carve.
• Before starting to carve, loosen the cooked meat from any outer, exposed bones.
• Cut across the grain of the meat, which usually means cutting at a right angle to the main bone.

### A GUIDE TO MEAT CUTS

Cuts of meat and their names vary enormously across Britain and throughout Europe and the United States. Some butchers and supermarkets in this country now stock a good range of Continental cuts. If you are unsure of a particular description it's best to ask. The following cuts are most commonly available.

### BEEF

Beef is still the first choice for roasting, but influences from abroad and changes in our eating patterns are encouraging us to use it in many other ways too.
• TOPSIDE A very lean cut with little fat, so it is usually sold with a layer of fat tied around it. Great for roasting and braising. Also sold sliced for making beef olives.
• RIB Both fore rib (the end of the ribs) and rib are sold on the bone or boned and rolled. Rib is more fatty than topside. It is usually roasted and served hot or cold.
• SIRLOIN This is another tender cut, sold either on the bone or boned and rolled for roasting. Sometimes it is sold with the fillet still attached, otherwise this is removed and sold separately as fillet steak.

Porterhouse steak is cut from the thick end of the sirloin and can weigh as much as 800 g (1 1/2 lb). When it is cooked on the bone it is called T-bone steak. Minute steak is very thin steak from the upper part of the sirloin.
• FILLET OF TENDERLOIN The ultimate joint for roasting and making Beef Wellington, fillet is the small 'eye' on the inside of the rib bone. It is extremely expensive, but very lean and tender. Fillet is best served rare. Chateaubriand is a thick slice of steak cut from the middle of the fillet, that serves 2 people. Tornedos or filet mignon steaks are also cut from the fillet.
• ENTRECOTE By definition, this is the part of the meat between the ribs. However, a slice cut from the sirloin or rump is sometimes sold by this name.
• RUMP STEAK A lean tender cut, taken from the hind quarter. Suitable for grilling or frying.
• FLASH FRY STEAKS Cut from the thick flank, topside or silverside, these steaks are beaten and passed between spiked rollers to make them tender.
• SILVERSIDE Another lean, boneless joint sold for roasting, but it can be dry and tough if cooked in this way. Traditionally it is salted and boiled. Uncooked salted beef is an unpalatable shade of grey, but it soon becomes pink when cooked.
• BRISKET Sometimes sold on the bone, but more commonly boned and rolled; it may also be salted. Brisket is best braised or pot roasted, but it can be roasted.
• CHUCK AND BLADE STEAK A lean cut which is usually sold sliced or cubed for braising, stewing and pie fillings. Look for some marbling of fat throughout.
• THICK FLANK (TOP RUMP) Another lean boneless cut for pot roasting and braising. If thinly sliced it can be fried.

• THIN FLANK Suitable for braising and stewing.

• NECK AND CLOD For stewing or mince.

• SHIN AND LEG Lean meat with lots of connective tissue. Needs slow, moist cooking such as stewing or casseroling.

## VEAL

Veal comes from young calves so it is a very tender, lean meat. The palest (and most desired by some) comes from baby milk-fed calves; as the animals get older they supplement their diet with grass and the meat darkens. Veal production is a dubious and at times inhumane practice. If you are happy to eat veal you should at least try to buy it from a butcher who uses a reliable supplier.

Despite its tenderness veal does not roast well; because it is so lean it tends to dry out. The most common cuts are as follows:

• LEG A prime cut, sold sliced as escalopes.

• FILLET The most expensive cut, generally sold in a piece for roasting. Follow recipes carefully because it tends to dry out. If possible, ask your butcher to lard it for you or marinate for 1 hour before cooking.

• KNUCKLE OR OSSO BUCO Meat and bone ready sawn into 5 cm (2 inch) pieces for stews and of course the Italian speciality, Osso Buco.

• LOIN Usually sold as cutlets and chops. It may also be boned and sold as entrecôte steak, or rolled for roasting.

• BREAST Usually the cheapest cut. Sold boned and rolled and sometimes ready stuffed for roasting.

• PIE VEAL Diced trimmings. This needs long slow cooking.

• LIVER AND KIDNEYS Calf's liver and kidneys are considered to be superior to all others. Calf's liver is mild and tender. Can be sautéed or grilled.

## LAMB

Think of lamb and you'll probably think of Spring; new potatoes, young peas and mint from the garden. Although home-produced lamb is at its best in the Spring, there is a good supply all year round owing to imported New Zealand lamb. Today's lamb is leaner than ever thanks to new ways of dividing the carcass, many influenced by French butchers. Shoulders and legs of lamb are now cut into steaks, and minced lamb is more widely available.

• LEG Probably the most popular cut for roasting, the leg has plenty of lean meat. It is usually sold with the bone in, but some butchers now sell ready boned legs. After boning it can also be 'butterflied' – spread flat for grilling or barbecuing – so that it cooks quickly and easily.

• SHOULDER Sold whole or halved for roasting. Chops or steaks can also be cut from the shoulder for grilling or braising.

• LOIN The loin consists of both chump and loin chops. Chump chops have a small round bone in the centre, and loin chops a small T bone. Loin steaks are simply loin chops with the bone removed. The whole loin can also be roasted in one piece either on or off the bone.

• SADDLE OF LAMB OR DOUBLE LOIN This is a really large joint for roasting consisting of the whole loin from both sides of the lamb. It is sometimes sold sliced into butterfly or Barnsley chops.

• FILLET OF LAMB This is also cut from the loin; it is very lean and can be roasted, or cooked en croûte rather like a fillet of beef.

• RACK OF LAMB Formerly known as best end of neck, this is sold as a whole roasting joint consisting of 6-8 chops or cutlets. Usually chined by the butcher to make serving easier, the tips of the cutlet bones are then scraped of all fat and meat to look attractive. The cut used for Guard of Honour and Crown Roast.

• LAMB CUTLETS Individual cutlets are popular for grilling and frying. Boned and rolled cutlets are called noisettes; these neat portions of lean meat are excellent grilled or fried.

• SCRAG AND MIDDLE NECK These are usually sold as neck cuts on the bone for stewing and braising in dishes like Lancashire Hotpot and Irish Stew. The main 'eye' of the middle neck is sold as neck fillet for grilling and frying.

• BREAST OF LAMB Generally sold ready boned and rolled and sometimes stuffed, breast of lamb is tender enough to roast, but because it contains a lot of connective tissue it is best cooked slowly and thoroughly. Riblets are cut from the breast for grilling.

• LIVER Suitable for frying or braising. To tone down the strong flavour, soak in milk for 1 hour before cooking, if wished.

• KIDNEY Lamb's kidney is darker than calf's and smaller. It is best quickly fried or grilled.

• HEART Whole hearts can be stuffed and braised or casseroled. Before cooking, wash thoroughly, trim away any fat and tubes and snip the cavity walls. Leave to soak for 1 hour in clean salted water. Rinse and drain.

• BRAINS Lamb's brains have a delicate flavour. They are usually sold in sets (one portion). Before cooking, soak for 2 hours in cold water or milk to remove all traces of blood.

• SWEETBREADS These are part of the lamb's thymus gland. They need to be soaked as above before cooking.

## PORK

The pork of today is leaner than it has ever been and it's available in a variety of quick-cooking cuts. Pork must always be well cooked: it should never be served rare or medium. Use a meat thermometer to check the internal temperature of roast pork; a reading of 85°C (180°F) indicates that it's well cooked. Alternatively, insert a skewer into the thickest part of the joint and the juices should run clear.

Part of the attraction of roast pork is the crackling. For good, crisp crackling score the rind, pat it dry, then rub it with oil and a generous amount of salt. Don't baste the rind as it cooks or it will not crisp. For moist methods of cooking like stews and casseroles it's best to remove the rind.

• LOIN A popular joint for roasting either on the bone or boned, stuffed and rolled. It usually has a good layer of crackling. It may also be cut into loin chops which sometimes have the kidney attached, or loin steaks (boned loin chops).

• LEG This large joint is usually sold divided into the fillet end and the knuckle or shank end. Both are good for roasting. The fillet end is sometimes cut into leg steaks for grilling or frying.

• SHOULDER OR HAND SPRING Another joint for roasting, or using diced in pie fillings, curries and casseroles.

• TENDERLOIN OR PORK FILLET This lean and really versatile cut is excellent for cubing and making kebabs for grilling. When thinly sliced it is perfect for pan-frying. Escalopes are thin, batted-out slices cut across the grain from the fillet or the leg.

• SPARE RIBS These are cut from the belly or the ribs. Spare rib chops can be casseroled or braised, while trimmed American or Chinese spare ribs are less meaty and often cooked in barbecue sauce.

• BELLY A long thin cut streaked with fat. It may also be sold as a boned and rolled joint.

• LIVER Pig's liver has a strong flavour, which can be toned down slightly by soaking in milk for 1-2 hours before cooking. It is really only suitable for including in pâtés and terrines.

## BACON AND HAM

Bacon is quite simply pork that has been preserved or cured. But, as a meat, bacon is almost in a category of its own. For some, the smoky flavour and aroma as it cooks are irresistible. Moreover bacon is highly versatile. Use it grilled until crisp in salads, to top baked potatoes, or in sandwiches. Cook it until the fat runs, and toss with vinaigrette and lentils, or use it to flavour pasta dishes, stews and casseroles.

There are several methods of curing bacon which all produce different flavours. Basically the meat is injected with brine solution which colours, flavours and preserves the meat. A side of bacon may be cured whole or cuts – such as the middle – may be cured separately. After curing it may be smoked. Unsmoked bacon is known as 'green' bacon.

Ham, strictly speaking, is the hind leg of a pig cut from the whole side, then cured and matured separately. Gammon is the name given to whole hind legs cut from a side of bacon after it has been cured. Cooked gammon is now frequently described as ham.

### Cuts of Bacon, Ham and Gammon

Throughcut (middle) rashers are the back and streaky joined together. Back, streaky and throughcut rashers are virtually interchangeable in recipes, although streaky is obviously much more fatty. If you are trying to reduce your fat consumption look out for 'fat reduced' bacon. Always drain grilled or fried bacon on kitchen paper after cooking.

Check whether the recipe states smoked or unsmoked bacon. Smoked bacon will lend a smoky flavour to foods it is cooked with and in some dishes this may be too strong.

Ham has a subtler more delicate flavour than bacon, but it is equally versatile. Hams are usually sold ready cooked; if not, cook as bacon. Some of the best known cures are York, Suffolk, Honey-roast, Cumberland and Virginia. Some hams, such as the Italian Parma ham, French *Bayonne* and Spanish *Serrano* are eaten raw.

• COLLAR OF BACON Taken from the shoulder, then boned and rolled, this is a good joint for boiling or braising. It may need to be soaked before cooking.

• FOREHOCK OF BACON This cheap cut is sold with the bone in or boned and rolled. It has a good flavour and is fairly lean. Use in pot roasts, braise with vegetables or simmer it.

• GAMMON Buy gammon raw as a whole or half gammon or as smaller cuts which are known as middle, corner and gammon hock. Most are sold boned, ready to boil, braise or bake.

Gammon steaks and rashers are cut after boning and are suitable for grilling or frying.

### Cooking Bacon and Gammon Joints

To remove excess salt, soak large joints overnight in frequent changes of cold water. Green or mild cure joints need only 4-6 hours' soaking or none at all – ask your butcher's advice. Simmer in water, with a few vegetables for flavour, for 20-25 minutes per 450 g (1 lb) plus 20 minutes. For joint over 4.5 kg (10 lb) allow 15-20 minutes per 450 g (1 lb) plus 15 minutes.

# POULTRY AND GAME

Poultry is the general name given to all domesticated birds bred for the table: chickens, ducks, geese, turkeys and guinea fowl. Strictly speaking, game is any wild bird or beast which is hunted for food, but the term is now used rather loosely to include some farm animals, such as rabbit and venison. Guinea fowl, which used to regarded as game, is now farmed extensively so it is classified as poultry.

### Choosing Poultry and Game

A grain diet and the freedom to roam in the open air produces the best flavoured poultry. At last consumers are realising this and some farmers are being encouraged to move away from intensive battery farming methods to produce free-range birds. In response to this the EC has introduced a set of guidelines stipulating free-range farming conditions such as the maximum number of birds per square metre; feed content; and the degree of open air access allowed. The aim is to ensure that birds labelled as such really are free-range.

True free-range chickens can be identified by calluses on their feet – unfortunately most birds are sold ready trimmed so this is impossible to check. Rely on your butcher or read supermarket labels instead. With all birds look for a moist, unbroken skin with no dark patches, and a nice plump breast. In young birds the breast will be pliable. When choosing duck look for a plump bird with a good light-coloured skin. Poultry that's past its best rapidly develops an 'off' smell. It should not be eaten if it smells anything other than fresh. If buying from a supermarket, check the sell-by date.

When choosing game look for soft, plump breast meat and unscarred feet. Badly callused feet indicate an old bird. A flexible breastbone and short spurs are also signs of youth. Young pheasants and partridges have a large pointed tail feather; in older birds it is rounded. Avoid any bird that has been badly damaged by shot.

### Handling and Storing Poultry

It is vital that poultry is handled, stored and cooked correctly, because most, if not all, raw poultry contains low levels of salmonella and campylobacter, the bacteria responsible for food poisoning. Provided that poultry is correctly stored these bacteria will remain at low levels. As long as it is then cooked thoroughly they will be killed by the heat and ren-

dered harmless. Always use the following guidelines:
• If buying frozen poultry, check that it's frozen solid. If buying fresh, ensure that it's well chilled and within the sell-by date.
• Transfer poultry to the refrigerator or freezer as soon as possible after purchase. In warm weather it's advisable to carry it home in an insulated cool bag.
• Remove the giblets from fresh poultry, put the bird on a plate to catch any drips then cover and store in the refrigerator for up to 2 days.
• Frozen poultry will keep for up to 3 months. Frozen chicken should be thawed at cool room temperature, not in the refrigerator. Pierce the wrapping and put the chicken on a plate to catch any drips. Remove the giblets as soon as they are loose.
• Always check that poultry is completely thawed before cooking: make sure that there are no ice crystals in the body cavity and that the legs are quite flexible. Once thawed, cover and refrigerate, but cook as soon as possible. For turkey thawing times, refer to the chart on page 347. Never re-freeze raw poultry.
• To avoid cross-contamination, always wash your hands before and after preparing poultry. NEVER use the same utensils for preparing raw and cooked poultry without first washing them thoroughly in hot soapy water. It's advisable to keep a separate chopping board for preparing raw poultry.
• Stuff the neck end only. Do not stuff the body cavity or the heat may not penetrate fully to kill the salmonella bacteria.
• Always cook poultry thoroughly until the juices run clear. Cool leftovers quickly, refrigerate and use within 2 days.

### *CHICKEN*

For taste, versatility and nutritional value, chicken is hard to beat. It's full of protein and B vitamins and once the skin is trimmed away, it has very little fat. It is therefore not surprising that this white meat is so popular and available in so many different shapes and sizes, both fresh and frozen. All of the chickens and cuts described below are also available as free range birds.
• Oven-ready chickens range in weight from 1.4-3.2 kg (3-7 lb). Allow at least 375 g (12 oz) per person. These are suitable for roasting, casseroling, braising and barbecuing.
• Corn-fed chickens are a distinctive yellow colour because they are reared on a diet of maize. They can

be cooked in the same way as oven-ready chickens.
• Poussins are 4-6 week old chickens. They weigh about 450-575 g (1-1¹/₂ lb). One poussin will serve 1-2 people. If serving 2 the bird is usually halved along the breastbone.
• Spring chickens are 12 week old birds weighing about 1.1 kg (2¹/₂ lb). One chicken will serve 2-3 people.
• Boiling fowl are older tougher birds weighing 2.3-3.2 kg (5-7 lb). Only really suitable for casseroling or for making stock, they are not as widely available as they used to be.
• Guinea fowl are lean golden-coloured birds weighing about 900 g-1.8 kg (2-4 lb). They are interchangeable with oven-ready or corn-fed chickens.
• Chickens are also available ready jointed into halves, quarters, breasts, thighs and wings. Chicken breast fillets are the lean white breast meat sold with or without the skin. When skinned and flattened they are known as escalopes. With the wing bone attached they are known as supremes. Cook carefully; if overcooked the lean meat becomes very dry.

### TURKEY

Once limited to Christmas, turkey is now available all year round both whole and as a boned roast; you can also buy turkey breast as escalopes, and even thighs and drumsticks for roasting. Free-range turkeys are also becoming more commonly available.
• Oven-ready turkeys are available fresh and frozen in sizes ranging from 2.3 kg (5 lb) to an enormous 13.5 kg (30 lb). For a guide to thawing and roasting turkey see below.
• Self-basting turkeys have a basting ingredient such as butter injected under the skin to keep them moist during cooking.

### JOINTING AND BONING POULTRY

All types of chicken and turkeys are treated in much the same way; size being the only difference. Poussins and spring chickens are best left to your butcher to bone because they're a bit fiddly.

Before you start, thoroughly wash your hands and make sure that the work surface is scrupulously clean. Use a very sharp knife or poultry shears.

### Jointing

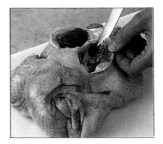 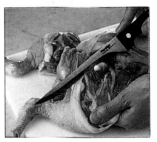

1 Put the bird breast side down and with the tip of a knife cut round the two portions of oyster meat (which lie against the backbone).

2 Turn the bird over and cut through the skin where the thigh joins the body. Cut right down between the ball and socket joint, being careful to keep the oyster meat attached to the leg. Repeat with the other leg.

3 If liked, separate the thighs from the drumsticks by cutting through at the joints. Trim off the bone end from the drumsticks.

### ROASTING TURKEY (FRESH OR FROZEN)

| Oven-ready weight | Approximate thawing time (at cool room temperature) if applicable | Cooking time (without foil) | Cooking time (foil wrapped) | Approx. no of servings |
|---|---|---|---|---|
| 550 g-1.4 kg (1¹/₄-3 lb) | 4-10 hours | 1¹/₂-1³/₄ hours | 1³/₄-2 hours | 2-4 |
| 1.4-2.3 kg (3-5 lb) | 10-15 hours | 1³/₄-2 hours | 2-2¹/₂ hours | 4-6 |
| 2.3-3.6 kg (5-8 lb) | 15-18 hours | 2-2¹/₂ hours | 2¹/₂-3¹/₂ hours | 6-10 |
| 3.6-5 kg (8-11 lb) | 18-20 hours | 2¹/₂-3¹/₄ hours | 3¹/₂-4 hours | 10-15 |
| 5-6.8 kg (11-15 lb) | 20-24 hours | 3¹/₄-3³/₄ hours | 4-5 hours | 15-20 |
| 6.8-9 kg (15-20 lb | 24-30 hours | 3³/₄-4¹/₄ hours | 5-5¹/₂ hours | 20-30 |
| 9-11.3 kg (20-25 lb) | 30-36 hours | 4¹/₄-4³/₄ hours | not recommended | 30-40 |
| 11.3-13.5 kg (25-30 lb) | 36-48 hours | 4³/₄-5¹/₂ hours | not recommended | 40-50 |

4 Turn the chicken over again, breast side down and, using poultry shears, cut down firmly through the back into the body cavity between the back-bone and one shoulder blade, leaving the wing attached to the breast.

5 Repeat on the other side. Then cut right the way through the ribcage, parallel to the backbone on both sides. Pull the back section away.

2 Put the bird breast side down and cut straight down the mid-dle to the backbone. Carefully pull and cut the flesh away from the carcass on each side of the cut until you get to the joints.

3 Holding one leg in each hand, press firmly outwards to release the ball and socket joints. Cut through the ten-dons and scrape the meat back from the bone. Pull out the bone, using the knife to help free it as you pull.

6 Turn the breast with the wings still attached, skin side up. Remove the wing portions by cutting through at a slight diagonal so that some of the breast is attached to the wing.

4 Cut through the ball and socket joints con-necting the wings. Holding the outside of the wing bone in one hand, cut through the tendons and scrape the meat from the bone. Pull the bone free.

5 Cut the meat away from both sides of the breast until you reach a point where the skin and bones meet without any flesh in between. Being very careful not to puncture the skin, pull the carcass away (you may have to use the knife to help you but take care as the skin is very delicate).

## Spatchcocking

Small chickens, poussins and game birds can be spatchcocked – split and flattened so that they can be grilled, barbecued or baked quickly and evenly. Using poultry shears, cut the bird along the back, each side of the backbone, then remove the backbone. Snip the wishbone in half and open out the bird. Push down on the breastbone with the heel of your hand to break the bone and flatten the bird. Thread a skewer through one leg and out through the other side, then thread a second skewer through the wings.

### Boning Whole Birds

Choose a bird with a skin that's intact. A good sharp boning knife makes things easier. Hands, work sur-face and knife must be scrupulously clean. If boning a frozen bird, make sure it is thoroughly thawed before you start. Use the carcass and bones for stock.

1 Remove the giblets if necessary. Cut off the wings at the second joint. Remove the par-son's nose. Cut out the wishbone.

## STUFFING POULTRY

A well-seasoned stuffing mixture adds flavour and moisture and helps keep the bird in a neat shape. Ensure that the bird is thoroughly thawed before stuffing. Loosely stuff the neck end only; stuffing the cavity can inhibit heat penetration and pose a health risk. Fill the bird with cold stuffing; if it is warm the bird must be cooked at once. Do not be tempted to overfill with stuffing; remember that it will swell as it absorbs fat and moisture from the bird during cook-ing. Bake any excess stuffing in a separate dish. Roast the bird soon after stuffing.

## TRUSSING POULTRY

Trussing keeps the bird in a neat compact shape for even roasting. It also keeps in the stuffing and makes carving easier. You will need a trussing needle threaded with fine cotton string.

1 Remove giblets. Remove wishbone, if desired (it makes carving the breast easier). Fold the neck skin under the body, then fold the wing tips back and under so that they hold it in position. Put the bird on its back and push the legs well into the sides.

2 Push the trussing needle into the bird through the second joint of one wing right through the body and out through the corresponding joint on the opposite side.

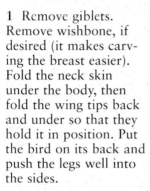

3 Insert the needle again in the first joint of the wing, pushing it through the flesh at the back of the body (catching the wing tips and the neck skin) and out through the opposite side. You should be back near where you started in step 2. Cut the string. Tie the two ends together.

4 Re-thread the needle. To truss the legs, push the needle in through the gristle at the right side of the parson's nose. Pass string over the right leg, over the left leg, then through gristle at the left side of the parson's nose. Take it behind the parson's nose and tie ends together. The bird should sit upright in a compact shape.

## CARVING POULTRY

Chickens and turkeys are carved in much the same way, although with large turkeys the breast is usually carved first (right through the stuffing) and the legs are removed afterwards and carved separately. Leave the bird to stand in a warm place for about 10-20 minutes before carving, then remove the trussing string.

1 Put the bird, breast side up, on a carving board and cut down between the leg and breast on one side.

2 With a carving fork, spear the bird through the thigh (on the opposite side to the cut) and use this to help tilt it cut side upwards. Cut round the oyster meat on the underside.

3 Cut right through the leg joint, keeping the oyster meat attached. Halve the leg by cutting through the joint.

4 If the wishbone was not removed before cooking, cut it out. Make a horizontal cut above the wing joint and along through the breast – this makes it easier to carve complete slices off the breast.

5 Carve slices from the breast, parallel to the breastbone. Repeat on the other side. Serve each person with portions of dark leg meat and white breast meat.

349

## DUCK

Duck is much fattier that chicken or turkey with a high proportion of bone to meat. Commercially produced duckling is generally sold for eating when it is around 8 weeks old; after this time it is known as duck (although in most recipes the terms duck and duckling are interchangeable). Wild duck (mallard) has a much richer flavour than farmed species.

Ducklings are generally sold whole, both fresh and frozen, for roasting, although portions are becoming more widely available. Breast fillets or *magrets de canard* are suitable for roasting, or for grilling or frying rather like steak. They are generally served cooked until just pink (medium or even rare), while roast duck is more commonly served thoroughly cooked. To serve a roasted duck cooked medium-rare the breast can be carved and served first and the legs returned to the oven for further cooking.

## GOOSE

Goose is even richer and fattier than duck. It is usually roasted on a rack so that the fat can drain off as it cooks. Before cooking, check the cavity for any fatty deposits and remove them but don't throw them away; save them along with any fat collected during cooking, for roasting potatoes – they will be absolutely delicious!

When buying goose, avoid any with deep yellow fat as this indicates an old bird. Instead look for a light skin and a good plump breast. Allow about 700 g (1½ lb) per person.

## GAME

To protect species of game their sale is restricted to certain seasons (see right), although hare, rabbit and wood pigeon are considered such pests that they may be hunted at any time. As game becomes more readily available, both fresh and frozen, it is regaining popularity. Many supermarkets now stock a good selection and prices are reasonably stable.

Most game needs hanging to tenderise the flesh and develop its characteristic 'gamey' flavour. The length of time depends on the species of bird or animal, weather conditions and personal preference. Always check with your butcher or game dealer as to the age of the game and how well it has been hung. A bird that has been hung and is ready for cooking can be stored for 1-2 days in the refrigerator, or it can be frozen.

If you are given game, you can hang it yourself in a cool, dry, airy place. Hang the bird by the neck without plucking or drawing it. Check it frequently and cook it as soon as the tail feathers will pluck out easily. In warm or damp weather check it more frequently and watch for signs of deterioration – a strong smell and a greenish tinge.

Purists say that young tender game is best roasted, then served with the traditional accompaniments, but it can also be barbecued and grilled. Game birds lack fat so to keep them moist they are barded before roasting, or the breast is covered with streaky bacon and basted frequently with butter. Large game birds are carved in the same way as chicken. Smaller birds are generally cut in half or served whole. Older game is usually much tougher and is therefore best marinated and casseroled or stewed or made into game pâté or pie.

### Grouse

Grouse are small so one bird is usually serve per person. Too small to carve, grouse are usually served whole or split down the middle. The young birds make the best eating. These can be distinguished by the soft, downy feather under the wings. Ptarmigan (white grouse) and capercaillie are members of the grouse family. Season: 12 Aug-10 Dec; except capercaillie: 1 Oct-31 Jan.

### Pheasant

Pheasant is regarded by some to be the most delicious of all the game birds. A brace of roast pheasant (one male and one female) served garnished with the tail feathers makes a spectacular centrepiece. For eating, the hen bird is considered to be the best. Although it is usually served roasted, pheasant also makes a good casserole. Oven-ready pheasants are also available frozen. Season: 1 Oct-1 Feb.

### Partridge

Partridge are smaller than pheasant and are considered to be superior in flavour by some, though they are less widely available. Season: 1 Oct-1 Feb.

### Quail

Quail has a good though not particularly gamey flavour. It is now a protected species, so all quail for sale in the shops is farmed. It's a tiny bird, so two are usually served per person. It can be roasted whole or spatchcocked (see page 348) and grilled, barbecued or fried.

### Woodcock

Woodcock are generally cooked whole (without drawing) with their heads still on. Traditionally, they are barded with bacon, roasted and served on toast. Because they are so small this is the best method of cooking. Season: 1 Oct-31 Jan.

## *ROAST GAME BIRD*

The rules for roasting are much the same for all game birds - keep the breast moist with streaky bacon rashers and cook at a fairly high temperature. Large birds are carved in the same way as chicken; smaller ones, such as partridge, can be cut in half; and the smallest of all, for instance quail, can be served whole, with 2 birds per person.

| BIRD | NUMBER OF SERVINGS | ROASTING TEMP/TIME |
|---|---|---|
| Grouse | 1 per person | 200 °C (400°F) mark 6 for 35-40 minutes |
| Partridge | 1 per person | 200°C (400°F) mark 6 for 40 minutes |
| Pheasant | Female birds 2 servings, male birds 3 servings | 230°C (450°F) mark 8 for 10 minutes, then 200°C (400°F) mark 6 for 30-50 minutes |
| Quail | 2 per person | 190°C (375°F) mark 5 for 15-20 minutes |
| Woodcock | 1 per person | 190°C (375°F) mark 5 for 15-20 minutes |
| Wood Pigeon | 1 per person | 230°C (450°F) mark 8 for 15-20 minutes |
| Wild Duck (Mallard) | 2 servings | 220°C (425°F) mark 7 for about 30 minutes |

### Wood Pigeon

Farmed pigeon meat is rich, dark, well flavoured and suitable for roasting. Wild pigeon is tough with a very strong flavour, so it's best in a casserole or pie.

### Venison

Venison is a lean, very dark, fine textured meat with a good flavour. The meat from mature deer aged about 2 years is considered to have the best flavour, although this is a matter of personal preference. Some like their venison well hung with a strong gamey flavour while others prefer the milder tasting farmed venison.

Cuts of venison are similar to lamb. Loin, saddle fillet and leg (haunch) are prime cuts for roasting and braising. Roast venison is usually served rare, in thick slices. Tenderloin chops, escalopes and medallions are cut from the boned loin or the haunch and are suitable for grilling and frying. The other cuts – shoulder, neck and breast – are only really suitable for stewing or braising. Smoked venison is also available. Because venison is such a lean meat, all cuts benefit from being marinated, before cooking. Strongly flavoured red wine marinades spiced with juniper and cloves work best.

### Rabbit and Hare

Although rabbit and hare belong to the same family, there is a good deal of difference in their flavour. Hare is usually hung for a few days to develop a strong gamey flavour, while rabbit is generally not hung and has a much milder flavour – rather like chicken. Wild rabbits can be more strongly flavoured.

Both hare and rabbit can be roasted. Very young hares (leverets) are often roasted whole. Like other game, they benefit from marinating and need constant basting during cooking to keep the flesh moist.

### *ROAST GAME BIRDS*

The following procedure can be used for nearly all game birds: wash the bird inside and out and dry on kitchen paper. If it is to be stuffed, put the stuffing in the neck end only. Pull the skin over the stuffing and truss the bird neatly to keep it in good shape. If you are not using stuffing, put half an onion or an apple inside the body cavity and season the inside well. Lean birds benefit from a little butter flavoured with lemon rind or herbs inside the cavity.

Lay streaky bacon rashers over the breast or smear with softened butter. Have the bird at room temperature before roasting. Calculate the cooking time according to the chart above. Baste frequently with butter and cover towards the end of cooking time if the breast is browning too quickly.

# EGGS AND CHEESE

Eggs are one of our most familiar, versatile foods with endless culinary uses. What's more they are a good source of protein and the vitamins A, D, E and K; they also contain iron. Eggs are quite low in calories too – the average egg provides about 80-90 calories. However, they are relatively high in cholesterol so nutritionists currently recommend that we restrict our consumption to about 3 per week.

In cooking we take their unique properties for granted. Apart from making tasty, fast food when simply poached, boiled or scrambled, eggs will lighten, thicken, bind, set and emulsify. However you are using them, it's vital to remember that they are extremely sensitive to temperature. Very cold eggs will curdle mayonnaise, so bring them to room temperature first. Similarly, eggs whisk to a greater volume if they are at room temperature. In cooked dishes they overcook or curdle very easily, so they must be heated slowly and gently.

When choosing eggs for cooking, remember that sizes do vary. Eggs are now graded following EC guidelines: size 1 is the biggest, weighing over 70 g, and size 7 is the smallest, weighing less than 45 g. It's advisable to use the size specified in a recipe – it can mean the difference between success and failure! Unless otherwise specified, size 2 or 3 eggs should be used for Good Housekeeping recipes.

Although supermarkets and shops now stock a wide range of eggs – free-range, barn eggs, eggs from grain-only fed hens (the 'vegetarian' egg), brown eggs (which are intrinsically no different from white) – most of the eggs sold in this country are produced by 'battery hens' which are raised by intensive farming methods. Hopefully, consumers will continue to increase the demand for free-range eggs to herald a decline in this cruel method of farming.

Although when we talk about eggs we generally mean hen's eggs, there are alternatives. However these are nowhere near as widely available, and for one reason or another they're not interchangeable in recipes. Quails are now farmed extensively so quails' eggs are becoming more widely available. Because of their size they are not suitable for everyday cookery but they are perfect for use as a garnish or in salads and canapés. They take about 2 minutes to soft boil; crack the shells under cold running water as soon as they are cooked to make them easier to peel.

Duck, goose and turkey eggs are larger and richer than hen's eggs. They must be thoroughly cooked as they are particularly susceptible to salmonella. Allow at least 10 minutes boiling time. Do not use them raw – in mousses, for example – or dishes cooked at low temperatures, like egg custard.

### Eggs and Salmonella

Eggs are susceptible to salmonella, one of the bacteria responsible for food poisoning. Since the great salmonella scare of the early nineties, we've all been advised to reappraise the way we store, handle and cook eggs at home.

For most of us, providing that the usual food hygiene rules are followed there is only a minor cause for concern. However, certain groups of the population should not eat lightly cooked eggs and, to be really safe, they should only eat eggs when cooked so that the yolk is set. This means that dishes like mousses, cold soufflés, mayonnaise and lightly cooked egg custards, should be avoided. People in the 'at risk' group are the elderly, pregnant women, babies and young children, those suffering from immune deficiency diseases or anyone that has or is recovering from a serious illness.

### Buying and Storing Eggs

When buying and storing eggs, note the following points:
• Always store eggs in the refrigerator or in a cool room. Never store them in a warm room or one that fluctuates in temperature. Keep the pointed end down to centre the yolk within the white.
• Buy eggs from a reputable source with a fast turnover. Never buy cracked or damaged eggs. Open the box in the supermarket and check each egg for cracks and the box for tell-tale wet patches.
• Check the date marked on the box and use eggs by the use-by date or within 2 weeks of purchase if there isn't one.
• If the egg is dirty, wipe it with a dry piece of kitchen paper and wash it just before use. However don't wash eggs and then store them for any length of time; washing destroys the natural protective coating and makes the shells more permeable.
• To test for freshness just before cooking: put the egg in a bowl of water, if it floats to the surface it is likely to be old (and possibly bad), because the size of the natural air pocket in the egg increases as it ages. If it stays at the bottom it is fresh.
• Do not keep foods that contain raw egg, such as

mayonnaise, for more than 3 days.
• Keep eggs well away from strong-smelling foods; they quickly absorb flavours and smells.

### COOKING WITH EGGS

It is often said that a sign of a good cook is someone who can boil an egg to perfection. Although this is relatively simple, the more skilful techniques used in egg cookery need some explanation. Many recipes call for separated eggs. Confident, experienced cooks will do this with a flourish, in one hand; but generally it is advisable to follow the method below.

#### Separating Eggs

**1** Crack the egg against the rim of a bowl. With your thumbs, crack open the shell, letting some of the white run out into the bowl.

**2** Over the bowl, tip the yolk from one half of the shell into the other until all the white is separated.

**3** If the yolk breaks and a little of it falls into the bowl, scoop it out with a teaspoon. If it gets mixed in the whites will not whisk. If you're separating several eggs, it's a good idea to transfer the whites to a different bowl as you go in case you accidentally break a yolk.

#### Whisking the Egg Whites

Professional cooks use an unlined copper bowl and a large balloon whisk for whisking egg whites. This creates maximum volume because the copper reacts with the whites to form a dense, stable foam. If you use a copper bowl always clean the inside of the bowl with a cut lemon to remove any accumulated toxic copper carbonate before you start. If a copper bowl is unavailable, opt for a balloon whisk or a hand-held electric whisk for the next best volume. Don't use a food processor with a whisk attachment because these rarely give as good results.

Bowls and whisks should be scrupulously clean; any trace of grease, water or egg yolk will hinder whisking and result in a poor volume. A pinch of salt or cream of tartar will stabilise the egg foam. Only whisk until the egg whites stand in soft peaks. Over whisking makes the eggs dry and granular; eggs whisked to this stage will not fold in evenly and tend to lose volume quickly. Once egg whites are whisked, immediately incorporate them into the other ingredients because otherwise they will collapse.

#### Folding in

Having whisked egg whites to a peak of perfection, don't waste all that time and energy with heavy-handed mixing. Use a large metal spoon (not a wooden spoon) and add a good spoonful to the mixture you're folding into to 'let it down' or lighten it slightly. Then add the egg white, using a cutting and folding action, until the whites are evenly incorporated. Allow a hot mixture to cool a little until it is just warm, before folding in the egg whites, or the delicate structure of the whites will collapse. Similarly, let a chilled mixture stand at room temperature until it is soft enough to fold into.

**1** If you are whisking egg whites to be folded into a mixture such as a soufflé or sponge, whisk only until they stand in soft peaks. The tips of the peaks should flop over gently when held up on the whisk.

**2** Always fold in whisked egg whites as lightly as possible, using a large metal spoon. Cut through the centre of the mixture and turn the spoon to scoop up the mixture and turn it in a rolling action.

#### Boiling Eggs

This is a misnomer since vigorous boiling produces a rubbery white. For best results, lower the egg(s) into a pan of simmering water using a slotted spoon. Ensure that the water covers the eggs completely or they will cook unevenly. A small pan is best so that the eggs don't move around too much. To centre the yolk (especially if you're using the egg as a garnish), spin the egg in the pan as it cooks.

Cooking times really do depend on personal

preference, the freshness of the egg and whether it's being cooked straight from the refrigerator or from room temperature. As a rough guide allow a minimum of 3½ minutes and a maximum of about 5½ minutes for soft-boiled eggs. If the egg does crack while it's cooking, add a little salt or vinegar to the water to coagulate the white and stop it running out.

Hard-boiled eggs take about 10-12 minutes. As soon as they are cooked, drain and rinse under cold running water then crack the shell on the side of the pan to cool the egg quickly and prevent an unsightly black line forming around the yolk. To peel hard-boiled eggs roll them across the work surface a couple of times and the shell should come off easily.

Eggs mollet have soft yolks and firm whites. To cook these, simmer for about 6 minutes, plunge into cold water, cool slightly and peel.

To coddle an egg, put it into a pan of boiling water, cover with a lid then remove from the heat and leave for about 8-10 minutes. It should be lightly set.

### Poached Eggs

Poached eggs are really easy to cook if you have an egg poacher. If you haven't, poach eggs in a deep frying pan filled with simmering water. Add 5-10 ml (1-2 teaspoons) vinegar to help the egg set. Use really fresh eggs; stale eggs will run all over the pan. As soon as you have dropped the egg in, swirl the water around it in a circular motion to contain the shape. Simmer gently until cooked, 3-5 minutes. It's best to cook only one egg at a time. Drain thoroughly and trim the edges before serving.

### Fried Eggs

Use the freshest eggs possible or they will run all over the pan. Heat the fat of your choice – dripping, bacon fat, olive or vegetable oil – until very hot before you add the egg to get a nice crisp base. To help the thicker middle set, carefully 'splash' a little of the hot fat over as it cooks.

### Making Omelettes and Pancakes

Vital to the success of both omelette and pancake making is a good heavy-based pan. Ideally it should be kept solely for pancake or omelette making and should never be washed or scrubbed, just carefully wiped out with kitchen paper after use. When buying a pan choose one that measures about 18-20 cm (7-8 inches) across the base with sloping sides and a non-stick coating. With a larger pan it is difficult to spread out the batter evenly. For best results, a new pan should be 'seasoned' before use. If available follow the manufacturer's instructions, otherwise fill the pan with oil and heat it gently until hot. Repeat this once or twice to seal the surface of the pan.

Before cooking, heat the pan; slow cooking makes pancakes and omelettes tough. Add a small amount of fat to the pan, heat again then tip out any excess. Always reheat and grease the pan between each one.

### CHEESE

Like eggs, cheese is amazingly versatile either as an ingredient or as a course or meal on its own. Although there are literally hundreds of cheeses they are all produced from milk – usually cow's milk but also goat's milk and ewe's milk. In fact during recent years goat's cheese has become popular on restaurant menus which in turn has encouraged supermarkets and delicatessens to offer a wider range.

Although many cheeses, are interchangeable in recipes as long as they are similar in texture, some cheeses have a particular property or flavour which is specifically required for certain recipes.

In cooking, it is important to realise that if semi-hard cheese is overheated it separates and the fat runs out. When adding cheese to a hot sauce remove the sauce from the heat before stirring in the cheese. When making cheese scones and breads use a well-matured cheese to get a good depth of flavour.

Because there are so many cheeses it is impossible to categorise them all, but for culinary purposes they can be divided into four groups: hard cheeses such as Parmesan and Pecorino; semi-hard cheeses including traditional favourites like Cheddar, Stilton, Edam, Cheshire and Lancashire; soft cheeses such as mould-ripened Brie and Camembert as well as the blue-veined Danish Blue; and finally fresh soft cheeses including cottage cheese, cream cheese, quark and curd cheese. Vegetarian cheeses made with non-animal rennet are now available in these categories.

In general, when choosing hard or semi-hard cheeses avoid pieces that look sweaty or dried at the edges. Soft cheeses, like Brie and Camembert, should be slightly springy to the touch and soft in the middle (or very soft verging on runny if for immediate consumption). Fresh soft cheeses, particularly goat's cheeses, should be eaten as fresh as possible. Check for signs of discoloration and a rancid smell.

When you get the cheese home, store it wrapped in greaseproof paper or foil in the refrigerator. Bring the cheese to room temperature before serving. Although in general cheese is high in calories and fat, it is a good source of protein, vitamins and minerals, particularly calcium. Lower-fat hard cheeses are produced from semi-skimmed milk and are ideal for those who are cutting down on fat in their diet.

# VEGETABLES

Never has the choice of vegetables been so good. Modern methods of production, transportation and refrigeration ensure that a constant supply reaches the shops no matter what the season. The influence of other cultures and cuisines brings 'exotic vegetables' such as yams, bamboo shoots and water chestnuts and genetic engineering brings us more and more hybrids and baby vegetables.

Traditionally vegetables are categorised into family groups. First are the brassicas, the cabbage family, which include Brussels sprouts, kohlrabi, cauliflower, broccoli and curly kale, as well as the many varieties of cabbage. Roots and tubers are the vegetables that grow underground, such as carrot, potato, turnip, beetroot, parsnip, Jerusalem artichoke and salsify. Pods and seeds takes in the many varieties of bean, along with peas, mangetout and sweetcorn. Vegetables fruits include the tomato, okra, aubergine and cucumber. Some would also put the avocado pear in this category but strictly it is a fruit rather than a vegetable. Leafy vegetables include the many varieties of salad leaves, which are described in more detail on pages 358–359.

Other categories are stalks and shoots – celery, asparagus, fennel and chard; squashes – marrow, pumpkin and courgette; and of course the much loved family of onions comprising garlic, leek and shallot, as well as red, white, Spanish and spring onion. Finally come mushrooms in all their many varieties and thistles – notably the globe artichoke – the thistle with the delicately flavoured heart.

When choosing vegetables look for a good bright colour, and crisp, firm leaves. Avoid those that show signs of discoloration or bruising, or that look shrivelled. Always look for firm root vegetables; those that are wrinkled and flabby have lost flavour and goodness. Don't buy potatoes with a green tinge to them as these are unfit for eating. At home always store potatoes in the dark or the exposure to light will turn them green. Resist buying the largest vegetables, particularly when choosing roots, since as they swell and enlarge they become tough and woody. Generally the younger and smaller the vegetable the sweeter and more tender it will be, although you may find that some of the baby vegetables lack flavour because they are so immature.

Store all vegetables in a cool, dark, well-ventilated place, preferably in a rack or in the bottom of the refrigerator. It is important that they are kept in the dark because light destroys vitamins B and C. Paper bags are preferable to plastic for wrapping; pierce holes in plastic bags and loosen or remove cling film to increase ventilation. Root vegetables should stay fresh for 5-6 days, and green vegetables for 3-4 days. Most vegetables freeze well if blanched beforehand. They are best used within 6 months, and cooked from frozen.

### ORGANIC FRUIT AND VEGETABLES
The demand for organic produce – obtained by farming methods which do not utilise artificial fertilisers or pesticides – is increasing. There is a growing awareness of the possible health risks of these chemicals and consumers are responding accordingly. Many supermarket chains now stock a reasonably good range of organic produce, but it tends to be rather expensive. This is because organic farming is labour intensive, yields are relatively low and there is a high demand for restricted supply.

### PREPARING VEGETABLES
If vegetables are incorrectly prepared they may not cook through in the stated time or they may spoil the appearance of the finished dish, so do pay attention to instructions given in recipes. Unless stated otherwise, in this book the weight of vegetables given relates to the unprepared weight, in other words the amount you should be buying.

#### Cleaning
Always shake or brush off loose earth before washing. With the exception of mushrooms, all vegetables must be thoroughly washed before cooking. To ensure that leeks are thoroughly cleaned, slit the green part in half lengthways and wash under cold running water to remove any accumulated grit inside. Brush or wipe mushrooms, rather than wash them, or they will soak up water and become spongy.

Vegetables with inedible skins, such as onion, thick-skinned roots and tubers, and large squash, must be peeled. If you're particularly worried about residual contamination from pesticides, peel vegetables with edible skins – washing is not enough.

#### Peeling and Cutting
A vegetable peeler or small paring knife is best for peeling. A really sharp knife and a good, heavy chopping board are essential for slicing and chopping.

Some recipes call for a specific method of preparation such as julienne or chiffonade. To cut into julienne the aim is to cut the vegetable into neat evenly sized pieces the shape of a matchstick. Simply cut into thin slices (which are the width of a matchstick), trim into 5 cm (2 inch) lengths, then stack the slices and cut lengthways again into strips. To make a chiffonade (usually of lettuce, rocket or basil) stack several leaves on top of each other, roll tightly then slice across the roll into fine strips.

Turned vegetables are popular on restaurant menus and are the hallmark of many classic French dishes, although at home they're best reserved for special occasions since they are wasteful and rather labour intensive. The aim is to 'turn' or carve chunks of vegetable into an elongated baton shape, usually with seven sides. A sharp paring knife is essential. Choose firm vegetables like carrots, courgettes, squash and turnips. Cut the vegetable into 5 cm (2 inch) lengths and trim off any sharp edges. Then working from the top to the bottom make a series of curved cuts around the vegetable, turning as you cut.

### Avoiding Discoloration
Some vegetables, notably celeriac, artichoke bottoms, Jerusalem artichokes and salsify, rapidly discolour once they are cut. To prevent this, peel and cut these vegetables with a stainless steel knife and then drop them into acidulated water immediately. To acidulate water, simply add the juice of 1 lemon to each 600 ml (1 pint) water.

### Dégorging
Vegetables such as aubergine, cucumber and gourd contain bitter juices which some people like to remove before cooking to improve the flavour of the finished dish and to reduce the amount of oil absorbed if the vegetable is to be fried. The French term for this technique is known as *dégorger*. Slice the vegetable (or prepare according to the recipe), then spread out in a large shallow dish or colander and sprinkle generously with salt. Leave for about 30 minutes to let the salt draw out the juices, then rinse very thoroughly and pat dry.

### Blanching
Vegetables are blanched before further cooking, so that they are slightly softened, or before freezing, to inhibit enzyme action. Since the cooking times are so short, different types of vegetables should be blanched separately, although the water may be reused. To blanch, bring a large pan of water to a rapid boil, drop in the vegetables (using a wire basket to make speedy retrieval easy) and cook according to the recipe – usually for just a minute or two. Drain and refresh under cold running water or in a large bowl of iced water to prevent further cooking and to retain the colour. Blanched green vegetables, such as French beans, broad beans and mangetouts, make good additions to salads.

### COOKING VEGETABLES
Once peeled, the vegetables begin to lose their vitamins. To reduce vitamin losses, don't prepare vegetables hours in advance and leave them soaking in water. Leave the skins on whenever you can. Cook with the minimum of water until just tender and use the cooking water in sauces, gravies and soups. Never add bicarbonate of soda to the cooking water as it destroys vitamin C, and try to get into the habit of using less salt. Vitamin losses continue after cooking, particularly when warm foods are left waiting around, so eat as soon as possible once cooked.

Most vegetables are best cooked until crisp and crunchy but no longer hard, however this is a matter of personal taste and many people still prefer them to be cooked until soft. Test during cooking with the point of a knife or preferably by tasting. Always test well before the estimated cooking time since vegetables are easily overcooked and ruined.

### Boiling
In most households this is still probably the most popular method of cooking vegetables. Green vegetables should be dropped straight into boiling water, while roots should be added to cold water and brought up to boiling point. Cook green vegetables with the lid off the pan so that volatile acids from the vegetables don't get trapped in the pan and cause discoloration. The vegetables should be barely covered with water. Do not fill the pan to the brim. To retain vitamins, boil potatoes in their skins and peel after cooking.

Serve boiled vegetables tossed in butter or olive oil and a few chopped fresh herbs. Alternatively flavour the butter or oil with garlic or aromatic spices, such as coriander or cumin. White sauce – either plain or flavoured with cheese, onion, egg or herbs – is also delicious with boiled vegetables. To make a tasty supper dish, coat the vegetables in a sauce of your choice, sprinkle with cheese and breadcrumbs and cook under a hot grill until browned and bubbling. Add strips of cooked ham, bacon or chicken for a really substantial dish.

If making a vegetable purée ensure that the vegetables are well drained after boiling, or you will end up with an unpleasant watery purée. Season generously with salt, pepper and a little cayenne or nutmeg. Moisten with cream or milk and melted butter or olive oil, or yogurt or fromage frais if you're watching your weight.

A food processor takes much of the effort out of puréeing but it is unsuitable for starchy vegetables, particularly potatoes, as it tends to pulverise them into a 'gluey' mess. Sieve vegetables which have fibres, strings or skin for an absolutely smooth purée.

### Steaming

If practised correctly, steaming will retain more nutrients than boiling. Use a metal or bamboo steamer, or a collapsible steamer fitted in a large saucepan. Cut vegetables into uniform sizes so that they cook evenly. Bring a 5 cm (2 inch) depth of water to the boil in the saucepan, then add the vegetables to the steamer in a single layer. Set the steamer about 5 cm (2 inches) above the water and cover with a lid. Steaming often takes longer than boiling since the vegetables are not in direct contact with the water. As with boiling, use the water for gravies and sauces.

### Sautéing

To sauté vegetables you will need a sauté pan or a large, preferably non-stick, heavy-based frying pan. Use olive oil, butter, bacon fat or even lard. Heat the oil or fat in the pan until it is really hot, then add the vegetables and shake the pan vigorously over a high heat until they begin to brown, then lower the heat and cook until tender. Aim for a dark golden brown, crisp crust and a soft succulent inside. Tough root vegetables should be parboiled before sautéing.

### Stir-frying

Stir-frying differs from sautéing in that it is traditionally done in a wok, although if you haven't got a wok a large deep frying pan can be use. Vegetables are usually cut into small evenly sized pieces, added to a little hot oil in the wok and cooked vigorously over a high heat so that they remain crisp and retain their colour. Slower-cooking vegetables, such as baby corn, carrots and onions, are added first, followed by fast-cooking vegetables, such as courgettes, mangetouts and mushrooms.

Flavourings such as garlic, chilli, ginger, five-spice powder and lemon grass are often stir-fried with the vegetables to add interest. For a moist stir-fry add a little soy sauce, sherry, oyster sauce or black bean sauce. Try sprinkling the cooked vegetables with a few sesame seeds, fried cashew nuts or toasted almonds before serving.

### Deep-frying

There is something irresistible about chips, however calorific they may be! Potatoes are still the most commonly deep-fried vegetable but many others, including mushrooms, broccoli, onions, peppers and courgettes, are suitable. A light batter or a coating of breadcrumbs is essential to protect the vegetables from the hot oil. As with all deep-frying the correct temperature is vital. Most vegetables are deep-fried at around 190°C (375°F) but follow directions in individual recipes. If possible determine the exact temperature of the oil with a thermometer. Drain deep-fried vegetables on crumpled kitchen paper as soon as they are cooked and serve immediately.

### Roasting

This is another favourite way to cook the ubiquitous potato, but most root vegetables can be roasted. For roast potatoes with really crunchy skins and light fluffy insides, parboil, drain thoroughly then shake the potatoes vigorously in the pan to roughen all the cut sides. Tip into a pan of really hot dripping, olive or vegetable oil, white vegetable fat or lard. Turn frequently during roasting so that they cook evenly.

Roast garlic – cooked until tender and delicately flavoured – makes a delicious accompaniment to roast meat. Alternatively it can be used to flavour the gravy. Simply put whole cloves, with the papery skins still attached, in the tin with the meat. To eat simply pop the succulent interior out of the crisp skin.

### Braising

A comforting wintry method of cooking vegetables in the oven, usually with aromatic herbs or spices and a little liquid. The vegetables are often left whole or just halved so that they can be cooked slowly and retain their shape. Traditional choices for braising are chicory, leeks, cabbage, onions and celery. Delicately flavoured braised vegetables make good accompaniments to grilled or roast meats, sausages and game.

### Grilling

The influence of Mediterranean cooking has brought grilled vegetables onto numerous restaurant menus. They are colourful, tasty and easy to prepare – making them the perfect starter. Halved radicchio and chicory are delicious grilled and flavoured with lemon juice. Peppers are grilled until the skins blacken and char, then left to cool so that the skins can be peeled off. Courgettes and aubergines are usually cut into fairly thick slices before grilling. Brush vegetables with olive oil as they cook. Serve warm or cold tossed in olive oil flavoured with garlic or herbs.

# SALADS

The days when a salad consisted of tired lettuce leaves, a sliced tomato and a limp piece of cucumber are over – or at least they should be. Market stalls, greengrocers and supermarkets now positively abound with brilliant displays of fruit and vegetables.

To start with, cast your eye over the varieties of salad leaves now on offer. Although leafy salad plants have been grown the world over for centuries the number of varieties produced commercially has until recently been disappointing. But now, new interesting well-flavoured leaves are appearing all the time, from the russet coloured loose-leafed Oak Leaf, frilly Lollo Rosso and Biondo to the delicate, lacy frisée and slightly bitter but hardier curly endive. Use them alone or in combination and look out for ready-prepared bags of mixed salad leaves in supermarkets: although these tend to be expensive they keep well and may work out cheaper than buying four or five different items. Other varieties worth looking out for are Batavia, Quattro Stagioni and dark red radicchio which has robust, tightly packed leaves and a strong bitter flavour. Use radicchio sparingly in salads, combined with other leaves.

Lamb's lettuce, also known as corn salad or mâche is now a popular salad leaf. It is not a true lettuce, but a weed native to Europe which is now cultivated mainly in France. It has a mild delicate flavour, making it a good foil for strong flavours, and the dainty, brightly coloured leaves are a useful garnish.

Chinese leaves are particularly crunchy but rather bland in flavour. They are best teamed with spicy, aromatic dressings, for example garlic and ginger, or they may be stir-fried.

Rocket (or roquette) has a delicious peppery taste and although it is expensive a little will add a distinctive flavour to a mixture of other leaves. Rocket is also extremely easy to grow. Serve it as a delicious salad on its own tossed with a little vinaigrette and sprinkled with shavings of Parmesan. Sorrel tastes similar to rocket but it is much stronger. Use a little in conjunction with other leaves or use to encase delicate fish mousses or rolled fish fillets.

Tender, baby spinach leaves are irresistible in salads. They are particularly good tossed with croûtons, crumbled blue cheese and crispy bacon. Chicory has a tightly packed head and elegant long leaves. It adds crunch and bitterness to a mixed salad or it can be braised or grilled.

With all these new varieties on offer it's easy to overlook the more familiar Cos (Romaine), Iceberg (Crisphead), Webb's Wonder, Butterhead and Little Gem. Cos with its large, crisp, mildly flavoured leaves is as essential to a Caesar Salad as eggs and Parmesan cheese. While an authentic 'BLT' (Bacon, Lettuce and Tomato Sandwich) would be incomplete without the crunch of Iceberg lettuce. The French know how to make the most of Butterhead and Little Gem lettuce by braising them with peas and onion for the classic *petits pois à la française*.

When choosing salad plants look for fresh, crisp leaves and a tightly packed head where appropriate. Avoid wilted or damaged specimens. Limp leaves can sometimes be crisped if immersed in a bowl of iced water. Store salad leaves in the refrigerator, loosely wrapped in the salad drawer. Lettuce with very delicate leaves will only remain fresh for a couple of days while the more robust varieties will keep for up to a week.

To prepare, pull off and discard any damaged outer leaves and wash thoroughly in several changes of water to remove all traces of earth and insect life. Drain thoroughly and dry in a clean tea towel or salad shaker.

### SALAD HERBS AND FLOWERS

Fresh herbs are an indispensable addition to any summer salad. Chives, basil, tarragon, mint and, of course, parsley and dill all have a particular affinity with salad ingredients. Break into delicate sprigs or chop roughly. Fresh basil may be shredded. Alternatively, chop the herbs finely and use to flavour the dressing.

To store fresh herbs, put them in a plastic bag; then, holding the bag in two hands by the opening corners, rotate it vigorously in the air to aerate and seal it simultaneously; knot the ends together then store in the refrigerator. This creates an environment in the bag which keeps the herbs fresh for several days. (Salad leaves may be stored in the same way.) If the herbs have long stems, treat them like flowers, placing them in a jug of water. They should keep like this for several days after which they will begin to lose their colour. Limp herbs may be revived by immersing in a bowl of iced water.

During the summer months a few edible flowers such as nasturtiums, violas, pansies, chive flowers and dandelions make a pretty addition to most salads. Fish and seafood salads are especially good with flowers of all kinds. Courgette flowers are much prized since they are large enough to stuff and deep-fry or bake; they make a delicious starter. Other more pungent flowers like roses and violets are usually crystallised and used to decorate cakes; these are really too overpowering to be used in salads.

Always pick flowers on a warm, dry day and choose those that are open but not full blown. Make sure that they are free from insects and contamination from pesticides. Although previously available only to those who grew them at home, edible flowers can now be found in supermarkets, greengrocers and delicatessens. Finally, it goes without saying that you should not pick wild flowers: some are protected by law but even those that are not protected are best left. Buying from a greengrocer or growing them in your garden ensures too that what you are sprinkling on your salad is edible.

## SALAD DRESSINGS

Apart from the freshness of the ingredients, vital to the success of any salad is a good dressing. The foundation of most good dressings is the oil. Virgin oils are those obtained from a first cold pressing. These unrefined oils have the strongest flavour and are therefore the most expensive. Good virgin olive oil with its rich green colour and distinctively fruity flavour is the starting point for many classic dressings.

Rich and mellow walnut, hazelnut and almond oils lend their own characteristic flavours to dressings. They're too strong to be used alone, so blend with a bland oil, such as sunflower or ground nut. A dash of sesame oil adds interesting oriental tones to salads, but avoid very dark-coloured brands as they tend to be overpowering and cloying. Oils gradually lose their flavour and become rancid, particularly nut oils, so store them in a cool dark place and adhere to the use-by date.

Vinegars now come in all sorts of flavours as well. As a change from the familiar wine vinegars, try cider, sherry or fruit vinegars or those flavoured with herbs, spices or garlic. Balsamic vinegar is wonderfully dark with a distinctive sweet-sour flavour that turns the humblest salad into something rather special. Use it in moderation because it is very strong. Both oils and vinegars can be flavoured at home with fresh herbs such as tarragon, chillies, or blanched cloves of garlic.

To make fruit vinegars mix 450 g (1 lb) soft fruit such as raspberries, strawberries or blackcurrants with 600 ml (1 pint) wine vinegar, then leave to stand for 3 days, stirring occasionally. Strain then add 50 g (2 oz) sugar, bring to the boil, cool and bottle in sterilised containers. Store in a cool dark place.

When making vinaigrette dressing the usual proportion of oil to vinegar is 3:1 but this can be varied according to how sharp you like your dressing and the ingredients in the salad. It's a good idea to make up a large batch and store it in the refrigerator ready for flavouring as desired. Vinaigrette will keep in a refrigerator for as long as 1 month providing it is just the basic mixture without added perishables, such as herbs.

## SLIMMERS' SALADS

If you're worried about calories or your fat intake, opt for low-fat yoghurt, fat-reduced mayonnaise or fromage frais based dressings flavoured with garlic, fresh herbs or lemon juice. Make salads based on crisp, virtually calorie-free salad leaves and crunchy vegetables. If adding cheese, make it Edam or cottage cheese. For a low calorie main course salad add strips of cooked skinned chicken, flakes of tuna fish (canned in brine rather than oil) or prawns. But remember that although prawns are low in calories they're surprisingly high in cholesterol.

## ASSEMBLING SALADS

Of course not all salads are based on leaves and raw vegetables. Today's salad can be hot, cold or warm and contain any combination of ingredients. As well as following the recipes in this book, experiment with your own combinations of vegetables, fruits, nuts, pulses, pasta, meat and fish, tossed with one of your favourite dressings. If making a salad based on robust ingredients like pasta, pulses or potatoes, add the dressing when everything is freshly cooked and still warm. Leave to cool, stirring occasionally, so that the flavours have time to be absorbed. Delicate leaf and herb based salads tend to wilt if dressed too soon so it is best to get everything ready and toss together at the last minute.

A well made salad should taste and look good. Presentation is all important. Either tear or chop salad leaves into manageable pieces, but don't make them too small. Aim for a balance of textures as well as colours and flavours. Choose an appropriate dish for serving; chunky salads or unruly leaf salads are best in a bowl, while salads containing a lot of neatly sliced ingredients look better displayed on a plate or platter. Add a subtle garlic flavour by rubbing the inside of the bowl or platter with a cut clove of garlic. And as a finishing touch to salads coated in creamy dressings apply a generous sprinkling of fresh herbs.

# MAYONNAISE

PREPARATION TIME 10-15 minutes
FREEZING Not suitable

MAKES 150 ML (5 FL OZ)
- *1 egg yolk (see note)*
- *2.5 ml ($^1/_2$ tsp) mustard powder or 5 ml (1 tsp) Dijon mustard*
- *2.5 ml ($^1/_2$ tsp) salt*

140 CALS/15ML (1 TBSP)
- *1.25 ml ($^1/_4$ tsp) pepper*
- *15 ml (1 tbsp) white wine vinegar or lemon juice*
- *about 150 ml (5 fl oz ) oil*

1 Put the egg yolk in a bowl with the mustard, seasoning and 5 ml (1 tsp) of the vinegar or lemon juice. Mix thoroughly.

2 Add the oil drop by drop to begin with, then in a steady stream, whisking constantly, until the sauce is thick and smooth. If it becomes too thick, add a little more vinegar or lemon juice.

3 When all the oil has been added, add the remaining vinegar or lemon juice gradually and mix thoroughly. Store for up to 3 days in a screw-topped jar in the refrigerator.

NOTE: The ingredients must be at room temperature. Never use eggs straight from the refrigerator as this may result in curdling.

If a recipe requires thin mayonnaise, thin it down with a little warm water, single cream, vinegar or lemon juice. Add the extra liquid slowly - too much will spoil the consistency.

USING A BLENDER OR FOOD PROCESSOR: Most blenders and food processors need at least a two-egg quantity of mayonnaise in order to ensure that the blades are covered. Put the yolks, seasoning and half the vinegar or lemon juice into the blender or food processor and blend well. If your machine has a variable speed control, run it at a slow speed. Add the oil gradually while the machine is running. Add the remaining vinegar and seasoning.

RESCUE REMEDIES: If the mayonnaise separates, save it by beating the curdled mixture into a fresh base. This base can be any of the following: 5 ml (1 tsp) hot water; 5 ml (1 tsp) vinegar or lemon juice; an egg yolk. Add the curdled mixture to the base, beating hard. When the mixture is smooth, continue adding the oil as before. (If you use an extra egg yolk you may find that you need to add a little extra oil.)

**Variations**

CAPER MAYONNAISE: Add 10 ml (2 tsp) chopped capers, 5 ml (1 tsp) chopped pimiento and 2.5 ml ($^1/_2$ tsp) tarragon vinegar. Caper mayonnaise makes an ideal accompaniment for fish.

CUCUMBER MAYONNAISE: Add 30 ml (2 tbsp) finely chopped cucumber and a little extra salt. This mayonnaise goes well with fish salads – especially crab, lobster and salmon.

BLUE CHEESE DRESSING: Add 150 ml (5 fl oz) soured cream, 75 g (3 oz) crumbled blue cheese, $^1/_2$ quantity vinaigrette (see below), 1 crushed garlic clove, and pepper to taste.

TARTARE SAUCE: Add 5 ml (1 tsp) chopped tarragon or snipped chives, 10 ml (2 tsp) chopped capers, 10 ml (2 tsp) chopped gherkins, 10 ml (2 tsp) chopped parsley and 15 ml (1 tbsp) lemon juice or tarragon vinegar. Allow to stand for at least 1 hour before serving, to allow the flavours to mingle.

CURRY CREAM SAUCE: Sauté 10 ml (2 tsp) chopped onion and 1 crushed garlic clove in 15 ml (1 tbsp) oil for 2-3 minutes. Stir in 10 ml (2 tsp) curry powder and 5 ml (1 tsp) tomato purée. Add 75 ml (3 fl oz) water, 1 lemon slice and 10 ml (2 tsp) apricot jam. Simmer for 5-7 minutes. Strain and allow to cool. When cold, whisk into the mayonnaise. Adjust the seasoning to taste.

# VINAIGRETTE

PREPARATION TIME 5 minutes
FREEZING Not suitable

MAKES 200 ML (7 FL OZ)
- *175 ml (6 fl oz) olive oil*
- *45 ml (3 tbsp) white wine vinegar*
- *salt and pepper*

90 CALS 15 ML (1 TBSP)
- *2.5 ml ($^1/_2$ tsp) caster sugar or thin honey*
- *10 ml (2 tsp) Dijon mustard*

1 Place all the ingredients in a bowl or screw-topped jar and whisk together or shake until thoroughly combined. Adjust seasoning to taste.

**Variations**

HERB VINAIGRETTE: Whisk 30 ml (2 tbsp) finely chopped mixed herbs, such as parsley, thyme and marjoram or chives, into the dressing.

GARLIC VINAIGRETTE: Crush 1 or 2 garlic cloves into the dressing. Stir in 15 ml (1 tbsp) snipped chives if desired.

# VEGETARIAN COOKING

An ever increasing number of people are choosing to eat more and more meatless meals based on ingredients like pasta, rice, pizza and vegetables. Many others – sometimes known as the 'demi-veggies' – choose to exclude red meat from their diets completely but still eat the occasional meal containing fish, shellfish or chicken. As for vegetarians, there are as many types of vegetarian diet as there are reasons for being one. Vegans are strict vegetarians, who won't eat any animal product whatsoever and that includes gelatine and in some cases honey. Less strict vegetarians eat cheese, butter and milk. Some also eat eggs.

The reasons for becoming vegetarian are numerous. Some look to it as a healthier way of eating; current research seems to suggest that many so-called 'diseases of Western civilisation' such as heart disease, strokes, obesity and high blood pressure are related to a diet that's high in animal fats. Others are influenced by their religion or choose to avoid meat because they're concerned about animal welfare. Many vegetarians are worried about the environment and believe that a vegetarian diet is a more economical method of food production in terms of the world's limited resources.

## *BALANCING A VEGETARIAN DIET*

Many people make the mistake of assuming that a vegetarian diet is automatically healthier than a carnivore's. This isn't always the case. It is not enough simply to stop eating meat; the nutrients that would have been obtained from meat must be derived from other sources. It's quite common for vegetarians to rely too heavily on dairy products – like cheese – which are high in saturated fats and calories.

As with any diet, variety is important. If a wide range of foods is eaten, a vegetarian diet is no more likely to be lacking nutritionally than any other diet. There are lots of good vegetable sources of protein such as beans, grain, nuts, tofu, quorn and TVP as well as dairy products. Animal proteins contain almost all of the essential amino acids and are regarded as 'complete protein' foods. With the exception of soya products, vegetable proteins are lacking or low in one or more of the essential amino acids. However, by eating certain foods together at the same meal any deficiency is overcome. This isn't as complicated as it sounds and tends to happen automatically when menu planning. For example, cereals should be eaten with dairy products, pulses or nuts: muesli with yogurt or milk; chilli beans with rice; nut roast made with breadcrumbs. Pulses and nuts should also be eaten with dairy products, for example, dhal with raita; nut burgers with a cream-based sauce; bean stew with cheese topping.

Vegetarians and vegans should be careful to regulate their intake of vitamins B12 and D, although contrary to popular belief a deficiency of either is unlikely. Both are found in dairy products and fortified products such as breakfast cereals. Anaemia or a lack of dietary iron is often discussed in relation to a vegetarian diet because meat and liver are commonly believed to be the best sources of iron. In fact, iron is found in a wide range of foods including leafy green vegetables, cereals, pulses, nuts, eggs and dried fruits – especially apricots. The absorption of iron is greatly increased if vitamin C rich foods are eaten at the same meal. It is decreased by the presence of tannin, which is found in large amounts in tea – so don't drink tea at meal times!

## *THE VEGETARIAN STORECUPBOARD*

Vegetarian alternatives to ingredients of animal origin are becoming increasingly available. You can now buy a wide range of cheeses produced using vegetarian rennet, for example. Other useful products include Agar-Agar and Gelazone which are alternatives for gelatine. Certain foods are particularly significant in a vegetarian diet; these are described below.

### Pulses

The term pulse covers all the various beans, peas and lentils which have been preserved by drying. Pulses are an important source of protein, carbohydrate and fibre in a vegetarian diet.

Pulses should be stored in airtight containers in a cool, dark place. They keep well, but after about 6 months their skins toughen and they take increasingly longer to cook, so buy them from a supplier with a fast turnover.

Before cooking, with the exception of lentils and split peas, all pulses should be soaked overnight in a large bowl of cold water. In the morning, drain them, bring to the boil in fresh water and boil rapidly for 10 minutes to destroy any toxins present. Although fast-boiling is not strictly necessary for all types of pulse it does them no harm and saves the problem of remembering which ones require it. After fast-boiling, lower the heat, cover and simmer until tender. The flavour can be subtly enhanced by adding a couple of bay leaves or garlic cloves, or an onion studded with a few cloves, to the cooking water. Add salt approximately 15 minutes before the end of cooking time. Salt added at the beginning of cooking tends to toughen the skins.

To save time the quick soak method works just as well. Put the beans into a saucepan, cover with cold water and bring to the boil. Boil rapidly for 10 minutes. Cover the pan and leave the beans to soak in the same water for 2 hours. Drain and cook in fresh water for the usual time (see chart below).

The weight of dried pulses approximately doubles during cooking, so if a recipe calls for 225 g (8 oz) cooked beans you will need to start with 125 g (4 oz) dried beans. Drained, cooked pulses will keep for several days in a covered container in the refrigerator. Alternatively, freeze them in usable quantities. Thaw overnight and use as freshly cooked beans.

• COOKING PULSES IN A PRESSURE COOKER
This cuts down on lengthy cooking times (see chart below). Overnight soaking is unnecessary: just cover the beans with boiling water and leave to soak for 1 hour. Drain, then weigh and transfer to the pressure cooker, adding 600 ml (1 pint) water for every 225 g (8 oz) soaked beans. The cooker must not be more than one-third full.

Bring to the boil, then skim off any scum that's risen to the surface. Lower the heat so that the beans are simmering gently, then put the lid on the pan. Bring up to pressure and cook for the time suggested below. Reduce the pressure slowly. Season with salt while warm.

Do not cook mixtures of different types of pulse at the same time. This is potentially dangerous as overcooked beans can rise up in the pan and block the safety valves and air vents.

### Canned Beans
Canned beans are a good quick alternative to cooking your own. It's a good idea to empty them straight into a sieve and rinse under cold running water before use. They tend to be rather soft, but some brands are definitely firmer and better than others, so shop around. Nevertheless they are all much softer than home-cooked beans so always add them towards the end of the recipe cooking time or they will disintegrate.

### Tofu
Also known as soya bean curd, tofu is made from a paste of soya beans which has been pressed into blocks. It is virtually tasteless but readily absorbs flavours when marinated in tasty dressings. It's really worth experimenting with tofu, since it is an excellent source of vegetable protein and contains no fat.

Silken tofu is soft and creamy and is useful for dressings, cheesecakes, sauces and dips. It adds bulk and texture, increases the nutritional value of these foods and takes on the flavours of the other ingredients. Firm tofu has been pressed for longer and can be cut into chunks for frying, grilling and inclusion in stews and curries, or it can be grated or chopped and made into burgers and roasts.

Tofu should be stored in the refrigerator. Once the packet is opened, keep the tofu immersed in a bowl of cold water in the refrigerator and it should remain fresh for up to 1 week if the water is changed daily.

### TVP (Textured Vegetable Protein)
TVP forms the bulk of most veggie burgers, and veggie mince and banger mixes. It's made from a mixture of soya flour, flavourings and liquid, which is cooked, then extruded under pressure and cut into chunks or small pieces to resemble mince. Unlike tofu it has a slightly chewy, meat like texture which makes it unappetising to some vegans and vegetarians; although for the same reason it may appeal to new vegetarians who miss the texture of meat. It is worth keeping a packet in the cupboard for emergencies because it's quite versatile, keeps well, and like tofu it is an excellent source of low-fat protein.

---

### COOKING DRIED PULSES

These times are approximate depending on the age of the pulse and the length of soaking time.

| TYPE | COOKING TIME | PRESSURE COOKING TIME (HIGH/15 LB PRESSURE) |
|---|---|---|
| Aduki beans | 30-60 minutes | 12 minutes |
| Black beans | 1½ hours | 20 minutes |
| Black-eye beans | 1½ hours | 12 minutes |
| Borlotti beans | 1 hour | 17 minutes |
| Butter beans | 1½ hours | 17 minutes |
| Cannellini beans | 1 hour | 25 minutes |
| Chick peas | 1½-2 hours | 20 minutes |
| Flageolet beans | 1 hour | 15 minutes |
| Haricot beans | 1-1½ hours | 20 minutes |
| Lentils | 30-60 minutes | 15 minutes |
| Mung beans | 40 minutes | 12 minutes |
| Red kidney beans | 1-1½ hours | 20 minutes |
| Soya beans | 3-4 hours | 30 minutes |
| Split peas | 45-60 minutes | 15 minutes |

# PASTA

It's difficult to remember what we did for fast, satisfying meals before pasta became readily available. Because it keeps well and is quick to cook, cheap and tasty, pasta has become one of our most popular foods. Nutritionally speaking pasta is high in fibre and low in fat and calories – it's the sauce that makes pasta dishes fattening. If you're watching your weight use low-calorie ingredients like vegetables, skimmed milk and low- or medium-fat cheese to replace full-fat equivalents, and keep the use of ingredients like olive oil, butter, olives and salami to a minimum.

## FRESH AND DRIED PASTA

Fresh pasta is now widely available in a good range of shapes and flavours, in supermarkets as well as delicatessens. It cooks in a matter of minutes and is considered superior to dried pasta. Of course, you can make your own at home following our recipe overleaf – homemade pasta is incomparable. The best flour to use is a very fine-textured soft wheat flour known as 'type 00'. This yields a dough which is easier to stretch by hand. Durum or hard wheat semolina flour is only really suitable if you are using a pasta machine which flattens, rather than stretches the dough. Both types of flour are available from Italian delicatessens.

If you make pasta frequently, it is probably a good idea to invest in a pasta machine to do the rolling and cutting for you. One of these machines will take all the hard work out of rolling and get the dough really thin. It will also ensure that the dough is cut into neat, uniform shapes, so that it cooks evenly.

Dried pastas are available in a bewildering range of sizes, shapes and flavours. The best are made from 100% durum wheat *(pasta di semola di grano duro)*; some include eggs *(all'uovo)*.

## Shapes, Sizes and Flavours

The choice of shape and size is a matter of personal taste but it's worth bearing in mind that some varieties – such as conchiglie (shells) – are particularly suited to holding lots of sauce, while other chunkier shapes – such as penne – are good with robust vegetable-based sauces. Fine spaghetti and noodles are excellent with delicate fish sauces, while tiny ditalini are perfect for soups and young children's meals. There are the classic recipes, such as macaroni cheese, spaghetti bolognese and spaghetti alla carbonara, but do experiment with your own combinations.

Coloured and flavoured pastas (fresh and dried) can add a new twist to a familiar meal. These are coloured with puréed vegetables; although the colours are fun the flavours are rarely pronounced. If you're looking for extra flavour choose those flavoured with garlic and herbs. Wholemeal pasta is made with wholemeal flour and has a rather heavy chewy texture. If you're trying to increase your intake of dietary fibre you may prefer to eat plain pasta with a high-fibre vegetable-based sauce.

### Quantities

It is difficult to give specific quantity guidelines for pasta since it really depends on how rich the sauce is, and even on the size and shape of the pasta – some are easier and quicker to eat than others! Of course appetites, particularly for pasta, vary enormously, too. As a very rough guide allow about 75-125 g (3-4 oz) uncooked weight, per person.

## COOKING PASTA

All pasta, fresh and dried, should be cooked until *al dente* – firm to the bite, definitely not soft, and without a hard, uncooked centre. The most important thing to remember is that pasta requires lots of fast-boiling salted water; a small pan containing insufficient water will produce unevenly cooked stodgy pasta. Some cooks add a little olive oil to the water in the belief that it will prevent sticking, but this is not necessary. Fresh pasta will cook in a few minutes, while dried pasta usually takes around 8-12 minutes. Whether you're cooking fresh or dried pasta the time will depend on the size and shape; obviously, thin shapes like capellini (angel's hair) will cook more quickly than chunky or filled shapes. Manufacturers' recommended cooking times vary too. The only accurate way to determine when pasta is cooked is by tasting.

## SERVING SUGGESTIONS

Toss cooked pasta with the chosen sauce or butter as soon as it is cooked, or it will stick together as it cools. Always have warm plates or bowls ready as it quickly loses heat. If cooking pasta to serve cold, drain and rinse with cold water to prevent further cooking and rinse away surface starch. Toss with dressing while still slightly warm for optimum flavour. If you store the salad in the refrigerator, bring it to room temperature before serving.

Parmesan cheese is a must for serving with hot pasta although some seafood pasta dishes are better without it. Do buy a piece of Parmesan; the taste is far superior to the 'soapy' ready grated alternatives sold in tubs and packets. A well wrapped piece of Parmesan will keep in the refrigerator for several weeks. Rather than grating it on the fine side of the grater try using a cheese slice or swivel potato peeler to shave off large flakes of cheese. But, dieters be warned, just one tablespoonful (15 ml) of grated Parmesan adds an extra 70 calories!

Should you find yourself with leftovers, the only satisfactory method of reheating pasta is in the microwave. Both dressed and plain pasta can be reheated in this way without loss of texture or flavour. To reheat plain pasta, toss with a little olive oil, cover and cook on HIGH for about 2 minutes. Alternatively, toss plain leftover pasta with a well flavoured dressing and salad ingredients and serve as a salad.

## HOMEMADE PASTA

PREPARATION TIME About 25 minutes plus drying
COOKING TIME 2-3 minutes

**MAKES ABOUT 400 G (14 OZ)**

**335 CALS/100 G (3¹/₂ OZ)**

- *about 300 g (10 oz) white plain flour (preferably soft wheat flour 'type 00')*
- *3 eggs, size 2*
- *1.25 ml (¹/₄ tsp) salt*
- *15 ml (1 tbsp) olive oil*

1 Tip the flour onto a work surface. Make a well in the centre and break in the eggs. Add the salt and oil.

2 Using your fingers, gradually mix the flour from the edge of the pile into the eggs. Continue to knead all the ingredients together until you have a soft dough.

3 Once the dough has come together, knead it on a lightly floured surface for about 8 minutes, using both hands as if kneading bread. If it is very sticky, add a little extra flour. When you have finished, the dough should be smooth and elastic. Wrap in cling film and leave to rest for 30 minutes.

4 If using a pasta machine, put the dough through your chosen setting, sprinkling the shaped pasta lightly with flour to prevent it sticking. Alternatively roll out the dough as thinly as possible to a large rectangle.

5 For stuffed pasta, such as ravioli or tortellini, the dough must be used immediately while it is still soft. For tagliatelle, fettuccine, lasagne, cannelloni and pasta shapes, the dough must be left to dry before cutting: put the rolled out sheet of dough on clean tea towels for 10 minutes or until the surface of the pasta is dry to the touch.

**Variations**

Flavoured pastas are quite easy to make and they are delicious served with simple sauces.
GREEN PASTA: Cook 225 g (8 oz) spinach, drain thoroughly, then purée in a blender or food processor. Add with the eggs.
TOMATO PASTA: Add 15-30 ml (1-2 tbsp) tomato purée with the eggs.
HERB PASTA: Add 60 ml (4 tbsp) chopped basil with the eggs.

## *SHAPING NOODLES*

**1** Sprinkle the pasta with a little flour, then roll up like a Swiss roll.

**2** For tagliatelle cut off 5 mm (¼ inch) wide strips; for fettuccine cut narrower strips; for pappardelle cut 1 cm (½ inch) wide strips, using a fluted pastry wheel.

**3** After cutting, unfold and leave to dry for 5-10 minutes before cooking.

## *SHAPING PASTA QUILLS*

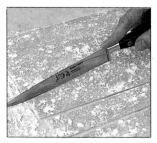

**1** Cut about a quarter of the rolled-out dough into 4 cm (1½ inch) squares. Keep the remaining dough covered so that it doesn't dry out.

**2** Take one pasta square, then lay the end of a wooden spoon or a round pencil diagonally across one corner of the square.

**3** Roll it up to make a quill shape. Leave to dry for about 30 minutes before cooking. Repeat with the remaining squares, and then with the rest of the dough.

## *SHAPING RAVIOLI*

**1** Prepare the filling ahead (see below). Put teaspoonfuls of filling at 4 cm (1½ inch) intervals across half of the rolled-out dough.

**2** Glaze the spaces between the filling with beaten egg or water.

**3** Cover with the other half of dough and press along the dampened lines.

**4** With a sharp knife or pastry wheel cut into squares between the filling. Lift onto a well floured baking sheet and leave to dry out for about 1 hour before cooking.

SUGGESTED FILLING: Sauté 1 finely chopped small onion and 1 crushed garlic clove in 15 ml (1 tbsp) olive oil until softened. Add 125 g (4 oz) cream cheese, 50 g (2 oz) finely chopped salami, 45 ml (3 tbsp) finely chopped watercress and seasoning to taste.

LASAGNE AND CANNELLONI: Cut the dough into rectangles measuring about 10 x 15 cm (4 x 6 inches).

NOTE: Fresh, unfilled pasta takes about 2-3 minutes to cook. When filled it takes about 5-8 minutes.

# RICE AND GRAINS

Rice is one of our staple foods. It contains protein and B vitamins, but no fat, and it is cheap and quick to cook. There are many types of rice, each with its own characteristics, and for many dishes it is important to choose the correct variety.

## TYPES OF RICE

• Brown rice is the whole grain with only the tough outer husk removed. Like other unrefined grains it is higher in fibre, B vitamins and protein than its refined counterpart. Because the bran is retained, the rice has a chewy texture and nutty flavour, and it takes longer to cook than white varieties.

• Long-grain white rice is brown rice that has been further milled to remove the bran and germ. When cooked the grains should be separate, quite dry and fluffy. Varieties include Patna and Carolina.

• Basmati rice is a wonderfully aromatic long-grain rice which was originally harvested mainly in the foothills of the Himalayas. It is the perfect accompaniment to curries and other spicy dishes, and is used to make a pilaf. Brown basmati rice is also available.

• Thai rice is a newcomer to our supermarkets. The large plump grains are extremely fragrant with a slightly sweet flavour.

• Arborio rice is a special short-grain variety from Italy which is essential for an authentic risotto. It has the unique ability to absorb a lot of liquid during cooking without turning mushy.

• Glutinous rice is another Asian variety which is also known as sticky rice. It has oval cream-coloured grains which cook into a sticky mass. It is a vital ingredient in Japanese sushi.

• Short-grain pudding rice is perfect for a rice pudding. The small grains absorb lots of liquid during cooking, producing a soft and creamy result.

### Cooking Rice

Contrary to popular belief, cooking rice isn't difficult. Some of the 'speciality rices' are cooked in specific ways: the liquid is usually added gradually to arborio for a risotto; pudding rice is usually baked slowly in a low oven; glutinous rice is steamed; but in general long-grain rice varieties can be treated in the same way. Many cooks like to wash or rinse the rice before cooking to remove excess starch. With some varieties this is not necessary, but others – particularly basmati – tend to be very starchy and may contain small pieces of grit so washing is advisable. Simply put the rice in a sieve and wash under cold running water until the water runs clear, shaking the sieve and picking out any bits of grit.

To cook the rice you will need a large saucepan and plenty of fast-boiling salted water. Sprinkle the rice into the boiling water and keep the heat high until the water returns to the boil. Stir once with a fork to loosen any rice grains that have sunk to the bottom, lower the heat and cook, uncovered, fairly vigorously. As long as you have sufficient water the rice will not stick.

There are so many varieties of long-grain rice on the market that it is impossible to give exact cooking times. Most varieties take a minimum of 10 minutes; to test, pick out a few grains and taste. When cooked, drain in a sieve and rinse with boiling water to remove excess starch. Fluff up the grains with a fork to serve.

The alternative method relies on accurately estimating the volume of liquid to that of rice (usually double liquid to rice). It is a little trickier because the rice has a habit of sticking to the pan, so you need to use a pan with a really solid base, and control the heat carefully. Keep a careful watch on the time and resist lifting the lid during cooking because this lets precious steam escape. Rice can also be cooked by this method in the oven, usually at about 180°C (350°F) mark 4, but it will take much longer. If converting a white rice recipe to use brown rice, don't forget to add extra liquid and increase the cooking time.

Rice may be cooked in advance, stored in the refrigerator and reheated in the microwave or in the oven – in a well-buttered covered dish.

## GRAINS

The interest in wholefood and healthy eating means that a better range of grains can be found in supermarkets than ever before. Grains are high in vitamins. They are also extremely versatile and can be used for making all sorts of dishes. Try them as a change from rice or potatoes as an accompaniment.

One of the most delicious and expensive grains is wild rice. It is not as the name suggests a rice but the seed of an aquatic grass. It is dark brown in colour and has a strong, nutty flavour. Because of its cost, wild rice is usually mixed with other grains or rice. Look out for commercially prepared mixtures. Other useful grains include bulghur wheat, couscous, barley and maize, which is used for making polenta.

# PASTRY

The art of successful pastry making lies in light careful handling and accurate measuring. Except when making choux pastry, the golden rule is to keep everything cool – the kitchen, work surface, utensils ingredients and yourself!

There are three main types of pastry: shortcrust, puff and choux. Flan pastry and the classic French pâte sucrée are similar to shortcrust, though they are richer and pâte sucrée is mixed differently. (Recipes for these sweet pastries are on page 371.)

For most pastries, plain white flour is the best, as it gives a light, crisp result. Self-raising flour produces a soft spongy pastry, while using all wholemeal flour tends to give a heavy pastry.

Puff pastry is made with strong flour which contains extra gluten to strengthen the dough and enable it to be rolled and folded intensively. A little lemon juice is usually added to puff pastry to soften the gluten and make the dough more elastic.

Traditionally shortcrust pastry is made with a mixture of lard and either butter or margarine, but more often nowadays white vegetable fat replaces lard, or all butter or margarine is used instead. For a rich flavour, butter is the best, although for savoury pastries margarine gives good results. Generally the firmer block margarine should be used in preference to soft-tub margarine. Be careful when adding the water to the dough: too much will make the cooked pastry tough while too little will make a dry dough that's hard to handle and is crumbly when cooked.

## MIXING PASTRY

Most pastries involve rubbing the fat into the flour. To do this, cut the fat into small cubes then tip them into the flour and salt. Mix them round briefly to evenly coat the exposed surfaces with flour, then using your fingertips and picking up small amounts at a time, rub the fat and flour together until the fat breaks down into small pieces. Try to do this as quickly and lightly as possible and don't use your palms or you will end up with a sticky mess.

Sprinkle the water evenly over the mixture and stir it in with a round-bladed knife. You may need to add a little more or a little less than stated in the recipe since the absorbency of different flours varies, so don't add the liquid all at once. Collect the dough into a ball and knead lightly for a few seconds. If it feels very sticky, simply sprinkle with a little extra flour.

## USING A FOOD PROCESSOR

Shortcrust pastry can be made very quickly and successfully in a food processor. It's important to pulse the machine or turn it on in short bursts only so that the dough doesn't get overworked. Don't try to make too much pastry at one time, or you will overload the machine.

## READY-MADE PASTRIES

If you haven't the time or inclination to make your own pastry, choose from the good range of ready-made pastries now available – both frozen and from the chilled cabinet. Ready-made wholemeal and plain, shortcrust, puff, flaky and filo pastries are widely available. For real time saving look out for ready-rolled sheets of puff pastry, and before buying check the quantity required (see below).

## PASTRY QUANTITIES

It is important to note that where a recipe specifies a weight of pastry, the quantity refers to the weight of flour rather than the combined weight of the ingredients. For example, if a recipe calls for 225 g (8 oz) shortcrust pastry you will need this amount of flour and 110 g (4 oz) fat because the correct proportion of flour to fat is 2:1.

When buying ready-made pastry remember that the weight specified on the packet is the combined weight of the ingredients and not the flour weight. As a guide, a 375 g (13 oz) packet of shortcrust pastry is approximately equivalent to homemade pastry made with 225 g (8 oz) flour. Two 375 g (13 oz) packets of ready-made puff pastry are roughly equivalent to homemade pastry made with 450 g (1 lb) flour.

## ROLLING OUT PASTRY

Dust the work surface and the rolling pin – never the pastry – with as little flour as possible. Roll the dough lightly and evenly in one direction only. Always roll away from you, using light, firm strokes and rotate the pastry frequently to keep an even shape and thickness. Roll it out until it is quite thin; very thick pastry is unpleasant to eat, but avoid over-rolling or stretching the pastry as you roll or it will shrink badly during cooking.

## LINING A FLAN CASE

Loose-based metal flan tins are ideal because they transfer heat rapidly and pastry tends to cook better in these than in china dishes. The removable base makes it easier to transfer the baked flan to a serving plate. Alternatively use a flan ring placed on a baking sheet, a sandwich tin or a fluted china flan dish. If cooked in a china dish the flan is generally served from the dish.

**1** Roll out the pastry until it is about 5 cm (2 inches) larger than the flan tin all round. Use the rolling pin to help you lift the pastry over the tin.

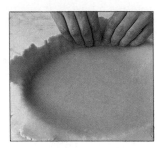

**2** Lift the edges of the pastry so that it falls down into the tin, then gently press the pastry against the edges of the flan tin so that there are no gaps between the pastry and the tin.

**3** Turn any surplus pastry outwards over the rim and trim the edges with a sharp knife.

## BAKING BLIND

If a recipe instructs you to bake blind, it means that you should bake the pastry case (or cases) without any filling. The pastry may be partially cooked before adding the filling, or it may be completely cooked if the filling doesn't require further cooking.

Fully baked pastry cases will keep for several days in an airtight tin or they may be frozen.

**1** Line the flan tin or dish with pastry. If you have time, chill the pastry case for 20-30 minutes to rest the pastry and help reduce shrinkage. Prick the pastry base with a fork, then line with grease-proof paper or foil.

**2** Fill with ceramic baking beans or dried pulses. Small pastry cases don't need lining; it should be sufficient to prick these with a fork.

**3** For partially baked cases, bake at 200°C (400°F) mark 6 for 10-15 minutes until the case looks 'set'. Carefully remove the paper or foil and the beans and bake for a further 5 minutes until the base is firm to the touch and lightly coloured. Pastry cases which need complete baking should be returned to the oven for about 15 minutes until firm and golden brown.

## COVERING A PIE DISH

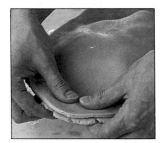

**1** Using the inverted pie dish as a guide, roll out the pastry until 5 cm (2 inches) larger than the pie dish. Cut a 2.5 cm (1 inch) strip from the outside of the pastry. Place on the moistened rim of the pie dish and brush with water.

**2** Fill the dish generously, so that the surface of the filling is slightly rounded; use a pie funnel if insufficient filling is available. Use the rolling pin to help lift the pastry lid into position. Press the edges together to seal.

**3** Using a sharp knife held at a slight angle away from the dish, trim off excess pastry. Knock up the edges and finish as desired (see right).

### FINISHING TOUCHES

Decorative edges and applied pastry shapes look attractive. Remember to glaze the decoration as well as the pie or flan

KNOCK UP: This seals the edges and prevents the filling leaking out. Press your index finger along the rim and holding a knife horizontally, tap the edge of the pastry sharply with the blunt edge of the knife to give a 'flaky' appearance.

FLUTED OR SCALLOPED EDGE: Press your thumb on the rim of the pastry and at the same time gently draw back the floured blade of a round-bladed knife about 1 cm (½ inch) towards the centre. Repeat around pie at 2.5 cm (1 inch) intervals.

CRIMPED EDGE: Push your forefinger into the rim of the pastry and using the thumb and forefinger of the other hand gently pinch the pastry that is pushed up by this action. Continue around the edge of the pie.

FORKED EDGE: Simply press all around the edge of the pie with the back of a floured fork.

LEAVES: Cut 2.5 cm (1 inch) strips from pastry trimmings, then cut these diagonally into diamonds. Use the back of a knife to mark veins.

OTHER DECORATIONS: Although leaves are the traditional decoration for pies, different shapes can be cut freehand or using cutters as desired. Holly leaves and berries are ideal for festive pies.

## SHORTCRUST PASTRY

This plain short pastry is probably the most widely used of all pastries. If preferred, omit the white fat and use 125 g (4 oz) butter or margarine. For shortcrust pastry, the proportion of flour to fat is 2:1, or twice the quantity. Therefore, for a recipe using quantities of shortcrust pastry other than 225 g (8 oz), simply use half the quantity of fat to the flour weight specified.

PREPARATION TIME 10 minutes
FREEZING Suitable

MAKES 225 G (8 OZ)
- *225 g (8 oz) white plain flour*
- *pinch of salt*
- *50 g (2 oz) butter or margarine, chilled and diced*

175 CALS/25 G (1 OZ)
- *50 g (2 oz) lard or white vegetable fat, chilled and diced*

1 Mix flour and salt together in a bowl. Add the fat to the flour. Using your fingertips, rub the fat lightly into the flour until the mixture resembles fine breadcrumbs.

2 Add 45-60 ml (3-4 tbsp) chilled water, sprinkling it evenly over the surface. (Uneven addition may cause blistering when the pastry is cooked.)

3 Stir in with a round-bladed knife until the mixture begins to stick together in large lumps. With one hand, collect the dough mixture together to form a ball.

4 Knead lightly for a few seconds to give a firm, smooth dough; do not overhandle the dough. Wrap in cling-film or greaseproof paper and chill in the refrigerator for about 30 minutes.

5 To roll out the pastry, sprinkle a very little flour on a work surface and the rolling pin (not on the pastry) and roll out the dough evenly in one direction only, turning it occasionally. The usual thickness is 3 mm (⅛ inch). Do not pull or stretch the pastry.

**Variations**

WHOLEMEAL PASTRY: Follow the recipe for Shortcrust Pastry, replacing half of the white flour with plain wholemeal flour. You may need a little extra water due to the absorbency of wholemeal flour.

NUT PASTRY: Follow the recipe for Shortcrust Pastry, stirring in 40 g (1½ oz) very finely chopped, shelled walnuts, cashew nuts, hazelnuts or almonds before adding the water.

CHEESE PASTRY: Follow the recipe for Shortcrust or Wholemeal Pastry, stirring in 125 g (4 oz) finely grated Cheddar cheese, or 45 ml (3 tbsp) freshly grated Parmesan cheese, and a pinch of mustard powder before adding the water.

SESAME PASTRY: Follow the recipe for Shortcrust or Wholemeal Pastry, stirring in 40 g (1½ oz) toasted sesame seeds before adding the water.

HERB PASTRY: Follow the recipe for Shortcrust or Wholemeal Pastry, stirring in 45 ml (3 tbsp) chopped mixed herbs before adding the water.

NOTE: Shortcrust pastry can be baked straight away, but it is better if allowed to 'rest' in the refrigerator for about 30 minutes before baking. Bake at 200°C (400°F) mark 6, unless otherwise specified.

## PUFF PASTRY

The richest of all the pastries, puff requires patience, practice and very light handling. Whenever possible it should be made the day before use. It is not practical to make in a quantity with less than 450 g (1 lb) flour weight. This is equivalent to two 375 g (13 oz) packets.

PREPARATION TIME 40 minutes, plus resting
FREEZING Suitable

**MAKES 450 G (I LB)**
- *450 g (1 lb) strong plain flour*
- *pinch of salt*
- *15 ml (1 tbsp) lemon juice*

**270 CALS 25 G (I OZ)**
- *450 g (1 lb) butter or margarine, chilled*

**1** Mix the flour and salt together in a bowl. Cut off 50 g (2 oz) of the butter and flatten the remaining butter with a rolling pin to a slab 2 cm (³/₄ inch) thick.

**2** Cut the 50 g (2 oz) butter into small pieces, add to the flour and rub in. Using a round-bladed knife, stir in the lemon juice and about 300 ml (10 fl oz) chilled water to make a soft, elastic dough.

**3** Quickly knead the dough until smooth and shape into a round. Cut through half the depth in the shape of a cross. Open out to form a star.

**4** Roll out keeping the centre four times as thick as the flaps. Place the slab of butter in the centre of the dough.

**5** Fold the flaps envelope-style and press gently with a rolling pin. Roll out to a rectangle measuring about 40 x 20 cm ( 16 x 8 inches).

**6** Fold bottom third up and top third down, keeping the edges straight. Seal edges. Wrap in greaseproof paper and 'rest' in the refrigerator for 30 minutes.

**7** Put the pastry on a lightly floured work surface with the folded edges to the sides, then repeat the rolling, folding and resting sequence 5 times.

NOTE: Shape the pastry as required, then leave to 'rest' in the refrigerator for 30 minutes before baking. Brush with beaten egg before baking at 220°C (425°F) mark 7, unless otherwise stated.

# PATE SUCREE

Pâte sucrée keeps its shape: it shrinks very little and does not spread during baking. Although it can be made in a bowl, the classic way to make this pastry is on a flat, cold surface, preferably marble.

PREPARATION TIME 10 minutes, plus resting
FREEZING Suitable

MAKES 125 G (4 OZ)
- *125 g (4 oz) white plain flour*
- *pinch of salt*
- *50 g (2 oz) butter (at room temperature)*

255 CALS/25G (1 OZ)
- *2 egg yolks*
- *50 g (2 oz) caster sugar*

**1** Sift the flour and salt onto a work surface. Make a well in the centre and add the butter, egg yolks and sugar.

**2** Using the fingertips of one hand, pinch and work the sugar, butter and egg yolks together until well blended.

**3** Gradually work in all the flour to bind the mixture together.

**4** Knead lightly until smooth, then wrap the pastry in foil or clingfilm and leave to rest in the refrigerator or a cool place for at least 30 minutes. Roll out as for Shortcrust Pastry (see page 369).

# SWEET FLAN PASTRY

This is made by the same rubbing-in method as short-crust pastry, but beaten egg is used instead of water. It is usually sweetened with sugar and is ideal for flan cases and small tarts.

PREPARATION TIME 10 minutes, plus resting
FREEZING Suitable

MAKES 125 G (4 OZ)
- *125 g (4 oz) white plain flour*
- *pinch of salt*
- *75 g (3 oz) butter or margarine, chilled and diced*

250 CAL /25G (1 OZ)
- *5 ml (1 tsp) caster sugar*
- *1 egg, beaten*

**1** Sift the flour and salt into a bowl. Rub in the fat until the mixture resembles fine bread-crumbs. Stir in the sugar.

**2** Add the egg, stirring with a round-bladed knife until the ingredients begin to stick together in large lumps.

**3** With one hand, collect the mixture together and knead lightly for a few seconds to give a firm, smooth dough. Wrap the pastry in foil or clingfilm and leave to rest in the refrigerator or a cool place for at least 30 minutes. Roll out as for Shortcrust Pastry (see page 369).

# CAKE-MAKING

Once in a while there's something wonderfully uplifting about baking a cake, whether it's a spectacular gâteau or a simple sponge. However health-conscious we may be, few can resist the aroma of a freshly baked cake. The following notes should help you to achieve perfect results with your home baking.

## ESSENTIAL INGREDIENTS

The following ingredients are commonly used in baking recipes, in addition to a wide variety of flavourings, including spices, essences, nuts, dried fruit, and chocolate. Remember to check the use-by dates on these items before use.

• FAT: Butter gives a rich flavour and colour which many prefer, but the flavour of margarine has improved enormously in recent years. Soft-tub margarine, which can be used straight from the fridge, is ideal for all-in-one methods.

If you are using butter (or one of the hard 'block' margarines) bring it to room temperature first. Alternatively microwave on LOW for about 1 minute but watch carefully – if it melts you'll have to start all over again.

Avoid using low-fat spreads: many contain high proportions of water and, although they look like margarine, they do not behave identically during cooking. Oil can be used in suitably proportioned recipes only.

• SUGAR AND SWEETENERS: Sugar is needed for texture and volume as well as flavour. Caster sugar is generally the best choice since it has small regular granules which dissolve easily. Granulated sugar can be used for rubbed-in cakes but, like icing sugar, it is unsuitable for creamed or whisked mixtures. Other sugars lend a particular effect: demerara makes a delicious crunchy topping, while dark Barbados sugar imparts a rich colour and distinctive flavour.

Golden syrup, honey, treacle and malt extract are generally added for flavour only and are used in addition to sugar. Sugar substitutes and artificial sweeteners cannot be substituted for sugar in cakes.

• EGGS: Avoid using eggs straight from the refrigerator – a cake mixture is much more likely to curdle if it's made with cold eggs. Eggs act as a raising agent in many cakes so it's important to select the right size – use size 2 eggs unless otherwise stated. Using the wrong size could result in failure.

• FLOUR: Self-raising flour is used in many cake recipes as it conveniently includes a raising agent.

Plain flour can be converted to self-raising, by blending it with baking powder. To every 225 g (8 oz) plain flour, use 15 ml (1 level tbsp) baking powder for scones; 10 ml (2 level tsp) for a plain cake mixture; and 5 ml (1 level tsp) for a rich fruit cake mixture. Cake flour is now widely available; its slightly lower gluten content is deemed to produce lighter cakes, but in practice the difference is minimal.

Wholemeal flour is nutritionally preferred to white flour but produces cakes with a darker colour and denser texture. If you wish to use wholemeal flour, a mixture of white and wholemeal with a little extra baking powder works best. If you sieve it don't forget to tip in the bran from the sieve or valuable fibre and nutrients will be wasted.

## CAKE-MAKING METHODS

The following standard mixing methods employ different techniques which largely determine the texture of the cake. Some recipes use more than one method – for example, creamed cakes sometimes have whisked egg whites folded in.

• CREAMING: This is the traditional method used to make a classic Victoria sandwich. Softened fat makes creaming considerably easier, as does a hand-held whisk or a mixer. As soon as the fat and sugar are creamed to a pale-coloured mixture, fluffy and light in texture, you can start adding the beaten egg. Don't be tempted to add it all at once or the mixture will curdle, producing a dense cake. If the mixture looks as if it is about to curdle, add a spoonful of the sifted flour. Finally fold in all of the flour with a large metal spoon.

• ALL-IN-ONE: For speedy last-minute cakes, this is the ideal method. Simply throw all the ingredients together in a bowl and beat thoroughly. If using a food processor, don't over-process or you will beat out all the air. Soft-tub margarine or softened butter are the best fats to use. It's prudent to add a little extra raising agent to compensate for the lack of creaming.

• WHISKING: This is the method used to produce the classic fatless sponge. Because the cake relies on the volume of air trapped in the egg mixture to make it rise, the eggs must be beaten really thoroughly. This is virtually impossible unless you use an electric hand-held whisk, an electric table-top mixer or a good rotary whisk plus strong arms and a lot of patience! Standing the bowl over a pan of simmering water helps to increase volume and stabilise the foamy mass. Keep the bottom of the bowl clear of the water or you will end up with scrambled eggs! The whisked mixture is ready for the flour when you can lift the beaters and write the numeral 8 on the surface with the trail of mixture.

• MELTING: Cakes made by this method usually contain a high proportion of treacle, golden syrup, honey or malt extract and it is vital that they are measured accurately; if you add too much the cake will be dense and it will probably sink in the middle. If the measurements are given in tablespoons, use a warmed measuring spoon, preferably metal. Alternatively put the saucepan on the scales, set the dial to zero then spoon in the required amount.

This measured syrup or treacle is then heated gently with fat and sugar until melted; cool slightly before mixing with the dried ingredients. The mixture should have the consistency of a thick batter; it should find its own level when poured into the tin. For best results wrap these cakes in greaseproof paper, then overwrap with foil and store for 1-2 days before cutting.

• RUBBING IN: As the name suggests these cakes are made in the same way as shortcrust pastry, by rubbing the fat into the flour with the fingertips. Once you have rubbed in the fat, add the liquid carefully – too much will result in a heavy doughy cake, while too little will make it dry. Remember that flour absorbencies vary; use the recipe as a fairly accurate guide but don't be afraid to add a little more or a little less. In general, for large cakes the mixture should be soft enough to drop from a spoon; for small buns it should be a little stiffer.

Because rubbed-in cakes are comparatively low in fat, they dry out and go stale quickly, so they are best eaten on the day of making.

### Cake Tins

Using the correct size tin can make all the difference between success and failure. It goes without saying that if you put a cake mixture in a tin that's too big you will end up with a pancake and if the tin is too small the mixture will spill out over the top. Because tins come in a confusing array of sizes – particularly loaf tins – a volume measurement is sometimes given as well. To check the capacity of a tin, simply fill with water from a measuring jug, noting how many litres (or pints) it will hold.

Grease tins and base-line with lightly greased greaseproof paper, or non-stick baking parchment which does not require greasing. We advise doing this even when using non-stick cake tins, to ease turning

out. For rich mixtures and fruit cakes, line the sides of the tin, too.

For large rich fruit cakes, stand the tin on a double thickness of brown paper and tie a band of brown paper around the outside of the tin to prevent the outside overcooking.

### What Went Wrong?

Unfortunately it's not always easy to determine why a cake hasn't come out looking like the picture. It is important to measure everything accurately – using scales and measuring spoons – and to use the right size tin. Once the cake is in the oven resist the temptation to open the door until at least three quarters of the cooking time has elapsed – a sudden gush of cold air will make it sink in the middle. If your cake appears to be browning too quickly, cover it with greaseproof paper towards the end of cooking.

Here are some other common problems and possible causes:

CLOSE, DENSE TEXTURE
• Too much liquid.
• Too little raising agent, or raising agent past its use-by date.
• Insufficient creaming of the fat and sugar.
• Creamed mixture curdled.
• Flour folded in too vigorously.

PEAKED AND CRACKED TOP
• Oven too hot, or the cake was too near the top of the oven.
• Not enough liquid.
• Tin too small.

SUNKEN FRUIT
• Fruit too sticky or too wet.
• Mixture too soft to support the weight of the fruit.

SUNK IN THE MIDDLE
• Wrong size tin.
• Inaccurately measured ingredients (gingerbread in particular).
• Oven too hot or too cool, or cooking time too short.
• Oven door opened too soon.

### Storing Cakes

Make sure that the cake is completely cold before you put it into a cake tin or plastic airtight container. If you haven't a large enough container, wrap in a double layer of greaseproof paper and overwrap with foil. Avoid putting rich fruit cakes in direct contact with foil; the fruit may react with it. Most cakes freeze well; they are best frozen undecorated. If you want to freeze a finished gâteau, open freeze, then pack in a rigid container.

## COVERING A RICH FRUIT CAKE

The easiest way to give a celebration cake a professional-looking finish is to cover it with fondant icing. Before applying the icing you need to cover the cake with almond paste or marzipan. This creates a smooth foundation for the icing.

## APRICOT GLAZE

Before applying the almond paste you need to brush the surface of the cake with a glaze. To make apricot glaze, simply place 125 g (4 oz) apricot jam in a small saucepan with 30 ml (2 tbsp) water and heat gently, stirring, until the jam begins to melt. Bring to the boil and simmer for 1 minute. Strain through a nylon sieve and use while warm.

## COVERING A CAKE WITH ALMOND PASTE

For recommended quantities of almond paste see the chart below.

1 If the cake has an uneven top, cut it level. Turn the cake over so the flat bottom becomes the top. Sift some icing sugar onto a clean work surface.

2 Roll out half the almond paste slightly larger than the top of the cake. Using the cake tin as a guide, cut the paste to fit. Brush the top of the cake with warm apricot glaze.

3 Lift the almond paste onto the cake and smooth over, neatening the edges. Place on a cake board, which is 5 cm (2 inches) larger than the cake.

4 Cut a piece of string the same height as the cake with its almond paste top, and another to fit around the side of the cake. Roll out the remaining almond paste and, using the string as a guide, trim the paste to size. Brush the sides of the cake with apricot glaze.

5 Roll up the almond paste strip loosely. Place one end against the side of the cake and unroll to cover the sides of the cake. Use a pallete knife to smooth over the sides and joins of the paste. Flatten the top lightly with a rolling pin. Leave the cake to dry out for about 2 days before applying the icing.

## ALMOND PASTE AND FONDANT ICING QUANTITY GUIDE

| SQUARE TIN | ROUND TIN | ALMOND PASTE | FONDANT ICING |
|---|---|---|---|
| 12 cm (5 inch) | 15 cm (6 inch) | 350 g (12 oz) | 350 g (12 oz) |
| 15 cm (6 inch) | 18 cm (7 inch) | 450 g (1 lb) | 450 g (1 lb) |
| 18 cm (7 inch) | 20 cm (8 inch) | 550 g (1¼ lb) | 700 g (1½ lb) |
| 20 cm (8 inch) | 23 cm (9 inch) | 800 g (1¾ lb) | 800 g (1¾ lb) |
| 23 cm (9 inch) | 25 cm (10 inch) | 900 g (2 lb) | 900 g (2 lb) |
| 25 cm (10 inch) | 28 cm (11 inch) | I kg (2¼ lb) | 1 kg (2¼ lb) |
| 28 cm (11 inch) | 30 cm (12 inch) | I .1 kg (2½ lb) | 1.1 kg (2½ lb) |
| 30 cm (12 inch) | 33 cm (13 inch) | 1 4 kg (3 lb) | 1.4 kg (3 lb) |
| 33 cm (13 inch) | 35 cm (14 inch) | 1.6 kg (3½ lb) | 1.6 kg (1½ lb) |

## *COVERING A CAKE WITH FONDANT ICING*

For recommended quantities, chart (page 374).

1 First cover the cake with almond paste and allow to dry. Sprinkle a clean work surface with cornflour and dredge your rolling pin. Roll out the icing until it is 12-15 cm (5-6 inches) larger than the cake top.

2 Supporting the icing on a rolling pin, place it centrally over the top of the cake, allowing the icing to drape over the sides. Press the icing onto the sides of the cake.

3 Work it with your hands sprinkled with cornflour or icing sugar, from the centre of the cake; gently ease the icing down the sides to give an even covering.

4 Trim the excess icing from the base. Smooth icing, using a circular movement with the fingers. Leave for about 2 days to dry before decorating.

## ALMOND PASTE

You can either make your own almond paste, following the recipe below, or buy it ready-made. When buying ready-made choose the white variety, rather than the yellow one, as it won't discolour the icing.

PREPARATION TIME 10 minutes
FREEZING Suitable

**MAKES ABOUT 450 G (1 LB)**          **135 CALS/25 G (1 OZ)**
- *225 g (8 oz) ground almonds*
- *125 g (4 oz) caster sugar*
- *125 g (4 oz) icing sugar*

- *1 egg*
- *5 ml (1 tsp) lemon juice*
- *5 ml (1 tsp) sherry*
- *1-2 drops vanilla essence*

1 Place the ground almonds, caster sugar and icing sugar in a bowl and mix together. In a separate bowl, whisk the egg with the remaining ingredients and add to the dry mixture.
2 Stir well to mix, pounding gently to release some of the oil from the almonds. Knead until smooth.

NOTE: If you wish to avoid using raw egg to bind the almond paste, use a little water instead.

## FONDANT ICING

Fondant icing - or moulding icing - provides and easy to apply covering. It is also used to mould decorations. Ready-to-roll icing (ready-made fondant) is used in the same way.

PREPARATION TIME 15 minutes
FREEZING Not suitable

**MAKES ABOUT 450 G (1 LB)**          **95 CALS/25 G (1 OZ)**
- *400 g (14 oz) icing sugar*
- *1 egg white*

- *50 g (2 oz) liquid glucose (available from chemists)*

1 Sift the icing sugar in a large bowl. Make a well in the centre and add the egg white and glucose. Beat these ingredients with a clean wooden spoon, gradually pulling in the icing sugar.
2 When the mixture becomes stiff, turn onto a surface sprinkled with icing sugar. Knead thoroughly to a smooth paste.
3 If necessary, store tightly wrapped in clingfilm in a cool place.

# BREAD-MAKING

There really is nothing quite like the aroma and taste of homemade bread. Unfortunately bread-making is one of those traditional tasks that many believe to be difficult, but in fact it's never been easier. Fast-action dried yeast is now readily available and simple to use; it speeds up bread-making dramatically. You will also find that many supermarkets and health food shops now stock a good range of bread flours.

Once you've mastered the basic techniques there is nothing to stop you baking your own creations and imitations of commercially produced speciality breads at a fraction of the cost.

### Yeast

Yeast is one of those fantastic ingredients with unique properties. Although not difficult to use, it is a living organism and must be handled in the right way in order to work effectively. When you buy yeast it is alive, but inactive. Only when it is mixed with a warm liquid does it become active and release the gases that should make the dough rise. Yeast is available in a number of different forms which are interchangeable in recipes, providing that the method is adjusted accordingly.

• FRESH YEAST: Although good health food shops continue to stock fresh yeast, it is becoming more and more difficult to buy. Should you manage to find a supplier, check that the yeast is firm, moist and creamy coloured with a good 'yeasty' smell. If it is dry and crumbly with discoloured brown patches then it is probably stale and it won't work. Fresh yeast is easy to use – simply blend with a little of the liquid specified in the recipe, add the remaining liquid, then mix into the flour. It will only stay fresh for about 3 days if stored in the refrigerator, but it freezes well – freeze in usable quantities for up to 3 months.

• FAST-ACTION DRIED YEAST: Also called easy-blend dried yeast, this product has revolutionised bread-making. It is sprinkled directly into the flour and the liquid is mixed in afterwards. After kneading, the dough can be shaped straight away and only requires one rising. However, for enriched doughs – particularly heavily fruited ones – better results are obtained if the dough is given the traditional two rises. Always make sure you adhere to the use-by date on the packet – fast-action dried yeast won't work if it's stale.

• DRIED YEAST: Because fast-action yeast works so well, it largely seems to have replaced 'ordinary' dried yeast in the shops. If, however, you use 'ordinary' dried yeast blend it with the liquid (see below) and leave it in a warm place for about 15 minutes or until a frothy head (similar to the head on a pint of Guinness) develops. This shows that the yeast is active. If it refuses to froth, then it is probably past its use-by date; discard and start again with a fresh packet of yeast.

• YEAST QUANTITIES: As a rough guide 15 g ($^1/_2$ oz) fresh yeast, a 7 g sachet ($1^1/_2$ tsp) fast-action (easy-blend) dried yeast, or 15 ml (1 tbsp) dried yeast is enough to rise 750 g ($1^1/_2$ lb) flour. If you add more than this, the dough will not rise any higher and the bread is likely to have an unpleasant yeasty taste. However, if the dough is enriched with sugar, butter or nuts the rise is more difficult and you will usually need more yeast.

### Liquid

Ordinary dried yeast (not the fast-action type) needs sugar to activate it. If using milk the natural sugars present in the milk will be enough; if using water add a pinch of sugar. No matter which variety of yeast you are using, the liquid should be just warm or tepid: it should feel slightly warm to the fingertips. If it is too hot it could kill the yeast; if too cold the yeast will not begin to work. Always regard any quantity of liquid specified in a recipe as a guide because flour absorbency varies from brand to brand.

### Flour

A variety of different flours is used for bread-making. 'Strong' flours give the best results because they are high in gluten – the substance which stretches the dough and traps air in it as it cooks, to give an open texture. Ordinary plain flour can be used for bread-making, but because it is lower in gluten it produces a close-textured crumbly loaf. Bread made with wholemeal flour has a distinctive flavour and texture; it is also an excellent source of fibre. It is, however, heavier than white bread. If you want a high fibre, lighter loaf use brown (wheatmeal) flour, or half wholemeal and half white flour.

Stoneground flour takes its name from the specific grinding process – between stones – which heats the flour and gives it a slightly roasted, nutty flavour. Both stoneground wholemeal and brown flours are available. Granary flour is a strong brown flour, with added malted wheat flakes, which give it a distinctive flavour. Rye and buckwheat flours also make interesting breads, but as these are both low in gluten, they should be mixed with a strong flour for best results.

### Other Ingredients

Salt improves the flavour of bread, but it also slows down the action of yeast, so don't add too much. Use the amount specified in the recipe as a guide – if you are trying to reduce your salt intake use less, or a low-sodium salt instead.

Some recipes call for a little fat to be rubbed into the flour before the yeast is added. This helps the keeping quality of the bread and imparts extra flavour, but too much fat will slow down the action of the yeast.

### Mixing and Kneading the Dough

Some recipes recommend warming the flour and mixing bowl in advance. If using fresh or 'ordinary' dried yeast or if you are working in a very cold room this helps speed things up a little, but otherwise it isn't really necessary. After mixing the yeast and liquid into the dry ingredients to make a soft dough, the dough must be kneaded. Vigorous kneading is required to strengthen the gluten in the flour, make the dough elastic and ultimately to achieve a good rise. If you omit this stage, the dough will not rise. There's nothing difficult about kneading and it doesn't take long – about 5-10 minutes.

Turn the dough onto a floured surface, fold it firmly towards you, then quickly and firmly push it down and away from you with the heel of your hand. Give it a quarter turn and continue kneading until the dough feels elastic and smooth: it shouldn't be sticky.

As an alternative to kneading by hand you can use a mixer with a dough hook attachment, or a food processor. In both cases it is essential to avoid overloading the machine; follow the manufacturer's instructions for quantities.

### Rising

Put the kneaded dough into a clean bowl and cover with a clean tea towel, an oiled polythene bag or oiled clingfilm to prevent a skin forming. Leave in a warm place until the dough has doubled in size and springs back when pressed. The time it takes to rise will depend on the surrounding temperature. If you put the bowl near a warm oven or in an airing cupboard, rising can take as little as 30 minutes, while at cooler temperatures it may take over an hour. Don't be tempted to put it somewhere hot to speed things up; you will end up with a badly shaped, uneven-textured loaf, or you could even kill the yeast. For a slower rise leave the dough in the refrigerator overnight; bring it to room temperature in the morning before shaping.

### Knocking Back and Proving

The risen dough is 'knocked' back to smooth out any large pockets of air. A brief kneading is sufficient just 2-3 minutes before shaping as required. Leave the shaped dough once again in a warm place until it has doubled in size and springs back when pressed. This proving stage is quicker than the first rising.

### Baking

Bread is baked in a hot oven to kill the yeast and halt its action. If the bread shows signs of browning too quickly, cover with foil. When cooked, the bread should be well risen, firm to the touch and golden brown; if you turn it over and tap it on the bottom the loaf should sound hollow. To crisp large loaves all over, return them to the oven upside down for about 10 minutes. Always remove bread from the tins before cooling on wire racks.

### Storing Bread

Bread which contains lots of fat or sugar should keep well for 3-4 days, but ordinary plain bread stales fairly quickly. It is best stored in a dry, well ventilated bread bin. If stored in the refrigerator, bread will stale more quickly. Bread freezes well for a short time – up to 1 month – after which the crust begins to deteriorate and lift off. Frozen or slightly stale bread can be freshened in a warm oven. Quick yeastless breads – leavened with baking powder or bicarbonate of soda rather than yeast – tend to stale quickly. They are invariably at their best eaten fresh and warm from the oven.

# WHOLEMEAL BREAD

PREPARATION TIME 25 minutes, plus rising
COOKING TIME About 35minutes
FREEZING Suitable

**MAKES I LOAF**
- *15 g (¹/₂ oz) fresh yeast or 7 g sachet (1¹/₂ tsp) fast-action dried yeast*
- *150 ml (5 fl oz ) tepid milk*

**1700 CALS/LOAF**
- *450 g (1 lb) wholemeal plain flour*
- *5 ml (1 tsp) salt*
- *5 ml (1 tsp) caster sugar*
- *25 g (1 oz) butter or margarine*

**1** If using fresh yeast, blend with the milk. Mix the flour, salt and sugar in a bowl, and stir in the fast-action dried yeast if using. Rub in butter. Make a well in the centre; pour in the yeast liquid or milk and about 175 ml (6 fl oz) tepid water. Mix to a soft dough.

**2** Turn out the dough onto a lightly floured surface and knead for about 10 minutes until smooth and elastic. If using fresh yeast place in an oiled bowl and cover with oiled cling-film. Leave to rise until doubled in size and sponge-like in texture.

**3** Knock risen dough down, then knead again on a lightly floured surface for 3-4 minutes until smooth. The dough is now ready for shaping (see right). After shaping it can be lightly scored to produce a pattern on the crust.

**4** Cover the shaped dough with oiled cling-film and leave in a warm place to rise. Free-shaped dough will double in size, dough in tins should rise to the rims; this takes about 45 minutes depending on size and room temperature.

**5** Glaze (see below). Bake at 220°C (425°F) mark 7 for 20 minutes. Reduce the temperature to 180°C (350°F) mark 4 and remove bread from tin if using. Bake for a further 15 minutes. To test, tap the bottom crust; the bread should sound hollow. Cool on a wire rack.

• GLAZING: For a deep golden shiny finish brush the shaped dough with beaten egg before baking. Brushing with water gives a crisp crust, while milk produces a soft crust.

**Variations**
LIGHT WHOLEMEAL BREAD: Use 225 g (8 oz) strong plain white flour and 225 g (8 oz) wholemeal plain flour with about 150 ml (5 fl oz) tepid milk and l50 ml (5 fl oz) tepid water.
SOFT WHITE BREAD: Use all strong plain white flour with 200 ml (7 fl oz) tepid milk and 90 ml (3 fl oz) tepid water.
NUTTY WHOLEMEAL BREAD: Use 425 g (15 oz) Granary flour with 25 g (1 oz) oatmeal. For additional texture add 75 g (3 oz) mixed sesame and sunflower seeds. Mix with about 150 ml (5 fl oz) tepid milk and 200 ml (7 fl oz) tepid water.

## SHAPING
TRADITIONAL TIN LOAF: Flatten the dough to an oblong the length of a 900 g (2 lb) loaf tin but three times as wide. Fold the bottom third up over the centre and the top third down. Press down well. Turn over, then place in the lightly greased tin.
ROUND: Shape the dough into a ball. For a smooth top, knead the edges of the round repeatedly into the centre and press down. Turn over and place seam-side down on a lightly greased baking sheet or in a deep 15-18 cm (6-7 inch) greased cake tin.
BATONS: Divide the dough in half and shape each piece into a long roll with tapering ends, about 35 cm (14 inches) long.
PLAIT: Divide the dough into three. Shape each piece into a roll 30 cm (12 inches) long. Pinch ends together and plait loosely. Pinch the other ends.
COTTAGE LOAF: Cut one third off the dough. Knead both pieces well and shape into rounds. Place the smaller round on top of the larger one, on a baking sheet. Push the handle of a wooden spoon down through the middle. Glaze with salt water.

# PRESERVES

There can be no finer or more satisfying sight than a pantry stacked full of homemade jams, jellies, chutneys and pickles. These preserved delights can bring to life the most mundane or humble meal and they're infinitely superior to and cheaper than commercially prepared equivalents.

### PRESERVING EQUIPMENT

If you make a lot of preserves, it's worth investing in a proper preserving pan: the sloping sides help maintain a fast boil and reduce the chances of everything boiling over. Choose a pan made from stainless steel, tin-lined copper or lined aluminium. Don't use unlined aluminium particularly when cooking acidic fruits or pickles.

If you don't have a preserving pan use a large heavy-based saucepan instead. Note that if you use a saucepan rather than a preserving pan the preserve will take much longer to reach the setting point.

For jelly making, you will need a jelly bag for straining the juice from the cooked fruit, although you can improvise with a large piece of muslin. Whatever you use, it should be scalded with boiling water before use. If the jelly bag doesn't have a stand, suspend it from the legs of an upturned chair or stool. Leave until the dripping has stopped.

### PRESERVING INGREDIENTS

• PECTIN is naturally present in fruit, and reacts with sugar and acid to set jams, jellies, marmalades and conserves. Some fruits such as cooking apples, lemons, Seville oranges, gooseberries and damsons are high in natural pectin and acid; eating apples, raspberries, blackberries, apricots and plums have a medium pectin and acid content; while cherries, grapes, peaches, rhubarb and strawberries score low on both counts.

Fruits with a low or medium pectin content should be cooked with a fruit high in pectin to achieve a set. Lemon juice is most commonly used since it is rich in both pectin and acid; 30 ml (2 tbsp) lemon juice to 1.8 kg (4 lb) fruit should be enough. Alternatively use 'sugar with pectin' (see below) or commercially produced bottled pectin.

• SUGAR acts as a preservative as well as helping to achieve a set, so it is important to use the amount stated in the recipe. Granulated sugar is fine for most preserves. Caster sugar or brown sugar can also be used, but brown sugar will lend a distinctive flavour and darker colour that are more suited to chutneys and pickles. Perfectionists insist that preserving sugar gives a clearer more sparkling finish to jams, jellies and marmalades, so you may prefer to use it. 'Sugar with pectin' contains apple pectin and tartaric acid. Preserves made with this should reach setting point in just 4 minutes.

• VINEGAR acts as a preservative in pickles and some chutneys. Virtually any vinegar is suitable – red, white, or flavoured providing that the acetic acid content is 5 per cent or more.

### TESTING FOR A SET

Jams, jellies, marmalades and conserves are cooked sufficiently when setting point is reached. There are various tests to determine this. Remove the pan from the heat while you are testing.

• TEMPERATURE TEST: The preserve is ready when the temperature registers 105°C (221°F) on a sugar thermometer.

• SAUCER TEST: Drop a spoonful of the preserve onto a chilled saucer and leave to cool. Push your finger through the jam: if the surface wrinkles, the preserve is ready.

• FLAKE TEST: Using a wooden spoon, lift a little of the preserve out of the pan. Let it cool slightly then tip the spoon so that the preserve drops back into the pan; if the drips run together and fall from the spoon in a 'flake' rather than as drips, it is ready.

### YIELDS AND POTTING PRESERVES

It is difficult to give accurate yields since they vary from batch to batch. So that you can have enough jars prepared, the recipes in this book give a rough guide wherever possible. All preserves should be potted into scrupulously clean containers. Wash jars or bottles in really hot soapy water, rinse thoroughly, then dry in a warm oven. Stand them upside down on a clean tea towel until the preserve is ready. Aim to pour hot jam or marmalade into the jars while they are still warm, to reduce the chances of the glass cracking, and fill them almost to the top. If potting jam, jelly, marmalade or conserve, cover with a waxed disc while the preserve is piping hot or else completely cold, then seal with a dampened clear disc secured with an elastic band. If you seal while the preserve is warm, mould will grow on the surface. Chutneys and pickles are covered in the same way. For long-term storage, cover the jar with a screw top as well.

# COOKING UTENSILS AND EQUIPMENT

A well-equipped kitchen does not mean one which contains every possible gadget and appliance. The most important considerations when choosing cooking utensils and equipment are frequency of use and quality. You should concentrate on buying a small number of high-quality but very practical tools which will stand the test of time rather than a larger number of lower quality items, many of which may never be taken out of the kitchen drawer

Pots and pans and knives are arguably the most indispensable items used in cooking. And, while they are not strictly essential as all cooking tasks can be performed by hand if necessary, food preparation machines can make such a difference when you are cooking large quantities or involved in a time-consuming task that they should be seriously considered when you are equipping your kitchen.

Following are some general guidelines on how to choose what you need:

### POTS AND PANS

The key factor here is the material from which a cooking pot or pan is made. This determines how quickly and evenly it conducts heat to the food and how easily it will burn.

• ALUMINIUM conducts heat evenly. Medium and heavy gauge aluminium are suitable for most types of hob but lightweight aluminium is suitable only for gas and has a short life as it tends to distort.
• CAST IRON conducts heat well. It is thick, heavy and good for long, slow cooking at low temperatures. Because cast iron is heavy, it is not suitable if you have problems lifting things and it is also liable to break if dropped on a hard floor surface.
• COPPER conducts heat very well and is preferred by many professional chefs. It must be lined with tin, nickel or aluminium to prevent the copper from reacting with very acid foods. Copper is expensive and needs regular cleaning.
• STAINLESS STEEL needs a layer of aluminium or copper bonded on to the base to help it conduct heat well. Pans of stainless steel are expensive, but they are also very durable and will, if looked after properly, last forever.

• VITREOUS ENAMEL is a coating applied to various metals to make them more attractive on the exterior and easier to clean on the interior. Painted enamel is inferior and chips easily. Look out for the trademark Vitramel™ which denotes good quality enamel and application.
• EARTHENWARE AND CERAMICS are not good conductors of heat although they do tend to retain heat well once hot. They are most suitable for use in the oven and should be set on a heat diffusing mat if used on top of the hob.

Aim for a good range of sizes in building up a collection of pans, so that you can choose the right size of pan for the task in hand. Food will not cook properly if the pan is too big or too small for what is in it.

### KNIVES

There are few cooking tasks which cannot be achieved with a sharp knife. The material from which a knife is made affects it sharpness and durability

• CARBON STEEL is easy to sharpen. However, it discolours on contact with acidic food and rusts easily. Dry carbon steel knives thoroughly after washing.
• STAINLESS STEEL does not discolour or rust easily. However, it blunts quickly and is difficult to sharpen.
• HIGH CARBON STAINLESS STEEL has all the advantages. It sharpens well and does not discolour or rust easily. Inevitably high carbon stainless steel knives are the most expensive.

Knives should be looked after well and the following guidelines will help to keep your knives in good condition:
• Always wash and dry them thoroughly after use.
• Do not keep knives all together in a drawer. Use a knife block which will prevent the blades from damaging each other.
• Sharpen them regularly.

As with pots and pans, aim to have a basic selection of good knives and acquire others when you can.

## FOOD PREPARATION MACHINES

The main point to consider when you are buying a machine is just how sophisticated you need it to be. It is easy to be tempted into thinking that you must have the most highly developed model on the market, but do stop to think whether you will really use all those functions, and remember that the machine and any attachments will have to be cleaned and stored somewhere.

### Food Processors

A machine which slices vegetables, grates cheese, blends soups, mixes cakes, chops nuts, purées fruit, kneads bread and whisks cream sounds like the perfect kitchen companion. Most food processors are supplied with a metal blade, a shredder/grater and a slicer disc as standard. In general, the more you pay, the larger the capacity of the bowl and the more attachments you get. Top-of-the-range models also offer greater power and optional extras such as extra shredders, a chipper, a fruit press, a mill, an ice cream maker, a Parmesan disc and a julienne disc. How much use you make of these clearly depends on the scale and kind of cooking you do. There are, however, a number of essential features which you should look for when buying:
• Measurements on the feed tube and bowl
• Variable speeds (although you do not need more than three) and a pulse (a short burst of high speed) for greater control
• Adjustable slicing discs
• Non-slip feet
• Flex storage
• Reversible discs, to save on storage space
• Safety-locking lid

In addition, there are some particularly useful features offered by more expensive food processors which you may consider paying more for:
• Mini chopping bowls for small quantities of food
• Drip-feed lid/feed tube which allows liquids to be added to the bowl while the processor is running (useful when making mayonnaise)
• Different feed-tube sizes - a double-feed tube is useful for foods of different sizes and a wide semi-circular feed tube is good for large items.
• Integral storage for attachments
• Finger grips on attachments
• Dishwasher-safe attachments
• Liquidiser attachment for fine, smooth purées
• Citrus press or juice extractor
• Blade storage compartment or box

### Blenders

A blender, which may also be an attachment to a food processor, is generally used for puréeing and liquidising. It purées more finely than a food processor and is especially good for mayonnaise. Blenders are not recommended for dry chopping, however. There are two types of blender to choose from:
• Goblet blenders, in which the cutting blades are at the bottom. Check the height of the blades before you buy as some are too high to cope with one-yolk mayonnaise and small amounts of food. Most goblets carry measurements down the side so you can check the quantity you are working with and add as necessary. A handle on the side of the goblet is useful for lifting it off the base when it contains hot liquid.
• Hand-held blenders, which require more effort than goblets but which are very portable.

### Mini-choppers

These are useful for chopping small amounts of nuts, herbs or vegetables and can also blend small amounts of liquid. They cannot compete with full-sized food processors on larger quantities.

### Food Mixers

These are particularly useful for mixing cakes, kneading dough and whisking, as food processors are not very good at incorporating air into mixtures such as egg whites, sponges or cream. They can be either hand-held or table-top models.
• Hand-held mixers may come with a bowl and stand and operate without being held. Or they may simply consist of a motorised head into which a selection of mixers, whisks and beaters can be fitted. There is little advantage in buying the type with a bowl and stand as these then have to be stored somewhere. Beaters alone can be used in a suitable bowl of your own.
• Table-top mixers are large and take up a lot of space. They can deal with large quantities of mixture such as bread dough or fruit cake, however, and can be left to operate without supervision.

### Other Utensils and Equipment

In spite of the huge range of kitchen tools and equipment on the market, the number of utensils which are needed on a day-to-day basis is relatively small. If you are interested in a particular area of cooking, such as cake decorating or preserving, you may want, or need, to add more specialist tools to your collection to help in specific tasks.

# EATING FOR HEALTH

During the last 20 years or so we have all become more aware that 'we are what we eat', and that a healthy, balanced diet is the cornerstone of a healthy lifestyle – one which will help ensure that we remain fit in later life.

There is no longer any doubt that the food we eat can have an important effect on our health. Conditions such as arthritis, heart disease, and even cancer are now all known to be linked to diet, so the importance of making sure we are getting enough vitamins, minerals, trace elements, essential fatty acids and fibre from the food we eat cannot be stressed enough.

## FIVE STEPS TO A HEALTHY DIET

Recent research on healthy eating suggests that following these guidelines would improve our health.

1 Eat at least five portions of fruit and vegetables (in addition to potatoes) a day
2 Reduce total fat intake
3 Increase fibre intake
4 Reduce salt intake
5 Aim to get almost half the daily intake of calories from complex carbohydrates found in starchy foods such as bread, potatoes, rice, pasta and breakfast cereals.

This doesn't mean being condemned to a life of eating lettuce leaves and cottage cheese. It simply means that we need to eat more of some foods – such as fruit and vegetables – and less of others, such as those which contain large amounts of fat and sugar.

Eating a wide variety of foods is very important to ensure that all the nutrients necessary for good health are included in the diet. Foods can be divided into four main groups, and you should try to eat food from each group each day. The key to a healthy diet is to get the balance right.

## FRUIT AND VEGETABLES

Basically, the more you eat from this group the better. Most people in the UK need to double the amount they already eat in order to reach the recommended level. Fruit and vegetables are low in fat and calories (the only notable exceptions being avocados and olives). They contain useful amounts of fibre, particularly soluble fibre – a good intake of which can help reduce high blood cholesterol levels. Most fruit and vegetables contain vitamin C, the richest sources being citrus fruits, kiwi fruit, strawberries and peppers.

The highly coloured fruit and vegetables such as apricots, pumpkin, spinach, red peppers and carrots are a good source of beta carotene, which the body converts into vitamin A. Beta carotene and vitamin C are antioxidant vitamins – a good intake of these will help protect against heart disease and certain types of cancer.

### Getting the most from vegetables

Many of the vitamins in fruit and vegetables can easily be destroyed during storage, preparation and cooking. To get the highest nutritional value from fruit and vegetables always try to:

• Buy little and often rather than in huge quantities. Look for firm, shiny-skinned produce, avoid limp wilting greens. Buy from a shop that you know has a quick turnover.
• Store vegetables in a cool dark place, ideally for no more than 3 days.
• Never leave vegetables standing in water before cooking.
• Do not add bicarbonate of soda to the water when cooking vegetables.
• The best way to cook vegetables in order to preserve their vitamins is to use cooking methods that require little or no water as boiling vegetables in large quantities of water can destroy up to 70% of the vitamin C. If you do boil vegetables, keep the water to an absolute minimum, do not add the vegetables until it is boiling and then, once the vegetables are cooked, use the remaining water to make gravy, sauce, soup or stock.
• Cut vegetables into large chunks so less surface area is exposed (vitamin C is lost when cut surfaces come into contact with the air). Keep peeling to a minimum, since the highest concentration of vitamins is found directly under the skin.
• Eat vegetables as soon as you can after they are cooked. Keeping food warm results in more vitamins being lost.

## CARBOHYDRATE FOODS

Bread, grains, rice, breakfast cereals, pasta and potatoes come under this heading. They provide fibre, protein, vitamins, (particularly those from the B group) and minerals such as calcium and iron. They are foods to fill up on – and should provide the bulk of our calories. To meet current healthy eating targets most people need to double their present intake. Many people mistakenly believe that foods from this group are fattening – in fact they're low in fat and those which contain appreciable amouts of fibre will help satisfy the appetite. However, it is worth remembering that if foods from this group are combined with large amounts of fat they will become extremely calorific – 125g (4 oz) boiled potatoes contain only 80 calories compared with the same weight of chipped potatoes which contain 250 calories!

## MILK AND DAIRY PRODUCTS

Foods from this group (including cheese, yogurt, fromage frais) are a major source of calcium – essential for strong bones. They also provide protein, vitamins A, D, B1, B2, B6 and B12. Most dairy products also contain large amounts of saturated fat and for this reason they should only be eaten in moderation. Using reduced-fat varieties such as skimmed milk, fromage frais and low-fat cheese can help to control fat intake.

## PROTEIN FOODS

This group includes meat, poultry, fish, eggs, nuts and pulses (beans and lentils); foods which provide protein, fat, vitamins and minerals.

Fish is an excellent source of protein and vitamins A and D. Recent studies have shown that people who eat oily fish two or three times a week have a significantly lower rate of heart disease.

Beans and pulses are naturally low in fat and an excellent source of protein, soluble fibre, and vitamins, particularly those from the B group.

Meat provides protein, vitamins and minerals, particularly iron and zinc. It is certainly not necessary to avoid red meat completely in a healthy diet but neither is it necessary to eat meat every day. Always choose the leaner cuts of meat and trim away any visible fat before cooking. Use smaller quantities of meat in stews and casseroles and bulk them out with vegetables or pulses.

Eggs provide protein, vitamin A, vitamin B1, B2, B12 and folic acid. Egg yolks are known to be a rich source of cholesterol; however, it is the amount and type of fat in the diet rather than the level of cholesterol in individual foods which will effect blood cholesterol levels. Because of the risk of salmonella poisoning the Department of Health recommends that dishes containing raw or lightly cooked eggs should be avoided, particularly by young children, the elderly, pregnant women and anyone with an immune deficiency disease.

## FATS AND OILS

Small amounts of fat are necessary in our diet to provide essential fatty acids and to allow the absorption of fat-soluble vitamins. Fat also helps to make our food palatable – it gives texture and flavour to foods. However, most people in the UK eat far too much fat. For good health we should aim for a balance between the three different types of fat – saturated, monounsaturated and polyunsaturated. Olive oil, peanuts and peanut oil, avocado pears and rape seed oil all contain high levels of monounsaturated fats. Vegetable and seed oils and oily fish provide mainly polyunsaturated fatty acids.

Saturated fatty acids are found predominantly in animal products such as the fat in meat and dairy produce. Diets which contain high levels of saturated fat are known to increase the risks of heart disease and certain types of cancer. However, this does not mean that these foods need to be avoided completely – simply that they should be eaten in moderation.

## SUGAR

Like fat, sugar helps to make food palatable and, also like fat, most people eat more of it than is recommended for good health. Sugar provides calories but nothing else in the way of protein, fibre, vitamins or minerals. Contrary to popular belief brown sugar and honey have no nutritional advantage over white sugar although some people prefer the taste. Like fat it's not necessary to avoid sugar completely but it makes good sense to think about the amount of sugar that we eat – it provides 'empty calories' – calories which most people could do without.

## SALT

Although sodium is an essential part of all body cells, the average daily intake of salt is 12 times higher than the amount needed. In fact, if we didn't add salt to anything we cooked or ate, our needs would still be met from the small amounts which occur naturally in most foods. Much of the salt we eat is added to foods during cooking or at the table, so one of the easiest ways to reduce salt intake is to stop adding it at the table. An appetite for salty foods is a learned preference. Many people add salt to their food out of habit, often without even tasting the food first. By trying not to add salt to food at the table you can significantly reduce your intake and therefore continue to use small amounts in cooking.

# FREEZING

Freezing is an easy and convenient way to preserve fresh food, allowing you to save and store for later use the wealth of seasonal delicacies that are available fresh for only a short time of the year. Whether you freeze ingredients in their basic state or made up into complete dishes, you will find a well-stocked freezer an invaluable help for producing nutritious meals with the minimum of fuss - especially if you also own a microwave for rapid thawing and reheating.

### TIPS FOR EFFICIENT FREEZING
• Freeze only food of the best quality. Never freeze food that looks blemished or old.
• Handle the food as little as possible.
• Never put any foods that are still slightly warm into the freezer, as a rise in temperature causes frosting up and deterioration of other foods will result.
• Never freeze more than one tenth of your freezer's capacity in any 24 hours, as this will also cause the internal temperature to rise.
• When freezing large quantities, use the fast-freeze option.
• Pack and seal food with care. If moisture or cold air is allowed to come into contact with the food it will begin to deteriorate. Cross flavouring might also occur.
• Be sure to wrap non-packaged foods well before freezing. Solid foods must be packaged tightly, with as little air as possible. Wrap items in foil or freezer film; ordinary clingfilm is not suitable for the freezer. Freezer film can also be used as a lining for acidic foods which should then be over-wrapped in foil.
• Where possible use square containers to store food in the freezer; they stack better than round ones and therefore waste less space.
• Interleave any items of food that might otherwise stick together with pieces of greaseproof paper, polythene, foil or freezer film.
• When freezing liquids always leave room for expansion, as frozen liquid expands by about one-tenth of its volume and will push the lids off containers that have been overfilled.
• Freeze single and double portions for easy use.
• Keep you freezer as full as possible. If necessary add loaves of bread to fill up spaces. Empty spaces require more energy to keep cool.
• Make sure food is clearly labelled and dated.

Always use up old stocks first. To help you do this it is a good idea to keep a freezer log book, adding items (with the date) as you freeze them and deleting them as they are consumed.
• Do not re-freeze food once it has been thawed, unless it has been subsequently cooked.
• Check your freezer is operating correctly with a freezer thermometer. It should read -18°C (0°F).

### FREEZER STORAGE CHART
This chart is a guide to approximate maximum storage times for certain types of food. Always follow the manufacturer's instructions.

*VEGETABLES*
blanched vegetables (most types) 10-12 months
mushrooms and tomatoes 6-8 months
vegetable purées 6-8 months

*FRUIT*
fruit in syrup 9-12 months
open frozen fruit 6-8 months
fruit purées 6-8 months
fruit juice 4-6 months

*FISH*
white fish 6-8 months
oily fish 3-4 months
fish portions 3-4 months
shellfish 2-3 months

*MEAT AND POULTRY*
beef and lamb 4-6 months
pork and veal 4-6 months
offal 3-4 months
sliced bacon/other cured meat 2-3 months
ham and bacon joints 3-4 months
chicken and turkey 4-6 months
duck and goose 4-6 months
venison 4-6 months
rabbit and game 4-6 months
sausages, sausagemeat 2-3 months
minced beef 3-4 months

*PREPARED FOOD*
soups and sauces 3 months
stock 6 months
prepared meals 4-6 months
    if highly seasoned 2-3 months
bread 2-3 months

pastries 3-4 months
cakes 4-6 months

*DAIRY PRODUCE*
cream 6-8 months
butter (salted) 3-4 months
cheese (hard) 4-6 months
cheese (soft) 3-4 months
ice cream, mousses etc 3-4 months

### FREEZER EMERGENCIES
The most common freezer emergency is loss of power. This can be as a result of a power cut or someone inadvertently turning the freezer off. If there is a power cut, don't panic; if you leave the freezer door closed the food should stay frozen for about 30 hours (48 hours in a chest freezer). If possible, wrap the freezer with a blanket to increase insulation.

If you have advance warning of a power cut, turn on the fast-freeze switch, making sure the freezer is full to capacity. Towels or rolled newspaper can be used to fill any gaps.

Do not re-freeze any food you suspect may have begun to thaw.

### FREEZING FRESH VEGETABLES
Vegetables can be very successfully frozen, but only if they are really fresh - no more than 12 hours after they were picked. Blanching the vegetables before freezing will help to preserve their colour, flavour and texture.

To blanch vegetables, bring a large pan of water to the boil and immerse the vegetables up to 450 g (1 lb) at a time. Bring back to the boil and keep the vegetables immersed for the required time - delicately textured or leafy vegetables such as spinach, mangetout and sliced courgettes will only need about 10 seconds, while firmer varieties such as broccoli and cauliflower florets, green beans and peas will need to be blanched for 1 minute. Root vegetables like carrots should be sliced and blanched for 2-3 minutes, while whole dense vegetables like globe artichokes and small beetroot need 4-5 minutes.

Once blanched, immediately remove the vegetables and plunge into a bowl of iced water. The blanching water can be used 6-7 times and the iced water refreshed with more ice as necessary. The vegetables can be put into a blanching basket for this part of the operation, but if you do not have one a suitable strainer or a large piece of muslin will do.

### FREEZING FRESH FRUIT
First, check that the fruit you wish to freeze is properly ripe and in peak condition, free from any blemishes. Any overripe fruit should be puréed before freezing. With fruits such as apples you will have to cook them first before puréeing, but fruits such as peaches and raspberries can be puréed in their fresh form.

Before freezing the fruit, consider how it will eventually be used. Small fruits which do not need peeling are best frozen as they are; remove any stalks if necessary, and open freeze by spreading them on trays lined with non-stick paper, then transfer to polythene bags. They will not stick together, enabling small quantities to be removed as needed.

Firm fruits and any which have a tendency to discolour should be frozen in a syrup made with 450 g (1 lb) sugar to 1 litre (1¾ pints) water and the juice of 1 lemon. The fruits can be left whole, halved or sliced into the cool syrup as appropriate. For fruits such as grapefruit and pineapple omit the lemon juice and substitute any juice from the fruit.

### THAWING FROZEN FOOD
Thawing must be done thoroughly and efficiently to ensure food is safe to eat.
• Never leave food to thaw in a warm environment; this is the ideal breeding ground for harmful bacteria. Instead, let the food thaw gradually in the refrigerator or in a cool larder.
• Cover food loosely while thawing.
• Make sure large items such as joints of meat are thoroughly thawed before cooking. The legs of poultry should be able to move freely.
• Dispose of any liquid which seeps from thawing meat and poultry. Do not allow it to come into contact with other food.
• Cook food as soon as possible after it is thawed.
• If thawing frozen food in a microwave, follow the manufacturer's instructions.
• Only use the microwave if you plan to eat or cook the food immediately.

# FOOD SAFETY

Everyone knows that eating well-prepared nutritious meals composed of lots of delicious fresh ingredients will keep us strong and healthy. However, food that is not hygienically dealt with – prepared on a dirty work surface, kept for too long or incorrectly stored – can also be our enemy, causing anything from mild stomach upset to chronic food poisoning.

## FOOD POISONING

Although food poisoning is rarely life-threatening, it can be very unpleasant and may cause serious illness in vulnerable groups. People who are particularly at risk include:
• Children under 2 years old
• Pregnant women
• Elderly people
• Anyone who is already ill or convalescing
• Those with an impaired immune system
• Anyone taking drugs which suppress their body's natural defences, such as transplant patients, people receiving chemotherapy or taking large doses of steroids.

Correct food storage and hygienic preparation of ingredients is important for the prevention of food poisoning. Following a few simple guidelines will help make your kitchen a safer place for preparing and storing both raw and cooked ingredients.

## KITCHEN HYGIENE

• Wash down work surfaces regularly with a mild detergent solution or multi-surface cleaner.
• Use rubber gloves for washing up, so that the water can be hotter than hands can bear. Leaving dishes to drain is more hygienic than drying them with a tea towel.
• Keep raw and cooked foods separate. If possible use different chopping boards and utensils for cooked and raw produce. Wash knives and kitchen utensils in between preparing raw and cooked foods. Never put cooked or ready-to-eat foods onto a surface which has just had raw food on it.
• Always wash your hands before handling food and again between handling different types of food (raw and cooked meat, for example). Cover any cuts with a waterproof plaster.
• Use absorbent kitchen paper to wipe up spills from meat or poultry juices, and dispose of it immediately.
• Keep pets away from work surfaces.

## STORAGE

• Always check to see if the manufacturer has given any storage advice. This is important even with familiar foods. As manufacturers have started to remove some of the additives from foods and reduce sugar and salt, storage requirements may have changed.
• Never keep goods beyond their 'use-by' date.
• Keep your cupboards, refrigerator and freezer scrupulously clean.
• Once opened, canned foods should be treated as though fresh. Transfer the contents to a clean container, cover and keep in the refrigerator.
• Transfer dry goods such as sugar, rice and pasta into moisture-proof containers. Old supplies should be used up before new ones are started and containers washed out and dried thoroughly before refilling.

## REFRIGERATOR STORAGE

• Use a refrigerator thermometer to check that your refrigerator is operating at the correct temperature, between 1-5°C (34-41°F).
• Always store cooked and raw foods on separate shelves in the refrigerator. Place raw foods at the bottom and cooked foods at the top.
• Never put hot food into the refrigerator as this will cause the internal temperature to rise.
• Avoid overfilling the refrigerator as this restricts the circulation of air and prevents it from working properly. Do not leave the door open longer than necessary. Defrost the refrigerator regularly.

## COOKING AND RE-HEATING FOOD

• Remember that to kill any food poisoning bacteria present food needs to reach a temperature of 70°C (158°F) for at least 2 minutes.
• Never eat undercooked pork or poultry.
• Always reheat food until it is 'piping hot', 63°C (145°F) or over. Never re-heat food more than once.
• Cooked food should be cooled as quickly as possible before placing it in the refrigerator or freezer. Small quantities will cool quite quickly but larger quantities should be either divided into smaller portions, or transferred into a container with a large surface area. During warm weather place the container into a bowl of iced water. Do not cover the food while it is cooling. Ensure the food is cooled within 1½ hours.

# GLOSSARY

A brief guide to cooking methods, terms and ingredients.

**Agar-agar** A tasteless white powder, made from seaweed, which has useful gelling properties and can be used as a vegetarian substitute for gelatine.

**Antipasto** Italian phrase for a varied selection of hot or cold foods served as an appetiser.

**Arrowroot** Can be used as an alternative to cornflour as a thickening agent in liquids, such as sauces and glazes. Arrowroot gives a clear gloss, unlike cornflour which produces an opaque sauce.

**Aspic jelly** Savoury jelly used for setting and garnishing savoury dishes.

**Au gratin** Describes a dish which has been coated with sauce, sprinkled with breadcrumbs or cheese and finished by browning under the grill or in the oven. Low sided gratin dishes are used.

**Bain-marie** A low-sided container which is half filled with water kept just below boiling point. Containers of food are placed in it to keep warm or cook without overheating. A bain-marie is used for cooking custards and other egg dishes and keeping sauces warm. No special container is needed; a roasting tin will do. The term is also sometimes applied to a double boiler.

**Baking** Cooking in the oven by dry heat.

**Baking blind** The method used for cooking flans and tarts without their fillings.

**Baking powder** A raising agent consisting of an acid, usually cream of tartar and an alkali, such as bicarbonate of soda which react to produce carbon dioxide. This expands during baking and makes cakes and breads rise.

**Barding** Covering dry meat or the breast of poultry or game birds with pieces of bacon or fat to prevent the flesh drying out during roasting.

**Basting** Spooning the juices and melted fat over meat, poultry or game during roasting to keep it moist. The term is also used to describe spooning over a marinade.

**Bean curd** Also known as tofu and widely used in vegetarian and oriental cooking. It is made from a pressed purée of soya beans and sold fresh, dried and in cans.

**Beating** A method of incorporating air into an ingredient or mixture by agitating it vigorously with a spoon, fork, whisk or electric mixer. Also used to soften ingredients.

**Béchamel** Classic French white sauce, which is used as the basis for other sauces and a variety of savoury dishes.

**Beurre manié** Equal parts of flour and butter kneaded together to form a paste.

Used for thickening soups, stews and casseroles. It is whisked into the hot liquid a little at a time at the end of cooking.

**Bicarbonate of soda** Sometimes used in baking to act as a raising agent.

**Blanching** Immersing food briefly in boiling water to whiten it, as in sweetbreads, or to remove the skin, such as peaches and tomatoes. Vegetables which are to be frozen and kept for a certain length of time are blanched to destroy enzymes and preserve the colour, flavour and texture.

**Blanquette** Stew usually made from white meat, such as veal or poultry, cooked in a white sauce enriched with cream and egg yolk.

**Blender** An electric machine usually consisting of a goblet with rotating blades in the base. Used for puréeing wet mixtures and grinding dry ingredients. Ideal for making fresh breadcrumbs.

**Boning** Removing the bones from meat or poultry, cutting the flesh as little as possible, so that it can be rolled or stuffed.

**Bottling** The term used for preserving food or preserves in glass jars under sterile conditions.

**Bouquet garni** Small bunch of herbs – usually a mixture of parsley stems, thyme and a bay leaf – tied in muslin and used to flavour stocks, soups and stews.

**Braising** A slow cooking method used for cuts of meat, poultry and game which are too tough to roast. It is also good for some vegetables. A pan or casserole with a tight-fitting lid should be used so that little liquid is lost through evaporation. The meat is first browned, then cooked on a bed of chopped vegetables (called a *mirepoix*), with just enough liquid to cover the vegetables. It may be cooked on the hob or in the oven.

**Brining** A method of preserving by immersing food in a salt and water solution.

**Brioche** An enriched yeast dough mixture baked in the shape of a cottage loaf. French in origin and usually eaten warm for breakfast.

**Brochette** Fish, meat or vegetables, cooked on a skewer or spit.

**Broth** The liquid produced by boiling meat or fish bones in water for a long time. Also sometimes called stock.

**Brûlée** A French term, literally meaning 'burnt' used to refer to a dish with a crisp coating of caramelised sugar.

**Calorie** A scientific term used in dietetics to measure the heat and energy-producing quality of food.

**Canapé** Small appetisers, usually served with drinks and often consisting of a topping on a bread or pastry base.

**Candying** Method of impregnating pieces of fruit or peel with sugar to preserve them.

**Caramel** Substance obtained by heating sugar syrup very slowly to a rich brown colour.

**Carbonade** Rich stew or braise of meat which includes beer.

**Casserole** Strictly speaking, a dish with a tight-fitting lid used for cooking meat and vegetables. Now applied to the food cooked in this way.

**Celsius** Also known as Centigrade. A scale for measuring temperature in which the freezing point of water is 0° and the boiling point 100°. Now used for the oven settings on electric cookers, replacing the Fahrenheit scale which is gradually becoming obsolete.

**Chantilly** A classic French whipped cream which is slightly sweetened and may be flavoured with vanilla.

**Charcuterie** The French term for cooked pork products, such as hams, sausages and terrines.

**Charlotte** A hot or cold moulded dessert. For a hot charlotte the mould is lined with bread and for a cold charlotte it is lined with sponge fingers.

**Chasseur** Literally translated means 'hunter style'. Describes dishes cooked with mushrooms, shallots and white wine.

**Chaudfroid** A cold dish of jellied fish, poultry or game that is coated in a thick Béchamel-based or brown sauce, set under a layer of aspic.

**Chilling** Cooling food without freezing.

**Chining** Applied to joints of meat, this means severing the rib bones from the backbone by sawing through the ribs close to the spine. Joints such as loin or neck of lamb, veal or pork are best chined as this makes them easier to carve into chops or cutlets after cooking.

**Chorizo** Spanish sausage made of smoked pork and pimiento. Sold ready cooked.

**Chowder** An American dish somewhere between a soup and a stew, usually based on fish, e.g. clam chowder.

**Citric acid** A mild acid which occurs naturally in citrus fruit. Commercially produced citric acid is used mainly for preserving soft fruit drinks and in home wine making.

**Clarifying** Process of removing sediment or impurities from a food. Butter and dripping may be clarified so that they can be used for frying at higher temperatures.

To clarify butter, heat until melted and all bubbling stops. Remove from the heat and stand until the salt and sediment have sunk to the bottom, then gently pour off the fat, straining it through muslin. Chill and use as required. Clarified butter is also known as ghee.

To clarify dripping, melt the fat, then strain it to remove any particles. Pour over two to three times its volume of boiling water and allow to cool. The fat will rise to the top and become firm. Lift it off and wipe the underside with absorbent kitchen paper to remove any sediment.

Clarifying also means to clear a liquid or jelly, such as consommé, usually by adding egg white. The coagulation of the egg white throughout the liquid gathers up all the impurities and forms a scum on the surface which can be discarded.

**Clotting** A gentle heat applied to cream which produces the thick clotted cream of the south-west of England.

**Cocotte** Small earthenware, ovenproof container of single portion size. Also called a ramekin.

**Coddling** Method of soft boiling eggs.

**Colander** Perforated metal or plastic draining basket.

**Compote** Mixture of fruit stewed in sugar syrup. Served hot or cold.

**Concasser** A French term used to describe food that is finely or roughly chopped. It is most often applied to skinned, seeded and chopped tomatoes.

**Conserve** Whole fruit jam.

**Consistency** Term used to describe the texture of a mixture, e.g. firm, dropping or soft.

**Consommé** Concentrated stock which has been clarified.

**Cornstarch** American name for cornflour.

**Coulis** A French term applied to a purée of vegetables, fish, poultry or fruit.

**Court bouillon** Seasoned liquid in which meat, poultry, fish or vegetables are boiled or poached.

**Couscous** Processed semolina in tiny pellets. Staple food in North African countries.

**Crackling** The crisp skin on roasted pork.

**Cream of tartar** (tartaric acid) A raising agent which is an ingredient of baking powder and self-raising flour.

**Creaming** Beating together fat and sugar until the mixture is pale and fluffy and resembles whipped cream in texture and colour. Used in cakes and puddings which contain a high proportion of fat and require the incorporation of a lot of air.

**Crêpe** French term for a pancake.

**Crimping** Decorating the edges of a pie, tart or shortbread by pinching it at regular intervals to give a fluted effect. The term may also refer to trimming cucumber, radishes, etc with a canelle knife or fork to produce a deckled-cut finish.

**Croquette** Mixture of meat, fish, poultry, cooked potatoes or vegetables bound together and formed into roll or cork shapes, coated with egg and bread crumbs and shallow or deep-fried.

**Croûte** A circle or rectangle of fried or toasted bread on which game and some main dishes and savouries are served. The term may also refer to a pastry crust, usually crescent shaped, served with savoury dishes.

**Croûtons** Small pieces of fried or toasted bread which are served with salads and soup.

**Curd** The parts of milk which coagulate when natural fermentation takes place, or when a curdling agent, such as rennet or an acid is added. The term also refers to a creamy preserve made from fruit (usually lemon or orange) and sugar, eggs and butter.

**Curdle** To separate fresh milk or a sauce either by adding acid (such as lemon juice) or by heating excessively. Also used to refer to creamed mixtures which have separated when the egg has been beaten in too quickly.

**Cure** To preserve fish, meat or poultry by salting, drying or smoking.

**Daube** Braising meat or vegetables in stock, often with wine or herbs.

**Deglaze** To heat stock, wine or other liquid with the cooking juices left in the pan after roasting or sautéing meat, stirring to dissolve the sediment.

**Dégorge** To draw out moisture from food, e.g. salting aubergines to remove bitter juices.

**Dhal** The Indian collective term for pulses.

**Dice** To cut food into small cubes.

**Dough** A thick mixture of uncooked flour and liquid, usually combined with other ingredients. The term is used to refer to mixtures such as pastry, scones and biscuits as well as those made with yeast.

**Drawing** Removing the entrails from poultry and game.

**Dredging** Sprinkling food with flour, sugar or other powdered coating. Fish and meat are often dredged with flour before frying, while cakes, biscuits and pancakes may be sprinkled with caster or icing sugar after cooking.

**Dressing** Plucking, drawing and trussing poultry and game. The term is also used to describe garnishing a dish, and coating a salad.

**Dripping** Fat obtained from roasting meat or pieces of fat which are rendered down deliberately (see also Rendering).

**Dropping consistency** Term used to describe the correct texture of a cake or pudding mixture just before cooking. Test for it by taking a spoonful of the mixture and holding the spoon on its side above the bowl. The mixture should fall off of its own accord within 5 seconds.

**Drying** Preserving food by dehydration. This is usually done commercially for foods such as rice, pasta and pulses, but it is possible to dry herbs and fruit at home.

**Dust** To sprinkle lightly with flour, cornflour or icing sugar.

**Egg and crumbing** Method of coating fish, rissoles, croquettes, etc before frying or baking.

**Emulsion** A mixture of two liquids which do not automatically dissolve into each other, e.g. oil and water. They can be made to emulsify by vigorous beating or shaking together, as when combining oil and vinegar in a French Dressing.

**En croûte** Term describing food which is wrapped in pastry before cooking.

**En papillote** A French term applied to food which is baked in baking parchment or greaseproof paper for a brief period and served in the parcel.

**Enzyme** Substances present in all foods which have not been subjected to processing. They work within foods continuously and are responsible for changes in food condition. Most enzymes are killed by cooking (see also Blanching).

**Escalope** A thin slice of meat, such as veal, turkey or pork, cut from the top of the leg and often egged and crumbed, then fried or grilled.

**Espagnole** Classic French rich brown sauce, used as the basis for other sauces.

**Extract** Concentrated flavouring which is used in small quantities, e.g. meat extract, yeast extract.

**Fahrenheit** System of measuring temperature which is being replaced with Celsius. Its freezing point is 32° and boiling point 212°.

**Farce** Alternative French term for stuffing.

**Fermenting** Term used to denote chemical changes deliberately or accidentally brought about by fermenting agents, such as yeast or bacteria. The process is utilised for making bread, yoghurt and wine.

**Fillet** A term used for the undercut of a loin of beef, veal, pork or game; boned breasts of birds; and boned sides of fish.

**Fines herbes** Classic French mixture of chopped herbs, i.e. parsley, tarragon, chives and chervil.

**Flambé** Flavouring a dish with alcohol, usually brandy or rum, which is then ignited so that the actual alcohol content is burned off. Christmas Pudding and Crepes Suzette are traditionally flambeed.

**Folding in** Method of combining a whisked or creamed mixture with other ingredients by cutting and folding so that it retains its lightness. Used mainly for meringues, soufflés and certain cake mixtures. Use a large metal spoon.

**Fondue** Dish cooked at the table over a fondue burner into which the diners dip food speared on long pronged fondue forks.

**Fool** Cold dessert consisting of puréed fruit with whipped cream or custard blended into it.

**Forcemeat** Stuffing for meat, fish or vegetables.

**Fricassée** White stew of chicken, rabbit, veal or vegetables, finished with cream and egg yolks.

**Frosting** American term for icing cakes. Also refers to the decorating of fruits, flowers and the rims of glasses, by coating with a fine layer of sugar.

**Frothing** Dredging the surface of roast meat, usually game, with flour and heating to a brown colour in a hot oven.

**Frying** Method of cooking food in hot fat or oil. There are various methods: shallow-frying in a little fat in a shallow pan; deep-frying where the food is totally immersed in oil; dry frying in which fatty foods, such as bacon and sausages, are cooked in a non-stick pan without extra fat; see also Stir-frying.

**Galantine** A dish of white meat which has been boned, sometimes stuffed, then rolled, cooked, pressed and glazed with aspic to be served cold.

**Garnish** A decoration, usually edible, such as parsley or lemon, which is added to a savoury dish to enhance its appearance.

**Gelatine** An animal-derived gelling agent sold in powdered form in sachets, and as leaf gelatine.

**Genoese** Sponge cake made with a whisked egg mixture enriched with melted butter.

**Ghee** Clarified butter widely used in Indian cookery (see also Clarifying).

**Glacé** French word meaning iced or glossy.

**Glaze** Food used to give a glossy coating to sweet and savoury dishes to improve their appearance and sometimes flavour. Ingredients for glazes include beaten egg, egg white, milk and syrup.

**Gluten** A protein constituent of wheat and other cereals. The amount present in flours varies and accounts for the different textures of cakes and breads.

**Grating** Shredding cheese, carrots and other hard foods with a grater or food processor attachment.

**Griddle** A flat, heavy, metal plate used on top of the cooker for cooking scones, crumpets etc.

**Grinding** Reducing foods to small particles in a food mill, pestle and mortar, electric grinder or food processor. Foods ground include coffee beans, nuts and spices.

**Grissini** Long, slim, brittle Italian bread sticks.

**Gut** To clean out the inside of a fish, removing all the entrails.

**Hanging** Leaving meat or game suspended in a cool, dry place to allow air to circulate around it to tenderise the flesh and develop the flavour.

**Hors d'oeuvre** Often used as a term for a starter but, strictly speaking, means a selection of cold foods served together as an appetiser.

**Hulling** Removing the calyx from soft fruits, e.g. strawberries.

**Infusing** Method of imparting flavour to a liquid. Flavourings, such as aromatic vegetables, herbs, spices, vanilla pod or coffee beans, are added to milk or water, sometimes brought to the boil, then left to soak.

**Jardinière** Refers to dishes garnished with mixed fresh spring vegetables or green peas and sprigs of cauliflower.

**Jugged** Traditional method of cooking hare in a tall covered pot until very tender and rich dark brown in colour. The blood is added at the end of the cooking time.

**Julienne** Vegetables or fruit rind cut into very fine strips to use as a garnish or ingredient.

**Kebab** General name for a dish comprising cubes of meat, fish, shellfish, fruit and vegetables which are cooked on skewers under a grill or on a barbecue.

**Knead** To work dough by pummelling with the heel of the hand.

**Knock back** To knead a yeast dough for a second time after rising, to ensure an even texture.

**Kosher** Food prepared according to orthodox Jewish laws.

**Kugelhopf** A sweetened yeast cake which contains dried fruit and is baked in a special deep fluted tin.

**Langues de chats** Literally means cats' tongues. Small thin flat crisp biscuits served with ice creams and mousses.

**Larding** Inserting small strips of fat bacon into the flesh of game birds, poultry and dry meat before cooking. It is done with a special larding needle.

**Leaven** The raising agent in dough, usually yeast or baking powder.

**Liaison** Term used to describe any combination of ingredients which is used for thickening or binding. The ingredients of a liaison are usually flour, cornflour, arrowroot, rice or potato flour or egg yolk.

**Macédoine** The French term for a mixture of fruit or vegetables cut into even-sized dice. Usually used as a garnish.

**Macerate** To soften and flavour raw or dried foods by soaking in a liquid.

**Marinate** To soak meat, poultry or game in a mixture of oil, wine, vinegar and flavourings to tenderise it and add flavour. The mixture, which is known as a marinade, may also be used to baste the food during cooking.

**Marmite** A French metal or earthenware pot used for long slow cooking of casseroles on top of the stove or in the oven.

**Medallions** French term for small rounds of meat, usually beef or veal.

**Meunière** A French term which refers to food cooked in butter, seasoned with salt, pepper and lemon juice and finished with parsley. Usually applied to fish dishes.

**Milling** Reducing to a powder or paste (see also Grinding).

**Mincing** Chopping or cutting food into very small pieces. It may be done with a knife, a manual mincing machine or in a food processor.

**Mirepoix** A mixture of cut vegetables, usually carrot, celery and onion, with a little added ham or bacon, used as a bed on which to braise meat.

**Mocha** A term which has come to mean a blend of chocolate and coffee.

**Monosodium glutamate (MSG)** A powder with little flavour of its own, but which enhances the flavour of ingredients it is added to. A principal ingredient in processed foods and Chinese cookery.

**Noisettes** Neatly trimmed and tied boneless pieces of lamb, not less than 1 cm (1/2 inch) thick, cut from the loin or best end of neck.

**Panada** A thick roux-based sauce used for binding croquettes and similar mixtures.

**Parboiling** A term used to describe boiling food for part of its cooking time before finishing it by another method.

**Paring** Thinly peeling and trimming vegetables or fruit.

**Pasteurising** Sterilising milk by heating to 60°-92°C (140-180°F) to destroy bacteria.

**Pâte** The French word for pastry familiar in *pâte sucrée*, a sweet flan pastry.

**Pâté** A savoury mixture made from minced meat, flaked fish and/or vegetables cooked to form a solid mass. Smoked fish pâtés are rarely cooked.

**Paunching** Removing the stomach and intestines of a rabbit or hare.

**Paupiettes** Slices of meat or fish rolled around a stuffing, usually braised or fried.

**Pectin** A naturally occurring substance found in most fruit and some vegetables which is necessary for setting jams and jellies.

**Pickling** Preserving raw fresh or lightly cooked food in vinegar.

**Piping** Forcing cream, icing, mashed potato, cake mixtures or meringue through a nozzle fitted into the end of a nylon or greaseproof paper piping bag.

**Pith** White lining under the rind of citrus fruit.

**Plucking** Removing feathers from poultry and game.

**Poaching** Cooking food gently in liquid at simmering point, so that the surface of the liquid is just trembling.

**Pot roasting** A method of cooking meat slowly in a covered pan with fat and a little liquid.

**Potage** The French term for a thick soup.

**Praline** Almonds caramelised in sugar, then crushed and used to flavour sweet dishes.

**Preserving** Keeping food in edible condition by freezing, canning, pickling, crystallising, irradiation, drying, smoking etc.

**Pressure cooking** Cooking food quickly in steam under pressure.

**Prosciutto** Italian raw smoked ham.

**Proving** The term used for leaving bread dough to rise after shaping.

**Pulses** The generic name given to all dried peas, beans and lentils. These are valued for their high protein and fibre content.

**Purée** Fruit, vegetable, meat or fish which has been pounded, sieved or liquidised to a smooth pulp. Purées often form the basis for soups and sauces.

**Quenelles** Fish, meat or poultry which has been blended to a fine forcemeat, shaped into rounds or ovals, then cooked in liquid and served either as a garnish for soup or as a main course.

**Ramekin** Individual round ovenproof dish.

**Réchauffé** French term for reheated leftovers.

**Reducing** Fast-boiling a liquid in an uncovered pan to evaporate water and produce a more concentrated flavour.

**Refresh** To pour cold water over blanched and drained vegetables to set the colour and stop the cooking process.

**Rendering** Extracting fat from meat trimmings by cutting them into small pieces and heating in a cool oven at 150°C (300°F) mark 2 until the fat runs out and can be strained.

**Rennet** A substance extracted from a calf's stomach which will curdle or coagulate milk. The process is also used for junket and cheese making. Vegetarian rennet is also available.

**Rice paper** Edible paper made from the pith of a Chinese tree. Used as an edible base for sticky baked goods such as macaroons.

**Roasting** Cooking meat by dry heat in an oven or over an open flame.

**Roulade** Meat, cake or soufflé mixture rolled around a filling.

**Roux** A mixture of equal amounts of fat and flour cooked together to form the basis of many sauces.

**Rubbing in** Method of incorporating fat into flour when a short texture is required. It is used for pastry, cakes, scones and biscuits.

**Salmis** A stew made from game birds; the bird is partly roasted and then cooked with wine or port.

**Salting** A method of preserving food in dry salt or a brine solution.

**Sautéing** Cooking food in a small quantity of fat in a sauté pan (a frying pan with straight sides and a wide base), which browns the food quickly.

**Scalding** Pouring boiling water over food to clean it, loosen hairs or remove the skin. Food should not be left in boiling water or it will begin to cook. It is also the term used for heating milk to just below boiling point, to retard souring or to infuse it with another flavour.

**Scalloping** Decorating the double edge of a pastry pie with small horizontal cuts which are pulled up with the back of a knife to produce a scalloped effect.

**Scoring** To cut narrow parallel lines in the surface of food to improve its appearance or help it cook more quickly.

**Searing** Browning meat quickly in a little hot fat before grilling or roasting.

**Seasoned flour** Flour mixed with a little salt and pepper, for dusting meat and fish before frying.

**Seasoning** Adding salt, pepper, herbs and spices to a dish to enhance flavour.

**Shredding** Grating cheese or slicing raw vegetables into very fine pieces or strips.

**Sieving** Pushing food through a perforated sieve to get a soft, even texture.

**Sifting** Shaking dry ingredients through a sieve to remove lumps.

**Simmering** Keeping a liquid just below boiling point.

**Singeing** Using a flame to burn off any residual traces of feather on plucked game or poultry.

**Skimming** Removing froth, scum or fat from the surface of stock, gravy, stews and jam. Use either a skimmer, a spoon or absorbent kitchen paper.

**Smoking** The process of curing food by exposure to wood smoke.

**Souring** Adding acid, often in the form of lemon juice, to cream to give it a sour taste.

**Sousing** Pickling in brine or vinegar.

**Spit** Rotating rod on which meat, poultry or game is cooked either in the oven or over a fire.

**Steaming** Cooking food in the steam of rapidly boiling water.

**Steeping** Covering food with hot or cold water and leaving it to stand either to soften it or extract its flavour and/or colour.

**Sterilising** Destroying bacteria in foods by heating.

**Stewing** Long, slow cooking method where food is placed in liquid which is kept at simmering point. Good for tenderising tougher cuts of meat.

**Stir-frying** Quick method of frying in shallow fat. The food must be cut into small, even-sized pieces and moved around constantly until cooked. Stir-fried food is usually cooked in a wok.

**Stock** The liquid produced when meat, bones, poultry, fish or vegetables are simmered in water with herbs and flavourings for several hours to extract their flavour.

**Suet** Hard fat found around the kidneys in beef or mutton. Sold in packets. Used in pastry and steamed puddings. A vegetarian alternative is available.

**Sweating** Gently cooking food (usually vegetables) in melted fat in a covered pan, until the juices run.

**Syrup** A concentrated solution of sugar in water, used in making sorbets, drinks and fruit juices.

**Tenderising** Beating raw meat with a spiked mallet or rolling pin to break down the fibres and make it more tender for grilling or frying.

**Tepid** The term used to describe temperature at approximately blood heat, ie 37°C (98.7°F).

**Terrine** China or earthenware dish used for pâtés. Also used to refer to the food cooked in it.

**Texturised vegetable protein (TVP)** Meat substitute made from vegetables, usually soya beans. It generally takes on the flavour of anything it is cooked with.

**Truffle** Rare black or white fungus of the same family as the mushroom. Due to the cost, truffles are used mainly for garnishing.

**Trussing** Tying or skewering into shape before cooking. Applied mainly to poultry and game.

**Unleavened** Bread without a raising agent.

**Vanilla sugar** Sugar in which a vanilla pod has been stored to release its flavour.

**Vol-au-vent** A round or oval puff pastry case which is filled with diced meat, poultry, fish or vegetables in sauce.

**Whipping (whisking)** Beating air rapidly into a mixture either with a manual or electric whisk.

**Wok** Chinese pan used for stir-frying. The food cooks on the sloping sides of the pan as well as in the rounded base.

**Zest** The coloured outer layer of citrus fruit which contains essential oil.

# INDEX

# P